Library of
Davidson College

STALIN'S POLICY TOWARDS INDIA

The International Relations Library

Agwani, M.S., *The Gulf in transition* (176 pp, 1937). Appadorai, A., *Contemporary India: essays in domestic and foreign policy* (251 pp, 1988). Appadorai, A. and M.S. Rajan, *India's foreign policy and relations* (709 pp, 1985). Bandyopadhyaya, J., *Climate and world order: an inquiry into the natural cause of underdevelopment* (178 pp, 1983). Bandyopadhyaya, J., *North over South: a non-western perspective of international relations* (290 pp, 1982). Bandyopadhyaya, K., *Burma and Indonesia: comparative political economy and foreign policy* (250 pp, 1983). Baral, J.K., *International politics: dynamics and dimensions* (348 pp, 1987). Benner, J., *Structure of decision: the Indian foreign policy bureaucracy* (214 pp, 1984). Chakravorty, S.R. and V. Narain, *Bangladesh*: Vol. 1 *History and culture* (220 pp, 1986), Vol. 2 *Domestic politics* (218 pp, 1986), Vol. 3 *Global politics* (in press). Chakravorty, S.R., *Bangladesh: the nineteen seventy-nine elections* (138 pp, 1988). Kamath, P.M., *Indo-US relations: dynamics of change* (194 pp, 1987). Nayak, P., *Pakistan: society and politics* (239 pp, 1984). Noorani, A.G., *India, the superpowers and the neighbours: essays in foreign policy* (273 pp, 1985). Phadnis, U. and E.D. Luithui *Maldives: winds of change in an atoll state* (179 pp, 1985). Phadnis, U., S.D. Muni and Kalim Bahadur, *Domestic conflicts in South Asia*: Vol. 1 *Political dimensions* (191 pp, 1986), Vol. 2 *Economic and ethnic dimensions* (201 pp, 1986). Rajan, M.S., V.S. Mani and C.S.R. Murthy, *The Nonaligned and the United Nations* (384 pp, 1987). Ramakant, *China and South Asia* (200 pp, 1988). Sen Gupta, B., *Soviet perspectives of contemporary Asia* (201 pp, 1984). Sen Gupta, B., *Regional cooperation and development in South Asia*: Vol. 1 *Perceptional, military and nuclear arms race problems* (277pp, 1986), Vol. 2 *Political, social, technological and resource aspects* (267 pp, 1986). Sen Gupta, B., *The Persian Gulf and South Asia: prospects and problems of inter-regional cooperation* (244 pp, 1987). Sen Gupta, B., *SAARC-ASEAN: prospects and problems of inter-regional cooperation* (in press). Sharma, K.L. *Society and polity in modern Sri Lanka* (189 pp, 1988).

STALIN'S POLICY TOWARDS INDIA

1946-1953

SURENDRA K. GUPTA
PITTSBURG STATE UNIVERSITY
PITTSBURG, KANSAS 66762

South Asian Publishers
New Delhi

Copyright © South Asian Publishers, 1988

All rights reserved. No part of this
publication may be reproduced in
any form or by any means, without the
written permission of the publishers.

ISBN 81-7003-093-5

Published by South Asian Publishers Pvt. Ltd.
36 Netaji Subhash Marg, Daryaganj, New Delhi 110002
and printed at Prabhat Press, 20/1 Nauchandi Grounds,
Meerut 250002. Printed in India.

Preface

Despite a number of excellent studies on Soviet-Indian relations written by Western as well as Indian scholars, Stalin's policy towards India still remains a largely neglected field. Some scholars have dismissed it altogether. For example, Roger Kanet, a leading American scholar on Soviet policy towards the developing countries, argues that Stalin's policy towards the Third World—in which he also includes India—was one of "total isolation" and was based on Moscow's "lack of knowledge and experience in these areas." In the same vein, Adam Ulam, in his long biography of Stalin, dismisses the Soviet ruler's policy towards this region by saying that he showed "scant interest" in the Third World. Writes Ulam, "...he could not be bothered with Nehru, Sukarno and Nasser." Those—as in the case of Robert H. Donaldson, Zafar Imam, Hemen Ray, and V.S. Budhraj—who have made an attempt to write on this period have done so only as a part of or an introduction to a larger work. Consequently, their analyses do not explore this early period in Soviet-Indian relations as fully as it richly deserves. After all, it was during this period that the first encounters between Moscow and New Delhi took place at several international forums, including the United Nations, and in their direct dealings with each other. It was also under Stalin that Moscow evolved its policy towards nonalignment, a movement which was later embraced by the majority of the countries in the Third World. This study seeks to fill this gap in the existing literature on Moscow's policy towards India and the Third World.

In approaching the subject, I have given less importance to either the interest shown in India by a number of Russian Orientalists of the Tsarist period or the journeys made by such travellers as Afanas Nikitin, which are often cited by some in the Soviet Union and India as laying the foundation of the relatively friendly ties that later developed between the two countries. I also have avoided detailed discussion of how various strategies to foster Communism in India were discussed at a number of meetings of Comintern. Soviet ideology will be discussed in the introductory chapter but only as a part of a discussion of the roles of ideology and national interest in Soviet foreign policy and to determine what role, if any, Moscow's attachment to Communist ideology played in the development of Soviet-Indian relations.

Since any relationship between two different countries depends on the need and willingness of both, it has been considered necessary to look at Indian foreign policy as it was formulated by Jawaharlal Nehru, first as Vice President of the Interim Government between September 1946, and August 1947, and then as independent India's Prime Minister and Minister of External Affairs. As a newly-liberated country, India needed external assistance for its economic development, as well as weapons for its armed forces. Although, therefore, Nehru boldly declared that India's policy was not to join one side or the other in the Cold War, he could not afford to be totally neutral between the West and the Soviet Union. A complicating factor would be the Kashmir issue. Brought before the UN by India itself in the hope that its charge of Pakistan's invasion of the state would be supported by everyone, it quickly found that the issue was drawn out in endless debates for several years, with very few countries accepting India's position in a forum that was dominated by the US and England.

The above considerations in Indian foreign policy have necessitated a detailed discussion of US-Indian relations. If the US was in a position to provide both economic assistance and diplomatic support on Kashmir, it also had its own strategic interests in the region. How to secure those interests, of course, depended on the perceptions and policies of those who at different times ran the administration in Washington, but a policy towards India had to be considered as a part of America's approach to the Communist world, which also came to include China after Mao Tse-tung's victory in 1949. Therefore, although, the main thrust of this study remains a discussion of the evolution of Soviet policy towards India under Stalin, it has been attempted with the backdrop of changes in US-Indian relations.

I have incurred many debts in completing this study. My greatest debt is to Professor Robert M. Slusser, Emeritus Professor of History at Michigan State U niversity. It was in his courses and seminars at the Johns Hopkins University that I first learned how to understand and interpret Soviet foreign policy, not always an easy task. His valuable suggestions at various stages of my work were most helpful. I am also grateful to him for contributing a foreword to this study. It is also a pleasure to acknowledge my appreciation to Dr. Charles A. Barker, now Emeritus Professor of History at The Johns Hopkins University. Over the years, he has taken keen interest in my work and was most helpful in obtaining financial support on several occasions.

Various foundations provided funds to enable me to complete this study. I would like to record my grateful thanks to the Edward W. Hazen Foundation in New Haven, Connecticut; Asia Foundation in San Francisco, California; the Truman Library Institute in Independence, Missouri; and the National Endowment for the Humanities in Washington, DC. Pittsburg State University provided me money to obtain some badly-needed microfilms of Indian newspapers, and I am deeply appreciative of the Administration, especially Dr. James E. Gilbert, Vice President for Academic Affairs, for its support.

Some findings of this study were presented at a seminar on Stalin at the University of Massachussetts in Amherst in summer 1980. I am very thankful to Dr. Robert H. McNeal, who directed the seminar, for this opportunity and his many helpful comments. Dr. R.G. Gidadhubli, Director of the Centre of Soviet Studies at Bombay University invited me to give a seminar on Soviet-Indian relations at the Centre in August 1983. I am grateful for his hospitality and for many critical but helpful comments offered by various members of the seminar.

Several of my colleagues in the history department at Pittsburg State University read all or some chapters of this study. I should like to record my appreciation to Professors Martin Campion, James B.M. Schick, Thomas R. Walther and Judith Shaw. Dr. Dudley T. Cornish, the former chairman, and Dr. Robert Ratzlaff, the present head, were helpful in providing some released time from my teaching duties.

One could not have found a better professional typist than Mrs. Debbie Ware, who cheerfully typed several drafts of this study and, on occasions, saved me from some serious errors. Her assistants,

viii PREFACE

Lori Reith and Mary Schneider carried part of the burden, and both of them deserve much credit.

Over the years, I have done research at various libraries in the United States and abroad. The libraries at The Johns Hopkins University, Harvard University, and the University of Kansas provided me excellent facilities. I used the Chester Bowles Papers at the Sterling Memorial Library at Yale University, and I am grateful to its staff for all their assistance. The Oral History Project at the Nehru Memorial Museum & Library in New Delhi was very useful, and I am grateful to its director and staff for making it possible for me to use some of the material. A scholar at a small university like Pittsburg State depends considerably on inter-library loan services, and I am very appreciative of the help provided by Ms. Cynthia Pfannenstiel and Ms. Leah Bevan of the Leonard H. Axe Library in getting some important books and articles from other collections.

In my case the traditional thanks to one's wife have meaning in more than one sense. Swarna not only typed the first draft, but has been a source of constant encouragement and inspiration. My children, Archana, Shailen and Raju reminded me of my unfinished work on this study, when I often drifted away to fulfil other commitments, and I am deeply appreciative of their love and concern.

Pittsburg, Kansas   SURENDRA K. GUPTA
March 1988

Contents

PREFACE v

I. Determining Factors in Soviet and Indian Foreign Policies 1
II. Beginnings of Cooperations 14
III. The Cold War: Moscow Evaluates India's Nonalignment Policy 49
IV. India's Further Estrangement from Moscow 85
V. Search for New Policies 131
VI. From the War in Korea to the Peace Treaty with Japan: Moscow Reconsiders India's Nonalignment 170
VII. New Directions in Soviet Policy towards India (1952–53) 244
VIII. Conclusions 270

BIBLIOGRAPHY 277

INDEX 288

I

Determining Factors in Soviet and Indian Foreign Policies

...Our orientation in the past and our orientation at the present time is towards the USSR, and towards the USSR alone. (*Stormy Applause*) And if the interests of the USSR demand rapprochement with one country or another which is not interested in disturbing peace, we adopt this course without hesitation.—Joseph Stalin, in his report to the Seventeenth Congress of the Communist Party of the Soviet Union, 26 January 1934.

The task of analysing Soviet foreign policy and interpreting the public statements of Soviet Officials, as well as the vast literature published in the country, is a formidable task. Every country, to a great extent, also carries some burden of the past. The Soviet Union is the inheritor of a centralized state which underwent territorial expansion almost in every direction and, over a span of centuries, was transformed from the small state of Muscovy into one of the largest empires in the world. It even used its Orthodox Christian and Slavic links to expand in Eastern Europe,[1] at the time ruled by an alien, Islamic Empire. In case of Asia, apart from other motivations for territorial expansion, there also was an ideological group, *Vostochniki* (Easterners), towards the end of the nineteenth century. Although there were many strands in their thought, the dominant group emphasized the similarities between the Russians and Asians and pointed to St. Petersburg's historical mission to liberate them. As Prince Esper Esperevich Ukhtomskii, one of the most articulate exponents of their ideology, said:

Asia—we have always belonged to it. We have lived its life and felt its interests. Through us the Orient has gradually arrived at consciousness of itself, at a superior life.... We have nothing to conquer. All these peoples of various races feel themselves drawn to us, and are ours, by blood, by tradition, and by ideas. We simply approach them more closely. This great and mysterious Orient is ready to become ours.[2]

This tradition of using ideology either for territorial expansion or spread of power and influence, be in Europe or Asia, was the legacy of the Tsarist regime to the new revolutionary Soviet state which came into existence as a result of the Bolshevik Revolution of November 1917. For the old ideologies, there was now a new one—that of Marxism-Leninism—which looked out at the world with certain hope and confidence as a playground for future revolutions. In the Marxian framework of history, there was hardly any scope for doubt, only of time, regarding the victory of socialism throughout the world. The new Soviet state, shortly after it came into existence, quickly established the Communist International (Comintern) to fulfil its historical obligation to promote revolutions in other countries. The famous Indian Communist leader M.N. Roy, who later abandoned Marxism to become a radical humanist, attended these early meetings of the Comintern in Moscow and was one of the most important members of the organization.

IDEOLOGY AND NATIONAL INTEREST IN SOVIET FOREIGN POLICY

The role of Communist ideology in the actual conduct of Soviet foreign policy has baffled outside observers and policy-makers in other countries since the founding of the Comintern. Is promoting revolutions with the purpose of overthrowing capitalism the main preoccupation of the Soviet state? A scholar's task is made more complicated when, along with talk of peaceful coexistence and peace, Soviet writers emphasize Moscow's continuing commitment to ideological goals. For example, writing in 1973, when the relationship between Russia and America was glowing under the sun of detente, Boris Dmitriev, a noted Soviet historian, described the policy of peaceful coexistence as "an unalterable truth for Soviet people," but then added:

It would be useless for anyone to expect that the Soviet Union would weaken in the ideological field or give away its principles for the sake of short-term benefits. Striving to implement the policy of peaceful coexistence, our country resolutely rejects appeals from Western circles to "smooth over" ideological differences and even to renounce altogether the fundamental principles of socialist ideology.[3]

In an authoritative piece on peaceful coexistence, a Soviet writer in *Great Soviet Encyclopedia* also echoes Dmitriev's argument on the continuing relevance of Communist ideology. In chiding those who believe that somehow emphasis on ideology would fade away, he says:

The liberal group of bourgeois ideologists, and the Social Democrats and revisionists, lean towards a very expansive interpretation of the potential of peaceful coexistence, which is viewed as a way to distinguish the political and ideological struggle between capitalism and socialism and bring about the convergence of the two systems. At best, this point of view is utopian. The struggle of the two systems is rooted in deep-seated social processes and in the opposition of the fundamental principles of the organization of society.... The policy of peaceful coexistence does not and cannot solve the cardinal social problems of our time and cannot prevent political and ideological clashes....[4]

With quotations of this type, one can easily come to the conclusion that the main goal of Soviet foreign policy is to promote Communist revolutions with the purpose of establishing Moscow's domination in the world. In fact, some have done that very often. Many in the West still talk about Russia's "master plan" or its "blueprint for world conquest," in which Communist ideology as a tool would play a decisive role.[5] This, however, would be a simplistic view and the result of what an American scholar, Samuel Sharp, labelled some years ago "the doubtful art of quotation."[6] The two essays quoted above put equal emphasis on peaceful coexistence, and one can cite both Lenin and Stalin equally to justify the emphasis on revolution or peaceful coexistence.

To get out of this difficulty, one must look at the development of Soviet foreign policy as it has evolved since 1917, and the principles that have guided Moscow in its actual dealings with other countries.

In the beginning, setting up a department to deal with foreign affairs appeared rather odd to Russia's revolutionary leaders. It was no wonder that Leon Trotsky, who was chosen by Lenin to become the People's Commissar for Foreign Affairs in his first cabinet, described his job in a very light-hearted manner when he said, "I will issue a few revolutionary proclamations to the peoples of the world and then shut up the shop."[7] But a war was on and the Bolshevik leaders needed to get out of it in order to save and consolidate the revolution at home. So the arduous task of negotiating a peace treaty with Germany was undertaken. Revolutionary slogans could not do the job when the Germans—after their initial terms offered at Brest-Litovsk were considered too humiliating by the Bolsheviks and rejected by them—decided to march farther into Russian territory. Lenin, who had earlier advised acceptance of the German terms, now criticized those who still counted on the coming German proletarian revolution. Threatening to resign if the German terms were not accepted, he said forcefully:

Stalin is wrong when he says that it is possible not to sign. These conditions must be signed. If you do not sign them, you will sign the death warrant of the Soviet power within three weeks.... The German revolution is not yet ripe. That will take months. The terms must be accepted.[8]

Faced with the thrust of the marching German army and Lenin's ultimatum to resign, the Bolshevik leaders now voted to accept Germany's conditions for peace, later formalized in a treaty signed at Brest-Litovsk in March 1918. Excepting Russia's occupation by the Mongols several centuries earlier, this was the most humiliating event in all of Russian history.

In justifying acceptance of the German conditions as the only way to achieve peace, Lenin also argued that it would free the Bolsheviks "from both warring imperialist groups," enabling Russia to utilize the war for its own purposes.[9] As E.H. Carr perceptively remarks, "From this recognition of the pragmatic value of the division in the enemy camp it was only a short step to the conscious exploitation of it as an asset of Soviet foreign policy, and to the abandonment of any doctrinal assumption of the uniform and unvarying hostility of the capitalist world."[10]

The belief of many Bolshevik leaders that revolutions in many other countries were around the corner suffered another blow during the Soviet-Polish War of 1920-21. Provoked by the Poles, the Red Army soon took the lead and, as it entered the Polish territory, hoped for a proletarian revolution to greet the incoming liberators. But there was no revolution, and the Polish people—all of them as Poles regardless of their social background—decided to fight back and succeeded in pushing the Red Army back. As Alvin Rubinstein rightly remarks, "With this defeat of the Red Army, Russian expectations of an imminent world revolution ended."[11] The Treaty of Riga of 18 March 1921, that ended the war, was thus another reminder to the Soviets that they would have to deal with the world as it was, not what appeared through their ideological prism. Always a pragmatist, Lenin now argued for trade relations with the capitalist countries because the new Soviet state needed to obtain "as soon as possible the machinery needed for our broad plan to rehabilitate our national economy."[12]

A year later, the Soviets signed the famous Rapallo Treaty with Germany, to be followed by the Berlin Treaty of 1926. These two treaties laid the foundation of economic—and, to some extent, military—cooperation between Communist Russia and non-Communist Germany. The treaties proved useful to both sides and the Soviets would have liked to continue the relationship even after the advent of Hitler, but it was the Nazi dictator who turned his back on Moscow,[13] thus creating a crisis in Soviet foreign policy. Stalin still tried to assure Hitler that Russia was not against fascism per se and would be ready to have dealings with the new Germany. As he stated in very clear terms, "...fascism is not the issue here, if only for the reason that fascism in Italy, for example, has not prevented the USSR from establishing the best relations with that country."[14]

Hitler's decision to ignore Stalin's conciliatory gestures now forced Russia to turn to the West. It is in the context of this shift in Soviet foreign policy that Moscow's desire to seek U.S. recognition, the decision to join the League of Nations, and Litvinov's many statements expressing Moscow's desire to participate in a European collective security system should be seen. A corollary of this policy was also the decision to de-emphasize ideological goals by Comintern. The main danger to the Soviet Union now came from Nazism, not capitalism. So the need was to mobilize everyone, regardless of one's ideological affiliation, to create a new united front to prevent war. At Comintern's Seventh Congress held in Moscow in 1935, the new policy was approved. Trotsky was not far from truth when he declared that it was, in fact, "the liquidation congress" of Comintern.[15]

The policy of seeking rapprochement with the West, however, failed as both London and Paris sought to buy peace at Munich by agreeing to accept Hitler's demand for the Czech territory of Sudetenland. The Soviets, who were not present at Munich, now switched back to Germany, eventually entering into a non-aggression pact with the Nazis in 1939. Ideology had thus become almost irrelevant in the 1930s in solving Russia's security problems.

One more development of the 1930s within Comintern, one which was to have a significant impact on Indian politics, should be noted. This was the increasing subservience of Comintern to Moscow's needs and policies. The trend was already obvious under Lenin, when he sought to change Comintern's policies to suit Russia's needs. In forceful and unambiguous language, Comintern issued a new programme in 1928 telling the foreign communist parties that their first and foremost duty was to support the Soviet Union. As the programme stated:

In view of the fact that the USSR is the only fatherland of the international proletariat, the principal bulwark of its achievements and the most important factor for its international emancipation, the international proletariat must on its part facilitate the success of the work of socialist construction in the USSR and defend her against the attacks of the capitalist powers by all means in its power....

In the event of the imperialist states declaring war upon and attacking the USSR, the international proletariat must retaliate by organizing bold and determined mass action and struggle for the overthrow of the imperialist governments with the slogan of: Dictatorship of the Proletariat and alliance with the USSR.[16]

As we have seen, this use of Comintern for the interests of the Soviet state was carried a step further at Comintern's Seventh Congress in 1935. And to suit the needs of Russia's alliance with the West against the Axis powers after 1941, Stalin decided to disband it in 1943.

Another aspect of the role of ideology that needs to be noted is the relationship between Russia and a country ruled by a bourgeoisie which is actually engaged in the task of suppressing internal Communist movements. This has always depended on how important the development of friendly ties with that country are considered by the Soviet leaders. This has especially been the case with those countries lying on the periphery of Russia. To have friendly governments there has been considered far more important for Soviet security interests than their internal class structure or the policy of the ruling bourgeoisie towards domestic communist parties. The precedent for this approach, in fact, was set in Lenin's time. To quote a perceptive Western scholar:

No matter that the leaders of the nationalist movements, such as Kemal in Turkey, were anti-Communist in some instances; that they suppressed their native Communists; that their programme went no further than independence and national development under bourgeois banners. Rapprochement with them and the governments formed by them, or even with established Eastern governments disposed to throw off Western tutelage, was a defencive Soviet interest in that it fostered the rise of friendly states on Russia's periphery. Thus, the Foreign Commissariat (Narkomindel) under Chicherin pursued with Lenin's most active support a fundamentally anti-British diplomacy of friendship with non-Communist Turkey, Afghanistan, and Persia.[17]

This aspect of early Soviet foreign policy would be especially applicable in deciding an appropriate policy towards countries like India. What mattered to the Soviets was India's attitude towards the West, particularly the United States, even if New Delhi was not as favourably inclined towards Moscow as it might have liked. This approach also helped the Russians to adopt a far more flexible policy towards the nonaligned movement than the United States has been able to do to this day. As an Indian scholar has rightly remarked, "...Soviet leaders came to view India's nonalignment as one regards a glass half-full. Washington regretted a glass half-empty."[18]

There were, in sum, four main considerations regarding the role of ideology in Soviet foreign policy. First, although the Soviets started their rule in Russia with confident expectation that their revolution would be followed by revolutions in other countries, the revolutions either did not take place at all, or if they did, they quickly dissipated. Ideology, therefore, became increasingly irrelevant for Soviet security interests. Second, the Soviets were forced to have diplomatic dealings with the capitalist countries on a traditional basis, even granting trade concession to some of them. Third, because ideological goals abroad no longer served Soviet national interests, Comintern increasingly became a tool of Soviet foreign policy. And, finally, in case of countries lying on Russian periphery, Moscow even ignored their suppression of internal Communist movements if they were otherwise prepared to have friendly relations with the Soviet Union.

Ideology's Destabilizing Role

Although Moscow's allegiance to an ideology which sees itself as the wave of the future is seen as Russia's desire to dominate the world, it is often forgotten that this emphasis on ideology may actually hurt Soviet interests. If it had not been for the fear the Western capitalist countries felt at the victory of Soviet Communism, they would not have intervened in the Russian Civil War that followed the Bolshevik Revolution. Again, Russia's effort to encourage revolutions in British colonies stood in the way of getting a trade agreement with London, which the Soviets badly wanted. Eventually, Moscow did get an agreement in 1921, but it had to assure the British that Russia would no longer engage in anti-British propaganda, would close the school set up in Tashkent for the training of Asian Communists, and would not promote revolutions in British colonies.[19]

It is not only the Western capitalist countries that have shown reluctance in dealing with Russia because of its attachment to an expansionist ideology, even many Asian nationalist leaders have had difficulty in dealing with Moscow for the same reason. When Sun Yat-sen, the great Chinese nationalist, turned to the Soviets in the early 1920s to ask for assistance for the purpose of unifying his country, he was afraid that Russians might utilize the alliance to overthrow his party, the Kuomintang, and support the Chinese Communist Party. So in the Sun-Joffe agreement of 1923, he made sure that the Soviets would give a commitment that it was "not possible to carry out either Communism or even the Soviet system in China."[20]

Russia is often blamed for promoting revolutions in several Asian countries, including India and Indonesia, in the late forties through the newly established Cominform, but it should also be noted that as far as the Russian interests were concerned, they were actually hurt and not helped by these Communist outbreaks, regardless of the fact whether they were dictated from Moscow or were the outcome of indigenous factors. In Indonesia, Sukarno and other nationalist leaders even refused to establish diplomatic relations with the Soviets, and in India Nehru's perception of Russian links with Indian Communists, as we shall see below, was an important factor in his negative approach towards the Soviet Union.

INDIA'S NEEDS AND OBJECTIVES

Although pursuit of such idealistic goals as disarmament, the promotion of world peace of human rights, of which Nehru and other Indian officials talked about a great deal, is important, our concern here is with more concrete objectives directly related to the economic and security needs of the country. Ultimately, such considerations always prove decisive in the formulation and conduct of a country's foreign policy. Nehru himself stressed this in the very first year of India's independence:

Whatever policy you may lay down, the art of conducting the affairs of a country lies in finding out what is most advantageous to the country. We may talk about international goodwill and mean what we say. We may talk about peace and freedom and earnestly mean what we say. But in the ultimate analysis, a government functions for the good of the country it governs and no government dares do anything which in the short or long run is manifestly to the disadvantage of that country.[21]

A major goal of Nehru's government was to bring about the country's economic development, for which some external sources for technology and machinery had to be found. Even Lenin, as we have seen, did not hesitate to turn to the West. In case of India, many, if not the majority, in the country would have had no qualms in turning to the Soviets, but Moscow, devastated by war and trying to recover itself, was not in a position to provide much economic or any other assistance at this time. The decision to turn to the West would, therefore, be easily made, because with the West India also shared a common commitment to democratic ideals and there was no danger of any ideological subversion of the Indian political system.

While India would have no hesitation in turning to the West, especially the United States, the biggest obstacle would be whether India could agree to a formal alliance with Washington. A large country like India could not become a militarally of the United States as many European countries did because India's historical experience with the West was different. Moreover, a major goal of Nehru and other Indian leaders, which was shared universally by all Indians, was to assert India's separate identity in international affairs. If the United States would have looked back at George Washington's Farewell Address of 1796, which was basically a call for an independent foreign policy, it would have understood the rationale of India's decision to follow a pro-Western foreign policy but not to the extent as to become an ally in the Cold War. So India chose neither neutrality, which symbolizes passivity, nor alliance but nonalignment, which gave the country freedom to act. But each time India made a pro-Western move—as when it decided to join the British Commonwealth in 1949—the hopes were raised in Washington that such a step might be a precursor to India's eventually becoming a part of an Asian military alliance on the lines of the Atlantic Pact. Such a development would have been contrary to India's perception of its role in world affairs and would have been opposed by a large section of the population.

As noted above, many Asian leaders in recent history approached Russia rather hesitatingly and with apprehension because of their fear that Moscow intended to promote Communist revolutions in their countries. In case of Nehru, such hesitation and apprehension were the results of what he experienced during his participation in India's freedom struggle. His first experience with the communist methods took place when, while in Europe in 1927, he joined the League Against Imperialism and became a member of its Executive Committee. As S. Gopal, Nehru's biographer, notes when he found that the Communists were trying to dominate it, Nehru "became one of the leaders of an effective resistance."[22] Later, he was expelled from the League as it came to be dominated by the Communists and as Comintern ended a policy of cooperation between the Communists and other parties.

More than the working style of the Communists, what bothered Nehru the most was their subservience to Moscow. While acting in opposition to the Communists in the League Against Imperialism, he developed a feeling of "the strongest objection to being led by the nose by the Russians or by anybody else."[23] Later, in 1929, he opposed the idea of Indian Trade Union Congress joining Comintern because that would "mean an adoption of their methods in their entirety,"[24] implying that the organization, as controlled by the Soviets, hardly allowed any freedom of action.

For Indian nationalists like Nehru, the most painful aspect of the activities of Indian Communists during World War II was their subservience they showed to Moscow's desires. They supported the Nazi-Soviet Non-Aggression Pact in 1939, and called the war that resulted from it "imperialist." Their tune, however, changed when Hitler invaded Russia in 1941, and the wartime alliance between the Soviet Union and the Western powers came about. The British war effort in India now needed to be supported because it was bound to help Russia. But the British had undertaken their war effort by signing up India on the Allied side on their own and jailing all the important Indian nationalist leaders, including Nehru. As Arun Shourie has recently shown in his well-researched pieces on the activities of Indian Communists at this time,[25] it was the Indian Communist leaders who took the initiative in offering their cooperation to the British with the purpose of supporting the Russians. So between the goals of Indian nationalism and helping Russia, Indian Communists chose to ignore the cause of Indian nationalism. At the end of the war, Nehru was a member of the Committee that recommended the expulsion of Indian Communists from the Congress Party.

Nehru's belief that Indian Communists were directed from Moscow played an important role in his approach to Russia during the early years of independence, especially at a time when his government was busy suppressing an armed Communist rebellion in Central India. The Soviets—as we have seen in case of their dealings with Kemal Ataturk of Turkey—would have been prepared to deal with him regardless of what the Indian Communists were doing or how New Delhi was dealing with them. Perhaps a cordial relationship with Moscow could have been used to persuade Moscow to put a leash on the party. If Moscow directed their activities, it could also lead them in the other direction if such a policy would serve Soviet interests. Such a sophistication in approaching the Russians would no doubt come, but only later when Nehru would be instrumental in persuading Nikita Khrushchev to disband Cominform. His daughter, Indira Gandhi, would often use her links with the Soviets to curb Indian Communists or use them for her own political gains. At this time, however, Nehru remained deeply suspicious of Soviet intentions and was reluctant to respond more favourably to Moscow's overtures even when such a response would have been in India's interests.

NOTES

1. See Ivo J. Lederer, "Russia and the Balkans," in *Russian Foreign Policy*, ed. Ivo J. Lederer (New Haven, 1962), pp. 418-43.
2. Cited from Andrew Malozemoff, *Russian Far Eastern Policy 1881-1904* (Berkeley and Los Angeles, 1958), pp. 43-44.
3. Boris Dmitriev, "What Is Peaceful Coexistence," *Coexistence* 10 (March 1973): 31-32.
4. A.E. Bovin, "Peaceful Coexistence," in *Great Soviet Encyclopedia* (New York: Macmillan, Inc., 1977), 16: 626. The encyclopedia was originally published in Russian in Moscow in 1974 under the title, *Bol'shaia sovetskaia entsiklopediia*.
5. See a recent critical discussion of this view by Alexander Dallin, "A Soviet Master Plan? The Non-Existent 'Grand Design' in World Affairs." in *The Gorbachev Era*, eds. Alexander Dallin and Condoleeza Rice (Stanford, 1986), pp. 167-77.
6. Samuel Sharp, "National Interest: Key to Soviet Politics," in *Soviet Conduct in World Affairs*, ed. Alexander Dallin (New York, 1960), p. 48.
7. Cited from E.H. Carr, *The Bolshevik Revolution, 1917-1923* (New York, 1961), 3: 16.
8. Ibid., p. 40.
9. Ibid., p. 42.
10. Ibid.
11. Alvin Z. Rubinstein (ed.), *The Foreign Policy of the Soviet Union* (New York, 1960), p. 45.
12. Lenin's "Report on Concessions to the Communist Party Faction at the Eighth Congress of Soviets of the RSFSR, 21 December 1920," ibid., p. 72.
13. Rubinstein quotes a despatch sent to Hitler on 20 February 1933, by his ambassador in Moscow, Herbert von Dirksen, urging "the continuance of the present friendly policy." But Hitler ignored the advice. Ibid., p. 87.

14. Ibid., p. 89.
15. Cited in E.H. Carr, *The Twilight of Comintern, 1930–1935* (New York, 1982), p. 427.
16. Cited in Rubinstein, *The Foreign Policy of the Soviet Union*, pp. 103–4.
17. Robert C. Tucker, "The Emergence of Stalin's Foreign Policy," *Slavic Review* 36 (December 1977): 572.
18. Surjit Mansingh, *India's Search for Power, Indira Gandhi's Foreign Policy, 1966–1982* (New Delhi, 1984), p. 132.
19. Carr, *The Bolshevik Revolution, 1917–1923*, vol. 3, p. 288.
20. Cited in Rubinstein, *The Foreign Policy of the Soviet Union*, p. 92.
21. Jawaharlal Nehru, *Independence and After* (New York, 1950), pp. 204–5.
22. Sarvepalli Gopal, *Jawaharlal Nehru: A Biography* (Cambridge, 1976), 1: 105.
23. Ibid., p. 105.
24. Ibid., p. 132.
25. Arun Shourie, "What the Communists Did to Sabotage the Quit India Movement," *Illustrated Weekly of India* (Bombay) 105 (25–31 March 1984): 6 13; "Who Called Gandhi 'Decadent'? Who Described Subhas Bose as 'A Traitor and Quisling'? Who Accused Jayaprakash Narayan and Others of Being 'Vultures, Dirty Vampires'?" ibid., 1–7 April 1984, pp. 6–13; and "What Were the Actual Reasons for Betraying the Freedom Struggle? What Motivated the Communists? Why Did They Double Deal?" ibid., 8–14 April 1984, pp. 26–33.

II

Beginnings of Cooperation

> Russia goes to the East as an equal not as a conqueror or a race proud superior. Is it any wonder that she is welcomed?—Jawaharlal Nehru, in a speech at All-Bengal Students' Conference, Calcutta, 22 September 1928 (Dorothy Norman, ed., *Nehru, the First Sixty Years*, New York, 1965, I, 166).

Even though in the pre-independence period Jawaharlal Nehru's primary concern was to fight for India's liberation, the momentous world events of that time not only attracted his attention but in some cases—such as the democratic cause in the Spanish Civil War—he found himself emotionally involved. This also made him reflect on the role that an independent India might play in world affairs. In fact, an outline of a foreign policy had already begun to emerge in his mind even before he assumed any governmental position.[1] But it was in his capacity as Vice-President of the Viceroy's Executive Council and the Member for External Affairs that he made the first official declaration of India's foreign policy. In a nationwide broadcast on 7 September 1946, he said India would participate in international conferences as a free nation "with our own policy and not merely as a satellite of other nations." She would cooperate with other nations in the cause of peace and progress, but would keep away from the power-politics of groups aligned against each other. Then, while sending his greetings to the United States "to whom destiny has given a major role in international affairs," and whose power he hoped "will be utilized for the furtherance of peace and freedom everywhere," Nehru spoke of the Soviet Union in warm words:

To that other great nation of the modern world, the Soviet Union which also carries a vast responsibility for shaping world events, we send greetings. They are our neighbours in Asia and inevitably we shall have to undertake many common tasks and have much to do with each other.

We are of Asia and the people of Asia are nearer and closer to us than others.²

THE SOVIET UNION AND THE INTERIM GOVERNMENT'S FOREIGN POLICY

Soviet press comments on the formation of the Interim Government in India and on Nehru's declaration announcing his intention to pursue an independent foreign policy had two aspects.³ As regards Nehru's declaration, they adopted a wait-and-see attitude but severely criticized the British for granting this "concession" to India. In an article in *Izvestiia*, A.M. D'iakov quoted Nehru's statement on foreign policy and his warm words for the Soviet Union, but added:

Indian papers close to the National Congress have greeted the formation of the new government and have called it the first national government of India. However, a number of papers of more leftist tendency have expressed doubt that the new government will be able to pursue an independent foreign and internal policy.⁴

But this doubt was in no way reflection on Nehru or the Congress Party which, according to D'iakov, enjoyed "the support of the majority of the people of India." It was because of the nature of the Interim Government which had very limited authority and was far from being an independent government.⁵ D'iakov went on to quote Nehru's own statement that the setting up of an Interim Government did not mean the achievement of Indian independence or the end of their struggle for it.⁶ An article in *New Times* said that the few anti-Soviet elements in the country who did not desire relations with the Soviet Union were actually British-inspired, and not connected with Nehru or the Congress Party.⁷

However, D'iakov severely censored the British government. The new step was characterized as nothing but a manoeuvre "to use in new forms the old policy of dividing the ranks of the national liberation movement."[8] It was implied that the "direct action"[9] launched by the Muslim League was British-inspired, because the champion of this new strategy was Firoz Khan Noon who had been a member of the Viceroy's Executive Council, and who for many years "faithfully and truthfully served British imperialism." Thus, D'iakov in a rather sympathetic tone towards the Nehru Government, accused the British of "ulterior motives," for after inviting the Congress Party to form the Interim Government they were, on the other hand, encouraging the Muslim League in its anti-Congress activities, with the purpose of making Nehru's government responsible for the severe economic plight of India and for the civil strife which had been provoked by the British policies.[10]

First Official Contact

The Interim Government soon approached various countries for the purpose of establishing diplomatic relations. In Europe this task was entrusted to V.K. Krishna Menon, who had been the Secretary of the India League in London and a personal friend and collaborator of Nehru for over a decade. In a press conference in New Delhi on 26 September 1946, Nehru said that India so far had no direct diplomatic contact with her northern neighbour, the USSR, as she had with the United States, and he proposed to explore the possibilities because, besides the importance of the USSR, "it is always desirable to have neighbourly relations with neighbours."[11]

Menon met the Soviet Foreign Minister, V.M. Molotov, on 28 September 1946, in Paris where he was attending the Paris Peace Conference.[12] A Reuters dispatch from Paris said that "the purpose of Mr. Menon's interview was to gain Soviet support to India's new Central Government to offset, particularly in foreign relations, the predominant British influence."[13] Later, upon his return to London, Menon himself explained the purpose of his visit to Paris:

I went to Paris to see M. Molotov...because the Government of India cabled to him to consider what assistance the Soviet people should give in the present food crisis.* Secondly, I visited M. Molotov

---

* Exceeding Nehru's instructions, Menon, on his own, also raised with Molotov the question of some Soviet military experts visiting India. This perturbed not only the British government but also several of Nehru's collea-

because the policy of the Indian Government—announced both when Pandit Nehru assumed office afterwards—is that the new Government will open up relations with all the countries as soon as practicable. The Government of India, having sent that message to Molotov, I was asked to see him and follow it up.[14]

As regards food aid, Menon added, Molotov gave him the impression that the Soviet Union was "quite anxious" to assist, but her own scarcity in this area might prevent her from doing so. "It looks as though Russia will not be in a position to help until 1947."[15] Referring to newspaper reports that the purpose of his meeting with Molotov was to seek Russia's support against the British, Menon said that "It is mischievous to suggest that we are asking support of any one country to offset another." India's policy, he said, did not envisage partial or exclusive relationships, but friendliness towards all.[16]

The purpose of Menon's visit to Paris was later confirmed by Nehru in the Constituent Assembly. Nehru said:

...the conversations with M. Molotov were very friendly and he expressed his willingness to exchange diplomatic representatives with India. (*Hear, hear and cheers.*) It was proposed that this matter be gone into further in Moscow in December next.[17]

While the official contact thus took place between the Interim Government and the Soviet Union, a section of the Indian Muslim League, which was agitating for a separate state of Pakistan and which had not joined the Interim Government, declared that it would seek assistance from the Soviet Union. *New Times* quoted a statement by Firoz Khan Noon to the effect that if the Hindus and British did not accede to their demand, they would turn to the Soviets.[18] In early September, the Sind Provincial Muslim League passed a resolution stating that "like the Jews who are fighting for their homeland with the support of the American people, Indian

---

gues in the Congress party. It is interesting to note that Nehru did not oppose Menon's move, although he cautioned his emissary to keep those people in India in mind who might be critical of such overtures to Moscow. Nehru to Menon, 13 October 1946; cited in Sarvepalli Gopal, *Jawaharlal Nehru: A Biography*, vol. 1, 1889–1947 (Cambridge, 1976), p. 336.

Muslims should secure the support of Soviet Russia and bring their question on the international plane."[19] Later Yusuf Abdulla Haroon, President of the Sind Provincial League, in an interview in London, told of his plans to go to Paris to see Molotov to appeal for Soviet support in raising their demand before the UN and the Paris Peace Conference. He said that the Muslim League should send "a very strong deputation to Moscow to explain and propagate the Muslim claim."[20]

Apparently Haroon was not able to see Molotov.[21] In the meantime, Mohammed Ali Jinnah, the President of the Muslim League, was reported to have disclaimed any association with this attempt.[22] The Soviet press itself deprecated any such idea, and labelled it a part of anti-Soviet propaganda which was "obviously inspired by the British] and rather crudely fabricated."[23] The Soviet view of the Muslim League's demand for a separate state of Pakistan, especially in contrast to the attitude of the Communist Party of India, had been quite consistent all through this period, and it did not fail to please Indian nationalist opinion which stood for a united India.[24]

The Soviet View at the Paris Peace Conference

The first test of whether India would follow an independent foreign policy or not came at the Paris Peace Conference which met from 29 July to 15 October 1946, for the purpose of negotiating peace treaties with the Axis satellite countries. By this time the wartime entente between the Soviet Union and the Western powers was already dead in everything but in name, and it was at this conference that the clash between their interest first became apparent. India was one of the twenty-one participating nations at the conference, but when it convened the Indian delegation was named by the British administration in India; the Interim Government had not yet come into existence. Since the personnel of the delegation could not be changed in the middle when the Interim Government assumed power in early September,[25] Nehru had to work through the delegates who were not only appointed by the British but were already working in close collaboration with them. This inevitably created some constraints for the Indian leader in his task of directing their activities from New Delhi.

The clash between the two viewpoints took place at the outset over voting procedure. Russian insistence that a two-thirds majority be required for all recommendations was rejected by 15 to 6, India voting with Great Britain and other powers.[26] The two other issues that created bitter dispute between the Western powers and the Soviet Union concerned the settlement of the territory of Trieste and the rights of navigation on the Danube. In regard to Trieste the French compromise proposal, supported by Great Britain and the United States and opposed by the six Soviet-bloc countries, was approved on 9 October 1946. It provided that a free port of Trieste be set up under the protection of the Security Council of the United Nations.[27] India voted with the US and Britain.[28] As regards the Danube, the conference again, in face of the bitter opposition of the Soviet Union and its satellites, approved by 14 to 7 a French proposal providing for freedom of navigation of the Danube. India again voted against the Soviet Union.[29]

The effect of the above decisions on Soviet interests has been summarized by an Indian scholar:

Trieste and Danube are the two main gates through which commerce between the Balkan countries and the West is carried on. The internationalizing of these gateways exposed the Soviet Union to security risks, as they exposed the Crimea and Southern Russian ports to naval attacks by the West.[30]

It was natural, therefore, that India's vote in favour of these decisions was displeasing to the Soviet Union.

At a press conference on 26 September 1946, Nehru had said that the Indian delegation at Paris, "has, *wherever possible*, followed an independent line of fair compromise, and has supported those proposals which seemed to offer the solution most generally equitable."[31] But of course the crucial vote on the internationalization of the Danube, on which India changed her earlier stand, was to come later. In April 1947, while proposing the ratification of the Peace Treaties in the Constituent Assembly, Nehru stated that "by our signing these treaties, we did not line up with any particular bloc." He also referred to the difficulty of considering a given question at the conference not "on its merits" but "from the point of view as to whether a decision helped one bloc of Powers or another bloc." In such a situation a country like India, "which tried to steer a middle course and to consider every question on [its] merits," would be criticized by both parties.[32]

In this case, because India had voted against the Soviet Union, she met with bitter criticism from Molotov. Speaking in the plenary session of the conference on 14 October 1946, he referred to the "efforts on the part of a definite group of delegations to hold a dominant position and to dictate its decision without any regard for the opinion of a considerable number of other delegations," creating "a rather embarrassing situation for the delegations of small countries." In support he specifically cited the problem of navigation on the Danube and said that while on the question of calling a conference no proposal could gather two-thirds of votes in the Economic Commission, the situation was reversed at the plenary session where:

The voting...yielded a majority of 14 votes against seven in favour.... India, Ethiopia and certain other States proved to be among those 14. It would seem these States could have adopted a more object- ive, more sober-minded and more responsible attitude toward the Danube States. Yet this did not happen.

Why, indeed, had India to insist on the settling of these problems, for instance in the peace treaty with Rumania? What interests of India, what interests of Indians are affected by the convocation of a Danube Conference of one or the other kind, on which Britain and the United States so strongly insist?...

...We have been...confronted with an impermissible situation in which the Indian delegation merely performed its colonial duty of voting at the will of another country—at the will of great Britain.[33]

An Even more critical comment came from A.M. D'iakov. In an article in *Pravda* he referred to Nehru's earlier declaration of his intention to follow an independent foreign policy and to establish collaboration between India and the Soviet Union, and then wrote:

...The membership of the Indian delegation in the organization of the United Nations has been changed and some progressive leaders have been included.

However, the new Indian Government did not dare to change the membership of its delegation at the Paris Peace Conference;

where the Indian delegation conducted itself as a loyal vassal of British imperialism.

....

Once again we are forced to doubt the ability of the Interim Indian Government to achieve that "independent" course as regards foreign policy which it has announced.[34]

This was undoubtedly a strong criticism of the Interim Government, especially considering D'iakov's September 27 article in *Izvestiia*, but still there was no criticism of Nehru, whom D'iakov distinguished from other leaders of the Congress Party.[35] Molotov's attack was also directed to the other Great Powers who exerted pressure on smaller countries.[36] The fact that India was not yet fully independent had made her more susceptible to such pressure. Had it been "the voice of an independent India," "of a representative of true India," said Molotov, "we would have expected more objective voting on the part of India...." And he added, "The time is not far remote, however, when other and happier days will come for India."[37]

INDIA AND THE SOVIET UNION AT THE UNITED NATIONS

1. *The issue of racial discrimination in South Africa* India and the Soviet Union came closer to each other's viewpoint at the first session of the United Nations General Assembly where, on questions such as the treatment of Indians in South Africa, the future of South West Africa, the trusteeship agreements, and the principle of unanimity of the Great Powers in the Security Council they found themselves in substantial agreement. India's delegation included some members whom A. D'iakov called "progressive" leaders: Vijayalakshmi Pandit, V.K. Krishna Menon, and Justice M.C. Chagla.[38] It was a delegation which, unlike the delegation at Paris, was appointed by the Interim Government, and its composition must have been largerly Nehru's own choice.

The practice of racial discrimination in South Africa[39] has been one of the worst forms of discrimination practised anywhere in modern times. It was a question that affected Indian sentiment very deeply. Indians had been first brought to South Africa as indentured labourers, through an agreement between the governments of India and Natal in the middle of the nineteenth century, to fill the need for labour in the sugar plantations in the Colony of Natal. This need arose as a result of the abolition of slavery by the British Parliament. But those who settled in South Africa were before long the victims of discriminatory practices. It was against these practices that Gandhi first started his historic passive resistance movement during 1907-1914. Soon, however, new discriminatory laws were enacted, resulting in strained relations between India and South Africa. Talks between them led to the Cape Town Agreement of 1927, reviewed and reaffirmed in 1932. Though the agreement provided relief for some time, there was soon recourse to other discriminatory laws. The Trading and Occupation of Land (Transvaal and Natal) Restriction Act of 1943 for the first time put statutory restrictions on Asiatics in Natal, barring them from acquiring land. In India the resentment against this law was so deep and widespread that the government enacted the Reciprocity Act in November 1944. Dr. N.B. Khare, a member of the government, declared in the Central Assembly, "I wish India was in a position to declare war against South Africa, here and now."[40]

The act of 1943 was to expire on 31 March 1946, and in spite of the protests of the Indian government, the discriminatory practices were embodied in the Asiatic Land Tenure and Indian Representation Act of 3 June 1946. India reacted sharply by severing trade relations with South Africa. She also submitted the issue to the United Nations on 22 June 1946, under Articles 10 and 14 of the Charter because, as India stated in her letter to the Secretary-General, "A situation...[had] thus arisen which...[was] likely to impair friendly relations between India and South Africa...."[41]

There could be no doubt as to which side Soviet sympathies and support would be on with regard to the question of race discrimination. Indeed, this was one of those questions which the Soviet Union had successfully used to criticize the Western countries and to make an appeal to the people in the colonial world.[42]

India brought this issue to the UN with great hope and feeling.[43] Mrs. Vijayalakshmi Pandit, Leader of the Indian delegation, said in a speech in the Assembly:

The issue we have brought before you is by no means a narrow or local one, nor can we accept any contention that a gross and continued outrage of this kind against the fundamental principles of the Charter can be claimed by anyone, and least of all by a Member

State, to be a matter of no concern to this Assembly of the world's people.

The bitter memories of racial doctrines in the practice of States and Governments are still fresh in the minds of all of us. Their evil and tragic consequences are part of the problems with which we are called upon to deal.[44]

Molotov, in his general speech to the Assembly, indicated his support for India:

Although India is a Member of the United Nations, and consequently, in accordance with the Charter, her relationship to Great Britain should be based on sovereign equality, have you not heard here in the General Assembly India's appeal for support and assistance? It is time that the just demands of India were recognized.[45]

Andrei Vyshinsky, Soviet Deputy Minister of Foreign Affairs, on behalf of the Soviet Union, came to India's support in the General Committee where the Union of South Africa argued that the question should not be taken up because it was "purely an internal one for South Africa...."[46] In the joint session of the Political and Security Committee where the issue was debated at considerable length,[47] India argued that it was a case of violation of the principles of the Charter and involved "a great moral problem."[48] In a resolution submitteed to the Committee, India requested the General Assembly to call upon the Union Government to "revise their general policy and their legislative and administrative measures affecting Asiatics in South Africa, so as to bring them into conformity with the principles and purposes of the Charter...."[49] South Africa denied that the Capetown Agreement of 1927 and the joint communique of 1932 were instruments "giving rise to treaty obligations." But she based her case mainly on Article 2, paragraph 7, of the Charter, and asserted that the question was wholly within the jurisdiction of the Union Government and thus one in which there could be no interference or control from outside.[50] In a resolution she proposed that the General Assembly seek an "advisory opinion" from the International Court of Justice as to whether or not, under the Article referred to above, the question came "essentally within the jurisdiction of the Union of South Africa."[51]

Both Great Britain and the United States, though saying nothing, approvingly or disapprovingly, on the basic question of the discriminatory legislation and practices in South Africa, supported the South African view that the question should be referred to the International Court of Justice. A resolution to this effect was submitted jointly by Britain and Sweden as an amendment to the Indian resolution.⁵²

Though India was warmly supported by many other countries, especially the countries of Asia, the Middle East and Latin America, the most eloquent and forceful support came from the Soviet Union. Andrei Gromyko, Soviet Permanent Representative in the Security Council, spoke in India's support in the joint session of the Political and Legal Committees.⁵³ Vyshinsky, later in the General Assembly, said that the South African effort to shift the issue to the juridical plane aimed at submerging it, "as the legal soil is very marshy."⁵⁴ But the Soviet Union, he said, did not want the question to be submerged. Even from the juridical point, he added, the agreements of 1927 and 1932 placed obligations on both parties, and thus there were no grounds to argue the case on the basis of paragraph 7, Article 2.⁵⁵ Speaking directly to the British delegate, Sir Hartley Shawcross, he added:

...The justice of which Sir Hartley Shawcross spoke should be secured, as he said, by the institution and organs specially created for this purpose. He had in mind the International Court of Justice, considering that the way to secure justice in the present question was precisely by the International Court. I disagree with Sir Hartley Shawcross....

The Soviet delegation considers that justice must indeed be secured and that it should be secured by an international court; but this international court is here, it is yourselves, it is all of us; it is our Organization which should deliver its verdict. This is what we want, this is what we demand.⁵⁶

Eventually India withdrew her resolution in favour of a milder and more conciliatory one proposed by France and Mexico, which, while stating that the "treatment of Indians in the Union of South Africa should be in conformity with the international obligations under the agreements concluded between the two Governments, due account being taken of the provisions of the Charter," simply requested India and South Africa "to report at the next session of the

General Assembly the action taken in its behalf."⁵⁷ This motion was carried by 24 to 19 with 6 abstentions, the USSR, Ukraine, and Byelorussia voting in its favour with India, and the US and Britain voting with South Africa against it.⁵⁸

When the French-Mexican resolution came before the General Assembly on 7 and 8 December for approval, South Africa tried to block it by asking that approval require a two-thirds majority under Article 18 of the Charter, because it had been argued, said the South African delegate, that the matter impaired relations between the two countries. The US and Britain supported the South African contention, while India and the USSR opposed it. It was, however, approved by a slight majority.⁵⁹ The French-Mexican resolution was able to secure 32 votes with 15 against and 7 abstentions, thus getting a two-thirds vote in its favour.⁶⁰

2. *The question of South West Africa* On two other issues—the question of South West Africa and the trusteeship agreements—India felt strongly, and here too her views largely coincided with those of the USSR.

Unlike other Mandatory Powers, who at this session of the UN General Assembly proceeded to place the mandated areas under the Trusteeship Council, the Union of South Africa proposed that the Assembly approve her annexation of the territory of South West Africa. She argued that the European population of the territory had expressed a desire for annexation through "normal democratic channels" in the form of the unanimous resolutions of the South West African Legislative Assembly, and the native population had done so "in an equally democratic but rather different form" through "consultation" by competent officials.⁶¹ The United Kingdom, just as in regard to the question of the treatment of Indians in South Africa, went all the way with South Africa. Her delegate stated that the people of South West Africa had "clearly expressed the wish to join the Union," and said it would be strange "if the United Nations were to gainsay the freely expressed wishes of the people."⁶² The United States did not go this far, but her delegate, John Foster Dulles, suggested postponement of the issue by saying that the data submitted by the Union Government "did not justify the approval by the Assembly during the current session."⁶³ Later Dulles said that the placing of former mandated territories under trusteeship was not compulsory.⁶⁴

Both India[65] and the USSR[66] vehemently opposed the incorporation of the territory by South Africa. Both submitted resolutions asking South Africa to prepare and submit a trusteeship agreement for South West Africa for the UN approval.[67] It was also at the suggestion of the USSR that India was included in the two sub-committees formed for considering this question and that of trusteeship agreements.[68]

The debate ended in the approval by the Assembly of a joint Danish-US-Indian resolution which represented a compromise between the US and Indian positions. It invited the South African government "to give further consideration" to the General Assembly resolution of 9 February 1946, regarding placing of mandated territories under trusteeship. On the question of the incorporation of the territory into South Africa, the resolution said that the data presented to the Assembly did not "justify" action for its approval.[69] The USSR voted for it while Britain, together with the South African government, abstained.[70]

3. *Trusteeship agreements* On the question of the approval of trusteeship agreements as submitted by the Mandatory Powers,[71] the views of India and the Soviet Union largely coincided. The Indian view was expressed by V.K. Krishna Menon:

There were violations of fundamental principles in these agreements for which the mandatory Powers were responsible. In the first place, the provision of the agreements concerning the establishment of military bases was a violation of the Charter. The establishment of such bases would be permissible only for the maintenance of collective peace, and should under these conditions be subject to the control of the Security Council. They were not in the interests of Trust Territories.

The second basic fault lay in the provision for administration as an integral part ... the declaration made in this regard had little value, as they were not part of the agreements. The agreements contained provisions to the contrary.[72]

One of the amendments submitted by India read:

The administering Authority shall administer the Trust territory on behalf of and solely for the benefit and in the interest of its people, and on the termination of the Trusteeship, all the powers of the Authority shall cease and it shall surrender the Territories together with all public property then existing... to the people whose sovereignty and whose right to self-government or independence shall always be recognized.[73]

The Soviet criticism of the draft agreements, though expressed in more critical words and going a little farther than India's, was in substance the same as had been expressed by the Indian delegates.[74] The US recognized, as Dulles said, that the agreements were not perfect, but he said "they reflected the terms and spirit of the Charter, and would continue to do so under the supervision of the Trusteeship Council, especially in regard to the political objectives of the System."[75] Great Britain, herself a Mandatory Power, and now submitting trusteeship agreements for Tanganyika, Cameroons, and Togoland, defended the agreements.[76]

In the Trusteeship Committee which eventually approved the draft agreements, only India and Chile joined the six countries of the Soviet bloc in voting against them. However, India abstained when they came up before the General Assembly, as she did not want to hinder the establishment of the Trusteeship System; the Soviet Union still voted against their approval.[77]

4. *The veto in the Security Council*   India supported the Soviet stand on the question of the veto in the Security Council. It was the Soviet Union which had made the maximum use of this right during the past year. The United States and Great Britain were able to muster majority support for their views; they therefore, though still accepting the veto in principle, were less enthusiastic about it. They sought some way in which the Soviet use of the veto could be checked or limited.

It is not necessary here to go into the details of the discussion and the various proposals which were put forward. The resolutions submitted by Cuba and Australia sought to limit the use of the veto privilege.[78] The United States supported the principle of unanimity of the Great Powers, but sought to limit it. Specifically, she wanted to exclude it from being applied to the peaceful process covered by Chapter VI of the Charter.[79]

The Soviet Union stood strongly against any change in this

regard.⁸⁰ In the debate in the Political Committee Vyshinsky defended the unanimity principle of the Great Powers and recalled that it was first proposed by President Roosevelt in December 1944. He said that criticism of the Soviet use of the veto was "aimed at destroying this basic principle of the Charter and destroying the unity of the United Nations."⁸¹

India considered that the veto right was undemocratic and believed that it should not be used arbitrarily, but in her view it was necessary in the existing international situation. K.P.S. Menon said in the Political and Security Committee that

... the unanimity rule, though not very democratic, faithfully reflected the existing international situation.

He attributed the weakness of the League of Nations mainly to the absence of the United States of America and to the withdrawal of certain great Powers. The same mistakes must not be made again and it was therefore essential to encourage any measure which might contribute to unanimity among the great Powers.⁸²

Opposing both the Cuban and Australian resolutions, Menon said that the essential problem was not "to limit" the "field of application" of the veto but "to regulate" its use. This could be done, he felt, only by the "five great Powers themselves."⁸³

The Australian resolution, with much revision, was later passed by the General Assembly. The Soviet Union opposed it while India abstained.⁸⁴

5. *The Soviet proposal on military establishments* The General Assembly was faced with another Soviet proposal, one to which India gave her whole-hearted support while the US, Britain, and other countries opposed. In it the Soviet Union proposed that the members of the United Nations submit to the Secretary-General details of forces and other military establishments in former enemy as well as other territories.⁸⁵ The reason for this proposal from the point of view of Soviet interests was quite obvious in the changing international situation marked by increasing hostility between the two sides. India, however, gave her support on other grounds which were also to characterize her policy in this regard in the coming years. Mrs. Pandit, giving India's support to the Soviet proposal, expressed pleasure that its scope had been extended to former enemy

as well as non-enemy territories. She argued that secrecy regarding troop locations in time of peace only led to complications. The Indian view would have been opposed to stationing of foreign troops in time of peace anyway because, as Mrs. Pandit pointed out, Indian troops had been used as an instrument of pressure against the Indonesian nationals. She also supported the Soviet resolution as "a step towards a scheme for universal and well-regulated reduction of arms."[86] India was one of the very few countries to vote against the American and British amendments to the Soviet proposal. These amendments, almost nullifying the original purpose of the Soviet proposal, were approved by a sizable majority.[87]

The outcome of the above session of the General Assembly was important from the point of view of Indian-Soviet relations, and also of India's relations with the Western democracies, especially Britain and the US. It brought out in sharp relief some of the major issues which seemed important to the emerging independent India, eager to assert her voice in international affairs, and with her own ideas about the questions of war and peace in the contemporary world.

On the question of discrimination against Indians, Mrs. Pandit had said in the General Assembly, "The way this Assembly treats and disposes of this issue is open to the gaze not only of those gathered here, but to millions in the world, the progressive peoples of all countries, more particularly the non-European peoples of the world..."[88] An Indian wrote at the time when the question was still being debated in the UN, "The sincerity or otherwise of such fine phrases as 'human brotherhood,' 'the four freedoms,' 'dignity and worth of the human person' and the whole gamut of them of which so much has been told and heard in recent months will be clearly shown by how the U.N.O. decides the Indian case. The taste of the pudding, they say, lies in the eating."[89]

In India therefore there was great disappointment with both the United States and Britain, especially the latter, and a feeling of gratitude towards the Soviet Union. As Mrs. Pandit expressed it in the General Assembly:

When I spoke yesterday, I expressed a hope that the British Commonwealth would at least remain neutral in this controversy, which vitally concerns one of its most important members. But Sir Hartley Shawcross' speech has shattered my hopes. He has spoken in a manner which I consider to be entirely partisan, however full of dialectical skill it may have been.[90]

And for those who had supported India's case, she expressed the gratitude "not only of the people of India and of the Indians in South Africa, but of the millions in every country whose hearts have been warmed and whose minds are eased by this impressive expression of world opinion in defence of justice and fundamental human rights...We shall remember this and know, in a way that cannot be forgotten, that justice, truth, and the oppressed have friends in every country and under every climate."[91]

Later, Mrs. Pandit accused Britain of "sabotaging everything that the Indian delegation brought up."[92] Another member of the Indian delegation, Lanka Sundram, said: "Britain's part during the debate will go down in history as unimpeachable testimony of her double-dealing with India."[93]

Indian press comments were equally bitter and full of disappointment. A prominent periodical of India, *Modern Review*, wrote:

USA and UK's support for Smuts in his advocacy for racial discrimination against the people of Asia has probably been the most notable feature of the South African debate. The high hopes that Asiatics had placed on these "arsenals and champions of democracy" have proved totally false at the first touch of reality. It is hardly a year since World War II was over and the delegates of the USA have tacitly disowned the "Four Freedoms" declaration which emanated from their country. As for Britain, it is strange that the representative of a Socialist government, that is apparently doing all it can to forge new ties and to eradicate old evils, should thus give the lie direct to all the claims of his government that the British Empire would henceforward be a Commonwealth of Nations on terms of equality with each other.[94]

It must be pointed out, however, that at least in official circles, Indian resentment was mainly directed against Britain. Even though the attitude of the United States disappointed them, it was thought that her policies were very much tied up with those of Britain and that an overwhelming fear of Communism was responsible for many of her actions in the United Nations.[95]

The support of the USSR on the question of discrimination naturally pleased India and strengthened her image of the Soviet Union as an anti-imperialist nation and one which stood for complete equality among races. Not only did Mrs. Pandit and other members of the Indian delegation openly thank the USSR in the United Nations; later Nehru also sent personal letters to the Soviet, Byelorussian, and Ukrainian governments to thank them for their support.[96]

It was suggested in some press comments in India that India's stand on the veto was a "responsive gesture" towards the USSR for her support on the South African question, and that by this action, India had "compromised" her position.[97] It is difficult to support this thesis because Nehru had stated India's position long before the South African issue was taken up by the UN General Assembly."[98] But coming as it did after the Soviet support of India in the South African debates, it must have been a contributing factor in prejudicing India's position in the eyes of some sections in the US.[99] John Foster Dulles, who had participated as a US delegate in debates on the trusteeship agreements, in a speech before the National Publishers' Association in New York charged that the Soviet leadership had encouraged "revolutionary movements" in colonial areas, and that throughout the colonial areas "there is growing a rebellion against the white man's assumption of racial superiority." He particularly referred to India where "Soviet Communism exercises a strong influence through the Interim Hindu Government."[100]

Dulles's remarks were widely carried by Indian newspapers, and both Nehru and Mrs. Pandit thought it necessary to reply. The former, in a statement on 20 January, expressed "surprise and regret" at Dulles's remarks and said that his description of the Interim Government "shows lack of knowledge of facts and want of appreciation of the policy we are pursuing."[101] Describing Dulles's statement as "complete misapprehension," Mrs. Pandit said, "Mr. Dulles represented the USA in the Trusteeship Committee where both India and the USSR strove hard to liberalize the trusteeship agreements submitted by the administering Powers. He therefore might have jumped to the conclusion that the Government of India was acting under Communist influence." Reiterating India's "independent" policy, she said, "India, far from blindly following alien influence, Communist or otherwise, will evolve her policy in accordance with her own interest and her own conceptions of right or wrong."[102]

In the Soviet press, especially in contrast to the criticism made after the Paris Peace Conference, there were favourable comments on Indian policy. An editorial in *New Times*, while criticizing the US and Britain for voting "as a bloc" in favour of South Africa, wrote that the outcome of the voting "represents a big moral victory for the democratic forces in the United Nations Organization."[103] The most favourable reference to Indian foreign policy, however, came in a Moscow radio broadcast by Bonsovai, a radio commentator, on New Year's eve:

The world is marching forward towards the triumph of genuine democracy. After 1946, there can be no return to a state in which the white third of mankind rules the world as F-M [Field Marshal] Smuts recommends. Whatever the tricks and ruses of champions of the colour bar, it is a fact recorded in the annals of 1946 that the oppressed nations have no intention of further accepting the position of political martyrs.

For the first time such nations as the Indians have begun taking an active part in international political life. And we note the constructive contribution to the work of the United Nations Assembly made by the Indian delegation with its consistently democratic stand...[104]

The Soviets Come to New Delhi

It was in this atmosphere of growing amicability between India and the Soviet Union that a delegation from the Soviet Academy of Sciences arrived in India in January 1947 to attend a session of the Indian Science Congress. India attached great importance to the participation of scientists from the US, the USSR, and other advanced countries as she looked forward to receiving their help and cooperation for scientific development in India, a point on which Nehru personally laid great emphasis. He was elected President of the Congress and touched on this theme when he spoke at a reception organized by the Congress in honour of the Soviet delegation:

For many years past we have looked with very great interest towards the Soviet Union for many reasons but more especially because of the tremendous achievements of the Soviet Union during the last quarter of a century or so. You are our neighbours and as neighbours and as neighbours we must...develop closer contacts with each other.

But apart from being neighbours, you have been pioneers in many fields and you have transformed the vast tracts of your country before our eyes with a speed that has astonished humanity. Inevitably, when we want to produce great changes in India, we want to learn from your example....Among the many things you have done is this tremendous flowering of science in the Soviet Union and the application of that science to the betterment of human beings...[105]

Professor V.P. Volgin, on behalf of the Soviet delegation, expressed the hope that their participation in the Congress would contribute to the strengthening of "the scientific bonds, cultural intercourse and friendly relations" between the two countries.[106]

The Soviet delegation's expressed desire for scientific cooperation with India made a deep impression. A correspondent of the *Hindustan Times* called it "a generous gesture in the true scientific tradition..."[107] The members of the delegation later visited Agra, Delhi, Banaras, Hyderabad and Aurangabad, and presented papers at some academic institutions. Later, the leader of the delegation, Professor Volgin, gave an account of their Indian journey in two articles published in the Soviet Union.[108] There was, no doubt, an attempt on the part of the delegation to propagate Communist ideas,[109] but in his articles Professor Volgin described India in most un-Marxist terms, speaking warmly of the welcome the Soviet delegation received, the beauty of Indian art and architecture and the life and customs of various places which they saw. As in other Soviet writings of this period, Nehru was distinguished from other Congress leaders as the "leader of the Left wing of the Indian National Congress..."[110]

The Soviet Union also sent a large delegation of the Soviet Transcaucasian and Asian republics—Armenia, Azerbaidzhan, Georgia, Kazakhstan, Kirghizia, Tadzhikistan, Turkmenistan and Uzbekistan—and a team of observers on behalf of the Soviet Union to an Asian Relations Conference held in Delhi in March-April 1947.[111] The conference discussed such subjects as national movements for freedom, migration, and racial problems, economic development and social services, cultural problems, and women's problems.[112] The massive representation of the Soviet Union—nine out of twenty-five countries—seemed quite out of proportion, and the invitation to them must have been sent at Nehru's own initiative.[113] He had spoken in the past of his fascination with the rapid modernization achieved in this part of Asia, which, perhaps, could provide not only an example but also a model to other regions aspiring towards this goal. In his inaugural speech at the conference he repeated this theme when he referred to the Soviet republics of Asia as those "which have advanced so rapidly in our generation and which have so many lessons to teach us..."[114]

The Soviets themselves picked up this theme. One example was the speech by Ibrahimoff, a delegate from Azerbaidzhan. He said:

History teaches that without national liberty and sovereignty, and especially without economic independence, neither a single country nor a single people can be really free. This has been proved in history from the example of the Soviet republics. Azerbaidzhan was formerly a colony of Tsarist Russia and before the great socialist Revolution it was one of the most backward corners of Asia where there prevailed a reign of feudal and patriarchal relations... The great October Revolution destroyed these forces as well as the conditions that gave birth to them. During the years of Soviet power, Azerbaidzhan became a prominent industrial republic. Soviet power has changed the face of Azerbaidzhan's villages. Azerbaidzhan is an example of the national cooperation of peoples.[115]

Madame Tairova, a delegate from Tadzhikistan, referred to the great advance accomplished under Soviet power in giving women their due place in society. She said, "Political, economic and domestic slavery and ignorance were the lot of our women before the Revolution. But for the Soviet system, I would not be standing here today on this dais, a free Tadzhik woman representing her free country. But for the Soviet system, I would not be what I am now, an engineer constructor and research worker."[116] Any suggestions made by the Soviet delegation for the specific problems discussed by the conference were based on the Soviet model.[117]

The offer and hope of scientific cooperation, together with the great achievements of modernization in the Soviet Asian republics, left a deep impression on the Indians.[118] They were also pleased with the presentation of an Uzbek robe and cap to Nehru by the Uzbek delegate.[119]

It may also be observed that whatever the Soviet press reported about the conference was accurate and without any criticism. It noted its resolution on the national independence movements and the discussion on racial discrimination, though emphasizing the suggestions and statements of the Soviet delegates.[120] It accurately reported the speech of Nehru at the concluding session in which he referred to the establishment of the Asian Relations Organization.[121] It apparently was also satisfied with the reception the Soviet delegation received in India and the impression it was able to make on the Indian people.[122]

Establishment of Diplomatic Relations

In the meantime the arrangements for establishing diplomatic relations between the two countries had been completed. As a sequel to the Menon-Molotov talks in Paris in late September 1946, and as announced by Nehru in the Constituent Assembly on 12 November 1946,[123] the Indian Interim Government in early December directed K.P.S. Menon, its Agent-General in China, to proceed to Moscow for this purpose.[124] India's eagerness for early diplomatic relations was again emphasized in early January by Nehru when he spoke at a reception in honour of the Soviet delegation to the Indian Science Congress.[125] The arrangements were agreed to in early April in talks between K.P.S. Menon and A.A. Petrov, the Soviet Ambassador to China.[126] An Indian government communique of April 13 stated:

Being desirous of maintaining and further strengthening the friendly relations existing between India and the USSR the Government of India and the Government of the USSR have decided to exchange diplomatic missions at Embassy level...[127]

For India, the establishment of diplomatic relations with the Soviet Union was a happy development. The Soviet press coupled the welcome with its denunciation of those British and Indian elements who did not desire friendly relations with the Soviet Union. An article in *New Times* welcomed it as "an event of no mean international significance," and considered it "a sign that India is moving toward an independent policy."[128] But in an apparent reference to those who opposed Nehru's policy of establishing friendly relations with the Soviet Union, the article said that "the British and Indian reactionaries" have been busy in their "anti-Soviet campaigns" "endeavouring to undermine the sympathy and interest of the Indian people for our country..." But, the article continued, "machinations of the foes of international peace and friendship" failed to prevent the establishment of diplomatic relations between the two countries.[129]

The increasing contacts between India and the Soviet Union drew some alarming comments from the West. A typical Western view was expressed by *Le Monde*, which remarked that since Britain was about to leave India, "the Soviet Government has more and more turned its eyes on that country."[130] It then said (echoing the earlier remarks of John Foster Dulles):

It is largely the Left-wing Hindu national movement which desires close understanding with the USSR of which one of the most eminent leaders is Pandit Nehru. It is this political celebrity who is the most active advocate of the Soviet Union in India...
The Soviet-Indian friendship is still only at its beginning... but one need only spend a few weeks in Moscow to notice that the Indian theme appears more and more frequently in the Press...[131]

One cannot say how the "beginning" of this seemingly warm relationship between Moscow and New Delhi would have developed in normal times, but the emerging Cold War soon changed the whole diplomatic environment. It was yet to be seen if in this worsening international climate, a country trying to steer an independent course—regardless of the fact whether it was coloured with a shade of pro-Western or pro-Soviet hue—could hope to establish a cooperative relationship with both Moscow and Washington.

NOTES

1. In his convocation address at Calcutta University on 9 March 1946, Nehru had said, ".. the position of India can never be that of one appended to any other country. As soon as she moves out of the orbit of subjection, immediately she jumps into a new orbit not only of independence but in a sense of the former intimate relationship with all the countries round about her. You cannot compel India to choose her friends. It is for India to decide finally what her future world outlook or foreign policy should be...." (*The Calcutta Review* 99 [April 1946]: 21). This theme was repeated in his speech before the Indian Council of

World Affairs in Bombay in August 1946, where he said that the first thing that India should do is to establish diplomatic relations with Asian countries "including the Asian Republics of the Soviet Union, which are on India's border." He also hoped that the Russians would participate in the forthcoming Asian Relations Conference (*New York Times*, 16 August 1946, p. 12).

2. *The Statesman* (Delhi), 8 September 1946, p. 5.
3. This point is emphasized here because some writers seem to take Soviet criticism of the Interim Government at this time as also the criticism of Nehru or the Congress Party. See, for example, David N. Druhe, *Soviet Russia and Indian Communism* (New York, 1959), pp. 271-72.
4. A. D'iakov, "K obrazovaniiu vremennogo pravitel'stva Indii," *Izvestiia*, 27 September 1946, p. 3.
5. Ibid. See also V. Bushevich, "Bor'ba Indii za nezavisimost'," *Mirovoe khoziaistvo i mirovia politika*, no. 9, 1946, p. 52. Bushevich wrote of the Interim Government that it was not responsible "even to the present Constituent Assembly which itself has no rights. The Viceroy, as before, preserves all his rights, including the right to veto. The Army, as before, is subordinated to the English Commander-in-Chief. The Government apparatus continues to be in the hands of English officials. Considering all this, it cannot be said that the Interim Indian Government possesses real authority."
6. D'iakov, "K obrazovaniiu vremennogo pravitel'stva Indii." See also Bushevich, "Bor'ba Indii za nezavisimost'."
7. "Different Voices but One Choir Leader," *New Times*, no. 18 (15 September 1946), p. 28. The article says, "It was announced by Nehru that this government intends to establish diplomatic relations with its neighbours, including the Soviet Union. But apparently there are some who do not relish the idea of normal relations between India and the Soviet Union." The article blames the British for these anti-Soviet elements because it is Britain which "wield[s] the baton that directs the chorus of heterogeneous voices in the present anti-Soviet campaign in India."
8. D'iakov, "K obrazovaniiu vremennogo pravitel'stava Indii." See also Ye. Zhukov, "Velikaia oktiabr'skaia revoliusiia i kolonial'nyi vostok," *Bol'shevik*, no. 20 (October 1946), pp. 43, 46. In analysis of the colonial policy of the imperialist powers, especially that of Britain, Zhukov said that their essential tactic towards the national liberation movement was to bring about a vision in it by isolating its "most active revolutionary elements." They do this by striking a bargain with "the most reactionary sections of the national bourgeoisie...." Thus, Zhukov added, "they have used the steadily strengthened reactionary tendencies of Kemalism in Turkey, the influence of Gandhism among the Indian national bourgeoisie, the betrayal of the counter-revolutionary right wing of the Kuomintang in China." But Zhukov did not suggest that in agreeing to participate in the Interim Government the Indian National Congress was

a party to such a bargain, though he said that this new step was, on the part of the British, a "'prophylactic' change" in face of the growing strength of the national liberation movement.

9. "Direct Action" was launched by Mohammad Ali Jinnah, leader of the Muslim League, after the Congress Party had agreed to join the Interim Government. August 16 was fixed as a day of demonstration and protest. In Calcutta it was marked by what came to be known as the "Great Calcutta Killing." It started a chain reaction of communal rioting first in Bihar and then in other parts of India. Percival Spear, *India, A Modern History* (Ann Arbor, 1961), pp. 415-16.

10. D'iakov, "K obrazovaniiu vremennogo pravitel'stva Indii."

11. *The Statesman*, 27 September 1946, p. 8. Commenting on Nehru's press conference, *The Economist* (London) wrote that there were no clear indications of the lines on which the relations between India and the Soviet Union were likely to develop, and it cautioned Congress that "as heir to the 'North-West Frontier' and neighbour of Afghanistan, [it] is taking over a legacy of problems in which there were always possibilities of serious foreign complications for any Indian Government." ("Indian Foreign Policy," *The Economist*, 5 October 1946, pp. 539-40).

12. *New Times*, no. 20 (15 October 1946), p. 31.

13. Reuters despatch in the *Sunday Statesman*, 29 September 1946, p. 7. See also the *New York Times*, 29 September 1946, p. 34.

14. *The Statesman*, 1 October 1946, p. 5.

15. Ibid. 16. Ibid.

17. *The Statesman*, 13 November 1946, p. 5.

18. Quoted in "Different Voices but One Choir Leader," p. 28.

19. *The Statesman*, 10 September 1946, p. 6. See also "Muslims in India Look to Russia," ibid., 15 September 1946, p. 5.

20. *The Statesman*, 24 September 1946, p. 1.

21. A Reuters despatch from Paris published in the *Sunday Statesman*, 29 September 1946, p. 7, which gave the news of Menon's meeting with Molotov, said that Haroon "want[ed] to meet the Soviet Foreign Minister...in an unofficial capacity," but that the Muslim League leader had not arrived in Paris so far.

22. George E. Jones in the *New York Times*, 25 September 1946, p. 11, in a despatch from New Delhi quoted "a source very close to Mr. Jinnah" as saying "that the Muslim League president had disclaimed any association with the reported attempt of a Muslim League member now in Europe to interview Russian Foreign Minister Molotov in the hope of obtaining Soviet aid for the League. This source said that Mr. Jinnah did not seek or expect any aid from the Soviet Union."

23. "Different Voices but One Choir Leader," p. 28. For a Soviet view of the Muslim League's policy and tactics see D'iakov, "K obrazovaniiu vremennogo pravitel'stva Indii."

24. "Soviet Comment on Pakistan," *The Modern Review* 81 (January 1947): 9.
25. See "The Paris Peace Conference, 1946," *India Quarterly* 3 (January-March 1947), 66.
26. The conference approved a British compromise proposal providing that the two sets of recommendations—one supported by two-thirds and the other by a simple majority—would be forwarded to the Big Four for consideration. For discussion on voting procedure see *Chronology of International Events and Documents*, Supplement to *The World Today*, n.s. 3 (22 July-11 August 1946): 477-81.
27. For differences on this question between the Soviet Union on the one hand, and the US, the UK and France on the other, see the proposals of the four powers for a Draft Permanent Statute for the Free Territory of Trieste in *Paris Peace Conference, 1946: Selected Documents* (Washington, D.C.. 1947), pp. 1348-1442.
28. For Indian support of the French compromise proposal see the statement of Sir Samuel Runganadhan in *The Statesman*, 10 October 1946, p. 5.
29. *Keesing's Contemporary Archives* 6 (1946-1948): 8214; *Paris Peace Conference, 1946: Selected Documents*, pp. 821-24.
30. Sailendra Nath Dhar, *International Relations and World Politics Since 1919* (New York, 1965), pp. 331-32.
31. *The Statesman*, 27 September 1946, p. 8. Emphasis added.
32. Ibid., 12 April 1947, p. 6.
33. Text of Molotov's Speech in *Labour Monthly* 28 (November 1946): 348-56. For criticism of India, see pp. 350-51.
34. A. D'iakov, "The Situation in India," *Pravda*, 21 October 1946, p. 4; cited from *Soviet Press Translations* 2 (28 February 1947): 6-7 (hereafter cited as *SPT*).
35. Ibid., p. 6.
36. Molotov referred to this "pressure" when he spoke at the conference on 10 October: "There exist two diametrically opposite methods in international life. One method, well known from times of old, is the method of coercion and domination, for which all means of pressure are good means. The other method, which, it is true, is not yet widely developed, is the method of democratic cooperation based on the recognition of the principle of equality and the legitimate interests of all countries, big and small." Quoted in "The Problem of International Cooperation in the Light of Practical Experience," editorial in *New Times*, no. 24 (15 December 1946), p. 7. See also Z Lippai, "Pervye mirnye dogovory," *Mirovoe khoziaistvo i mirovaia politika*, February 1947, pp. 3-4.
37. Quoted in *Labour Monthly* 28 (November 1946): 350.
38. D'iakov, "The Situation in India," p. 6.
39. For the background of race discrimination against Indians in South Africa see UN, General Assembly, *Official Records*, Joint Committee of

the First and Sixth Committees, doc. A/68, "Memorandum of the Position of Indians in the Union of South Africa," pp. 53–81.
40. Cited in Karunakaran, *India in World Affairs, August* 1947-*January* 1950, p. 168.
41. UN, General Assembly, *Official Records*, Second Part, First Session, Joint Committee of the First and Sixth Committees, Annex 1, doc. A/149, p. 53.
42. For a characteristic Soviet article on this question see V. Borisov, "On the Subject of Race Discrimination," *New Times*, no. 8 (15 April 1946), pp. 3–6. The writer vehemently criticized racial discrimination in South Africa and added, "This objective [racial equality] is so much the closer to the hearts and minds of the Soviet people since in our country all forms of national oppression have been wiped out and relations between nations are based on the principle of complete equality." (p. 6.) Dmitri Z. Manuilsky, the Ukrainian delegate, later referred to this matter in the General Assembly when he said, "This delegation of India well knows that the Soviet Republics, which have solved the problems of nationality in accordance with the principle of self-determination, cannot take up any position other than that of the defence of the Indian population." UN General Assembly, *Official Records*. Second Part, First Session, Plenary Meetings, 49th meeting. 31 October 1946, p. 921. See also V. Borisov, "The British Colonial Empire as It Really Is," review of Alexander Campbell, *It's Your Empire* (London, 1945), *New Times*, no. 22 (15 November 1946), pp. 25–28; V. Borisov, "Rasovaia diskriminatsiia v Iuzhno-Afrikanskom Soiuze," review of John Burger, *The Black Man's Burden* (London, 1943). *Bol'shevik*, no. 22 (November 1946), pp. 66-72; B. Vronsky, "Race Discrimination in the Capitalist World," *Pravda*, 17 November 1946 (cited from *SPT* 2 [31 January 1947]: 7-9); and V. Berezhkoy, "Discrimination Against Indians in the Union of South Africa," a review of Shafa'at Ahmad Khan, *The Indians in South Africa* (Allahabad, 1946), *New Times*, no. 31 (30 July 1947), pp. 25–28. The apparent Soviet example of abolishing discrimination on the basis of race no doubt impressed the people in India and other countries of the colonial world, where the nationalist leaders and common people alike had personal and bitter experiences of this discrimination. S. Radhakrishnan, who later became India's president, was very much impressed by the absence of any discrimination on this basis in the Stalin Constitution of 1936: "Race equality is a part of the Stalin Constitution and Soviet practice. This cannot be said of two other groups, the United States of America and the British Empire. In the Soviet Union all, whether they belong to minority or a majority group, share in the benefits of a common economic system." Excerpt from Foreward to KS. Hirlekar, *Soviet Asia; The Power Behind USSR* (Bombay, 1945), p. iii. Shafa'at Ahmad Khan, India's Agent-General in South Africa during 1941–45 and later a member in Nehru's Interim Government, wrote, "The positive contribution of Russia to the solution of the racial problem must be studied by every statesman throughout the world...." *The Indians in*

South Africa (Allahabad, 1946), quoted in Berezhkoy. "Discrimination Against Indians," p. 27.

43. The question of the treatment of Indians in South Africa was an emotional issue in India. In regard to the question of South West Africa and trusteeship agreements, and in the coming years on the question of colonial territories, she felt she had an "obligation" to speak on behalf of the peoples who were not represented in the United Nations. See *India and the United Nations*, Report of a Study Group set up by the Indian Council of World Affairs (New York, 1957), p. 76.

44. UN General Assembly, *Official Records*, Second Part, First Session, Plenary Meetings, 37th meeting, 25 October 1946, p. 732.

45. Ibid., 42nd meeting, 29 October 1946, p. 834. Molotov's reference to India in his speech to the General Assembly was widely reported and commented upon in Indian papers. See, for example, "Recognise India's Just Demands—M. Molotov's Appeal to UNO Assembly," *Times of India*, 31 October 1946, p 5; "Molotov Pleads for India's Rights," *Hindustan Times*, 31 October 1946, p. 1; and "UNO Must Recognize India's Just Demands—Molotov's Address," *Amrita Bazar Patrika*, 31 October 1946, p, 1.

46. UN, General Assembly, *Official Records*, Second Part, First Session, General Committee, 19th meeting, 24 October 1946, p. 70. For Vyshinsky's statement in India's support, see ibid., pp. 70-71, 73.

47. See UN General Assembly, *Official Records*, Second Part, First Session, Joint Committee of the First and Sixth Committees, 21-30 November 1946, pp. 1-51.

48. Ibid., 5th meeting, 28 November 1936, pp. 44-45. See also ibid., 1st meeting, 21 November 1946, pp. 1-3, and ibid., 25 November 1946, pp. 8-11. There was much handshaking and intermingling among the Soviet and Indian delegates which, incidentally, did not remain unnoticed by the Western delegates in this era of the emerging Cold War. A Reuters despatch of 27 November reported that after the meeting that day, in which Mrs. Pandit had made a forceful speech, "M. Gromyko walked up to her in the delegates' lounge and, shaking her hand, said, 'I endorse your speech. We will vote for you because we believe you are right." (*The Statesman*, 28 November 1946, p. 1.)

49. Text of the resolution in ibid., Annex 1d, doc. A/C.1 & 6/3, 20 November 1946, p. 132.

50. Ibid., 1st meeting, 21 November 1946, pp. 3-4.

51. Text of the resolution in ibid., Annex 1e doc. A/C.1 & 6/8, 23 November 1946, p. 132.

52. Text of the joint amendment in ibid., doc. A/C.1 & 6/20, p. 43. The "Western dilemma" on this question was discussed by James Reston in the *New York Times*, 26 October 1946, p. 3, in his report, "Fixing of UN Scope Posed by South African Question—Dispute with India Shows Need to Delimit Purely Domestic Jurisdiction." Reston wrote, "This [Soviet support to India] pleased the Indians, of course. One of them remarked

that the Indian people would remember Mr. Vyshinsky's cooperation [in the General Committee on October 24], but it disturbed many other persons, including some Americans who turn pale or bright red at the thought that if Mr. Vyshinsky's argument is correct, the United Nations might have the power to discuss 'human rights and fundamental freedoms' of the Negroes in Georgia."

53. UN, General Assembly, *Official Records*, Second Part, First Session, Joint Committee of the First and Sixth Committees, 3rd meeting, 26 November 1946, pp. 28-29.
54. UN, General Assembly, *Official Records*, Second Part, First Session, Plenary Meetings, 52nd meeting, 8 December 1946, p. 1042.
55. Ibid., pp. 1043-44.
56. Ibid., pp. 1044-45.
57. Text of the resolution in UN, General Assembly, *Official Records*, Second Part, First Session, Joint Committee of the First and Sixth Committees, Annex 1f, doc. A/C.1 & 6/12, 26 November 1946, p. 138.
58. Ibid., 6th meeting, 30 November 1946, p. 51.
59. UN, General Assembly, *Official Records*, Second Part, First Session, Plenary Meetings, 52nd meeting, 8 December 1946, p. 1060.
60. Ibid., p. 1061.
61. UN General Assembly, *Official Records*, Second Part, First Session, Fourth Committee, Trusteeship, pt. 1, 14th meeting, 4 November 1946, p. 64.
62. Ibid., 19th meeting, 13 November 1946, p. 100.
63. Ibid., 20th meeting, 14 November 1946, p. 107.
64. UN, General Assembly, *Official Records*, Second Part, First Session, Fourth Committee, Trusteeship, pt. 3, Meetings of Subcommittee 2, 9th meeting, 28 November 1946, p. 49.
65. For the Indian view see UN, General Assembly, *Official Records*, Second Part, First Session, Fourth Committee, Trusteeship, pt. 1, 15th meeting, 5 November 1946, pp. 70-71, and ibid., 20th meeting, 14 November 1946, pp. 109-11.
66. For the Soviet view see ibid., 18th meeting, 11 November 1946, p. 89. In an English commentary broadcast over Moscow radio on 17 November 1946, K. Hoffman criticized the South African request as an abuse of its mandatory rights. The commentator said, "The claims put forward by F-M [Field Marshall] Smuts not only run counter to the United Nations principles but would be a setback even from the previous mandatory system of the League of Nations." (Reported in *The Statesman*, 18 November 1946, p. 5).
67. Text of Indian resolution in UN, General Assembly, *Official Records*, Second Part, First Session, Fourth Committee, Trusteeship, pt. 1, Annex 21, p. 287. Text of Soviet resolution in ibid.
68. Ibid., 20th meeting, 14 November 1946, pp. 118-20.
69. Text of the joint US-Danish-Indian resolution in UN, General Assembly,

BEGINNINGS OF COOPERATION   43

Official Records, Second Part, First Session, Plenary Meetings Annex 76, p. 1560.
70. UN General Assembly, *Official Records*, Second Part, First Session, Plenary Meetings, 64th meeting, 14 December 1946, p. 1327.
71. For origins of the international trusteeship system and a good summary of the Assembly discussion on the trusteeship agreements see Elizabeth H. Armstrong and William I. Cargo, "The Inauguration of the Trusteeship System of the United Nations," *Department of State Bulletin* 16 (23 March 1947): 511–21.
72. UN General Assembly, *Official Records*, Second Part, First Session, Fourth Committee. pt. 1, 26th meeting, 11 December 1946, p. 169. See also UN, General Assembly, *Official Records*, Second Part, First Session, Plenary Meetings, 61st meeting, 13 December 1946, pp. 1267–69.
73. UN General Assembly, *Official Records*, Second Part, First Session, Fourth Committee, Trusteeship, pt. 2, Subcommittee I, Annex 15, p. 284.
74. See N.V. Novikov's statement in UN, General Assembly, *Official Records*, Second Part, First Session, Plenary Meetings, 62nd meeting, 13 December 1946, pp. 1276–83.
75. UN General Assembly, *Official Records*, Second Part, First Session, Fourth Committee, Trusteeship, pt. 1, 26th meeting, 11 December 1946, p. 169. For disagreement between the US and India on the question of naval and military bases in the trust territories see ibid., 23rd meeting, 9 December 1946, pp. 143–44.
76. Ibid., 14th meeting, 5 November 1946, pp. 65–69.
77. Karunakaran, *India in World Affairs, August* 1947-*January* 1950, p. 206.
78. See the text of the Australian resolution in UN, General Assembly, *Official Records*, Second Part, First Session, First Committee, Annex 7e, doc. A/C.1/42 Rev. 1, p. 327; and the text of the Cuban resolution in ibid., Annex 7b, doc. A/C. 1/49 Rev. 1, 8 November 1946, p. 324.
79. For the US view see ibid., 33rd meeting, 1 December 1946, pp. 215–217. See also Blair Bolles, "US Favours Discussion to Clarify Use of Veto," *FPB* 26 (18 October 1946): 4.
80. The need of the veto right from the Soviet viewpoint was stated by Gen. Romulo of the Philippines Republic, who said, "Why do we not admit the plain fact that the Soviet Union, most steadfast of all in its opposition to efforts to eliminate the veto in the Security Council, has a valid reason for that opposition? We all know that the Soviet Union is in a hopeless minority..., a minority out of all proportion to the real power and influence of the Soviet Union in the modern world. We all know that this is the real reason for the Soviet Union's insistence that the veto be retained." UN, General Assembly, *Official Records*, Second Part, First Session, 61st plenary meeting, 13 December 1946, pp. 1251–52.
81. UN, General Assembly, *Official Records*, Second Part, First Session, First Committee, 20th meeting, 15 November 1946, p. 99. See also UN, General Assembly, *Official Records*, Second Part, First Session, Plenary

Meetings, 60th meeting, 13 December 1946, pp. 1235–44. For Soviet press criticism of the efforts to modify the unanimity principles, see "The Problem of International Cooperation in the Light of Practical Experience," editorial in *New Times*, no. 24 (15 December 1946), pp. 2–4, 7; A. Sokolov, "What Is Hindering International Cooperation?," *New Times*, no. 16 (15 August 1946), pp. 4–9; "International Cooperation in Our Day," editorial in *New Times*, no. 21 (1 November 1946), pp. 1–2; "The Security Council," editorial in *New Times*, no. 37 (10 September 1947), pp 1–3. *New Times* wrote that "In its present form the Security Council serves in some degree as a brake on the aggressive policy of the present-day bidders for world supremacy." (10 September 1947, p. 3.)

82. UN, General Assembly, *Official Records*, Second Part, First Session, First Committee, 23rd meeting, 18 November 1946, p. 120.
83. UN, General Assembly, *Official Records*, Second Part, First Session, First Committee, 23rd meeting, 18 November 1946, p. 121.
84. UN, General Assembly, *Official Records*, Second Part, First Session, Plenary Meetings, 61st meeting, 13 December 1946, p. 1264.
85. UN, *Yearbook of the United Nations*, 1946–47 (Lake Success, 1947), p. 135.
86. UN, General Assembly, *Official Records*, Second Part, First Session, First Committee, 26th meeting, 22 November 1946, pp. 137–38.
87. Ibid., 29th meeting, 27 November 1946, pp. 168, 171–74.
88. UN, General Assembly, *Official Records*, Second Part, First Session, Plenary Meetings, 37th meeting, 25 October 1946, p. 732.
89. Sudhansubimal Mookerji, "Why Anti-Indian Drive?," *The Modern Review* 80 (December 1946): 457.
90. UN, General Assembly, *Official Records*, Second Part, First Session, Plenary Meetings, 52nd meeting, 8 December 1946, p. 1045.
91. Ibid., p. 1046.
92. *The Statesman*, 22 December 1946, p. 1.
93. *The Statesman*, 4 December 1946, p. 7. Syed Raza Ali, a former High Commissioner for India in South Africa, while paying tribute "to those white countries which refused to be swayed by prejudice and expediency," criticized the attitude of the USA and Britain "who claim to be the champions of democracy, equality and liberty, which they so often dangle in the face of Soviet Russia." Reported in *The Statesman*, 2 December 1946, p. 5. See also Naresh Chandra Roy, *India and the United States of America* (Calcutta, 1954), p. 76.
94. "India wins at the UNO," *The Modern Review* 80 (December 1946): 412. See also "An Unholy Alliance," editorial in *Amrita Bazar Patrika*, 31 October 1946, p. 4.
95. See Mrs. Pandit's comment on the vote of the USA at a meeting in New Delhi on 21 December 1946, in *The Statesman*, 22 December 1946, p. 5.
96. See *Trud*, 9 March 1947; *New Times*, no. 11 (14 March 1947), p. 31;

New Times, no. 12 (21 March 1947), p. 31; and *The Statesman*, 17 March 1947, p. 4.
97. "India and the UNO," *The Modern Review* 80 (December 1946): 409–10.
98. See Nehru's press conference in New Delhi on 26 September 1946, in *The Statesman*, 27 September 1946, p. 8.
99. For the charge in some Anglo-American quarters that India "all along" took "a pro-Russian stand" at the UN, and Mrs. Pandit's reply to it, see *The Statesman*, 16 December 1946, p. 1.
100. *The Statesman*, 20 January 1947, p. 5. See also the *New York Times*, 21 January 1947, p. 11. This statement of Dulles is emphasized here because he was to be the architect of American military alliances in Asia, especially SEATO, which were so much to affect India's relations with the USA and the USSR. The impression which Dulles formed of the Interim India Government under Nehru apparently persisted with him for many years, to be somewhat modified only in the last few years of his secretaryship. Winston S. Churchill, another Western leader, had expressed similar view of the Interim Government. See Herbert L. Mathews, "Churchill Solidifies Party; Fears a Soviet-ruled India," *New York Times*, 6 October 1946, pp. 1, 32.
101. *The Statesman*, 21 January 1947, p. 1. Nehru referred to it again two days later, on January 22, while replying to a debate on the Objectives Resolution in the Constituent Assembly. He said, "Recently an American statesman criticized India in words which show how lacking in knowledge and understanding even the statesmen of America are. Because we follow our own policy, this group of nations thinks that we are siding with the other and that group of nations thinks that we are siding with this." *Jawaharlal Nehru's Speeches*, 1: 22.
102. *The Statesman*, 21 January 1947, p. 1. See also Lanka Sundram's letter in the *New York Times*, 2 February 1947, Section 4, p. 8. Sundram was a member of the Indian UN delegation and had just made a tour of the United States where he found "wrong and untenable impressions" by several leaders. Sundram wrote that Nehru's government was not a "Hindu" government, nor did Communism exercise any influence over it.
103. "The Problem of International Cooperation in the Light of Practical Experience," *New Times*, no. 24 (15 December 1946), pp. 3–4, 6. See also N. Sergeyeva, "The United Nations General Assembly," *New Times*, no. 1 (1 January 1947), p. 19. The writer, a *New Times* correspondent at the UN, wrote that the Indian delegation had "to withstand the bitter attack of the South African delegation and its British and American supporters." And because the South African and British delegations put up such a fight, the final passage of the resolution "was an all the greater triumph for its supporters, and especially for the Indian delegation." See also a Moscow radio commentary by M. Yermashev, in a Reuters despatch, "Russia Shares India's Victory," reported in *The Statesman*, 13 December 1946, p. 8.
104. Reported in a Reuters despatch, "Indian Contribution to UNO," from London, 31 December 1946, in *The Statesman*, 3 January 1947, p. 5.

105. *The Statesman,* 8 January 1947, p. 6.
106. Ibid.
107. "Science Congress Review," *Hindustan Times,* 11 January 1947, p. 5.
108. "Eighteen Days in India, an Interview with Academician V.P. Volgin," *Izvestiia.* 2 February 1947; cited from *SPT* 2 (15 April 1947): 11–12; and "Our Trip to India," *New Times,* no. 12 (21 March 1947), pp. 19–24.
109. For example see "Eighteen Days in India," p. 12. Volgin says, "In Benares, I delivered a lecture on 'The Development of the Concept of Socialist Property,' at the request of the Rector of the University. We were informed that the lecture was received with great attention. Each statement concerning the social structure of our great motherland was received eagerly and with great interest."
110. Volgin, "Our Trip to India." p. 19.
111. "Otkrytie Mezhaziatskoi konferentsii v Deli," *Pravda,* 24 March 1947, p. 4. For origins of the conference see *Asian Relations, Being a Report of the Proceedings and Documentation of the First Asian Relations Conference* (New Delhi, 1948), pp. 2–3; hereinafter cited as *Asian Relations.* See also G.H. Jansen, *Nonalignment and the Afro-Asian States* (New York, 1966), pp. 41–45.
112. *Asian Relations,* p. 4.
113. G.H. Jansen, an Indian journalist who has published an interesting account of various Asian and nonaligned conferences, also wondered at the presence of the Soviet Asian republics at the conference. He writes, "When asked today about the massive Soviet representation...the scholars of the Indian Council blandly reply that since the conference was meant to cover the whole of Asia, and since the Central Asian Republics were, and are, a part of Asia, they were invited. But this is disingenuous. Bandung was also supposed to comprise the whole of Asia, but the Soviet States were not invited." Jansen could also have referred to another Asian conference which met in New Delhi in January 1949, again at the initiative of India, to consider the question of Indonesia—a conference to which the Soviet Asian republics were not invited, and which was, as we shall see in Chapter Four, denounced in the Soviet press in the harshest terms. Agreeing that the invitations to the Soviet republics in 1947 were due to Nehru's "influence," Jansen writes of him, "In his early and enthusiastic writings about Russia, he is especially complimentary about the work of modernization that the Russians had carried out in hitherto backward parts of Asia. Further, as a historian, he may well have been influenced by the ancient links between India and the part of the world that was the homeland of the Moghul dynasty. And as a lover of words and phrases, he or anyone else for that matter, would have been interested to meet, for the first time, travellers from Merv and Bokhara and Samarkand." Jansen, *Nonalignment and the Afro-Asian States,* pp. 47–78.
114. *Asian Relations,* p. 22. 115. Ibid., pp. 35–35.

BEGINNINGS OF COOPERATION   47

116. Ibid., p. 60. See also ibid., pp. 47, 52–53, 62, 79, 102, 132–33, 149, 195, 229; and "Mezhaziatskaia konferentsiia v Deli," *Pravda*, 28 March 1947, p. 3.
117. For example, see the discussion on "Agricultural Reconstruction and Industrial Development," in *Asian Relations*, pp. 128–44.
118. See, for example, "Russian Delegation; Harbingers of Scientific and Economic Collaboration," in Kalidas Nag, *New Asia* (Calcutta, 1947), pp. 26–31. Dr. Nag was a prominent Indologist and had drafted a memorandum for the conference on "Cultural Problems." See *Asian Relations*, p. 289.
119. *Asian Relations*, p. 62. See also *The Statesman*, 25 March 1947, p. 7.
120. See "Na Mezhaziatskoi konferentsii v Deli," *Pravda*, 30 March 1947, p. 4 and 4 April 1947, p. 4. See also *New Times*, no 14 (4 April 1947), p. 32.
121. *Asian Relations*, p. 247; "Zakliuchitel'noe zasedanie Mezhaziatskoi konferentsii v Deli," *Pravda*, 5 April 1947, p. 4. See also *New Times*, no. 15 (11 April 1947), p. 31.
122. An article in *Pravda* quoted the growth in the ranks of Soviet friends in the East because of its "unselfish and consistent defense" of their "national independence and democratic aspirations." And it interpreted the "warm welcome" received by the Soviet scientists at the first Indian Science Congress and by the representatives of the Soviet republics at the Asian Relations Conference as evidence of "how deep is the esteem of Eastern Peoples for the Soviet state." N. Rubinstein. "An Aid to the Agitator and Propagandist, Friends of the Soviet Union Abroad," *Pravda*, 30 April 1947; cited from *SPT* 2 (15 October 1947): 179.
123. See note 17.
124. *The Statesman*, 1 December 1946, p. 10.
125. See *The Statesman*, 8 January 1947, p. 6. Nehru expressed the hope that "in the near future our two countries will be able to exchange diplomatic representatives (*cheers*) and that having done so, the door will be opened for closer contacts in many fields of beneficent human activity."
126. *Investiia*, 15 April 1947, p. 4.
127. *The Statesman*, 15 April 1947, p. 1. There was a similar announcement by the Soviet government. See "K ustanovleniiu diplomaticheskikh otnoshenii mezhdu Sovetskim Soiuzom i Indiei," *Izvestiia*, 15 April 1947, p. 4.
128. "Establishment of Soviet-Indian Diplomatic Relations," *New Times*, no. 16 (18 April 1947), p. 15.
129. Ibid. "Anti-Soviet" elements in India were denounced in another article published about a month earlier which also made a distinction between Nehru and these elements by quoting his speech of welcome to the Soviet delegation which attended the Indian Science Congress. "Anti-Soviet Slander in India," *New Times*, no. 11 (14 March 1947), p. 26.
130. Andre Pierre, "Entre Moscou et New Delhi: L'U.R.S.S, s'interesse beaucoup a l'Inde," *Le Monde*, 16 April 1947, p. 2.

131. Ibid. R.C. Menzies, at this time Leader of the Opposition in Australia, said that the political change in India would mean the increase of Russia's political influence affecting the whole political balance of the Middle East and Southern Asia. But he also put some faith in "the independent thought and power of growing Indian nationalism..." Quoted in the *Sunday Statesman*, 20 April 1947, p. 1.

III

The Cold War
Moscow Evaluates India's Nonalignment Policy

> ...there can be no compromise between the forces of democracy and those of imperialism, between the champions of peace and the warmongers either in domestic or international affairs.—Pierre Hentges in "The 'Third Force' in the Service of Imperialism," *For a Lasting Peace, For a People's Democracy*, 15 March 1948, p. 3.

While India was moving to the final phase of the achievement of her independence, with the agony and inevitable tragedy of partition, the world had also moved slowly but steadily towards a different kind of partition—division into two power blocs.[1] Thus began the Cold War between two blocs, one led by the United States and the other by the Soviet Union. It is the logic of every war that the warring powers seek allies in their struggle and tend to judge the policies of other countries on the basis of their attitude to this struggle; the more intense and fierce the war, the more rigid becomes the application of this rule. The Cold War, however, was not an ordinary war; it was—like the two global wars—a total war.

While the question as to when the Cold War really began may be debatable, it can be said with some certainty that President Truman's message to Congress on March 12, 1947,[2] heralding what came to be known as the Truman Doctrine, completed the process of the gradual erosion of the wartime cooperation between the US and the Soviet Union. Truman said that American aid was necessary for the survival of a free Greece—whose government was involved in a bloody conflict with leftist and Communist anti-government rebels—and for Turkey's independence (the British Government was soon to end her help to that strategic country). But the American President did not confine his promise of help only to these two countries.

Instead he said "that it must be the policy of the United States to support free peoples who are resisting attempted subjugation by armed minorities, or by outside pressure." The implication of the President's message was obvious: it was to combat internal communist terrorists and external Soviet and Communist pressure that American aid would be sent. The aid for Greece and Turkey, as had been recommended by Truman, was provided in a bill which became law on 22 May.[3] In the midst of these events, the Foreign Ministers' Conference, which met in Moscow in March and April 1947, ended without settling the German problem. Then, to ensure the European countries against economic collapse—which would certainly lead to increasing communist influence—the US Secretary of State, George Marshall, in a speech at Harvard University on 5 June,[4] launched the famous Marshall Plan.

The Soviets, whose policies—especially in Eastern Europe and Iran—had helped precipitate the Cold War, also hardened their attitude. An article in *Izvestiia* vehemently criticized the Truman Doctrine as "a fresh intrusion of the United States into the affairs of other States."[5] *New Times* said that although the direct purpose of Truman's message was to replace Britain in Greece and Turkey, these were "only stepping stones" in a much wider plan of American expansion. It added, "The real meaning of Truman's message is that it openly proclaims America's claim to supremacy and hegemony over the whole world."[6]

The initial Soviet response to the Marshall Plan, however, seemed favourable. The Soviets attended the conference which began in Paris on 27 June 1947, to discuss Secretary Marshall's proposals. But on 29 June Tass issued a statement criticizing the British and French proposals.[7] Shortly afterwards, on 2 July, Moscow withdrew from the conference. The sixteen non-Communist nations—without the participation of Eastern European countries—met in Paris on July 12 and reached agreement regarding the programme in a few weeks. In July and August, the Soviets signed a series of trade agreements with their East European allies.[8]

Thus by July 1947 the lines between the two power blocs had been clearly drawn. As a noted French writer observes, "The division of Europe really dates from this month of July 1947: on the one side the clients of the United States, on the other the satellites of the Soviet Union..."[9] The Cold War, writes Adam Ulam, now:

assumes the character of position warfare. Both sides become frozen in mutual unfriendliness. It was no longer a question of this or that political difference or of a contested territory; it was the totality of foreign policies of each side that became the object of attack by the other.[10]

It was this international atmosphere—and the chilly winds of the Cold War emanating from Europe and the United States—that greeted the birth of freedom in India. It was inevitable that the developments in Europe and in the Soviet-American rivalry would have increasing influence in determining Soviet attitudes and policies towards India. Speaking in Moscow on 20 May 1947, about three months before India became independent, a Soviet scholar, I.M. Lemin, had asked whether "the question of Indian independence [will] be decided 'a la Philippines' or 'a la Transjordan,' or will she become a genuinely independent and democratic country, one of the major, fully independent factors in Asian and world politics."[11] It was obvious that the Soviet answer to this question would largely depend on India's future course of action regarding the burning issues of the Cold War.

EUGENE VARGA AND INDIA

An indication that the ensuing world struggle—political and ideological—against the West was becoming the determining factor in Soviet policy came in May 1947 when at a meeting of the Institute of Economics of the Academy of Sciences a group of leading Soviet economists met to discuss Eugene Varga's recent book on the capitalist economy.[12] Although the main theme of the discussion was Varga's views on the effect of the Second World War on the economy of the capitalist countries, particularly the United States, there were some references to India and her relationship to Great Britain. Varga had said in his book that "the economic dependence upon England of some of her most important colonies [had] considerably decreased."[13] In fact, the effect of the war had been the transformation of Britain from a creditor to a debtor nation in its relationship with India. As Varga put it at the meeting:

...there is...a great difference between whether India must turn to the London banks and ask them for 1,000,000 pounds sterling credit as charity, for building railroads, and the present-day situation of India, when it presents England with the demand: you are our debtor—pay us 1,200,000,000 pounds sterling...it is impossible to deny that great changes have taken place. One cannot deny facts.[14]

Would this weakening of the British economic hold on India lead to political changes? Varga did not explicitly say so. But V.V. Reikhardt, who presented one of the most critical reports concerning Varga's book, found this implication in it:

The formulations given in the book are very unclear also because they contradict a multitude of facts cited by the author. But the chief thing is that from Yevgeny Samoilovich's [Varga's] propositions a conclusion can be drawn concerning the possibility of the colonies attaining independence by purely economic means.[15]

Varga, at this point, asked, "Do you think it will be like this to the end, that there will always be colonies?" Reikhardt replied, "No, I think the colonies can attain independence, but only in one way— the revolutionary..."[16]

However, the majority of the supported Varga on his views on India. M.I. Rubinshtein, Ya. A. Kronrod, I.N. Dvorkin and L.A. Mendel'son supported Varga's viewpoint that British imperialism had been sharply weakened.[17] In particular reference to India, V.A. Maslennikov, while supporting Varga's thesis, asked, "Can one really discard economic factors from the calculations? They are the basis for understanding political questions."[18] Varga himself said at the meeting:

...there is also a definite 'orthodox' point of view. The empires have remained empires, the colonies have remained colonies, everything has remained as it was before the war. I think this is also wrong...the fact that it is not England that is the creditor of India, Egypt, etc., but the contrary—that has some significance, has it not? It has, of course. The fact that the process of political liberation of the colonies is going on: that India has an ambassador among us and we have an ambassador in India—that is something new.* One cannot say that this signifies nothing.[19]

*Although diplomatic relations between India and the Soviet Union had been

THE COLD WAR 53

Officially, Varga had not yet been "disgraced" and forced to admit his error. Moreover, the publication of these reports did not take place until December 1947. Therefore it cannot be assumed that criticism of Varga's views on India's economic relationship with Britain by some Soviet economists represented the official Soviet view. At best, since it meant criticism of the British economic domination of India—i.e., of foreign capital which was soon to become a part of Soviet anti-imperialist strategy—criticism of Varga at this point indicated what Soviet thinking might be in case the Cold War did take a turn for the worse. More important for our present purposes was a remark of K.V. Ostrovitianov, chairman of the session and Corresponding Member of the Academy of Sciences of the USSR, who said, "One of the very great shortcomings in the teaching of political economy is *the separation of political economy from present-day events.*"[20] In fact, said Ostrovitianov, nothing—neither economic nor ideological nor political questions—could be separated from "present-day events." To be more specific, Ostrovitianov attacked Varga's premise that during the Second World War the struggle between the two systems had been suspended; he added that this struggle in fact should be "the fundamental, the initial methodological proposition in an analysis of capitalism, both of the war period and likewise of post-war development."[21]

THE SOVIET VIEW OF INDIAN INDEPENDENCE

In June 1947, events moved swiftly in India. Early in the month the British Viceroy, Lord Mountbatten, presented the plan of partitioning the country into Muslim-majority and non-Muslim (Hindus and Sikhs) majority areas of the country. The plan was subsequently accepted by both the Indian National Congress and the Muslim League.
The Soviet press, in the meantime, had continued to emphasize

---

established in April, the Indian Ambassador did not arrive in Moscow until August 6 (*The Statesman*, 8 August 1947, p. 4) and the Soviet Ambassador in New Delhi until December 21 (*Statesman Overseas Edition*, December 27 1947, p. 14). Therefore, Varga's reference to the two ambassadors, notwithstanding the fact that the report of these meetings was approved for publication on 8 December 1947, probably indicated merely that the two countries had already established diplomatic relations with each other.

the need for the unity of India, a viewpiont, as we have seen, also held by the Congress Party. A writer in *New Times* wrote that the duty of "true Indian patriots" was "to assuage and eliminate Hindu-Muslim" antagonism since the interests of the poor people in both the communities were the same; therefore, the article concluded, "the political unity of the Indian people is an imperative dictate of the times."[22] Another writer, I. Lemin, criticized the British proposals of 3 June to divide India and said they would lead to division not merely into two but several parts because of the princely and feudal states, in which the British would be able to retain their political, economic, and military control. Regarding the present situation in India, Lemin said, one could not deny that the establishment of diplomatic relations between the Soviet Union and India and the Asian Relations Conference "organized by Nehru's Government" were evidence of "large-scale improvement in the events in the colonial world and of the weakened position of England." But, as he had earlier said in his lecture of 20 May, he emphasized that it was yet to be seen whether the Indian people would be able to achieve "real independence"; only this, he added, would be of "decisive significance."[23]

Lemin's article was obviously written after the publication of the British proposals for partitioning India but before their acceptance by the Congress Party. If the Congress Party were to accept these proposals—as it quickly did—it was bound to be criticized by the Soviets on two points: first, acceptance was a compromise with the party's earlier stand—a position which had been consistently supported by Moscow—on the unity of India; second, in the climate of the Cold War the Soviet Union could hardly be prepared to accept a country as fully independent if it associated in any way with its enemy or enemies in the Cold War.[24]

However, even after the acceptance of the Mountbatten Plan by the Congress, Soviet comments were moderate and cautious in the beginning. A. D'iakov, one of the foremost Soviet experts on India, said that in the guise of these proposals the British were "in a new form" resorting to "the old method of divide—foment national dissension—and rule."[25] The acceptance of the division of the country by the Muslim League did not surprise D'iakov, since the League had agitated for Pakistan. But why did the Congress accept it? Here, although D'iakov was critical of the Congress for abandoning its past stand, he did not question the motives of its leaders. He wrote:

> We still do not know what their motives were, but from the comments in the Indian press it can be judged that certain political circles thought it better to consent without delay to at least a partial satisfaction of the demands for independence, rather than leave the whole question hanging in the air indefinitely.[26]

An article written by Yevgenii Zhukov, a member of the Soviet Academy of Sciences and Director of its Pacific Institute (1943-1950), went a step further.[27] In it Zhukov criticized Vallabhbhai Patel—a prominent Congress Party leader known for his anti-Communist views—as "the most reactionary of all the Congress leaders, whose speeches usually begin and end with the stereotyped phrase that the main danger in India is Communism."[28] Zhukov called Gandhi "an apostle of the backwardness of India" and "an inveterate enemy of the people" whose "role of a preacher of universal conciliation means the ideological disarmament of the people and contributes to the blocking of all reforms in India."[29]

Although Zhukov was using quite harsh words in criticizing Patel and Gandhi, the criticism of these two Indian leaders in the Soviet press was nothing new. The departure lay in Zhukov's characterization of Nehru who, he said, "personally belongs to a privileged higher caste in India and is himself a very rich person—a millionaire." The Soviet writer added, "In the past Nehru was known by his anti-English statements but recently he has undergone a significant evolution to the Right."[30] The main evidence offered for this assertion was Nehru's acceptance of the British proposal for the partitioning of India. Zhukov did not criticize Nehru's foreign policy or say that the Indian leader wanted any kind of military alliance with the British. Also, while he offered a new interpretation of the Asian Relations Conference—that it was an effort on the part of the Indian big bourgeoisie to capture Asian markets through Indian leadership under the old slogan of Pan-Asianism—Zhukov gave credit to Nehru for organizing it, even quoting his statement that the Asians could learn from the rapid development of the Soviet Asian Republics. Zhukov concluded his discussion of the conference by saying that it was still "an evidence of the profound changes that have taken place in Asia."[31]

Blame for wanting a military alliance with Britain was, however, put on a few elements among the Indian capitalists. In a Moscow radio broadcast on 29 June, which was apparently based on the above-cited article, Zhukov said, "Certain Indian capitalists are inclined towards even a military alliance with Britain."[32]

Zhukov not only confined his attacks on the "big bourgeoisie", he also clearly said that there were "progressive left-wing" elements in the rank-and-file of the Congress. In a departure from the earlier outright Soviet condemnation of the Muslim League and its demand for Pakistan, Zhukov said it too had such elements.[33] He said that while the demand for Pakistan apparently had been put to Jinnah "from outside with the aim of producing a split in the united anti-British front in India," it was regarded in a somewhat different way by the Muslim masses. "Sometimes," said Zhukov, "under the slogan of Pakistan an anti-imperialist struggle developed."[34]

The new Soviet interpretation of the birth of Pakistan was quite significant, especially in view of the worsening international situation. Not only did Moscow hope to draw all sections of India except the "big bourgeoisie" to its side, the same hope was also held out for Pakistan.

Several Soviet specialists on India met in a joint session on Indian Studies of the Sections of History and Philosophy, Literature and Language, and Economics and Law of the Academy of Sciences of the USSR on 14-18 June 1947.[35] (Zhukov's article, quoted above, was one of the papers presented at the session.[36] Apparently, only his paper was published at the time.)

Others who presented papers on India at the joint session included V.V. Balabushevich,[37] S.M. Mel'man[38] and A.M. D'iakov.[39] Their papers, together with that of Zhukov, are indicative of the debate then being conducted among Soviet scholars as to whether only the big bourgeoisie in India or the whole of the bourgeoisie had turned reactionary.

Balabushevich criticized the right wing of the Congress Party for starting a new trade union organization to oppose the one dominated by the Communists. He said that it was not surprising that some of the leaders of the new organization "have been coming forward with anti-Soviet declarations."[40] He also criticized the right wing of the Congress for passing several laws against the workers in 1947 and—in language that was current at the time of publication of his paper (1949)—said that the division of India was "the result of a deal of the Indian bourgeoisie and landowners with the British imperialists."[41] He concluded by saying that "the Indian bourgeoisie and the leadership of the Indian National Congress have gone over completely to the camp of reaction and imperialism."[42]

S.M. Mel'man also referred to a "deal" of the Indian bourgeoisie and the leadership of the Congress Party "with English imperialism."[43] However, unlike Balabushevich, he stigmatized only "the Indian big bourgeoisie" as having gone completely over "to the camp of reaction and imperialism."[44]

A.M. D'iakov, in a generally accurate paper, referred to the declaration of the Congress Party of 1929 (Nehru had been the President in the year) calling for the "complete independence" of India, and to its insistence on the unity of India throughout its history as well as in its discussions with the Cabinet Mission in 1946, and asserted that in 1947 the Indian capitalists, being afraid of the growing mass movement, had led "the leadership of the National Congress...to make a deal with the English Government...."[45] Although he concluded by condemning "the selfishness and treachery of the Indian bourgeoisie which for the sake of its profits is ready to sacrifice the indepence of its country,"[46] D'iakov, at one point, made a distinction between the big bourgeoisie and the petty bourgeoisie. Speaking of the acceptance of the partition of India by the Congress Party, he said, "This tendency to compromise gave rise to a significant cleavage between the leadership of the Congress and its left, petty-bourgeois wing."[47] Again he wrote that when the All-India Congress Committee met to approve the partition plan, "...it was adopted...only by an insignificant majority, and that too under the pressure of the leading leaders of the Congress, including Gandhi."[48]

We must conclude, therefore, that the June 1947 debate on the role of the Indian bourgeoisie remained inconclusive. Since the Soviet scholars at this time were allowed to hold differing opinions on this important subject, we cannot say that Balabushevich's view that all of the Indian bourgeoisie had gone over to reaction and imperialism represented the official Soviet attitude in mid-1947. Another important point to be noted—and perhaps more significant in our discussion of Soviet-Indian relations—is that there was no criticism of Nehru's foreign policy at the joint session. In fact, D'iakov made a clear distinction between the foreign and domestic policies of the Nehru Government. (In the Cabinet, it may be noted,

Nehru directed foreign affairs, while domestic affairs were largely under the control of Patel.) D'iakov, while he said that in early 1947 "The Nehru Government *in internal policy* began to pursue a reactionary line, standing openly for the defence of the Indian bourgeoisie," also spoke of several acts of the same government in foreign affairs which were "opposed to the interests of British foreign policy measures."[49]

THE FIRST INDIAN AMBASSADOR IN MOSCOW AND INDIAN INDEPENDENCE DAY

When the first Indian Ambassador, Mrs. Vijayalakshmi Pandit, arrived in Moscow on 6 August 1947,[50] the Soviets, as we have seen, were quite critical of the Indian leaders for many of their actions in domestic affairs, including their acceptance of the British proposal for the division of India. For this, even Nehru had been criticized. But they had nothing yet to complain of as far as Nehru's foreign policy was concerned. In fact, as D'iakov's paper presented at the June session of the Academy of Sciences had shown, a clear distinction between these two aspects of Nehru's government had been carefully kept. The Soviets still hoped that India would be sympathetic to Soviet policies in international affairs.

The choice of Mrs. Pandit as ambassador seemed to encourage this hope. It was a delegation led by her which had made the first, fruitful encounter with Soviet representatives at the UN General Assembly a year earlier. The Soviets therefore were delighted at her appointment. A Reuters despatch from Moscow stated that her appointment, because of her past record, "is felt here to be a happy one in the interests of Soviet-Indian relations."[51]

Soon after her arrival Mrs. Pandit was given good embassy quarters, an unusual courtesy in the conditions that prevailed in the Soviet capital. *Time* magazine, with a slight touch of sarcasm, wrote:

The practical rewards she [Mrs. Pandit] was enjoying in Moscow last week were earned by her defence of Russia's use of the veto, her hostility to Britain and occasional cracks at the US...while other nations were still waiting to be allotted suitable embassy quarters in the crowded capital, newly arrived Mrs. Pandit went straight to the head of the diplomatic queue, was promptly given a well-kept brick residence by Soviet officials.

The Hindi daily *Aja*, however, was very much gratified, reporting that "The Soviet Union has given so much importance to the Indian Embassy that it has provided it with a permanent building; usually the embassies get a permanent building in the Soviet capital only after they have been there for a year."[53]

On 9 August, Mrs. Pandit was received at the Soviet Foreign Ministry by Andrei Vyshinsky, Deputy Minister of Foreign Affairs, and had "a cordial conversation with him."[54] on 13 August, two days prior to the declaration of Indian independence, she presented her credentials to Soviet President N.M. Shvernik at the Kremlin.[55] On 15 August, a representative of the Soviet Foreign Ministry attended the flag-hoisting ceremony and celebration at the Indian Embassy and expressed the greetings and good wishes of the Soviet Government for the newly independent country.[56] The Indian Ambassador gave a press conference on the same day which, together with her message, was carried in full by both *Pravda* and *Izvestiia*.[57] In her message to Tass, as published by the Soviet papers, Mrs. Pandit referred to India's emergence into freedom after a long period of dependence and said that "new India" wanted to continue her past tradition of sending "emissaries of peace and goodwill" by establishing friendship with other nations. She then referred to India's "special links" with the Soviet Union, observing that both had shown the capacity to harmonize diverse races and civilizations. On the basis of this friendship, said Mrs. Pandit, both India and the Soviet Union could work together to establish "a century of freedom, justice and peace for humanity."[58]

Izvestiia also published a detailed account of the independence day ceremonies in New Delhi, referring to 15 August as "the first day of independence after the transfer of power by England."[59] V.M. Molotov, the Soviet Foreign Minister, in a personal congratulatory message to Nehru, said, "*As Prime Minister of independent India*, please accept congratulations on my own behalf and on behalf of the Soviet Government. On Indian independence day, I also send the hearty greetings of the Soviet Government to the people of India."[60] Apparently pleased with Molotov's message and expressing hopes of cooperation with the Soviet Union, Nehru said in reply:

I am most grateful to you...for the message of congratulations that you have sent me on behalf of the Soviet government and on your own behalf on the occasion of the celebration by the people of India of the achievement of their independence. We shall always be proud of this day and earnest and steadfast in our endeavour to devote this freedom to the social and economic betterment of our own people and the promotion of peace and justice throughout the world. In the realization of our international aims we look forward to the cooperation of the government and the people of the USSR...[61]

The crucial question, however, still remained unanswered: What would be the foreign policy of independent India? Would she support Soviet policies or side with the Anglo-American bloc? As the Soviets prepared for their first major moves in Europe to counter the Truman Doctrine and the Marshall Plan and prepared their broad "anti-imperialist" strategy, this question must have been given considerable weight in the Kremlin. Soviet expectations had been clearly expressed by a Soviet journalist, N. Baltiisky, in *New Times* in early June in his reply to an Indian reader. Baltiisky wrote:

...The Soviet Socialist State, by its very nature, is alien to imperialist ambitions, respects and upholds the principles of equality and self-determination of nations, and is a reliable bulwark of universal peace. It is therefore only natural that progressive democrats in other countries should be in full sympathy with the consistently democratic policy pursued by the Soviet Union in international affairs.[62]

THE COLD WAR INTENSIFIES: RUSSIA'S RESPONSE

In July 1947, George F. Kennan, under the pseudonym of "X", wrote the celebrated article, "The Sources of Soviet Conduct," in which he said that "...the main element of any United States policy towards the Soviet Union must be that of a long-term, patient but firm and vigilant containment of Russian expansive tendencies."[63]*

---

* In his *Memoirs*, Kennan protests against being considered the author of the "doctrine of containment" in the form in which it became the basis of Washington's policy. His emphasis, he says, was on containing Russian power and not Communism in general in every part of the globe. Also, it was more a

What would Russia do at this return of the United States to Europe with all its power, economic and military?

In face of the tough posture and firm policies of the West, the Kremlin could perhaps adopt a policy of conciliation and appeasement in settling all outstanding issues. But, as Louis Halle has pointed out, fear has been "the prime driving force" in the history of the Russian state from its very inception in the ninth century. This, together with the Communist belief that the "capitalist-imperialist ruling circles" might at a certain stage wage a war to destroy the Soviet Union, created a kind of "persecution-mania" in the minds of the Soviet leaders.[64] Did not Truman say that America would support "free peoples" everywhere? Was there anything to prevent the Americans from using the atomic bomb to reinforce this support? To quote Halle again, all this

...could only aggravate the fear of encirclement that had haunted Moscow for so many centuries. Who would say that it did not mean the use of the atomic bomb to enforce the American conception of freedom all around the globe? We Americans knew that we intended no such thing, but the Russians had a less benign picture of our character and our intentions.[65]

Moscow's first response to Western moves came in Eastern Europe, where she felt the need for tightening her control on the ruling Communist parties so that they would be completely subservient to Moscow and thus united in the defence of the Soviet state.

The Soviet response was accompanied by some of the most abusive and vituperative language used since the days of Hitler. An article by Boris Gorbatov in *Literaturnaia gazeta* accused Truman of "straining for the laurels of the corporal from Munich."[66] Another Soviet commentator, V. Vishnevsky, criticized a speech by General Dwight Eisenhower at a convention of the American Legion, saying that he called on Americans "to prepare for a new total war, for a war to full exhaustion and destruction." Vishnevsky said the convention was reminiscent of "the Nuremberg gatherings of the Hit-

---

political threat to be contained by political means—a point which, he says, he should have made clear in his article. See Chapters 13 ("The Truman Doctrine") and 15 ("The X-Article") in George F. Kennan, *Memoirs*, 1925–1950 (New York, 1967). See also Louis J. Halle, *The Cold War as History* (New York, 1967), p. 285.

lerites."[67] Such examples were soon to become common in Soviet journals and newspapers.

In order to provide an organizational machinery for tightening Soviet control over the Communist parties of Europe, reptesentatives of the principal European Communist parties met in Wiliza Gora (Upper Silesia), Poland, on 22 September 1947. There they agreed to establish the Communist Information Bureau, known as the Cominform.* A newspaper to be published on behalf of the new organization bore the appealing title, *For a Lasting Peace, For a People's Democracy*.

The key address on the international situation at the meeting was delivered by A.A. Zhdanov, member of the Soviet Politburo and a close associate of Stalin.[68] In his long speech Zhdanov put forward his famous "two camps" thesis. Speaking of the changes that had taken place on the international scene in the postwar years, he said:

...A new alignment of political forces has arisen...the division of the political forces operating on the international arena into two major camps; the imperialist and anti-democratic camp, on the one hand, and the anti-imperialist and democratic camp, on the other. The principal driving force of the imperialist camp is the USA. Allied with it are Great Britain and France.... The imperialist camp is also supported by colony-owning countries such as Belgium and Holland, by countries with reactionary anti-democratic regimes, such as Turkey and Greece, and by countries politically and economically dependent on the United States, such as the Near Eastern and South American countries and China.[69]

As for the "anti-imperialist and democratic camp," Zhdanov said:

* Milovan Djilas, who attended the meeting in Poland as a Yugoslav delegate, says that the idea of an agency "that could facilitate the coordination and exchange of views among the Communist parties" was discussed as early as 1946; it was, however, dropped then primarily because the Soviets thought the time was not yet ripe for it. Explaining the reasons for its revival in 1947, Djilas says, "It ripened in the fall of 1947, most probably in connection with the Marshall Plan and the solidification of Soviet domination over Eastern Europe." (Milovan Djilas, *Conversations with Stalin*, New York, 1962, pp. 128-29).

The anti-fascist forces comprise the second camp. This camp is based on the USSR and the new democracies. It also includes countries that have broken with imperialism and have firmly set foot on the path of democratic development, such as Rumania, Hungary and Finland. Indonesia and Vietnam are associated with it; it has the sympathy of India, Egypt and Syria....[70]

The official Soviet view of Indian foreign policy, up to this point, is unmistakably clear; Zhdanov's statement shows that India's policy was still considered to be sympathetic to the Soviet Union, and by no means was she considered a partner or even supporter of the opposite camp.

Zhdanov advocated an anti-imperialist strategy to suit the prevailing circumstances of the Cold War, aiming at uniting all possible elements in the struggle. In the section of his address dealing with "The Tasks of the Communist Parties in Uniting the Democratic, Anti-Fascist, Peace-Loving Elements to Resist the New Plans of War and Aggression," Zhdanov stated that "...Communist must support all the really patriotic elements who do not want their countries to be imposed upon, who want to resist enthrallment of their countries to foreign capital, and to uphold their national sovereignty."[71] He added that they should "...unite their efforts on the basis of a common anti-imperialist and democratic platform, and gather around them all the democratic and patriotic forces of the people."[72]

Although Zhdanov did not specify what these "democratic and patriotic forces" would be, we can assume that they would include the "anti-imperialist" elements of the bourgeoisie. Although Zhdanov was speaking specifically in reference to Europe, there was no reason why this would not also apply to Asia. Thus Nehru, despite the fact that he had been described by Zhukov as "personally a rich man," could still qualify as a member of Zhdanov's "democratic and patriotic forces" as long as he followed an "anti-imperialist" foreign policy.

In an important lecture delivered in Moscow on 30 October 1947, i.e., about a month after Zhdanov's address, the Soviet historian I. M. Lemin also spoke of the "two currents, two courses in international affairs," but he described the "anti-imperialist" camp in much broader terms than Zhdanov had done. He said:

The Soviet Union, countries of people's democracy, democratic, progressive circles in all the countries follow the same course. It is directed at the creation of a durable, just and democratic postwar order, based on regard for the rights, sovereignty, independence and security of all nations, on international cooperation of all peace-loving states, independent of their differences in ideology and social organization.[73]

Lemin was thus using approximately the same words which were to become current in the relatively more tolerant Khrushchev era. But, one must hasten to add, the Soviet Union, at this point, had no use for nonalignment, neutrality, or a "third force" of Indian or any other variety. Referring to the "Third Course" of the British Labour Party, Lemin warned that the struggle was "between American expansionism and the Soviet policy of peace and security"; the choice for all "peace-loving" peoples was therefore quite evident. The Third Course, said Lemin, was "a myth."[74]

THE COLD WAR AT THE UN AND INDIA'S POLICY

It was in the midst of tough Western postures and anti-Soviet moves and the rising crescendo of Soviet criticism of Western policies and leaders that the second session of the UN General Assembly was convened at Lake Success on 16 September 1947. By this time the Cold War had already begun to dominate all discussions in the corridors of the United Nations,[75] and it was inevitable that it should affect all major issues to be debated by the Assembly.

1. *The election of non-permanent members to the Security Council*
One of the first items on the Assembly's agenda was the election of three non-permanent members of the Security Council to replace Australia, Brazil, and Poland, whose terms were to expire by the end of the year. The Soviets naturally wished that Poland should be replaced by a nation from their own group. It was even reported at the time that they were bargaining with Latin American delegates that the Soviets would support another Latin American country (Argentina) in return for Latin American support for the Ukraine, whose name they proposed to replace Poland.[76] India was attending the UN for the first time as an independent nation; she was eager to play an active role and make her voice heard at Lake

Success. She also felt that the Indian Ocean area should find representation in the Security Council.[77] But her entry disturbed the arrangement that had been working well so far in the election of the non-permanent members of the Security Council.

India's candidacy led to intense discussions in the US delegation at the UN as well as in the State Department.[78] Since the Soviets had supported one country from Latin America, some of the Latin American delegations approached the US to press for Washington's support for the Ukraine.[79] But the US eventually decided to back India. Giving reasons for American support, Loy Henderson, then Director of the Office of Near Eastern and African Affairs in the State Department, said that at this session of the UN General Assembly India had "shown a tendency to follow [a] fairly independent and moderate course." He then added:

India at [the] present time is at foreign policy crossroads. Stimulated by foreign powers interested in creating chaotic conditions in colonial world of Asia and Africa, India could conceivably become [a] dangerous [and] disruptive force. Alternatively, India's genuine interest in dependent peoples could, given friendly collaboration between India and countries sincerely interested in political and economic advancement [of these] peoples, play a stabilizing role in South Asia. India's election to SC with support of US would tend to orient India in latter direction.[80]*

The US was thus pleased at India's performance at the UN. She

---

* It is interesting to note that when, in 1946, India sought US vote for a seat in the Security Council, Washington declined to support her. At the time, Girija Shankar Bajpai, then India's Agent General in the US, met both Dean Acheson and Loy Henderson to plead India's case. (See Memorandum of Conversation, by the Acting Secretary of State, 8 November 1946, in *FRUS* 1946 [Washington, DC, 1969], 5: 97; and *FRUS* 1946 [Washington, DC, 1972], 1: 216–17).

The reasons for US stand in 1946 were the same as in 1947—India's foreign policy vis-a-vis the Soviet Union. While Washington was pleased with India's stand in 1947, in 1946 it was not. Explaining why the US should not support India, John Foster Dulles, a member of the US delegation, stated that it would be a mistake to switch from Belgium to India because New Delhi "was much more apt to be in the Soviet bloc than was Belgium." (Minutes of the Thirteenth Meeting of the United States Delegation..., 1 November 1946, *FRUS* 1946 [Washington, DC, 1972], 1: 220), now calculated that by supporting India's candidacy for the Security Council, Washington would be able to push India further in the direction of the West. The British, on the other hand, appeared "not at all displeased that the Indians have maneuvered themselves... into a position in opposition to the Soviet Union."[81]

At the UN, the first ballot took place on 30 September. Both Argentina and Canada were elected; for the third seat neither India nor the Ukraine got two-thirds of the votes, although the Ukraine got a few more, evidence that the Latin American countries had voted for her. The delegates voted five times again on the same afternoon, but although the Ukraine picked up a few more votes, she still did not get enough to win.[82] The members were now tired after voting seven times during the day and wanted adjournment.[83] Vyshinsky not only opposed this move but, despite the objections of the President, also made a strong appeal for the Ukraine's case. Said Vyshinsky:

...I should like to put the question directly and honestly: what is happening? The Slav countries have an indisputable right to have their own representative in the Security Council in addition to the representative of the Soviet Union.[84]

The Assembly met again next day, 1 October 1947, to vote on this issue and did so twice, but without resolving the deadlock.[85] Since Vyshinsky had spoken the day before in support of the Ukraine, Mrs. Pandit spoke for India:

India offered herself as a candidate to the Security Council since we, and many others, felt that with the withdrawal of Australia, the Indian Ocean area would remain without representation and Asia itself would be greatly under-represented. It was because we felt that there was a fundamental principle involved, one which is recognized in the Charter itself, that of a geographical distribution in the allocation of seats, that we stood for this seat....[86]

The President said he had allowed Mrs. Pandit to speak because Vyshinsky had also been permitted to do so earlier. But Vyshinsky wanted to refute Mrs. Pandit's argument in favour of "geographical distribution" and became angry when the President stopped him from doing so. He said, in reference to the Indian delegation, "I am entitled to expect that the President had authority enough to interrupt the other speaker too."[87] The issue, however, still remained unresolved.

The Soviets saw some hidden strings behind the action of India.[88] B. Izakov and Yu. Zhukov, the two *Pravda* correspondents in New York, reported that the US was using the issue "to isolate" the Soviet Union and "to further subjugate the United Nations to its influence." For this purpose, they argued, the US has put forward the name of India "as a rival of the Ukraine."[89] They did not yet attack India directly, but said, "The Indian delegation, apparently without investigating properly the situation which has arisen, has allowed itself to be converted into one of the pieces on the chess-board of American diplomacy."[90] The *Izvestiia* correspondent, B. Vronsky, also blamed India for allowing itself to be used by the US delegation. He wrote:

...Everybody knows perfectly well that India least of all wanted to disturb the settled principles of the selection of the Security Council. Still less did she want to stand against the Ukraine which has made so many sacrifices in the name of freedom and independence of the peoples of the whole world and for saving world civilization.

In view of this it seems that the Indian delegation is in the present position not because of its own will, most likely, the hidden machinations of the American and British delegations are responsible for this.[91]

Thus the logic of the Cold War had begun to work in India's case in her first move at the UN as an independent country. To the Soviets, an action which did not side with them or went against them must have been inspired by the "Anglo-American bloc."

In India, the incident gave rise to some anti-Soviet feeling. A Hindi daily, *Āja*, wrote that so far India and the Soviet Union had worked "in the international conferences as a united front against the reactionary powers for the defence of democratic principles," but the clash between India and the Ukraine over the Security Council seat showed "the first possibility of a clash of interests of India and the Soviet Union on the international stage." The paper also suggested that by supporting India the Soviets would not only have avoided tension but would have won a powerful supporter.[92]

Nataraja, the political commentator of *Āja*, replied to the criticism of India in the Soviet press on this question:

> ...India has always had, and will always have, sympathy for Russia. But it will be in her own interest to forget the talk of a political chessboard and pieces.* She may use the Ukraine, Poland or her other satellites in any way she likes, India doesn't have anything to say in this regard. [But] Russia will have to change her old conceptions about India, otherwise due to the fault of her own eye-sight she might lose the sympathy of her real well-wisher—India.[93]

The Statesman also resented the "unpleasant and uncalled-for remarks" of Vyshinsky and "the malicious comments" of the Soviet press and stigmatized Russia for trading votes with the Latin American countries "in spite of her otherwise unfriendly relations with them."[94]

India was still in the race for the Security Council seat when the General Assembly took up the question again on 20 October. Even after two ballots, the deadlock between India and the Ukraine persisted.[95]

Seeing that there was no way out, India finally decided to withdraw from the race.[96] Therefore, when the Assembly met on 13 November to vote again, the Ukraine was duly elected.[97] While giving the reason for India's withdrawal, Mrs. Pandit criticized what she called "secret diplomacy" through which the allocation of seats was privately arranged before the balloting. Although she said she did not desire "to offend any of the Powers concerned,"[98] her remarks were evidently directed against the Soviet Union.

The Soviet Union held to her belief that India's entering the race against the Ukraine and clinging to her candidacy for one and a half month was at the instigation of the "enemies" of the Soviet Union in the United Nations. Writing after the victory of the Ukraine, a Soviet writer stated, "Anglo-American diplomacy thus suffered another defeat."[99]

2. *The problems of Greece and Korea* Two international problems that had already become issues of the Cold War, Greece and Korea,

---

*Apparently a reference to the allegation made in the *Pravda* report of 7 October 1947.

were now taken up by the UN General Assembly. India's policy on these questions, as we shall see, had a considerable effect on Soviet-Indian relations.

In Greece, the government was dealing with an open revolt led by the Greek Communists. Although the rebellion had started soon after the end of the Second World War, the crisis deepened in 1946 with renewed activity of the rebels. There is some evidence that they were supported by Yugoslavia, Bulgaria, and Albania, and enjoyed the advice and indirect support of the Soviets.[100] The Greek Government was helped by the British Army and later by military aid from the United States.[101] Thus an internal conflict, like so many other postwar issues, quickly assumed international dimensions.

Since the Security Council, where the Soviet Union made frequent use of its veto, had been unable to bring about an end to the conflict, it was brought by the United States before the General Assembly. After a heated debate, the Assembly eventually passed a resolution, originally moved by the US but slightly amended by France and Great Britain, which called upon Albania, Bulgaria, and Yugoslavia "to do nothing which could furnish aid and assistance to the said guerrillas."[102] Although the US resolution was passed by a huge majority, India abstained.[103] The Soviet Union submitted a resolution which blamed the "hostile policy" of the Greek Government towards countries on its borders, "foreign interference in the internal affairs of Greece," and "anti-democratic forces grouped around the present Greek Government" as responsible for the existing situation.[104] As a solution, the Soviet resolution called for "the withdrawal of foreign troops and foreign military personnel" from Greek territory. India abstained on all but one on the paragraphs of the Soviet resolution, but on the last one, calling for the withdrawal of all foreign troops, she voted with the Soviets.[105]

Korea emerged from the Second World War with the northern portion (north of the 38th parallel) occupied by Soviet troops and the southern half by the US Army. Only cooperation and mutual trust between the two powers could ensure the emergence of a unified, independent Korea. In its absence, however, the Joint Commission which was appointed with this objective under the Moscow Agreement of 1945 failed to achieve anything. In the meantime, Moscow went about establishing a Communist regime in North Korea. In the South, a non-Communist if not democratic, regime was gradually coming into existence.

The US made several proposals to Moscow in the first half of 1947 looking towards the reunification of Korea. Nothing materialized, however, since the US suggestions were quite unacceptable to the Kremlin.[106]

The United States, which now brought the Korean question before the UN General Assembly, submitted a resolution recommending that "the occupying Powers hold elections not later than 31 March 1948," and that an assembly and a national government be established soon after the elections.[107] It also proposed the establishment of a United Nations Temporary Commission to facilitate and expedite the implementation of the provisions of the resolution, which included the withdrawal of the occupying forces after the establishment of a national government. A Soviet resolution, however, proposed to the US Government "the simultaneous withdrawal of their troops from southern and northern Korea respectively at the beginning of 1948, thereby leaving to the Korean people itself the establishment of a national government of Korea."[108]

India's behaviour on the Korean issue, unlike the silence she observed on the Greek question, was very active. From the very beginning, the Indian delegate, B.R. Sen, criticized the Soviet approach as one that would delay the achievement of Korea's independence.[109] On another occasion, Sen said that the Soviet resolution would "lead only to confusion, since there was no Korean Government which could take over the administration of the country."[110] Replying to the Ukrainian delegate D.Z. Manuilsky's statement that "It was impossible to hold free elections...in the presence of foreign troops and under the fictitious control of a United Nations commission,"[111] the Indian delegate said:

The argument of the USSR that the presence of foreign troops would be a hindrance to the holding of free elections in Korea, to say the least, was in contradiction with the assertion that free and unanimous elections had taken place in Northern Korea while USSR troops were present.[112]

This was indeed a very harsh attack on Manuilsky, one which he was not likely to forget. India not only criticized the Soviet resolution but also expressed her support for the American resolution, with some proposed changes. The Indian delegate proposed, among other things, that "the election should be held on the basis of adult suffrage... and by secret ballot."[113] In an amendment to the original US resolution, India also proposed that the elections should be held under the supervision of the UN Commission and not conducted by the occupying powers as provided in the resolution.[114] These suggestions were included in the revised US draft,[115] which was approved by the Political Committee.[116] At the suggestion of the US, India was also named as one of the members on the proposed commission.[117] In the General Assembly, therefore, India voted in favour of the revised US draft and against the Soviet resolution.[118]

Speaking for the Soviet Union, A.A. Gromyko said the proposed commission would only work as "a screen concealing the unilateral activities which are in fact being carried on by the United States of America in South Korea and which...are designed to convert Korea into an American colony..."[119] Thus in Soviet eyes, India, by being a member of the commission, would actually be serving US interests. Gromyko refused to participate in the voting on the American resolution.[120]

Manuilsky, whose statement was earlier criticized by the Indian delegate in the Political Committee, now said that he would "like to say a few words to our Indian friends." Reminding the Indians of the support the USSR had given them on the question of the treatment of Indians in South Africa, he said:

We deeply sympathize with the delegation of India in its fight against the South African policy of racial discrimination. We consider that the Indian delegation is defending an absolutely just cause which we, basing ourselves upon consideration of principles, will support in the Political and Security Committee today. We have the right, however, to ask this of the delegation of India: Are you not weakening your position in view of the treatment of the Koreans by the United States authorities, which is approximately the same as the treatment of the native population and the Indians by the Union of South Africa? In the circumstances, how can you justify your support of this resolution without contradicting yourselves?[121]

Manuilsky ended his long statement with an ominous warning: "by casting your vote in favour of the Korean Commission, you will create a new hotbed of discord, which will be fraught with grave consequences. Remember that!"[122]

3. *The US proposal for creation of the Little Assembly* During the preceding year, the Soviet Union had frequently used its veto in the Security Council, creating a deadlock and making it an ineffective body on most of the controversial issues. As we have seen, in the first session of the UN General Assembly in 1946, the United States, conscious of its majority both in the Security Council and the General Assembly, wanted some modification in this provision. It will also be recalled that it had not succeeded in its efforts. At the second session the US put forward a new formula: the formation of an Interim Committee, the so-called Little Assembly, consisting of one representative from each nation, with quite wide powers regarding questions of international peace and security for which, under the UN Charter, the Security Council had in fact "the primary responsibility."[123] The Committee was to meet after the last day of the current session of the Assembly and was to continue in existence until the opening of the next.

It was inevitable that the Soviet Union would bitterly oppose this American move; after all, the proposal calling for the creation of the Little Assembly was directed towards making Soviet opposition to Western proposals, at least to some extent, ineffective. India, it will be recalled, had supported the Soviet position on the right of veto in the first session of the General Assembly. She still thought that any change regarding this provision should occur only after an agreement among the Great Powers, but in the past year she had also seen the abuse of the veto by the Soviet Union, blocking the settlement of questions, such as Korea, in which she was intensely interested. India was therefore prepared to support the US proposal for a Little Assembly—as her delegate put it—"purely as an experimental measure."[124]

The US proposal, after some modifications,[125] was adopted on 13 november 1947.[126] India voted for the creation of the Little Assembly. A Tass dispatch, as was to be expected, said that the decision of the General Assembly would assist only "in turning the United Nations into a weapon of American policy."[127]

REASONS FOR SHIFT IN INDIA'S POLICY

Why did India change her stand on some of the issues on which she had voted differently in 1946? And why did she support the US on most of the major issues brought up at the 1947 General Assembly session? The explanation lies in India's domestic concerns and requirements. The brave talk of anti-colonialism and anti-racialism no doubt expressed some general principles of India's worldview, but Nehru, as Prime Minister, was now faced with more immediate and pressing problems at home. These were scarcity of food and need for outside assistance for the country's economic development. Any realistic foreign policy had to take these requirements into consideration. As Nehru himself said on 4 December 1947, a country's foreign policy is "ultimately...the outcome of [its] economic policy."[128]

In the past year, India had realized that the US was the only source of food imports. The initial approach to the Soviets had not brought any results.[129] On the other hand, Washington acted promptly to facilitate the export of grain for India at a time when the maritime strikes going on in the US created difficulties for such exports. In a letter to Secretary of State Dean Acheson, Nehru requested the US government to see that the strikes did not impede wheat exports to India in view of the difficult food situation in the country.[130] Acheson took swift action at Nehru's urgings and assured the Indian government that grain will continue to be shipped to India.[131]

A more important consideration, however, was the need for economic development in India. On a special mission to Washington as Nehru's envoy, Girija Shankar Bajpai told the Acting Assistant Secretary of State, Robert A. Lovett, that "India can expect no effective assistance from the USSR in its primary objective of developing and strengthening itself economically...." He then added, "In fact the US is the only country which is in a position to aid India."[132] It was with this realization that the Indian government had started discussions with the US ambassador in India, Henry F. Grady, only a month after achieving independence. This led the US ambassador to invite Stephen Bechtel of W.A. Bechtel & Co. of San Francisco to come to India and have talks with Nehru and other members of the Indian government.[133] Although there were no immediate positive results,[134] talks on this would continue in the future.

A minor factor in this pro-Western tilt in India's foreign policy was the unproductive and disappointing experience that its ambassador had in Moscow. Although Mrs. Pandit's initial welcome, in her own words, was "warm—red carpet, red roses, and assurances of friendship and esteem,"[135] she found the atmosphere in the Soviet capital stifling and full of suspicion of all foreigners.[136] The travel restrictions imposed on foreign diplomats were also applied in her case, and her application to seek the government's permission to travel to some of the Soviet republics brought no positive response.[137] She did visit Leningrad and was honoured with the presentation of a copy of the first Russian translation of *Ramayana*. And she was also welcomed warmly by the city of Moscow ("The new Indian ambassador was given a standing and, as far as we could judge, enthusiastic welcome. I felt very happy."[138]) on the occasion of its eighth anniversary, but politically she was not able to accomplish much. Stalin never invited her to the Kremlin, nor did she make any attempt to see him.[139] On the other hand, she got into friendly terms with the Western diplomats, including US ambassador General Walter Bedell Smith. A few months later at the UN, when an American diplomat asked her about her stay in Moscow, Mrs. Pandit

made a wry face and said that everything was most difficult there and although she should not reach conclusions on the basis of only one month's residence in the Soviet capital, she was already disillusioned. She said that she and her brother [Nehru] had changed their minds a great deal in the last year in respect to the USSR...[140]

India's policy had, in fact, been shifting towards the West for sometime. Although publicly it would be reflected only at the 1947 session of the General Assembly, New Delhi had already begun to express it through diplomatic channels. In February 1947, more than a month before the announcement of the establishment of diplomatic relations between India and the Soviet Union, and almost four months before Mrs. Pandit's arrival in the Soviet capital, Nehru's newly appointed ambassador to the US, Asaf Ali, told US Secretary of State George Marshall that "he hoped to see the political and economic development of his country flourish, and that if India became strong it would be a bastion for the world against the great northern neighbour which now cast its shadow over two continents, Asia and Africa."[141] And to emphasize India's changed policy at the 1947 General Assembly session, Bajpai told the State Department officials in Washington, D.C., in April 1948 that "India's position had been more accurately reflected in the 1947 UNGA than in the 1946 session."[142]

SOVIET VIEW OF INDIA'S PERFORMANCE

If one were to look at the Indian performance at this crucial session of the General Assembly with Soviet eyes, one could say with some justification that India had sided with the "Anglo-American bloc." Except on the Greek issue, on which India was mostly neutral, she had voted in favour of the US resolutions on Korea and the Little Assembly.

As the history of the Korean negotiations between the US and the USSR during 1945-1947 had shown, the Soviet Union was not prepared to accept the US solution of the problem. Now, with the passage of a UN resolution creating a commission to supervise elections in Korea, she was faced with the alternative of acquiescence or open defiance. There could be little doubt as to what her choice would be. With India not only voting for the creation of the commission but also included as a member of it and then made chairman of it, New Delhi was clearly pitted against Moscow's policies.

The veto right was the very basis of Soviet participation in the work of the UN. As Alvin Rubinstein has written:

The Soviet Union...joined the UN as an act of accommodation, not conviction. Stalin had no ideals or illusions concerning the nature of the UN, its capacity to safeguard Soviet security, or its domination by the Western Powers. Aware that the UN was ideologically and institutionally a creation of the capitalist West, Stalin agreed to membership only when the right to veto any moves inimical to Soviet interests was made a corner-stone of the new organization. The veto was a precondition for Soviet participation....[143]

In an editorial published just before the convening of the second session of the General Assembly, *New Times* had warned those who were trying "to abolish or restrict" the veto right. "In its present form," the editorial stated, "the Security Council serves in some degree as a brake on the aggressive policy of the present-day bidders for world supremacy."[144] But now the General Assembly had been able—with India voting in favour—to "restrict" the veto right of the Soviets.

While considering the possible effect of India's policy on the Soviet attitude, we have also to remember that it was a time when even the attitude of neutrality was not liked by either the Soviet Union or the United States.[145]

The Soviets and their supporters had continued to attack any talk of neutrality among socialists in Western Europe. A Yugoslav Communist, M. Pijade, for example, wrote in the Cominform paper that the position of a "third force" allegedly between capitalism and Communism, has always strengthened and even brought temporary victory to reaction in different countries, and is actually a total betrayal of the interests of the working class and servility to the bourgeoisie."[146] An editorial in the same paper said that the theory of the "third force" was only "a thinly disguised political trick, disguised to facilitate the expansion of the American imperialists...." It added that "the provocative splitting role for which this theory is a cloak" was becoming clear to "the democratic elements" in every country.[147] Mikhail Suslov presented the Soviet view at a Lenin Memorial meeting in Moscow on 21 January 1948. Criticizing those who did not like the Bolshevik "partisanship in ideology," Suslov said:

Lenin denounced the bourgeois preachers of 'neutrality,' non-partisanship in the arts as servitors of capital, whose talk about creative freedom only masks the dependence of art on the money bags. 'Non-partisanship in bourgeois society,' Lenin said, 'is only a fraud, a screen, a passive expression of affiliation to the party of the wellfed, to the party of the masters, to the party of the exploiters.'[148]

Indian policy had therefore not been what the Soviets had expected of Nehru. The doubts they had of India's independence had been further reinforced by India's selection of Lord Mountbatten—the last British Viceroy in India, who had presided over the partition of the country—as independent India's first Governor-General. As an East European premier reportedly told an Indian journalist, R.K. Karanjia, at the time, "...by permitting itself within the Empire and retain Mountbatten as Governor-General, India had mortgaged its independence to the British Devil and the American Dollar."[149] Karanjia, who visited several East European capitals towards the end of 1947, noted a decided change in the Soviet attitude towards India and its foreign policy.[150] K.M. Pannikar, a member of the Indian delegation at the second session of the UN General Assembly, described a conversation which he and the leader of the delegation, Mrs. Pandit, had with Manuilsky:

...Mrs. Pandit had asked of him the reason for this less cordial attitude of the Soviet Union to the Indian delegation this year. Manuilsky was frank. "What is your interest in Korea and Greece? To us these are vital areas for our defence. Why should India interest herself against our interest in these matters?"—such was the general line of his argument. It was clear that Russia had become uncertain of India's attitude and was generally suspicious of our approach to questions of vital interest to her.[151]

In a standard Soviet reference work, the *Diplomaticheskii Slovar'* (1950), Soviet displeasure at India's policy at the 1947 session of the General Assembly was unmistakably expressed. Regarding Mrs. Pandit, it stated:

...In the General Assembly, Mrs. Pandit successfully came forward with regard to the Indians in South Africa, but on a number of questions (Greek question, question of the election of non-permanent members of the Security Council) she took a position in support of the Anglo-American bloc....[152]

As we have seen, Yevgenii Zhukov was the first Soviet expert to provide a clear indication of Soviet displeasure with Nehru. But at that time, it must be noted, his criticism had been confined only to Nehru's acceptance of the British plan for the partition of India. Immediately after India's vote on the critical issues in the UN, however, Zhukov specifically voiced a critical view of Nehru's policy of neutrality. Writing in *Bol'shevik* in December 1947, Zhukov said:

In order to undermine the internal forces of resistance in the colonies and semi-colonies, imperialism and its agents as usual are mobilizing not only the old means—all possible religious and philosophic reactionary teachings—but are even modifying in conformity with the East, the 'theory' of the third force now fashionable in Europe....
According to this 'theory' the countries of the East are to preserve strict 'neutrality' in the struggle between two forces—Communism and imperialism. It is significant that the 'theory' of the third force has especially wide circulation and success among the Indian bour-

geoisie.... The meaning of the whole 'theory' consists in the fact that the imperialists and their accomplices are trying to slander the USSR and with this purpose are putting her on the same level with American imperialism.[153]

Thus Nehru, who in 1946 and early 1947 had been considered a "progressive" and a "democrat" by the Soviets, now in December 1947 had moved over into Zhdanov's "imperialist camp." In a report delivered in June 1949 at a joint meeting of the Learned Councils of the Economics Institute and the Pacific Institute of the USSR Academy of Sciences, Zhukov was to describe this change—or "metamorphosis," as he put it—in these words:

...Nehru...has turned from a left-wing Congressite and exposer of imperialism into a nimble servant of two masters, Britain and the USA, into an ally of the Indian princess and landowners, a bloody strangler of the progressive forces in India. But such is the logic of the class struggle: there can be no 'middle position' between imperialism and democracy.[154]

Thus the Soviets had no use for Nehru's nonalignment policy in its existing form; it was found to be serving the interests of "imperialism" and not of "democracy."

NOTES

1. See "Divided India a Prelude to Divided World," *The Modern Review* 82 (July 1947), 13–14.
2. *Department of State Bulletin* 16 (23 March 1947): 534–37.
3. See "An Act to Provide for Assistance to Greece and Turkey," ibid. 16 (1 June 1947), 1071–73.
4. Ibid. 16 (15 June 1947), 1159–60.
5. "Vystuplenie Trumena v kongresse," editorial in *Izvestiia*, 14 March 1947, p. 1.
6. "American Foreign Policy," editorial in *New Times*, no. 12 (21 March 1947), p. 2.
7. Text of the Tass statement is included in *Documents on International Affairs* 1947–48 (London, 1952), pp. 42–45.
8. Robert M. Slusser and Jan F. Triska, *A Calender of Soviet Treaties, 1917–1957* (Standord, 1959), pp. 233–36.

9. Andre Fontaine, *History of the Cold War; From the October Revolution to the Korean War* 1917–1950 (New York, 1968), p. 331.
10. Adam B. Ulam, *Expansion and Coexistence; The History of Soviet Foreign Policy*, 1917–67 (New York, 1968), p. 437.
11. I.M. Lemin, *Britanskaia Imperiia* (Moscow, 1947), p. 31. This is a verbatim record of a lecture delivered in Moscow on 20 May 1947.
12. Yevgenii [Eugene] Varga, *Izmeneniia v ekonomike kapitalizma v itoge Vtoroi mirovoi voiny* (Moscow, 1946).
13. Quoted by Varga in his concluding remarks on 21 May 1947, in *Soviet Views on the Post-War World Economy; an Official Critique of Eugene Varga's 'Changes in the Economy of Capitalism Resulting From the Second World War'*, trans. by Leo Gruliow (Washington, D.C., 1948), p. 122.
14. Ibid. 15. Ibid., p. 20. 16. Ibid.
17. Ibid., pp. 46, 74, 80, and 98–99. 18. Ibid., p. 72. 19. Ibid., p. 7.
20. Ibid., p. 2; emphasis added. 21. Ibid., p. 110.
22. N. Baltiisky, "Reply to Indian Readers," *New Times*, no. 23 (6 June 1947), p. 19.
23. I. Lemin, "Sovremennye problemy Britanskoi imperii," *Mirovoe khoziaistvo i mirovaia politika*, no. 6 (June 1947), pp. 10–11.
24. Even the US sometimes took this position in its attitude towards some Communist nationalists. For example, Loy Henderson, when he was US Ambassador in New Delhi, said, "It is impossible, in the opinion of the United States, for a Communist, in the Moscow sense of the term, to be a genuine nationalist. My Government is convinced that any movement headed by a Moscow-trained Communist such as Ho Chi Minh must be in the direction of subservience to a foreign state, not in that of independence or self-government." *New York Times*, 28 March 1950, p. 20.
25. A. Dyakov (D'iakov), "The New British Plan for India," *New Times*, no. 24 (13 June 1947), p. 14.
26. Ibid.
27. Ye. Zhukov, "K polozheniiu v Indii," *Mirovoe khoziaistvo i mirovaia politika*, no. 7 (July 1947), pp. 3–14.
28. Ibid., p. 10. 29. Ibid., pp. 10–11.
30. Ibid., p. 10. 31. Ibid., p. 14.
32. Moscow Radio, 29 June 1947, reported in *The Statesman*, 1 July 1947, p. 5.
33. Zhukov, "K polozheniiu v Indii," p. 10.
34. Moscow Radio, 29 June 1947, reported in *The Statesman*, 1 July, 1947, p. 5.
35. For a report of the joint session see Akademiia Nauk SSSR, *Uchenye Zapiski Tikhookeanskogo Instituta*, vol. 2, *Indiskii sbornik* (Moscow, 1949).
36. Ibid., p. 1.

37. V.V. Balabushevich, "Rabochii klass i rabochee dvizhenie v sovremennoi Indii," in ibid., pp. 5-28.
38. S.M. Mel'man "Ekonomicheskie posledstvii vtoroi mirovoi voiny dlia Indii," in Ibid., pp. 29-53.
39. A.M. D'iakov, "Poslevoennye Angliiskie plany gosudarstvennogo ustroistva Indii," in ibid., pp. 54–66.
41. Balabushevich, "Rabochii klass i rabochee dvizhenie," p. 27.
41. Ibid., p. 28. 42. Ibid.
43. Mel'man, "Ekonomicheskie posledstvii," p. 53. 44. Ibid.
45. D'iakov, "Poslevoennye Angliiskie plany," p. 62.
46. Ibid. 47. Ibid., p. 62. 48. Ibid., p. 65.
49. Ibid., p. 62. Emphasis added.
50. *The Statesman*, 8 August 1947. p. 4.
51. Reuters despatch from Moscow, 27 June 1947, in *The Statesman*, 28 June 1947, p 4. See also another Reuters despatch from Moscow, 2 August 1947, in ibid., 3 August 1947, p. 4.
52. "Robin Redbreast," *Time*, 8 September 1947, pp. 27-28.
53. "Hindi mem parichaya patra—Soviyata sarakara ke liye" [Credentials in Hindi – For the Soviet Government], *Aja*, 7 August 1947, p. 3.
54. *The Statesman*, 10 August 1947, p. 4.
55. Ibid., 14 August 1947, p. 7. 56. *Aja*, 18 August 1947, p. 4.
57. "Poslanie Vidzhaii Lakshimi Pandit, indiiskogo posla v Moskve," *Pravda* and *Izvestiia*, 16 August 1947, p. 4.
51. Ibid.
59. "Tseremonii v sviazi s ob"iavleniem nezavisimosti Indii," *Izvestiia*, 16 August 1947, p. 4.
60. "Molotova dvara badhai—Jawaharalala Nehru ko" [Molotov's Congratulations to Jawaharlal Nehru], *Aja*, 24 August 1947, p. Emphasis added. A copy of Molotov's telegram of 17 August 1947, was supplied to the author by the Soviet embassy in Washington, DC.
61. Nehru's telegram to Molotov, 21 August 1947; copy obtained by the author through the Soviet embassy in Washington, DC.
62. N. Baltiisky, "Reply to Indian Readers," *New Times*, no. 23 (6 June 1947), p. 19.
63. "X" [George F. Kennan], "The Sources of Soviet Conduct," *Foreign Affairs* 25 (July 1947): 575.
64. Louis J. Halle, *The Cold War as History* (New York, 1967), pp. 12-13, 145.
65. Ibid., p. 160.
66. Boris Gorbatov, "Garri Trumen," *Literaturnaiia gazeta*, 20 September 1947, p. 2.
67. V. Vishnevskii, "Podzhigateli voiny: Fashistskii Legion v Amerike," ibid., 24 September 1947, p. 1.

68. A. Zhdanov, "The International Situation," *For a Lasting Peace, For a People's Democracy*, 10 November 1947, pp. 2–4.
69. Ibid., p. 2.   70. Ibid.
71. Ibid., p. 4.   72. Ibid.
73. I. M. Lemin, "Bor'ba dvukh napravlenii v mezhdunarodnykh otnosheniiakh," verbatim record of a lecture delivered in Moscow on 30 October 1947 (Moscow, 1947), p. 24.
74. Ibid., p. 25.
75. See, for example, "The Cold War," editorial in the *New Statesman and Nation*, 23 August 1947, pp. 142-43 which reported that the atmosphere at Lake Success had been poisoned by the Cold War to such an extent that it would be surprising if the United Nations survived the Greek tragedy—at this time one of the most controversial issues between the US and Russia.
76. "India and the Security Council," *Statesman Overseas Edition*, 24 October 1947, p. 4.
77. See the Indian delegate's statements in the General Assembly on 1 October and 13 November in UN, General Assembly, *Official Records*, Second Session, Plenary Meetings, vol. 1, pp. 330, 749-50.
78. *Foreign Relations of the United States* 1947 (Washington, DC, 1973) 1: 122, 129-30, 134-38, 148-51, 153-58, and 160-64 (hereafter cited as *FRUS*).
79. Ibid., pp. 155-56.
80. Henderson to Charles Bohlen, 6 October 1947, ibid., p. 158.
81. Memorandum of Conversation [between G. Hayden of the US delegation and B. Cockram of the British delegation], 2 October 1947, ibid., p. 154.
82. UN General Assembly, *Official Records*, Second Session, Plenary Meetings, 92nd and 93rd meetings, 30 September 1947, pp. 320-26.
83. Ibid., 93rd meeting, 30 September 1947, pp 325-27.
84. Ibid., p. 327.
85. Ibid., 94th meeting, 1 October 1947, pp. 328-29.
86. Ibid., p. 330.   87. Ibid., p. 331.
88. See, for example, Tass despatch from New York, "Nedostoinye makhinatsii vokrug vyborov nepostoiannogo chlena Soveta Bezopasnosti," *Pravda*, 2 October 1947, p. 4.
89. B. Izakov and Yu. Zhukov, "Pochemu pravednik Karan krichit 'Karaul'?" *Pravda*, 7 October 1947, p. 4.
90. Ibid.
91. B. Vronskii, "Manipuliatsii amerikanskoi delegatsii," *Izvestiia*, 7 October 1947, p. 4.
92. "Rusa aura Bharata maim sangharsha ?" [Clash between India and the Soviet Union?], editorial in *Aja*, 4 October 1947, p. 2.
93. Nataraja, "Visva ki Rangasala maim—Savana ka Andha [On the World Stage—With Jaundiced Eyes]," *Aja*, 13 October 1947, p. 2. The Hindi proverb used here means that everything looks yellow to a jaundiced eye;

it has been used by the writer to point out the Soviet view of the world, including India.

94. "India and the Security Council," editorial in the *Statesman Overseas Edition*, 24 October 1947, p. 4.
95. UN General Assembly, *Official Records*, Second Session, Plenary Meetings, 109th meeting, 13 November 1947, p. 749.
96. *New York Times*, 12 November 1947, p. 1.
97. UN, General Assembly, *Official Records*, Second Session, Plenary Meetings, 109th meeting, 13 November 1947, p. 749.
98. Ibid., pp. 749–50.
99. A. Alekseev, "Vtoraia sessiia General'noi Assemblei Organizatsii ob'edinennykh natsii," *Mirovoe khoziaistvoi i mirovaia politika*, no. 12 (December 1947), p. 9.
100. See the letter allegedly written to General Markos, the Commander of the rebel forces, to Nico Zachariades, Secretary General of the Greek Communist Party, 10 February 1948, in *Documents on International Affairs*, 1947–48 (London 1952), pp. 318–20.
101. On US policy towards Greece, see Winifred N. Hadsel, "American Policy towards Greece," *Foreign Policy Reports* 22 (1 September 1947): 146–47.
102. UN, General Assembly, *Official Records*, Second Session, Resolutions, Resolution 109 (II), 21 October 1947, p. 13.
103. UN, General Assembly, *Official Records*, Second Session, Plenary Meetings, 100th meeting, 21 October 1947, pp. 461–62.
104. UN, General Assembly, *Official Records*, Second Session, Political Committee, Annex 15th, doc. A/C. 1/199, 27 September 1947, pp. 595–96.
105. Ibid., 73rd meeting, 13 October 1947, pp. 125–29.
106. Texts of these diplomatic exchanges are included in *Documents on International Affairs*, 1947–48, pp. 680–96.
107. UN, General Assembly, *Official Records*, Second Session, Political Committee, Annex 16b, doc. A/C. 1/218, 17 October 1947, p. 604.
108. Ibid., Annex 16g, doc. A/C. 1/232, 29 October 1947, p. 607.
109. Ibid., 90th meeting, 30 October 1947, p. 269.
110. Ibid., 91st meeting, 30 October 1947, p. 285.
111. Ibid., 92nd meeting, 4 November 1947, p. 292.
112. Ibid., p. 302.
113. Ibid., 91st meeting, 30 October 1947, p. 285.
114. Ibid., Annex 161, doc. A/C. 1/237, 4 November 1947, p. 609.
115. Ibid., Annex 16c, doc. A/C. 1/218 Rev. 1, pp. 605–6.
116. Ibid, 94th meeting, 5 November 1947, p. 307.
117. Ibid., p. 306.
118. UN, General Assembly, *Official Records*, Second Session, Plenary Meetings, 112th meeting, 14 November 1947, p. 858.
119. Ibid., 111th meeting, 13 November 1947, p. 829.

THE COLD WAR 83

120. Ibid., p. 832.
121. Ibid., 112th meeting, 14 November 1947, p. 853.
122. Ibid., p. 858.
123. See the US draft resolution in UN, General Assembly, *Official Records*, Second Session, Political Committee, Annex 17a, doc. A/C. 1/196, 26 September 1947, pp. 609-10.
124. UN, General Assembly, *Official Records*, Second Session, Political Committee, 76th meeting, 16 October 1947, p. 151. In an obvious reference to the Soviet criticism that it would be an attack on the privileges of the Security Council, the Indian delegate also said that he was satisfied that this would not happen. He then added, "It was true that the Interim Committee would deal with matters of peace and security, but only within the powers of the Assembly, and the Assembly had to some extent common jurisdiction on those questions," ibid., 9th meeting, 5 November 1947, pp. 317-18. The Soviets could hardly agree with this interpretation.
125. UN, General Assembly, *Official Records*, Second Session, Resolutions, Resolution 111 (II), 13 November 1947, pp. 15-16.
126. UN, General Assembly, *Official Records*, Second Session, Plenary Meetings, 111th meeting, 13 November 1947, p. 822.
127. "Reshenie sposobstvuiushchee prevrashcheniiu OON v orudie amerikanskoi vneshnei politiki," *Pravda*, 17 November 1947, p. 2.
128. *Jawaharlal Nehru's Speeches*, vol. 1, 1946-49 (New Delhi, 1949), p. 202.
129. See Chapter Two, note 15.
130. Text of Nehru's message is cited in George R. Merrel (US Commissioner in India) to Acheson, 20 September 1946, *FRUS*, 1946 (Washington, DC, 1969), 5: 94.
131. Acheson to Bajpai, 7 October 1946, ibid., pp. 94-95.
132. Memorandum of Conversation, by the Acting Secretary of State, 2 April 1948, *FRUS*, 1948 (Washington, DC, 1975), 5: 507.
133. Grady to Bechtel, 16 October 1947, Papers of Henry F. Grady, Harry S. Truman Library.
134. Henry F. Grady, "Adventures in Diplomacy," pp. 181-82, Papers of Henry F. Grady, Harry S. Truman Library.
135. Vijayalakshmi Pandit, *The Scope of Happiness: A Personal Memoir* (New York, 1979), p. 236.
136. Ibid., pp. 236-45.   137. Ibid., p. 241.   138. Ibid., p. 242.
139. See T.N. Kaul, *Diplomacy in Peace and War: Recollections and Reflections* (New Delhi, 1979), p. 15. Kaul served as First Secretary in the Indian embassy during Mrs. Pandit's tenure as ambassador.
140. Memorandum of Conversation, by Mr. Ray L. Thurston of the United States Delegation of Advisers, 8 November 1947, *FRUS*, 1947 (Washington, DC, 1973), 1: 164.

141. Memorandum of Conversation, by the Secretary of State, 26 February 1947, *FRUS*, 1947 (Washington, DC, 1972), 3: 148.
142. Memorandum of Conversation, by the Assistant Chief of Division of South Asian Affairs, 2 April 1948, *FRUS*, 1948 (Washington, DC, 1975), 5: 502.
143. Alvin Z. Rubinstein, *The Soviets in International Organizations* (Princeton, 1964), p. 3.
144. "The Security Council," editorial in *New Times*, no. 37 (10 September 1947), pp. 1–3.
145. For example India's neutrality on the Greek question created some displeasure in Western circles. See K.P. Karunakaran, *India in World Affairs, August* 1947-*January* 1950 (Calcutta, 1952), p. 278.
146. M. Pjade [Pijade], "The International Conference of the Socialist Parties in Antwerp," *For a Lasting Peace, For a People's Democracy*, 1 December 1947, p. 8.
147. "For Unity of the Working Class," editorial in ibid., 15 January 1948, p. 1. See also Pierre Hentges, "The 'Third Force' in the Service of Imperialism," ibid., 15 March 1948, p. 3.
148. "The Ideas of Lenin Illumine Path to Communism; Report Delivered by M.A. Suslov on 21 January 1948, at Memorial Meeting Held in Moscow on Occasion of 24th Anniversary of Death of V.I. Lenin," ibid., 1 February 1948, p. 3.
149. R.K. Karanjia, "The Foreign Policy of India," *New Statesman and Nation*, 3 January 1948, p. 6.
150. Ibid.
151. K.M. Panikkar, *In Two Chinas, Memoirs of a Diplomat* (London, 1955), pp. 10–11.
152. A. Ya. Vyshinsky (chief editor), *Diplomaticheskii Slovar'* (Moscow, 1950), 2: 315.
153. Ye. Zhukov, "Obostrenie krizisa kolonial'noi sistemy," *Bol'shevik*, no. 23 (December 1947), p. 63.
154. Ye. Zhukov, "Problems of the National-Colonial Struggle Since the Second World War," *Voprosy ekonomiki*, no. 9, 1949, quoted from *Current Digest of the Soviet Press* 1 (3 January 1950): 5.

IV

India's Further Estrangement from Moscow

Facts irrefutably prove that the Indian big bourgeoisie has willingly taken upon itself the role of a steward of Anglo-American imperialism by rallying all the reactionary elements in the countries of East Asia for the struggle against the national liberation movement of the oppressed peoples, against those forces that stand for [a] lasting democratic peace.—V.V. Balabushevich in "New Stage in the National Liberation Struggle of the People of India," presented in June 1949 at a joint meeting of the Learned Councils of the Institute of Economics and of the Pacific Institute of the USSR Academy of Sciences (cited from *Colonial Peoples's Struggle for Liberation*, Bombay, 1950, p. 57).

THE CONTINUATION OF THE COLD WAR

The year 1948 was not marked by any relaxation in the Cold War which had become a reality in the preceding year; instead mutual distrust and suspicion led to more rigid postures and both sides began to consolidate their positions in the areas they directly or indirectly controlled.

Moscow began by signing pacts of assistance and friendship with Rumania, Hungary, and Bulgaria on 4 February, 18 February and 18 March respectively. A Communist coup in Czechoslovakia took place on 25 February 1948, which the US, France, and Great Britain stigmatized as jeopardizing "the very existence of the principles of liberty to which all democratic nations are attached."[1] It was reported on 10 March that Jan Masaryk, the Czechoslovak Foreign Minister, had committed suicide,[2] and by June the country was completely in Communist hands.

On the question of Germany, the two sides found it difficult to agree on anything. They began the year by taking steps directed towards consolidating their positions in the areas under their occupation. Finally, on 20 March, Marshal Vasily Sokolovsky walked out of the four-power Allied Control Council of Berlin after accusing the three Western Powers of violating earlier agreements regarding Germany.[3] The Soviets followed this action by instituting the blockade of Berlin, which strained Western relations with Moscow still further.

The West also took significant steps to prepare itself for any military contingency. On 17 March, Great Britain, France, Belgium, the Netherlands and Luxembourg signed a 50-year treaty for collective self-defence in Brussels.[4] On the some day President Truman recommended to the US Congress early adoption of universal military training.[5] Washington also began to evolve a policy looking towards the creation of military defence pacts in Europe and elsewhere to meet any possible threat from Moscow. It had, in fact, encouraged the signing of the Brussels Treaty and it was hoped that the US would be associated with it before long.[6] On 11 June 1948, the US Senate passed the Vandenburg Resolution, which expressed faith in the "progressive developments of regional and other collective arrangements for individual and collective self-defence" and promised US "association with such arrangements."[7]

The US Department of State itself began to work on such an arrangement. Louis Halle, who was a member of the Policy Planning Staff in the office of the US Secretary of State at this time, writes that "sometime in 1948" Dean Rusk, then Director of the Office of United Nations Affairs in the State Department, called a meeting in which he asked "the Department to address itself to the question of preparing a treaty, modeled on the Rio Treaty, that might be entered into by such countries all around the world as were disposed to resist the expansion of the Soviet Union." Thus Washington was considering the establishment of collective defence pacts not only in Europe but also in other areas of the world. However, since the European situation was the main source of worry to the US at the moment, it was with regard to the defence of Europe that the Department of State moved most rapidly. In April 1949 the North Atlantic Treaty was signed by Denmark, Iceland, Italy, Norway, Portugal, Canada, and the US, in addition to the five Brussels powers. The treaty provided for full mutual armed assistance against "an armed attack against one or more of them [the signatories] in Europe or North America...."

What seemed to be a defensive alliance to the West could hardly be taken as such by Moscow. In a memorandum issued on the formation of the North Atlantic Treaty Organization (NATO), the Soviets said that the treaty was in fact "directed against the Soviet Union" and "designed to intimidate the states which do not agree to obey the dictate of the Anglo-American grouping of Powers that lay claim to world domination...."[10]

What could be the role of "neutrals" or "nonaligned" nations in such an international situation? In an editorial written on New Year's Day, an Indian newspaper, the *Statesman*, lamented, "Capitalism and Communism, the USA and Russia, democracy and totalitarianism seem to be fast shaping for a struggle in which room for neutrals is sharply contracting."[11]

As we have noted, the Soviet attitude towards the "third" course had been made clear in the preceding year. In 1949, in a particular reference to the "bourgeois nationalists" of countries like India, Ye. M. Zhukov said that it was only to disguise their real role as "agents of imperialism" that they "put forward the idea of 'neutrality' or the so-called middle line, middle path, between imperialism and Communism."[12] In fact, Zhukov added, the way in which this theory had been practised has already proved its falseness.[13] In an obvious reference to the actual application of this policy, he said, "Supporters of bourgeois nationalists invariably end with slanders against the USSR, against Communism, exposing themselves as agents of imperialism."[14] It was therefore apparent that Moscow would continue to judge Nehru's foreign policy not on the basis of his frequent assertions about India's independent line in world affairs but on his actual performance in this arena.

KOREA AGAIN: THE SOVIETS WATCH INDIA'S ROLE IN THE UN COMMISSION

The UN Temporary Commission, which, as we have seen, had been appointed in the autumn of 1947 at the suggestion of the US to supervise elections in Korea for the formation of a National Government, flew to Korea in January 1948. India, it will be recalled, had been chosen a member of the commission at US insistence; an Indian national had been named chairman. Since the Soviet Union had bitterly criticized the setting up of the commission, it was clear that she would not only not cooperate with it, but would also consider its activities as hostile to her interests in Korea.

The commission, however, arrived in Korea in early January and was accorded what its chairman, K.P.S. Menon, described as "an unforgettable reception,"[15] but one in which there was not a single Communist leader present.[16]

Menon put emphasis on the preservation of Korea's unity from the very beginning. In his first statement after arriving in Korea, he said:

The thirty-eighth parallel was not meant to divide Korea forever. It was considered to be a military necessity, though, in fact, that necessity never arose. Yet this minor military expedient has so far continued to be a major political obstacle in the way of the unification of Korea.[17]

On 15 January, in a public address in the Seoul Stadium, Menon said, "Whom God hath joined together, let no man put asunder."[18] He spoke in the same vein in a broadcast on 21 January, this time eliciting much praise from General John R. Hodge, Commanding General of the US forces in Korea.[19] He later wrote, "Korea was indivisible, whether one looked at the problem from an economic, political or historical point of view. Deep down in the heart of every Korean, whether in the North or the South, was this longing for unity."[20] But the Soviets could hardly be expected to look at this problem solely on the basis of these considerations. Having established a foothold in North Korea, Moscow was not prepared to let it come under any government in the South which it knew would be under US influence. Therefore, it was not interested in the kind of unity for which Menon and other members of the commission were working.

In an effort to establish contact with the Soviet authorities in the North, Menon sent a letter to Lieutenant General G.P. Korotkov, Commanding General of the Soviet Forces in Korea, on 16 January. In his letter Menon said that he was seeking a meeting with the Soviet general "to exchange appropriate courtesies."[21] Korotkov did not reply to Menon's letter; instead Soviet Deputy Foreign Minister Andrei Gromyko informed the UN Secretary-General:

...we find it necessary to remind you of the negative attitude taken by the Soviet Government towards the establishment of the United Nations Commission on Korea as already stated by the Soviet delegation during the second session of the General Assembly of the United Nations.[22]

A similar reply was also sent to the UN Secretary-General by the Ukrainian delegation.[23] Still retaining some hope that the Soviets might not be so inflexible, the commission sent three envelopes on 23 January addressed to General Korotkov and two to General Kim Il Sung, Chairman of the People's Committee of North Korea, containing copies of Menon's public speech in Seoul on 14 January, his broadcast on 21 January, and press announcements and discussions with Korean personalities.[24] But despite the efforts made by the American liaison officer stationed in Pyongyang to deliver these letters on 30 January, 31 January, 1 February, 2 February, and again on 3 February, the Soviet authorities still refused to accept them. The commission was finally informed by the US military authorities that the Soviets "would neither sign for nor accept the letters..."[25]

After being rebuffed by the Soviets, the commission decided to concentrate on studying the situation in South Korea.[26] The commission also continued to stress the theme of unification, an effort which, according to Menon, began to have some effect across the 38th parallel. Menon describes the reaction of the North:

...The Government of North Korea therefore began to abuse the Commission in choice language, as "hirelings of the American dollar," "puppets consisting of henchmen of American imperialists, bent on converting Korea into an American colony" and "brokers who want to fatten the pocket of the United States of America, as well as their own, by selling under false pretences, the small nations of the world, including Korea."[27]

The commission was therefore unsuccessful in establishing any contacts with the North. There was no other course left to it but to report to the Interim Committee of the General Assembly to seek its advice for further action. Since the Soviets had opposed the setting up of the committee in the preceding year, from their viewpoint, as Peter Calvocoressi has put, "an illegal commission was [now] seeking instructions from an illegal committee."[28]

The extent to which official Indian policy regarding Korea followed the American line is evident from the difference in viewpoints apparent at Lake Success between Menon, the Indian Chairman of the UN Commission, and P.P. Pillai, at this time India's Permanent Representative at the United Nations.

Although Menon's initial statements had been welcomed by US authorities in Korea, he was criticized by them when he did not favour Washington's desire to hold elections only in South Korea and establish a separate government in Seoul. Joseph Jacobs, the US political adviser, called him a member of the "British bloc" or "anti-American bloc."[29] Under Menon's direction—and supported by the Canadian, Australian, and Syrian delegates—the commission decided by a vote of 5 to 3 against holding elections only in the South.[30] Later, presenting the commission's report to the Interim Committee of the UN General Assembly, he spoke forcefully of the need for preserving Korea's unity. He also warned the committee that if the unity of Korea was not restored and if two states were allowed to come into existence in Korea, they were bound to come into collision with each other.[31]

Despite Menon's statement, the US decided to proceed with the holding of elections in the southern part of Korea and thereby to establish a pro-Western government there. When Menon informed the US that the Indian delegation at the UN had asked for instructions from New Delhi and had been told by the Indian government not to support the US move,[32] Secretary of State George Marshall decided to approach New Delhi directly. He instructed US ambassador Loy Henderson to meet the Indian officials, saying that the "Department earnestly hopes Indian delegation may be instructed to support US position."[33] Apparently, Henderson's direct approach and explanation of US position changed New Delhi's stand. He was able to report to Washington on February 26 that "the Indian delegation at the UN had been instructed to follow a policy 'in substance' the same as proposed by the US Government."[34]

Acting at the US suggestion, the Interim Committee now decided to instruct the commission to implement its programme in such parts of Korea as were accessible to it.[35]

It is interesting to note that both Australia and Canada voted against the US proposal, while the Indian delegate Pillai, as freshly instructed by New Delhi, supported it.[36] Writing years later, Menon was still critical of Pillai's vote, saying that "India had always taken pride in saying that she would put principle before expediency."³⁷

Within the commission also, India now supported the move to hold elections in the South. On 12 March, by a vote of 4 to 2 with two abstentions, the commission decided to hold elections on 9 May. India voted in favour along with China, the Philippines and El Salvador; Australia and Canada, in accordance with their stand in the Interim Committee, voted against the decision, while France and Syria abstained. Interestingly enough, Menon voted to implement the decision of the Interim Committee. But now he was "speaking as a delegate of India" and was obviously carrying out the instructions of his government.³⁸ Not only this, the new Indian chairman of the commission, Bahadur Singh, even praised the work of the American authorities regarding the arrangment of the elections.³⁹ The Soviet reaction to this move was naturally one of strong disapproval and condemnation. A Soviet writer later said, "All the Korean people in the North and in the South received the decision about separate elections with profound resentment."⁴⁰

Boycotted by the leftist and moderate parties and marked by much violence,⁴¹ the elections took place on 10 May. But the judgment of the UN Commission was that they represented "a valid expression of the free will of the electorate in those parts of Korea which were accessible to the commission and in which the inhabitants constitute approximately two-thirds of the people of all Korea."⁴² Consisting largely of the supporters of Dr. Syngman Rhee, a veteran nationalist but a conservative and a strong anti-Communist, the new national assembly adopted a constitution for the "Republic of Korea," and elected Rhee as President. The new government was formally inaugurated on 15 August, thus ending the American Military Government. It was clear from the statements of both General MacArthur and President Rhee that the authority of the new government would be regarded as extending over the whole of Korea.⁴³

Elections in the usual Communist style took place in North Korea in late August, leading to the establishment of a "Democratic Korean People's Republic". It too, like the government in the South, claimed jurisdiction over the whole of Korea.⁴⁴* Moscow accorded recogni-

---

* Of the Supreme People's Assembly in North Korea convened after the August elections, *Pravda* wrote that it "demonstrated the unanimous will of the Korean people to continue the struggle for the reunification of northern

tion to the new regime in early October and before long appointed an ambassador to Pyongyang.[45] Thus Korea was divided into two parts, one pro-US and the other pro-Soviet, making the problem of the unification of the country more difficult than ever.

The UN General Assembly in December 1948 was faced with the question, which of the two Korean governments should be recognized. A Czechoslovak resolution proposed that delegates of the People's Democratic Republic should be invited to participate in the debates on Korea, while China proposed that this invitation should instead be extended to the representatives of the Republic of Korea.[46] The committee rejected the Czechoslovak resolution and accepted the one proposed by China, India voting with the US on both occasions.[47] A joint resolution now moved by the US, China and Australia proposed that the Republican Government in the South be recognized as the only legitimate government of all Korea and provided for the setting up of a new UN Commission to supervise the withdrawal of the occupation forces and to "lend its good office to bring about the unification of Korea..."[48]* The Soviet Union, on the other hand, proposed that the old commission should be terminated and no successor appointed to it.[49] Jacob Malik, the Soviet delegate, told the Political Committee:

... Looking back on what had been done, it was clear that the Commission had helped the United States Government to achieve

---

and southern Korea into a single, independent, and democratic Korean state." Voicing Moscow's support for the unification of Korea under the Communists, the Soviet paper said, "The Soviet people and Soviet public opinion welcome the formation of the People's Democratic Government of Korea, discerning in it a significant and important step towards the unification of the entire Korean people." ("An Importont Historical Event in the Life of the Korean People," *Pravda*, 13 September 1948, p. 3; cited from *SPT*, vol. 3, 1 November 1948, 580).

* As in the case of holding separate elections in the South, India showed some reluctance to accept the US view that the Rhee government in Seoul be accepted as the "national" government of all of Korea. Again, it led to intense discussions between the US embassy in India and Indian foreign office, where Menon now served as Secretary for External Affairs. George Marshall spoke of a "substantial identity of views" on the Korean question between the US and India, and hoped that the "present attitude of Menon and GOI [Government of India] can be altered in our favour...." (The Secretary of State to the Embassy in India, 22 June 1948, *FRUS*, 1948, Washington, DC, 1974. 6: 1224). It is apparent that the US again succeeded in persuading India to drop its opposition and support Washington's position at the UN.

its aim of obtaining control of South Korea, so that it could become a springboard for military aggression in Asia and a field for exploitation by American monopolies..."[50]

The committee, however, adopted the three-power joint resolution and rejected the one proposed by the Soviet Union.[51] In the Plenary Session of the General Assembly, the US supported resolution was passed (India voting for it) with an amendment from Canada. The Canadian amendment proposed that the new commission should consist of all members of the old commission, excepting Canada and the Ukraine.[52] India thus continued to be a member of the UN Commission.

The members of the commission arrived in Korea at the end of January 1949 and were soon denounced by the Pyongyang radio as a "collection of hirelings of American imperialism."[53] In an effort to contact the North, the commission made a direct appeal to Moscow, requesting it to intercede with the northern government, an appeal which Moscow completely ignored.[54] Thus it appeared that there was no hope that the commission would be successful in achieving the unification of Korea. India, although hoping for the eventual unification of Korea, at the moment thought it best to support the US policy (and thus oppose the Russian stand) directed towards setting up a non-communist and pro-US government in the South.

The Soviet View of the Kashmir War

One of the questions that bedeviled Indian-Pakistan relations from their very inception as independent states was the question of Kashmir, a strategic area lying in the northwest of India. As we shall see, Kashmir was also to become an issue of the Cold War, thus complicating the problem further and making its solution more difficult.

When India was divided between India and Pakistan, the Instrument of Accession had provided that the rulers of the Indian States could join either India or Pakistan.[55]

In the course of time, the states surrounded by Pakistan territory joined Pakistan, and the states within India joined India, although this process of accession in some cases was not altogether smooth. Kashmir's case was unique. It was bordered by both India and Pakistan, although its larger border was with the latter. During

India's struggle for freedom it had also presented a unique example on the Hindu-Muslim question. While the Muslim League had a local organization in Kashmir—the Muslim Conference, which supported its policies—there was also the powerful National Conference led by Sheikh Abdullah, a Muslim leader, which opposed the League's policies based on religion, and supported the policies of the Indian National Congress for the creation of a united secular India. Sheikh Abdullah had also shared Nehru's ideas on socialism, an important fact to mention since in all Soviet writings of this period he was lauded highly.[56] Nehru himself had supported the National Conference, advising a prominent Hindu leader in Kashmir, Prem Nath Bazaz, to work under Abdullah's leadership.[57] Nehru had visited Kashmir in 1946, risking arrest, to support Abdullah, who had been imprisoned by the Hindu ruler of the state.[58]

At the time of partition, both India and Pakistan wished to acquire Kashmir. Apart from strategic considerations, Pakistan wanted Kashmir because it was an area with a Muslim majority. India's reasons were also based on the religious charactor of the Kashmiris, but for the opposite reason: the Indian leaders, especially Nehru, thought the accession of Kashmir would strengthen their efforts to set up a secular state in India in face of the opposition of those who wanted it to become a Hindu state.

The Maharaja of Kashmir hesitated, however, and did not accede to either India or Pakistan. Then, in October 1947, there was a full-scale invasion of the state when armed tribesmen from the Pakistani side entered. When they had reached the outskirts of Srinagar, the capital, the ruler decided to accede to India. In order to seek help from New Delhi, the ruler signed an Instrument of Accession and stated that he desired to set up an interim government under Sheikh Abdullah.[59] Lord Mountbatten, Governor-General of India, accepted the accession with one condition: "that, as soon as law and order have been restored in Kashmir and her soil cleared of the invader, the question of the State's accession should be settled by a reference to the people."[60] The offer was one made by India herself, although under the terms of the Instrument of Accession, Kashmir's accession had already become legal and final. Sheikh Abdullah came to New Delhi and asked for India's help on behalf of his organization, the National Conference.[61]

India claimed that Pakistan had planned the invasion of Kashmir to force its accession. Her case was based on this charge when she decided to bring the Kashmir issue before the UN Security Council in January 1948.⁶² Pakistan denied that she had been involved in any way, stating that she had rather tried to check the infiltrators who entered Kashmir after hearing tales of persecution of fellow Muslims by the Hindu government of the state.⁶³

Whatever the Indian or Pakistani claims might have been, it is worthwhile to see how the Western and the Soviet press reported these developments. It would at least show whether the policies, eventually decided on in Washington, London, or Moscow towards this question, were based on the merits of the case, or whether some other considerations were the determining factors.

The London *Times* published a report from its correspondent in India on 13 January 1948, which said:

That Pakistan is unofficially involved in aiding the raiders is certain. Your correspondent has first hand evidence that arms, ammunition, and supplies are being made available to the Azad Kashmir* forces. A few Pakistani officers are also helping to direct their operations... and however much the Pakistan Government may disavow intervention, moral and material support is certainly forthcoming.⁶⁴

On 29 January 1948, the *New York Times* published a long dispatch from Robert Trumbull, its correspondent in India and Pakistan. This was an account of an interview which took place in Lahore, Pakistan, with an ex-GI from New York, Russell K. Haight, who had fought for two months with the Azad Kashmir forces, but who was now leaving Pakistan. Russell instructed Trumbull to publish the interview only after receiving a coded telegram from him that he had left Pakistan, since otherwise he feared he might be murdered by the Pakistanis. In his dispatch, Trumbull reported that:

Mr. Haight said gasoline—a scarce and strictly rationed commodity—was supplied plentifully to the raiders by the Pakistan authorities. Mr. Haight also found Pakistan army personnel running the Azad Kashmir radio station, relaying messages through their own Pakistan Army receivers, organizing and managing Azad en-

---

*"Azad [free] Kashmir" was the name given by Pakistan to that part of Kashmir which she was able to occupy, and where she established a separate government—the Azad Kashmir Government.

campments in Pakistan, and supplying uniforms, food, arms and ammunition shipments.[65]

Thus the correspondents of the two most important papers of the Western world corroborated the Indian charge that Pakistan was involved in the tribal invasion of Kashmir.

The Soviet reporting on Pakistan's involvement was not very different from the reports of the London *Times* and the *New York Times*. Z. Petrunicheva, in a long article on Kashmir in which she gave a detailed background of the "National Movement in Kashmir," mentioned the Maharaja's policy of hesitation prior to the fateful days of October. But she says, "the events were hastened by the aggressive activities of Pakistan."[66] As regards the invasion, the Soviet author writes:

In the first week of October, only parts of a few detachments infiltrated into Jammu through the Punjab border. On October 22, the principality was invaded by nearly two thousand well armed Afridis...and also detachments of other border tribes.

The government and press of Pakistan depicted this invasion as the result of "spontaneous insurrection" by the border tribes [against] discrimination of the Muslim population by the Hindu government. In fact, this "spontaneous" movement was planned and organized by the authorities of Pakistan with the help of English advisers...

Participation of the Pakistani government in organizing the invasion is shown by numerous facts, for example: among those of the Baramula invaders who were killed were discovered the bodies of soldiers in the uniform of Punjab regiments of the regular army of Pakistan; the boxes with cartridges, wireless equipment, machine guns and other captured material, seized from the interventionists, had such clear and unequivocal inscriptions as 'military depot of Rawalpindi,' 'military business of Peshawar,' and even 'from Rawalpindi to Kashmir.'[67]

Another Soviet scholar, V. Balabushevich, wrote:

If we realize that the territory of the border tribes continues under British control, that the wellknown British agent, Kuli Khan, heads the invaders, and that, according to certain Indian newspapers, the attackers include both Pakistan and British officers as well, there remains little room for doubt as to who is the real instigator of the armed conflict in Kashmir.⁶⁸

A Soviet article published in 1949, written in sympathy with the Afghans for their struggle for liberation from Pakistan's control, said the following about the involvement of some of the Afghans in the invasion of Kashmir:

A number of Afghans in the frontier belt, attracted by the prospects of easy loot and deceived by Pan-Islam propaganda, were also utilized by the forces of imperialism and reaction in the recent war over Kashmir.⁶⁹

Two other Soviet writers, A. D'iakov⁷⁰ and T. Yershov,⁷¹ also gave details of Pakistan's involvement in the invasion.
What did Moscow say about India's role in Kashmir? To quote Petrunicheva again:

The National Conference also turned to the government of India with the request to allow Kashmir to enter the Indian Union. Sheikh Abdullah declared that the struggle against Pakistani intervention [and] for joining the Indian Dominion was the struggle for a free and democratic Kashmir. The Indian government expressed agreement with the request for the accession of Kashmir with the Indian Union and about rendering military help on the condition that this question would finally be decided by the people of Kashmir by means of plebiscite or referendum after the expulsion of the Pakistani interventionists.
The government of the Indian Dominion was aware that without the help of the people of Kashmir the Indian forces would not be successful in clearing the principality of the invaders, and wanted to use the authority of the National Conference over the popular masses of the principality for organizing resistance to Pakistani invasion.
Therefore, under one of the conditions for rendering military help, the Indian government provided for the recognition by the Maharaja of an Emergency Administration headed by Sheikh Abdullah.⁷²

Covering almost the same ground as Petrunicheva with regard to

India's acceptance of Kashmir accession and her attitude towards Abdullah's National Conference, another Soviet commentator, O. Orestov, wrote:

On the morning of 27 October, the first battalion of Indian troops landed on the Srinagar airfield, under enemy fire. Springing out of the planes that had brought them, the soldiers rushed out at once into battle. Together, the Indian regulars and the Kashmir Popular Guard drove the invaders back from the capital.[73]

If there was any criticism of India, it was a very mild one for not supporting Sheikh Abdullah and the National Conference fully and for trying to preserve the privileges of the Kashmir ruler.[74]

But why would the British, in Moscow's estimation, support Pakistan instead of India? Two answers were provided: first, because "in Pakistan reactionary elements are stronger than in Hindustan";[75] second, since Pakistan would be entirely dependent upon British and American support, "the Anglo-American strategists felt that, if they were to retain Kashmir as a strategic military base, they must get it included in Pakistan."[76]

Thus in its comparison of India and Pakistan, Moscow considered Pakistan as being more under the influence of Britain and the US. Therefore it could have been expected that Moscow would take a pro-Indian stand when New Delhi brought the charge of Pakistani invasion before the Security Council in early January.[77] But Moscow, together with the Ukraine, decided to abstain. Why did the Soviet Union adopt this attitude? Lieutenant General B.M. Kaul, Military Adviser to the Indian Delegation at the UN, tried to seek Soviet support but got an evasive answer from Gromyko:

I [along with Sheikh Abdullah] met Gromyko, who was Russia's principal spokesman at the Security council, at my request, at...the latter's residence. When asked whether he, on behalf of USSR, would support us in the Kashmir issue, he said, enigmatically, that when an astute people like the British had to pull out of India after their association with us for nearly two hundred years without fully understanding our problems, how then could his country, who got acquainted with our difficulties only recently, do better than the British, so far as grasping the Kashmir problem was concerned and be expected by us to take a concrete stand on this issue in haste.

After a long talk, during which Gromyko was generally cautious, he said that the Russian delegation would abstain from voting on the Kashmir issue in the Security Council.[78]

Gromyko, of course, was only trying to evade the issue and avoid giving a direct answer to Kaul. As the detailed and heavy coverage of the conflict in the Soviet press showed, there was no lack of understanding of the issue in Moscow. The real reason, no doubt, was that the Soviet Union saw no compelling reason to support a country which she found following the American line in Korea and other places. Had the Soviets found Nehru's foreign policy sympathetic to what they considered were their vital interests, it is probable that they would have supported India's case on Kashmir even at this stage. In fact, in September 1948, the Soviet ambassador in India told an Indian cabinet minister that Moscow would be willing ot help New Delhi on the Kashmir question.[79] It was, however, obvious that such help would mean a pro-Soviet orientation in Indian foreign policy, for which Molotov, on several occasions in Moscow, had pressed Mrs. Pandit.[80] Since India did not wish to alter its foreign policy—not beyond expressing its "intent to be neutral in case of conflict"—nothing came of the Soviet overture.[81]

Moscow and the Communist Violence in India

The year 1948 was one in which the Communists waged violent struggles in several countries of South and Southeast Asia. Since these outbreaks took place within a few months of the two important Communist conferences which were held in Calcutta in February-March—the Southeast Asia Youth Conference, 19-26 February, and the Second Congress of the Communist Party of India from 29 February to 6 March (both of which were attended by Soviet delegates and Communists from South and Southeast Asian countries)—it has been a matter of speculation as to whether or not it was Moscow that gave instructions to start these insurrections. There is "no tangible evidence," as Joseph Frankel concludes,[82] to suggest that Moscow did issue instructions to this effect to those Asian Communists who attended these conferences. In fact, a careful study of the Soviet writings on India of this period suggests that Moscow had not yet evolved any firm strategy regarding the Communist movement in India.

First, the difference among Soviet scholars on the role of the bourgeoisie in India, which, as we have seen, had been expressed in the papers presented at the Academy of Sciences in June 1947, continued at this time. Ye. Zhukov, in an article published in December 1947, still spoke only of the "big bourgeoisie" in India as having gone over to imperialism and said that the Communist party in many countries must unite, along with the proletariat and the peasantry, "part of the bourgeoisie, mainly the petty and middle bourgeoisie."[83] A. D'iakov[84] and V.V. Balabushevich,[85] on the other hand, continued to show hostility to the *entire* bourgeoisie, although these writers also occasionally singled out only the big bourgeoisie" in India for their condemnation. It thus seems that while Moscow, after its complete disappointment with Nehru's foreign policy, had given up what is known as the "right" strategy in regard to the Communist movement in India, it had not yet decided as to what strategy should be followed in the future.* Thus the Communist

---

* Depending on its needs in particular circumstances, the Soviet leadership has, in different periods, prescribed two main strategies—the "left" and the "right"—for Communist movements in other countries. Taking capitalism as Communism's main enemy, the "left" strategy has considered the entire native bourgeoisie as its enemy on a par with native feudalism and foreign imperialism. With socialist revolution as its immediate goal, it has sought what is described as a "united front below" with workers, poor peasants and also with petty bourgeois elements, asking them to join the Communist parties or cooperate with them in a "united action."

The "right" strategy, on the other hand, considers native feudalism and foreign imperialism (and Fascism) as Communism's main enemies. In this the goal of socialist revolution becomes subservient to the immediate goal of national liberation and the defense of democracy. In a "united action from above" the Communists are prepared to work with all anti-fascist, anti-feudal and anti-imperialist elements, including those from the bourgeoisie.

Organized as an all-India party in 1933, the Communist Party of India followed the then current "left" strategy of the international communist movement. On directions from outside, it shifted to the "right" strategy in 1935, returned to the "left" after the Hitler-Stalin Pact of August 1939, and went back on the "right" as a result of Hitler's invasion of the Soviet Union in 1941. This remained the CPI's line until the end of the war. However, after the war, while Moscow's approach continued to be the same until the end of 1947, it didn't give any firm and clear directions to the CPI. Thus left to itself, the CPI worked out its own course, depending on its evaluation of the conditions in India and the interplay of its factions. While it followed the "right" strategy from 1945 to July 1946, it adopted the course of the "left" (though still considering the left-wing in the Congress Party led by

Party of India (CPI) was left without any firm direction from Moscow. In fact, Moscow was too busy throughout 1948 and the first half of 1949 with Europe, which was the central arena of the Cold War at this time, to pay much attention of the Communist movement in India and other South and Southeast Asian countries.

Therefore, when the CPI eventually decided to adopt the "left" strategy, condemning the entire bourgeoisie, it was not at the direction of Moscow but as the outcome of such factors as internal discontent and factionalism. Indian Communists, like Communists everywhere, naturally looked to Moscow for guidance. It was apparent by December 1947, especially with the publication of Zhukov's article, that Moscow's attitude towards Nehru had changed with regard to both his domestic and foreign policies. As a firm believer in the "left" strategy, B.T. Ranadive had previously only grudgingly accepted P.C. Joshi's leadership and the "right" strategy of the CPI.[86] But now, since Moscow's own attitude towards Nehru had turned hostile, Ranadive thought it an opportune moment to challenge Joshi's leadership and the "right" strategy. As has been shown by John Kautsky, who has made a thorough study of the strategies of the CPI in this period, the "right" strategy was actually attacked for the first time at a meeting of the Central Committee of the CPI which was held in Bombay in December 1947.[87] It was at this meeting that a resolution was passed condemning the *entire* Indian bourgeoisie. Speaking of "...the upsurge of ... the peasant unrest in South India, Bihar, Orissa and Bengal, the strike struggles of the workers, the mass demonstrations against special Emergency Powers in Calcutta, the struggles of middle-class employees, and students," the resolu-

---

Nehru as "progressive"), returning to the "right" by the end of 1946, but giving it up again by December 1947.

Among the leaders of the CPI, B.T. Renadive led its leftist faction, even at times criticizing the party leadership when it followed a moderate course. Another leader, P.C. Joshi, the CPI's General Secretary from 1935 to 1948 and considered "outside the factional groupings," led the moderate course of the party in the post-war period and continued to advocate it even after its abandonment by the party in 1948.

For a fuller discussion of the two strategies followed by the CPI until the end of 1947, see Gene D. Overstreet and Marshall Windmiller, *Communism in India* (Berkeley and Los Angeles, 1960), Chapters 6–11. For Moscow's approach to the Communist movement in India and the CPI's course between 1945 and 1947, see also John H. Kautsky, *Moscow and the Communist Party of India* (New York, 1956), pp. 16–42.

tion said that "these are the forces that will grow and defeat Anglo-American imperialism and its reactionary allies."[88] The new strategy was incorporated in the Draft Political Thesis at the Second Party Congress in Calcutta, where Joshi was replaced by Ranadive as the CPI's General Secretary. Of the Indian bourgeoisie, the Political Thesis declared, it had "ceased to play an oppositional role"; that it had "turned its face away from the masses, and gone over to imperialism"; and that its embodiment, the Congress Party, had become "the avowed enemy of the national-democratic revolution." The Communist party, therefore, concluded that "the bourgeoisie cannot lead the democratic movement to victory," which must now be led only by "the working class."[89] For the form of struggle to achieve the goal of overthrowing Nehru's Congress government, the CPI commended Telengana's violent agitation, which had been going on for over a year, as a model. Ranadive declared, "... Telengana today means Communists and Communists mean Telengana."[90] Bhowani Sen, who became Ranadive's principal supporter, said in reference to Telengana, "That is the way the victorious people must march to freedom and real democracy." He added, "Therefore, we must respect this battle, this struggle inside Hyderabad, of the people of Hyderabad, as a struggle of a new type. We must be proud to say here at least there is the force that will achieve real Indian liberartion."[91]

We must therefore conclude that (1) Moscow at this time had not developed a specific strategy with regard to the Communist movement in India; (2) there is no evidence to show that the Soviets had any direct hand in either the adoption of the CPI's "left" strategy or the replacement of Joshi by Ranadive as the CPI's General Secretary; and (3) violent agitation in Telengana was already going on: it did not occur as a result of the change in the CPI's policy, although it was taken as a model to intensify violent agitation in other parts of the country.

Thus it was not the official Soviet policy at this time to overthrow Nehru's government. After all, even during this period of Communist violence in India, Stalin sent messages of felicitations to Nehru on 15 August 1948, the first anniversary of India's independence,[92] as well as on his birthday on 14 November 1948.[93] If Nehru's foreign policy had followed a "democratic" and "progressive" course, or if at this time Moscow had any real need of wooing India, it is possible that Moscow might have pulled strings to check the violent activities of the CPI. The CPI was thus allowed to indulge in violent uprisings in India without any opposition from Moscow, and also left to its own fate when the Indian Government took strong steps, including the use of the military, to put an end to its activities.[94]

COMMUNIST VIOLENCE AS A FACTOR IN SOVIET-INDIAN RELATIONS

If the intensified Communist violence in India in 1948 and 1949 does not seem to be a significant factor in Soviet policy towards India, the same cannot be said of India's foreign policy in general or her policy towards the Soviets in particular. In fact, many of the statements by Nehru and other Indian leaders made at this time showed that they were concerned not only with the Communist violence in India but also in the neighboring areas. K.S. Roy, a member of the Congress Party and Home Minister of West Bengal, where the government outlawed the Communist Party and took several other strong measures, said in a statement in the State Assembly on 28 September 1948:

Let us examine the situation just outside the border of India-SE Asia. It is apparent to every intelligent observer of current events that this preaching and preparation for violent seizure of power is not peculiar to India or Bengal. It is part of an international plan. If anybody has any doubt, let him look to China with 20 years of civil war, to the recents events in Java, and nearer home to Burma, where ministers after ministers are being assassinated by these forces of disorder. Burma today is torn by sanguinary civil war. We find anarchy creeping towards Bengal from Burma through Arakan, and I have no doubt that we would have the same experience here if we had not been alert from the beginning. Even now do not know what may happen if we allow the forces of disorder to get the upper hand.[95]

Vallabhbhai Patel, the Deputy Prime Minister, in a call to the Indian workers to fight the Communists, said, "The fire burning in certain parts of Asia today is bound to affect us, if we are not watchful."[96] In a dispatch to the *New York Times* from New Delhi in June, Robert Trumbull reported the deep concern of the Indian leaders at the increasing Communist violence in Asian countries.[97]

Moreover, not only the press in India[98] but even top Congress Party leaders, including Nehru, thought that the Communists were engaging in these activities at the dictation of Moscow. At a press conference in New Delhi on November 12, Nehru asked:

... Why did they [the Communists] take this wrong step? This could only be explained in two ways: either the Communist leadership in these countries was very immature and had no realization or appreciation of the countries, or *they acted under some orders from some other place*, which ignored these conditions. Perhaps, it was both.[99]

Then pointing out that one of the fundamental principles of Marxism or Communism was that it must take into account the conditions of a country wherein it functioned, Nehru said:

That was what Marx said and which [sic] Lenin had stressed. Even Stalin had repeated several times that one could not repeat in some country what had happened elsewhere. This was exactly what was being done, however, *presumably in furtherance of world policy*.[100]

In March 1949, while denouncing the Indian Communists for their attempt to stage a rail strike, Nehru said in Puri:

Any failure to maintain food supplies would have meant starvation to thousands of people, yet knowing this, the Communists tried to organize a strike. Their objective was not inspired by a national stand-point, but in favour of an interest outside India.[101]

In the same month, in a speech in the Parliament, Nehru said, "The House is well aware of Communist revolts in countries bordering on India. It was presumably in furtherance of the same policy that attempts were made in India to incite the people to active revolt."[102]

Nehru also felt irritated at the activities of the first Soviet ambassador in India. As Mrs. Pandit told some of the other ambassadors in Moscow, the Prime Minister was concerned at the fact that after his arrival in New Delhi, K.V. Novikov did not make any serious attempt to meet with the government officials: instead his main contacts, undertaken secretly, were with the Indian Communists.[103] Reporting from New Delhi, US Ambassador Grady also said that the Indian leader's criticism in the Soviet press, plus Novikov's pro-Communist activities, had "opened" Nehru's eyes and "his attitude towards Russia has definitely stiffened." Grady also reported that on March 23, H.V.R. Iyengar, Acting Secretary General of External Affairs, called the Soviet ambassador to question him about some foreign Communists coming into India. The Indian government also asked the Soviets to withdraw their trade commissioner from the Calcutta area because of his objectionable activities.[104]

This concern of Communist activity at home, as well as the perception that the Soviet government was behind these activities, affected Indian foreign policy deeply. After a long conversation with Prime Minister Nehru in Paris in October 1948, US Secretary of State Marshall noted that "it was clear that Nehru recognizes interaction of Soviet policy and world Communism."[105] More specifically, on such questions as Indonesia, the danger of these countries going under Communism, led New Delhi to cooperate with Washington. Shortly after the Communist uprising in the city of Madium in East Java in September 1948, R.K. Nehru, India's Minister in Washington, met the State Department officials to point out the dangers of Communist take-over and, consequently, the necessity of solving the Indonesian problem. As a State Department memo stated:

... Referring to his government's efforts to resist Communism in India and to the ominous character of Communist activity throughout Southeast Asia, the Indian Minister said that his government considered that the dilatory tactics of the Netherlands in negotiations would increase the prospects of Communist success in Indonesia...[106]

In later years, when the armed activity of the Indian Communists had been brought under control, Nehru could affort to adopt a more detached view about Communist rebellions in other countries, but the reality of an armed rebellion right at home at this time could not allow such a view. It is only by keeping in mind this fact of India's domestic scene in 1948 and 1949 that one can understand the pro-Western bias in Nehru's foreign policy. His decision to support the US policy in Korea, and in general to support Western policies in Europe, was partly the result of this reality. Eventually, India's decision to retain her links with Britain by joining the Commonwealth of Nations was also, in part, determined by this factor.

This understanding on the part of the Indian leaders of the Communist violence in India had other repercussions on India's relations with Moscow. As we have seen, great hopes were expressed in India in early 1947 for the development of cultural relations with

Moscow. The *Statesman* reported in October that a scheme had been initiated by the Indian Education Ministry to send about a dozen students to the Soviet Union for higher education. The report further said:

The Russian Government, it is understood, agreed to provide facilities on a reciprocal basis. The scheme had, however, to be dropped on the recommendation of the Ministry of Home Affairs, which did not consider the present time suitable for implementation.[107]

The Indian Government, it seems, had no intention of sending Indian students to the Soviet Union at a time when it was putting down a Communist rebellion inside India which it thought had been inspired by Moscow.

INDIA AND THE BRITISH COMMONWEALTH

The Independence Resolution adopted by the Indian National Congress on 31 December 1929, had declared that India's goal was Complete independence.[108] A few days later, on 26 January 1930, the majority of the Indians who followed the Congress leadership took a pledge which stated: "We believe...that India must sever the British connection and attain *Purna Swaraja* or Complete Independence."[109] Even on the eve of independence, the Indian Constituent Assembly, in its famous "Objectives Resolution," declared that India would be an "Independent Sovereign Republic."[110] Thus the goal of those who fought for India's freedom was to sever all ties with the British Empire and establish a completely independent republic after the attainment of freedom.

But there were indications in the postwar period that the Indo-British relationship was undergoing a fundamental change. Nehru, long an admirer of British institutions, found in Lord Mountbatten an individual with whom he was able to establish a close and personal relationship. He and other Congress leaders were also impressed with the fact that the British were after all sincere in their desire of giving up their *Raj* in India. The choice of Mountbatten as the first Governor-General was evidence of this changed outlook on the part of Indian leaders. In the new atmosphere, it seemed that India might not sever all ties with the British Commonwealth. Although rejecting the idea of "lining up with a certain set of Powers," Nehru at a press conference in Bombay on 26 April 1948, said that for economic and cultural purposes India could have "some sort of close relationship with the British Commonwealth."[111]

This tendency was offset considerably by the disappointment felt by India at the handling of the Kashmir question in the UN Security Council, where on this question even the US seemed to be guided by Great Britain,[112] and by the persistent reports of the involvement of British officers in the Kashmir War.[113] Reporting a 5 September meeting of the Congress Party, a dispatch in the *Statesman* said that although no decision was taken on Commonwealth links, the Party's attitude on this issue had become less favourable. According to the dispatch:

Among the recent factors which have hardened the Party's mind against Dominion Status are Britain's alleged unfriendly role in the Security council over the Kashmir dispute, [and] the alleged share of British officers in the Kashmir campaign...[114]

Despite this change, Nehru attended the Conference of Commonwealth Prime Ministers in London in October 1948, where he announced that India was eager to cooperate with the other members of the Commonwealth.[115]

But the problem was, could India remain in the Commonwealth as a republic? Since Great Britain and other members were anxious that India should stay in the Commonwealth, they agreed to change its character somewhat. At the Commonwealth Prime Ministers' meeting in April 1949, India was admitted to the Commonwealth as a republic by recognizing the British King "as the symbol of the free association of its dependent member nations and as such the Head of the Commonwealth." The "British Commonwealth" also became simply the "Commonwealth."[116]

To what extent did India ally herself with Western policies in the Cold War by her decision to remain in the Commonwealth? Nehru's statement at his press conference on April 26, as we have seen, envisaged only "economic and cultural" ties. But apparently there was much more to it than that. A dispatch in the *New York Times* stated, "...Sir Stafford Cripps and Foreign Secretary Ernest Bevin are especially eager to keep India in the Commonwealth for economic, political and strategic reasons."[117] That this report was not without foundation was evident from the Final Communique issued by the conference on 22 October which stated that the discussions covered many matters of common concern, "including international relations, economic affairs and defence," and that they showed "a substantial community of outlook among all the Commonwealth Governments in their approach to present world problems." The Prime Ministers, the Communique added, expressed their resolve "to work together and with other Governments to establish world peace on a democratic basis."[118] But this was not merely a general statement. In a particular reference to the British defence policies in Europe, the communique said:

The United Kingdom Government outlined the nature of its association with other Western European nations under the Brussels Treaty, as a regional association within the terms of the United Nations Charter. There was general agreement that this association of the United Kingdom with her European neighbours was in accordance with the interests of the other members of the Commonwealth, of the United Nations, and the promotion of world peace. It was agreed that other Commonwealth Governments should be kept in close touch with the progress of this cooperation with Western Europe.[119]

India not only supported British membership in the Western Union, established under the Brussels Treaty, she also agreed with the approach behind it: to deter Communist aggression by building up the armed forces. A statement issued on 20 October from the British Prime Minister's residence outlined this approach:

Defence and the maintenance of world peace were the subjects of discussion at the Prime Ministers' meeting this morning and afternoon.

The discussion was opened with surveys by the Prime Minister of the United Kingdom, the Minister of Defence, and the Chief of Air Staff as chairman of the Chiefs of Staff Committee.

In the discussion there was agreement that the danger of war must be met by building up armed forces in order to deter any would-be aggressor, and that freedom must be safeguarded not only by military defensive measures, but also by advancing social and economic welfare.[120]

It was India's support to these policies, and the hope that New Delhi would thus stand with the West in any confrontation with Moscow, that made her membership in the Commonwealth so welcome to the Western countries. The London *Economist*, in a leading article, observed that India's decision to continue her full membership "may perhaps be the most heartening news the liberal segment of the world had since Mr. Marshall's Harvard Speech."[121] In an editorial, the *New York Times* called it "a historic step...in setting a limit to Communist conquest...."[122] Even the South African Prime Minister, Dr. D.F. Malan, whose policy of *apartheid* had so often been criticized by India, in a statement in the South African House of Assembly upon his return from London, said that South Africa welcomed India's membership because "India is anti-Communist"[123] and because

India, like the rest of the world, is today taking her stand with the anti-Communist countries. She regards Communism in Asia or Communism which is trying to gain a foothold in India also, as a danger, just as we regard it as a danger. Well, there are common interests; there is a general, common outlook....[124]

Pointing out what the West would have lost if India had not become a member of the Commonwealth, Dr. Malan added:

...If we lose the goodwill of India, if we lose the cooperation of India, then not only the Commonwealth but the anti-Communist Western Powers will lose a foothold, an extremely important foothold in Asia, and that may have a tremendous influence and prove a tremendous disadvantage in the dangerous world situation with which we are faced today. That is what we stood to lose....[125]

What were India's reasons for joining the Commonwealth despite some strong opposition at home[126] both within and outside the Congress Party? In his long speech in the Indian Constituent Assembly upon his return from the conference (as on many other occasions), Nehru gave several reasons for India's decision, but at one place he said:

...If we dissociate ourselves completely from the Commonwealth, then for the moment we are completely isolated, and so inevitably by stress of circumstances, we have to incline in some direction or other....[127]

It seems, therefore, that the possibility of isolation in face of the Communist uprisings in many Asian countries—which, as we have noted, Nehru believed were Moscow-inspired—was very much in Nehru's mind when he and other Indian leaders were faced with this issue. In fact, even before the Commonwealth Prime Ministers' Conference of October 1948, the *Modern Review* had reported:

...India standing at the head of the Indian Ocean has a distinct part to play in the defence arrangements of the areas...stretching from Africa to Australia...Realists in India, among whom is the present Governor-General, Shri Chakravarti Rajagopalachari, appear to be of the opinion that in discharging this responsibility, India can get the most immediate help from Britain and her 'white' Dominions. These considerations may be weighing with them, and it is but natural that they should be pressing on the attention and consideration of the Nehru Cabinet...Military organization and foreign policy are interlinked. Let us not forget this fact.[128]

A correspondent of the *New York Times* wrote at the time, "Likewise, it is obvious that fear of Communist agitation from within and aggression from without caused Prime Minister Nehru of India to think twice about severing all ties with the Commonwealth."[129]

We must therefore conclude that the Communist danger as seen at that time was perhaps the most important, if not the only, factor in India's decision to join the Commonwealth; only this fact could explain her support to British membership of the Western Union and the Western buildup of armed strength in Europe to counter the Soviet threat.

It was therefore natural that the Soviets should be highly critical of Nehru's policy. Even an Indian writer said, "If India joins the Commonwealth, she will at once draw upon herself the enmity of the bloc of Powers dominated by Russia."[130]*

---

*T.N. Kaul says that in Moscow he and Mrs. Pandit's eldest daughter, Chandralekha, discussed the question of India's links with the Commonwealth and suggested to the Indian ambassador "that we get out of the Commonwealth." "In our youthful enthusiasm we drafted a telegram from her to the Prime Minister giving various reasons for our recommendation. Mrs. Pandit approved and sent it off. But Nehru had to keep wider considerations in mind

The Soviet press indeed followed closely the developments in London and New Delhi. It was difficult for Moscow to comprehend how India could recognize the British King as head of this new grouping (the Soviet press never used the word "Commonwealth," still calling it the "British Empire") as an "independent" republic. In a rather ironical comment, an editorial in *Voprosy istorii* spoke of the "particular form" of India's "independent" existence "which 'admits the power of the king over the republic."[131] An article in *Pravda* said that the new status of what it called a "dominion republic" "conceals the maintenance of imperialist domination in India" and "bears eloquent witness as to how transparent is India's 'independence." Asserting that the British could never leave the colonies, the article added, "The Labourite guardians of the integrity of the British Empire are inclined to follow the exact testament of Lord Beaconsfield, one of the founders of the Empire, who once said that 'colonies do not cease to be colonies from the fact that they are independent.' "[132]

The Soviet press also noted that India's decision to stay in the Commonwealth went against all past declarations of the Congress Party and Nehru. In a review of an Indian novel which had just been published in the Soviet Union, a Soviet writer quoted a statement of Nehru which he had made in the past at the time of his trial at the Gorakhpur prison. "I stand before you, Sir," Nehru was quoted as saying, "as an individual being tried for certain offences against the State. But I am something more than an individual also. I too am a symbol at the present moment, a symbol of Indian nationalism resolved to break away from the British Empire and achieve the independence of India." But, commented the Soviet reviewer, "Now, when Nehru himself has affixed his signature to the agreement concluded in London, leaving India within the British Empire, it is clear that his words were nothing but sheer demagogy."[133]

The Soviet press also did not accept Nehru's protestations made in defence of the agreement that India had not entered into any secret agreements or made any commitments which might influence her domestic or foreign policy. In this connection *New Times* referred to the 11 May House of Commons statement of British Foreign Secretary Bevin, in which he was quoted as saying that during the Lon-

---

than the mere reaction of the Soviet Government and rejected the recommendation." See Kaul, *Diplomacy in Peace and War: Recollections and Reflections* (New Delhi, 1979), pp. 11–12.

don Conference the Prime Ministers of Burma, India, Pakistan, and Ceylon had agreed to "help" the Government of Burma "to restore law and order" as quickly as possible. This, *New Times* added:

> lifted a corner of the veil concerning the major London decisions. It turns out that secret negotiations had taken place in London, and that the outcome of these negotiations was an alliance of the governments of India, Pakistan and Ceylon under [the] Anglo-American aegis. One of the functions of this alliance is to crush the democratic movement in the countries of Southeast Asia. At present its efforts are directed in the first place against the people of Burma, who are fighting for the liberty and independence of their country.
>
> In this newly formed anti-democratic bloc, India's rulers are taking a most active part....[134]

But from Moscow's point of view, the most important factor—and a matter of deep concern—was that India had given her support to the Western Union and the West's rearmament policy which, in the Kremlin's view, had been designed for aggression against the Soviet Union.[135] Therefore, the development from India's support of Western policies in Europe to her inclusion in an Asian pact similar to the Western Union or the North Atlantic Treaty must have seemed a real possibility in Moscow. D'iakov specifically noted the support which India gave to the Western Union.[136] The *New Times* article, which had spoken of the "anti-democratic alliance" of Britain, India, Pakistan and Ceylon for the suppression of "the national liberation movement" in Southeast Asia, also said that this was "only one of the stages in the inclusion of the countries of Southeast Asia in the Anglo-American system of military blocs."[137]

A Tass report from Sydney mentioned that talks for forming such a pact in the Pacific had indeed taken place in London. Quoting from an article published in *Tribune*, Tass said that there would hardly have been such a thick veil of secrecy if only the question of India's membership had been discussed.[138] Two days later, an article published in *Pravda* said that in the Anglo-American plans for the formation of an "aggressive bloc" in the Pacific, "India occupied one of the foremost places." The article added:

> ...This bloc is to be an elongation of the North Atlantic Treaty, a

weapon in the struggle against the movement for national liberation among the peoples of Asia and the countries of the Pacific, an attempt to create an Eastern hive of aggression against the Soviet Union.[139]

That this possiblity must have seemed a very real one to Moscow is evident even from some Western comments. While welcoming India's membership in the Commonwealth, the *New York Times* wrote that it opened up "the prospect of a wider defence system than the Atlantic Pact."[140] Discussing the relationship between the Commonwealth and the Atlantic Pact and the possibility that India might also accept and adopt the "approach of Anglo-American cooperation" as envisaged in the Pact, the London *Economist* said, "...what draws the Commonwealth most firmly and quickly together is a danger which transcends exclusively Commonwealth interests. That danger is as real in the Indian Ocean and the Pacific as it is in the North Atlantic sphere—the threat of militant Communism allied to the imperialism of Russia in its new Soviet form."[141] Thus, in the Soviet view, India, by becoming a member of the Commonwealth, became involved in the "plans directed towards establishing US world hegemony, towards depriving peoples of their national sovereignty and statehood."[142]

Moscow and the Asian Conference on Indonesia

The question of Indonesia's independence, as noted above, was one about which India was deeply concerned, and which brought out the pro-Western and anti-Communist bias in her nonalignment policy. The Soviets, in turn, reacted by attacking Nehru's foreign policy with increasing Vehemence.

After protracted negotiations, with the British playing a mediatory role, the Dutch and the Indonesian Rupublicans had reached an agreement—the Linggadjati Agreement—in November 1946 (formally signed on 25 March 1947) which looked to the eventual creation of an independent United States of Indonesia but linked with the Dutch in a Netherlands-Indonesian Union. But the Dutch soon decided to discontinue their efforts in implementing the agreement and in July 1947 began what they termed a "police action" against the Republican government. The UN however, intervened in the situation and in November 1947 decided to send a Committee of Good Offices to Indonesia; it was this committee which brought about a truce agreement—the Renville Agreement—in January 1948. The Dutch, however, in violation of this agreement, started their second "police action" in December. It was this worsening situation that confronted both India and the US towards the end of 1948.

Here was an issue on which the interests of the US and India did not seem to differ very much. Both wanted a free and non-Communist Indonesia, and while India had been quite outspoken in its condemnation of Dutch rule and its policy of suppression,[143] the United States also realized that nationalist sentiment was strong in Indonesia, and that only by respecting this sentiment could that area be saved from Communism.* The US, in fact, was one of the three members of the UN Good Offices Committee on Indonesia, and it was aboard the USS *Renville* that the truce agreement in January 1948 had been signed. When the Dutch decided to take action against the Republican leaders, the US member of the committee, H. Merle Cochran, criticized the Dutch.[144] But the Dutch were determined to force a settlement on their own terms and therefore proceeded with their military action.

The United States was also critical of the Dutch action when the matter came up before the Security Council; the US also cut down some of the aid to the Netherlands which had been assigned to her under the European Recovery Programme.[145]

In India, the Congress Party was having its annual session in Jaipur

---

* A large-scale Communist rebellion in Indonesia broke out in the city of Madium in September 1948 and quickly spread to other parts in Java. The Republicans, however, took effective action and were able to bring it under control. For the US, it now became quite clear that the Indonesian question must be resolved to the satisfaction of the Republicans in order to save the area from the Communist threat. In a strongly-worded aide-memoire to the Netherlands on 8 December 1948, Washington told the Dutch that if they did not resolve the issue, "The goodwill of the Indonesian people would necessarily in the course of the struggle be replaced by bitterness and enmity of leaders with whom no truce, no common understanding would be possible." Two weeks later, Robert Lovett, US Acting Secretary of State, told the American delegation at the UN that Dutch armed action was a "direct encouragement" to the spread of Communism in that area. He also said that it was a "serious blow" to the achievement of Indonesian independence "under moderate national elements." For the US aide-memoire of 8 December 1948 to the Netherlands see *FRUS*, 1948 (Washington, D.C., 1974), 6: 531–35. For the statement by Robert Lovett see the Acting Secretary of State to the Acting United States Representative at the United Nations (Philip Jessup) at Paris, 23 December 1948, in ibid. p. 598.

when the news arrived of the military hostilities in Indonesia. Reacting strongly against the Dutch action, Nehru said, "I warn the Dutch that they will not be able to achieve their object....The day of imperialism is over because no imperialist power can stay in Asia."[146] Then, while announcing the convening of a conference of Asian countries to discuss the grave situation, Nehru called the Dutch action "the most naked and unabashed aggression."[147] In a sharp criticism of the Western Powers, and also of the Western Union to which he had given his support at the Commonwealth Prime Ministers Conference in October 1948, Nehru said:

The world is divided more or less in rival power blocs. What do they stand for? What is their reaction to this attempt at the destruction of the Indonesian Republic? We have to confess with sorrow that the attitude of some Powers had been one of tacit approval or acceptance of this aggression. There is a Western Union of which Holland is a member. What does that Union stand for? Money has flown from the Western Union....[148]

But as US policy became clearer, and as the United States began to work for a solution of the problem in close cooperation with Nehru (it was reported that Loy Henderson, the US Ambassador in India, had several meetings at this time with the Indian leaders),[149] Nehru ceased to criticize the West. Not only this, he even tried to explain that the forthcoming Asian Conference would not be anti-Western. He said in Calcutta on January 14, 1949:

I want to make it perfectly clear that there is no idea of forming an Asian bloc against European countries or against America behind the Conference called by the Government of India....[150]

The *Statesman* report added, "The Prime Minister emphasized that this conference was not opposed to any country or people. It was not anti-European, anti-American or anti-Western...."[151] The US Ambassador in India publicly welcomed Nehru's Calcutta statement. He said that in view of Nehru's statement, his government "would consider that such a conference could have a constructive effect..." With apparent satisfaction, he added, "that [Nehru's] statement had made it clear that the Conference was to be held for no other purpose than to strengthen the UN and to strengthen world unity rather than weaken it."¹⁵²

When the conference finally met in New Delhi, from 20 January to 23 January, it lacked any anti-Western speeches and adopted a rather moderate aproach to the Indonesian problem. It did not issue any threats or asked for any sanctions against the Dutch; instead, it made recommendations to the Security Council and pledged the participants' "full support to the Council in application of any of these measures."¹⁵³* Its recommendations, among others, consisted of immediate and unconditional release of Republican political prisoners, withdrawal of Dutch troops from the Republican areas which they had recently occupied, the formation of an interim government representative of all Indonesian territories, elections for a Constituent Assembly, and the transfer of power to the United States of Indonesia by 1 January 1950.¹⁵⁴

Commenting on the approach adopted by the Asian Conference, the *Statesman* observed editorially:

...The Conference could easily have become a platform for provocative speeches and imprudent counsel. Insted it showed restraint. Since the Security Council was in session simultaneously, considering proposals sponsored by the USA and others, a clash of views was possible. But it was avoided...its detailed proposals differ not very widely from those which the Council itself was considering.¹⁵⁵

Not everybody was happy with the outcome, however, including the Indonesian Representative in the UN, Dr. D. Soemitro. He had said at a press conference in New Delhi on 11 January that he hoped the conference would result in extending the scale of sanctions against the Dutch by all the participating countries;¹⁵⁶ this the conference obviously failed to recommend. Dr. Soemitro therefore ex-

* It is interesting to note that Nehru's initial announcement on the convening of the conference had created great concern in Washington. The US feared that it might lead to a "split" between Asia and the West. (The Secretary of State to the Embassy in the Philippines, 11 January 1942, *FRUS*, 1949, Washington, DC, 1974, 7: 141.) The outcome of the conference, however, was deeply gratifying to the US. As Cochran told the Dutch officials in early February, the tone of the resolution adopted by the conference "had been kept comparatively moderate only through the skilful diplomacy on [the] part of American Ambassador [in] Delhi." (The Ambassador in Belgium to the Secretary of State, 9 February 1949, ibid., p, 217.)

pressed his disappointment with the outcome and blamed "heavy pressure of the Western Powers" for the failure of the conference to act more boldly.[157] Even an Indian author has written that the US "put all the diplomatic pressure" on Nehru and that "he [Nehru] could not stand up to the first real test of his own independence."[158] This may be true, but the US in this case was sincere in its support to Indonesian independence. Nehru's initial anti-Western outburst on this question was not anti-Western for its own sake; his goal also was the independence of Indonesia—and, more important, an anti-Communist Indonesia. He therefore could have adopted the only approach that he did to realize these objectives. The policies adopted by the US and India were eventually vindicated when power was transferred to the Indonesian Republic in December 1949. The question of Indonesia, in fact, showed that if India and the US could work in cooperation, the outcome would be good for them as well as for peace in Asia.

If the work of the Asian Conference in New Delhi turned out to be a symbol of US-Indian cooperation, it was just the opposite in India's relations with Moscow. One is struck by the interest the Soviets took in the conference and the coverage given to it in the Soviet press. In the first place, Moscow had reason to be indignant about this affair. To the Asian Relations Conference of April 1947 Nehru had invited not just one but several delegations from the USSR; in January 1949 he did not think it necessary to invite even one. Not only this, the countries now invited included Australia and New Zealand, which had not been invited in April 1947. None of the Asian Communists got invitations for the conference. Thus the Composition of the conference was in itself indicative of the change that had taken place in India's relations with the Western countries on the one hand, and with Moscow on the other, in the past two years. The London *Economist* noted, with apparent pleasure, some "significant and reassuring omissions." "The eight Soviet Asian Republics," it added, "that attended the 'cultural relations' conference of 1947 in New Delhi are missing;...Viet Nam, which has frequently appealed for Asia's help against the French in Indo-China, is omitted, as is Malaya. In fact, the united nationalist front which it may be Mr. Nehru's purpose to inspect is to include no Communists or fellow-travellers."[159] The Soviets, therefore, expressed their displeasure when they referred to the Delhi meeting as a "conference of a group of the countries of Asia and the Far East."[160] Discussing its composition, a Soviet commentator, B. Izakov, said:

...The tone of this conference was set by a group of British dominions composed of India, Australia and Pakistan, which relied upon the support of such countries dependent upon England as Burma, Iran, Yemen and others. It is indicative that no invitations were sent to representatives of the Asiatic countries which, like the Indonesian Republic, are fighting for their freedom and independence. The Republic of Viet Nam in particular was not invited.[161]

Regarding the recommendations the conference offered for the solution of the Indonesian problem, Izakov wrote, "Speaking at the first meeting of the Conference, the Indian Prime Minister, Nehru, thundered against 'the dying colonial regime of the last century' and called for 'measures to liquidate colonial bondage as a whole.' He affirmed that Holland will not be permitted to impose 'colonial control' upon Indonesia." But did the final resolution of the conference conform to these declarations of the sponsor? No, said Izakov, they had "nothing in common" with Nehru's declarations.[162]

But Soviet press coverage of the conference was not so much concerned with discussion of the Indonesian question as with the possibility that it might lead to the creation of a Pacific bloc. Covering the opening session of the conference, a Tass report said that the general impression of the first session was that the real purpose of the conference was to work for the creation of a union similar to the Pan-American and Western European Union.[163] Another Tass dispatch covering the work of the closing session of the conference pointedly noted Nehru's statement that although the conference had ended, it was only the beginning of their work.[164] In fact, the decision of the countries represented at the conference to maintain close ties among themselves and to consult with each other seemed to lend some truth to Soviet suspicions. In noting this decision of the conference, Izakov wrote, "In adopting this decision the participants in the conference mentioned as examples the Inter-American Union, the notorious Western Union and similar formations. Thus it is perfectly clear that the creation of a new political grouping of Southeast Asian countries was discussed in Delhi."[165] In a particular reference to India's role, Izakov said:

The special correspondent of the France Presse cabled from Delhi at the height of the Conference: "Observers at the Conference emphasize the identity of the viewpoints of India and England, which adhere to the opinion that the strengthening of the non-Communist nationalist forces is the best means to employ against the spread of Communism in Southeast Asia." These words express the very essence of the Conference in Delhi.[166]

Several other sources were also quoted by the Soviet press to show India's involvement in the formation of a Pacific bloc. Quoting the Indian Communist Party's newspaper *People's Age*, a *Pravda* report said that the primary objective of the conference was "to create an anti-Communist bloc, which will serve as an instrument of an imperialist war against the USSR, against the new democracy of China and the freedom of Asiatic peoples."[167] Further, the Indian Communist paper was quoted as saying that the Nehru Government would be joining this "dangerous" bloc, "which will serve essentially as a vanguard of colonizers for the suppression of the liberation struggle and for the conversion of India into a military base of imperialism."[168] An Australian paper was also quoted (the name of the paper was not mentioned) as referring to the Delhi Conference as "the first step towards the forming of an Asiatic bloc led by India."[169] Even the reports of the Western press were cited in support of this contention: "The British and American press had already stated earlier that Washington and London regarded India as 'the potential leader of a bloc of Asian States reaching down from Burma to Java.' It was evidently with a view to forming this bloc that the Delhi Conference was called."[170]

The Security Council on 28 January 1949, had passed a joint resolution submitted by China, Cuba, Norway, and the United States,[171] whose proposals about the release of Indonesian Republican political prisoners, formation of an interim government, elections for a Constituent Assembly, and the transfer of power, were almost on the same lines as had been recommended by the Delhi Conference. But the Dutch did not receive the resolution very well and put all sorts of obstacles in the way of implementing it. The participants of the Delhi Conference, therefore, met again in Delhi in April to press for the implementation of the above resolution of the Security Council.[172] Another meeting of these Asian countries in such a short time, and that too in Delhi, seemed to confirm the earlier suspicions of the Soviets regarding India's participation in the formation of an

Asiatic bloc. A Tass dispatch of 14 April from Delhi said that the very fact that a second conference had been called in Delhi was evidence of "the existence of a machinery of regional union of Asiatic countries with its permanent president in the person of Indian Prime Minister Nehru and with a permanent meeting place at Delhi."[173]

India's policy during 1948 and in the first half of 1949 had thus been increasingly pro-Western. An Indian correspondent, Iqbal Singh, wrote towards the close of 1948:

Although it is claimed that we are trying to steer a middle course in order to reduce the existing international tensions, there are signs that this middle path is deviating increasingly towards a point where it will be indistinguishable from the policies of the Western Powers and their campfollowers.[174]

Even an American observer noted in 1949, "In the shadow of two giants India declares independence from both power blocs, but leans towards the West on some important issues."[175] It was therefore natural for the Soviets to be critical of Nehru's nonalignment policy, which seemed to them to be very much aligned with the West. To summarize the Soviet charges against Nehru's foreign policy in this period, we might quote here a statement issued by a representative of the Communist-dominated All-India Trade Union Congress, R.M. Jambhekar. Jambhekar attended the World Peace Congress in Paris,* where he circulated a statement with the heading. "We shall Not Allow India to be Turned into a Base for the Anglo-American

---

* The Polish Communists had organized a World Congress of Intellectuals for Peace at Wroclaw, Poland, in August 1948, which elected an International Liaison Committee of Intellectuals for Peace with headquarters in Paris. This met in Paris on 24 February 1949, and decided on a series of meetings, one of which was a World Peace Congress to be held in Paris. As scheduled, it took place in the French capital in April 1949. The Soviets used the Peace Movement to mobilize popular opinion in Western Europe against the North Atlantic Treaty and other US policies in this area. For an excellent discussion of the origins of the Peace Movement and its use by the Soviets, see Marshall D. Shulman, *Stalin's Policy Reappraised* (Cambridge, 1964), Chapter IV, "The Peace Movement as an Instrument of Diplomacy."

The Indian government refused passports to those Communists or Communist sympathizers who wanted to attend the World Peace Congress in Paris, but some of them who were already in Europe were able to go. Jambhekar was one of them, and he was eventually elected a member of the World Peace Committee. On India's participation in the World Peace Congress, see Overstreet and Windmiller, *Communism in India*, pp. 411–12.

Warmongers."[176] Later, he sent his statement to *New Times* which devoted three full pages to publishing it under the title, "Indian Realities." On Nehru's foreign policy, Jambhekar said:

The Indian Government has officially announced an 'independent' foreign policy of 'neutrality', which is only a fig leaf to cover their servile collaboration based on hopes of securing loans for the joint exploitation with British and US monopolies of our working people and markets in Southeast Asia, the Middle East and Africa. The bait of huge loans and markets is held out to the Indian government as a price for playing [the role of] imperialism's gendarme in Southeast Asia.

The Government's official support of Western Union, the Anglo-US sponsored Commonwealth conference held in Delhi on Indonesia and Burma, the landing of Gurkha troops for Britain's robbery in Malaya, the latest schemes to construct India's 'civilian' airfields with Anglo-American financial and technical support, the recent tour by British and US technical experts, representing the oil barons of London and Washington, to study the prospect of large-scale petrol production in India, the Indian Government's recent utterances denouncing the national liberation struggles in Indonesia, Malaya, Viet-Nam, Siam and Burma, and their open hatred of the gigantic victorious march of the People's Army of Liberated China—all this openly reveals beyond any shadow of doubt that the Indian Government has been instructed by the Anglo-American axis to prepare the ground for an 'Indian Ocean Pact.' The pact is aimed against Southeast Asia's struggle for liberation, against the USSR, the unswerving champion of the freedom of all peoples....

Swallowing the bait of 'leadership of Asia' held out by their imperialist masters, the ruling circles of India are converting our country into a base for imperialism's war against the democratic revolution in Asia, against People's Democratic China, and against the great Soviet Union.[177]

The above words, although written by an Indian Communist, represent in mid-1949 the Soviet indictment of Nehru's foreign policy. Although Moscow had criticized Nehru's foreign policy as far back as December 1947, one finds that the events of 1948 and the first half of 1949 brought about an important change in Moscow's thinking: its re-evaluation of the role of India and Pakistan in the policies of the West. We have noted that writing in January 1948, one of the Soviet specialists on India, A. D'iakov, had said that the reason why the British helped Pakistan invade Kashmir was because the reactionary elements were stronger in Pakistan than in India.[178] Another Soviet commentator, writing in September 1948, had said that London and Washington supported Pakistan on this question because they hoped to get military bases in Kashmir.[179] But India's support to the West's alliances in Europe and its rearmament policy at the Commonwealth Prime Ministers' Conference in October 1948, followed by India's decision to join the Commonwealth in April 1949 and Nehru's role in the two Asian conferences on Indonesia in January and April of 1949, together with the persistent talk in the Western press itself that India might be included in an Asian Pact of the type of the Atlantic Alliance, seemed to change all this. In 1949, the same D'iakov, while criticizing both India and Pakistan for their decision to join the Commonwealth, observed, "The Indian government [thus] became the main agent of Anglo-American imperialism in South-East Asia."[180] This was a significant change, for upon this interpretation would depend Moscow's new diplomatic move towards the Indian subcontinent.

NOTES

1. *Documents on International Affairs*, 1947-1948 (London, 1952), p. 308.
2. "Masaryk Killed; A Suicide, Reds say," *New York Times*, 11 March 1948, p. 1. Although *Pravda* charged that "the wild campaign of defamation and falsehood conducted by the Western democracies against Masaryk" was responsible for his reported suicide ("The Suicide of Jan Masaryk," *Pravda*, 12 March 1948, p. 6; cited from *SPT*, vol. 3, 15 April 1948, p. 250), the Soviets were immensely pleased with the developments in Czechoslovakia. See B. Polevoy, "The Defeat of Reaction in Czechoslovakia," *Pravda*, 16 March 1948, p. 3; cited from *SPT*, vol. 3, pp. 243-45.
3. See Statement by Marshal Sokolovsky in *Documents on International Affairs*, 1947-1948, pp. 574-75.
4. For text of the Brussels Treaty, see ibid., pp. 225-30.
5. *The United States in World Affairs*, 1948-1949 (New York, 1949), p. 7.
6. Louis J. Halle, *The Cold War as History* (New York, 1967), p. 184.
7. *Documents on American Foreign Relations*, 1948 (Boston, 1950), pp. 583-84.
8. Halle, *The Cold War as History*, p. 183.
9. *Documents on International Affairs*, 1949-1950 (London, 1953), p. 258.

INDIA'S FURTHER ESTRANGEMENT   123

10. Memorandum of the Government of the USSR on the North Atlantic Treaty, 31 March 1949; cited from *Documents on International Affairs, 1949-1950*, pp. 39-40.
11. "New Year," editorial in *Statesman Overseas Edition*, 9 January 1948, p. 3.
12. Ye. M. Zhukov, "Obostrenie krizisa kolonial' noi sistemy posle vtoroi mirovoi voiny," in Ye. M. Zhukov (ed.), *Krizis kolonial' noi sistemy natsional 'no-osvoboditel' naia bor'ba narodov vostochnoi Azii* (Moscow, 1949), pp. 18-19.
13. Ibid., p. 19.   14. Ibid.
15. K.P.S. Menon, *Many Worlds: An Autobiography* (London, 1965), p. 252.
16. *New York Times*, 15 January 1948, p. 13.
17. "Koreans Greet UN Commission; Hear Indian Make Plea for Unity," ibid.
18. Menon, *Many Worlds*, p. 254.
19. Joseph Jacobs (US political adviser in Korea) to the Secretary of State, 24 January 1948, *FRUS*, 1948 (Washington, DC, 1974), 6: 1085.
20. Menon, *Many Worlds*, p. 254.
21. UN, General Assembly, *Official Records*, Third Session, Supplement No. 9 (A/575 Add.1), First Part of the Report of the United Nations Temporary Commission on Korea, vol. 2, Annexes I-VIII, p. 6.
22. Ibid.
23. Ibid., p. 7.   24. Ibid.   25. Ibid., pp. 7-8.
26. Menon, *Many Worlds*, p. 253.   27. Ibid., p. 256.
28. *Survey of International Affairs*, 1947-1948 (London, 1952), p. 318.
29. Jacobs to the Secretary of State, 12 February 1948, *FRUS*, 1948 (Washington, DC, 1974), 6: 1107.
30. Lieutenant General John R. Hodge to the Secretary of State, 14 February 1948, ibid., p. 1110.
31. Menon, *Many Worlds*, pp. 256-57. See also UN, General Assembly, *Official Records*, Third Session, Supplement No. 10 (doc. A/583), Reports of the Interim Committee of the General Assembly (5 January-5 August 1948), p. 19.
32. The Secretary of State to the Embassy in India, 24 February 1948. *FRUS*, 1948 (Washington, DC, 1974), 6: 1127.
33. Ibid., 1128.   34. Ibid.
35. UN, General Assembly, *Official Records*, Third Session, Supplement No. 10 (doc. A/583), Reports of the Interim Committee of the General Assembly (5 January-5 August 1948), p. 21.
36. Menon, *Many Worlds*, p. 257.   37. Ibid., pp. 257-58.
38. UN, General Assembly, *Official Records*, Third Session, Supplement No. 9 (doc. A/575), First Part of the Report of the United Nations Temporary Commission on Korea, vol. 1, pp. 28-29.
39. "US Aid to Koreans Lauded, "*New York Times*, 13 April 1948, p. 54,

General Hodge found Singh's views very "refreshing," apparently comparing him with Menon whose emphasis on Korean unity had been attacked by the US. See Jacobs to the Secretary of State, 8 April 1948, *FRUS*, 1948 (Washington, DC, 1974), 6: 1176-77.

40. F.I. Shabshina, "Korei a posle vtoroi mirovi voiny," in Zhukov (ed.), *Krizis kolonial' noi sistemy*, p. 274.
41. *Survey of International Affairs*, 1947-1948, p. 320; and *The United States in World Affairs*, 1948-1849 (New York, 1949), pp. 306-7.
42. UN, General Assembly, *Official Records*, Third Session, Supplement No. 9 (doc. A/575), First Part of the Report of the United Nations Temporary Commission on Korea, vol. I, p. 47.
43. The two statements are quoted in *Survey of International Affairs*, 1947-1948, p. 321.
44. "An Important Historical Event in the Life of the Korean People," *Pravda*, 13 September 1948, p. 3; cited from *SPT*, 3 (1 November 1948): 579-80.
45. "The Establishment of Diplomatic Relations between the Soviet Union and the Korean People's Democratic Republic," *Pravda*, 13 October 1948, p. I; cited from *SPT*, 3 (1 December 1948): 654-55.
46. UN, General Assembly, *Official Records*, Third Session, Part I, First Committee, 229th meeting, 6 December 1948, pp. 936-38.
47. Ibid., 230th meeting, 6 December 1948, p. 955.
48. UN, General Assembly, *Official Records*, Third Session, Part I, First Committee, Annexes to the Summary Records of Meetings, doc. A/C. 1/426, 6 December 1948, pp. 91-93.
49. Ibid., doc A/C. 1/427, Corr.1, 8 December 1948, p. 93.
50. UN, General Assembly, *Official Records*, Third Session, Part I, First Committee, 234th meeting, 8 December 1948, p, 998.
51. Ibid., 236th meeting, 8 December 1948, pp. 1025-26.
52. UN, General Assembly, *Official Records*, Third Session, Plenary Meetings, 187th meeting, 12 December 1948, p. 1042.
53. Quoted in *Survey of International Affairs*, 1947-1948, p. 327.
54. Robert D. Warth, *Soviet Russia in World Politics* (New York, 1963), p. 393.
55. S.L. Poplai (ed.), *Select Documents on Asian Affairs: India*, 1947-1950 (Bombay, 1959), 1: 75.
56. For example, a Soviet commentator wrote, "This [National] Conference, headed by Sheikh Abdullah, had always been in the lead in the people's struggle against the British colonizers, the feudal lords and the Maharaja, and it had the ready following of the population....Its ranks included both Moslems and Hindus." (O. Orestov, "The War in Kashmir," *New Times*, no. 40, 29 September 1948, p. 25.) For other references to Abdullah and the National Conference, see T. Yershov, "The Truth about Kashmir," a review of "Salute to Kashmir," by Romesh Chandra (an

Indian Communist writer), *New Times*, no. 10 (3 March 1948), pp. 24–29; and Z. Petrunicheva, "Natsional 'no-osvoboditel' noe dvizhenie v kniazhestve Kashmir," in A.M. D'iakov (ed.), *Uchenye zapiski Instituta Vostokovedeniia* (Moscow, 1950), 1: 157–224.

57. Jawaharlal Nehru to Prem Nath Bazaz, 7 July 1936, in Prem Nath Bazaz, *Kashmir in Crucible* (New Delhi, 1967), pp. 179–83.
58. Sisir Gupta, *Kashmir; A Study in India-Pakistan Relations* (Bombay, 1966), p. 64.
59. Maharaja, Jammu and Kashmir, to Governor-General, India, 26 October 1947; text in Poplai (ed.), *Select Documents*, 1, pp. 372–73.
60. Governor-General, India, to Maharaja, Jammu and Kashmir, 27 October 1947; extract in Poplai (ed.), *Select Documents*, 1, pp. 373–74.
61. Gupta, *Kashmir*, p. 124.
62. For an exposition of India's case, see UN, Security Council, *Official Records*, Third Year, Supplement for November 1948, Annex 28. Letter from the Representative of India to the President of the Security Council, 1 January 1948 (doc. S/628), pp. 139–44.
63. Government of Pakistan communique, 30 October 1947; cited from Poplai (ed.), *Select Documents*, 1, pp. 376–77. For the Pakistani view see also K. Sarwar Hasan, *Pakistan and the United Nations* (New York, 1960), pp. 98–102.
64. "Conflict Over Kashmir," *The Times* (London), 13 January 1948, p. 5. See also *The Economist*, 13 December 1947, p. 952.
65. Robert Trumbull, "Ex-GI, Kashmir Leader, Reveals He Quit After Murder Attempts," *New York Times*, 29 January 1948, p. 20.
66. Petrunicheva, "Natsional' no-osvoboditel' noe dvizhenie," p. 207.
67. Ibid., p. 208. For one of the first reports of the invasion in the Soviet press, see *New Times*, no. 45 (7 November 1947), p. 32.
68. V. Balabushevich, "What is Happening in India," *Trud*, 18 February 1948; cited from *SPT*, 3 (1 June 1948): 327.
69. I. Reisner, "On the Question of the Formation of the Afghan Nation," *Voprosy istorii*, no. 7 (1949); cited from *CDSP*, 1 (10 January 1950): 5.
70. A. Dyakov (D'iakov), "Partitioned India," *New Times*, no. 3 (14 January 1948), p. 8. See also D'iakov, *India vo vremia i posle vtoroi mirovoi voiny, 1939–1949* (Moscow, 1952), pp. 170–71.
71. Yershov, "The Truth about Kashmir," pp. 27–28.
72. Petrunicheva, "Natsional 'no-osvoboditel' noe dvizhenie," p. 210.
73. Orestov, "The War in Kashmir," p. 26.
74. Yershov, "The Truth about Kashmir," p. 29.
75. Dyakov (D'iakov), "Partitioned India," p. 8.
76. Orestov, "The War in Kashmir," p. 24.
77. India's move was reported in *New Times*, no. 2 (7 January 1948), p. 32.
78. Lt. General B.M. Kaul, *The Untold Story* (New Delhi, 1967), p. 99.

79. Sarvepalli Gopal, *Jawaharlal Nehru: A Biography*, vol. 2, 1947-1956 (Cambridge, 1979), p. 45. Gopal provides this information on the basis of his use of the Nehru Papers, which are at present closed to other scholars.
80. Telegram by the Chinese Ambassador in Moscow to the Chinese Ambassador in India, cited in Grady to the Secretary of State, 18 March 1948, *FRUS*, 1948 (Washington, DC, 1975), 5: 496.
81. Gopal, *Jawaharlal Nehru*, vol. 2, p. 45.
82. Joseph Frankel, "Soviet Policy in South East Asia," in Max Beloff, *Soviet Policy in the Far East, 1944-1951* (London, 1953), p. 209.
83. Zhukov, "Obostrenie krizisa kolonial 'noi sistemy," pp. 55, 57.
84. Dyakov (D'iakov), "Partitioned India," pp. 3-12.
85. V.V. Balabushevich, "Indiia posle razdela," *Mirovoe khoziaistvo i mirovaia politika*, no. 12 (December 1947), pp. 41-46.
86. Gene D. Overstreet and Marshall Windmiller, *Communism in India* (Berkeley and Los Angeles, 1960), p. 570,
87. John H. Kautsky, *Moscow and the Communist Party of India* (New York 1956), pp. 35-42.
88. Cited in ibid., p. 38.
89. "Political Thesis Adopted at the Second Congress, 28 February-6 March 1948," in M.B. Rao (ed.), *Documents of the History of the Communist Party of India*, vol. 7, 1948-1950 (New Delhi, 1976), pp. 49, 55.
90. "Review of the Second Congress of the Communist Party of India," in ibid., p. 197.
91. Ibid., p. 202.
92. "Stalin Felicitates India," *New York Times*, 17 August 1948, p. 9.
93. *Statesman Overseas Edition*, 20 November 1948, p. 6.
94. The Party was outlawed in several provinces, police raided the CPI offices, imposed a ban on its publications, and arrested Communists in large numbers. For some of these reports, see "Section 144 in Calcutta and Suburbs; West Bengal Ban on Communists," *Statesman Overseas Edition*, 2 April 1948, p. 5; "Arrests of Communists in East Punjab," ibid., 9 April 1948, p. 8; "Bombay Police Round up Communists—'Activities Dangerous to Public Safety,' " ibid.; "Communist Activities in Travancore," ibid., 16 April 1948, p. 8; "Communist Party HQ in Bombay Searched," ibid., p. 6; "Ban on Communists in Bhopal," ibid., 1 May 1948, p. 12; "Madras Warns Reds Against Disorder," *New York Times*, 14 May 1948, p. 8; "Troops Sent to Two Hyderabad Districts; 'Drastic Measures' to Quell Communist-inspired Trouble," *Statesman Overseas Edition*, 1 October 1948, p. 1; "Hyderabad Communist Parties Banned; Threat to State's Peace and Tranquility," ibid., p. 9; and "Arrests of Communists in India," ibid., 26 February 1949, p. 6.
95. *Statesman Overseas Edition*, 1 October 1948, p. 5.
96. Ibid., 25 December 1948, p. 9.

97. Robert Trumbull, "Red Surge in Asia Alerts New Delhi," *New York Times*, 19 June 1948, p. 4.
98. See, for example, "Communist Menace in India Diminishing," *Statesman Overseas Edition*, 16 October 1948, p. 8.
99. Ibid., 20 November 1948, p. 5; emphasis added.
100. Ibid., emphasis added. 101. Ibid., 19 March 1949, p. 6.
102. *New York Times*, 1 March 1949, p. 20.
103. The Ambassador in India (Grady) to the Secretary of State, 18 March 1948, *FRUS*, 1948, (Washington, DC, 1975), 5: 497. See also Walter Bedell Smith, US Ambassador in the Soviet Union to the Secretary of State, 20 March 1948, ibid., pp, 499–500. Mrs. Pandit told Smith that Nehru "had been deeply affronted by actions and attitude [of the] Soviet Ambassador [in] New Delhi."
104. Grady to the Secretary of State, 23 March 1948, ibid., p. 500.
105. The Secretary of State to the Acting Secretary of State, 16 October 1948, ibid., p. 517.
106. Memorandum of Conversation, by the Director of the Office of Far Eastern Affairs, 22 September 1948, *FRUS*, 1948 (Washington, DC, 1974), 6: 360. Similar fears were expressed by India's Consul and Vice Consul in Indonesia. See Charles Livengood, US Consul General at Batavia, to the Secretary of State, 17 September 1948; and Livengood to the Secretary of State, 20 September 1948, in ibid., pp. 342, 358.
107. "Scheme for Exchange of Students Dropped," *Statesman Overseas Edition*, 16 October 1948, p. 13.
108. C.H. Philips (ed.), *The Evolution of India and Pakistan*, 1858–1947 (London, 1962), p, 237.
109. Ibid., p. 238.
110. Nicholas Mansergh (ed.), *Documents and Speeches on British Commonwealth Affairs*, 1931–1952 (London, 1953), 2: 652–53.
111. *Statesman Overseas Edition*, 1 May 1948, p. 9.
112. For some of the Indian reports to this effect see "The United Nations and India," *The Modern Review* 84 (October 1948): 253–54; "Kashmir Dispute Before the UN," *Statesman Overseas Edition*, 5 March 1948, p. 1; and "Surakcha samiti maim talamatola [Delaying Tactics in the Security Council]," editorial in *Aja*, 31 January 1948, p. 2.
113. Lieutenant General B.M. Kaul, who commanded an infantry battalion in Kashmir in 1948, has cited in his autobiography an instance of the pro-Pakistani role of even the Indian Army Chief, General Bucher. Interestingly enough, at this time the Army Chiefs of both India and Pakistan were British Generals. See Kaul, *The Untold Story*, pp. 105–6.
114. "Congress Attitude to Dominion Status," *Statesman Overseas Edition*, 11 September 1948, p. 9.
115. "Dominions Affirm British Bond Anew," *New York Times*, 12 October 1948, p. 10.

116. Mansergh, *Documents and Speeches*, pp. 846-47.
117. "India Status Taxes Dominion Leaders," *New York Times*, 15 October 1948, p. 9.
118. Mansergh, *Documents and Speeches*, p. 1137.
119. Ibid., p. 1138,
120. "Armed Strength to Deter Aggression by Empire Prime Ministers, ' *The Times* (London), 21 October 1948, p. 4.
121. "New Statute," *The Economist*, 30 April 1949, p. 778.
122. "The Larger Commonwealth," editorial in the *New York Times*, 28 April 1949, p. 30.
123. Mansergh, *Documents and Speeches*, p. 862.
124. Ibid., p. 868.   125. Ibid., p. 862.
126. See, for example, "India should Leave Commonwealth; Resolution Adopted by Forward bloc," *Statesman Overseas Edition*, 8 October 1948, p. 5; "Socialist Chief [Jai Prakash Narain] criticizes Foreign Policy," ibid., 25 December 1948, p. 11; "'Outrage of National Sentiments'—Narendra Deo [an Indian Socialist leader]," ibid., 7 May 1949, p. 5; "India in the British Commonwealth," editorial in *The Modern Review* 85 (May 1959): 338-40. For criticism by the Congress Party members, see *Statesman Overseas Edition*, 25 December 1948, p. 5.
127. Mansergh, *Documents and Speeches*, p. 856.
128. "India's Place in British Commonwealth," *The Modern Review* 84 (July 1948): 6.
129. Raymond Daniell, "London Renewing Commonwealth Ties," *New York Times*, 1 May 1949, Section IV, p. 5.
130. K.K. Bhattacharya, "India Must Not Remain in the British Commonwealth," *The Modern Review* 85 (March 1949): 200.
131. "Urgent Tasks of Soviet Historians of the Orient," editorial in *Voprosy istorii*, no. 4, April 1949; cited from *CDSP* 1 (4 October 1949): 4.
132. V. Maevskii, "The Results of the Conference of Prime Ministers of the British Dominions," *Pravda*, 8 May 1949; cited from *SPT*, 4 (1 June 1949): 324.
133. N. Korobkov, "The Evil Thing" (a review of Bhabani Bhattacharya's *So Many Hungers*), *New Times*, no. 28 (6 July 1949), 24.
134. "Secrets Exposed," *New Times*, no. 22 (May 1949), 15.
135. See Molotov's reply of 9 May 1948, to an earlier statement made by US Ambassador W. Bedell Smith to the Soviet Foreign Minister in *Documents on International Affairs 1947-1948*, p. 158.
136. A.M. D'iakov, "Krizis angliiskogo gaspodstva v Indii i novyi etap osvoboditel' noi bor' by ee narodov," in Zhukov (ed.), *Krizis kolonial 'noi sistemy*, p. 110.
137. "Secrets Exposed."
138. "Gazeta 'Tribiun' o Londonskoi konferentsii prem'er-ministrov stran britanskoi imperii," *Pravda*, 6 May 1949, p. 3.

139. Maevskii, "The Results of the Conference," pp. 324-25.
140. "The Larger Commonwealth," editorial in the *New York Times*, 28 April 1949, p. 30.
141. "Commonwealth and Pact," leading article in *The Economist*, 26 March 1949, pp, 545-46.
142. I.D. Levin, "On the Essence and Significance of the Principle of Sovereignty," *Sovetskoe gosudarstvo i pravo*, no. 6 (June 1949); cited from *CDSP*, 1 (25 October 1949): 4.
143. Bimla Prasad, *The Origins of Indian Foreign Policy* (2nd ed.; Calcutta, 1962), pp. 248-49; K.P. Karunakaran, *India in World Affairs, August 1947-January* 1950 (Calcutta, 1952), pp. 219, 221.
144. *The United States in World Affairs* 1948-1949, p. 317.
145. Ibid., p. 318.   146. *New York Times*, 20 December 1948, p. 1.
147. Cited in Karunakaran, *India in World Affairs*, p. 229.   148. Ibid.
149. Statement of Dr. Soemitro, an Indonesian leader, cited in Hector Abhayavardhan, *Russo-American Rivalry in Asia* (Bombay, 1954), p. 76.
150. *Statesman Overseas Edition*, 22 January 1949, p. 8.
151. Ibid.   152. Ibid., p. 11.
153. Resolution Adopted by the New Delhi Conference, 23 January 1949, *Documents on International Affairs*, 1949-1950, p. 569.
154. Ibid., pp. 567-69.
155. "Plan for Indonesia," editorial in *Statesman Overseas Edition*, 29 January 1949, p. 3.
156. "Indonesian Memorandum for Asian Conference," ibid., 15 January 1959, p. 9.
157. Cited in Abhayavardhan, *Russo-American Rivalry*, p. 76.
158. Ibid., p. 75.
159. "Guests of Nehru," *The Economist*, 8 January 1949, p. 50.
160. "Konferentsiia gruppy stran Azii i Blizhnego Vostoka," *Pravda*, 22 January 1949, p. 4.
161. B. Izakov. "The Delhi Conference," *Pravda*, 30 January 1949, p. 3; cited from *CDSP* 1 (1 March): 27-28.
162. Ibid., p. 28.
163. "Konferentsiia gruppy stran Azii i Blizhnego Vostoka," *Pravda*, 22 January 1949, p. 4.
164. "Okonchanie raboty konferentsii stran Azii i Blizhnego Vostoka po indoneziiskomu voprosu." *Pravda*, 25 January 1949, p. 4.
165. Izakov, "The Delhi Conference," p. 28.   166. Ibid.
167. "Gazeta 'Piplz Eidzh' ob otvetakh Tovarishcha I.V. Stalina Smitu," *Pravda*, 9 February 1949, p. 4.
168. Ibid.

169. "Behind the Closed Doors of the Delhi Conference," *New Times*, no. 6 (2 February 1949), p. 17.
170. Ibid.
171. UN, Security Council, *Official Records*, Fourth Year, Supplement for February 1949, doc. S/1234, 28 January 1949, pp. 1–4.
172. *Survey of International Affairs*, 1939-1950 (London, 1953), p. 386.
173. "Na vtoroi konferentsii po voprosu ob Indonezii v Deli," *Pravda*, 16 April 1949, p. 4.
174. Cited in *The Modern Review* 84 (December 1948): 427.
175. Lawrence K. Rosinger, "India in World Politics," *Far Eastern Survey* 18 (5 October 1949): 5.
176. See "From Editorial Letter Box—Indian Realities," *New Times*, no. 23 (1 June 1949), p. 29.
177. Ibid., p. 31. 178. See above, note 75. 179. See above, note 76.
180. D'iakov, "Krizis angliiskogo gospodstva v Indii," pp. 110–11.

V

Search for New Policies

> Today, from Iran on the Persian Gulf, through Turkey, Greece, and Italy to France and the Scandinavian north, the dyke against the Communist flood has been built and is now in good strong condition. But we know from experience that floods cannot be contained by building a dyke on one side only.... Building the dyke on one bank of the river has forced the waters to overflow the lands on the other bank.— T.F. Tsiang, Delegate of Nationalist China, in the UN General Assembly, 22 September 1949.

The most important development in Asia in 1949 was the victory of the Communists in the Chinese Civil War. Starting in the early 1920's and passing through various periods of cooperation and conflict with the Kuomintang, but aiming always at its eventual destruction, the Chinese Communists were in control of most of China north of the Yangtze by March 1949. Their advance into southern China quickly followed. Taking Nanking in late April, they swiftly took Soochon and Hangchow, and by May 27 were in control of Shanghai. Canton and Chungking were also taken before long, and so were the remaining areas on the Chinese mainland. In Peking, the Chinese People's Republic was proclaimed, with Mao Tse-tung, the leader of the Chinese Communists, as chairman, while Chiang Kai-shek, who had waged a war against Mao and his forces for so long, fled to Formosa and vowed to fight the new Communist regime from there.

The Search for a New Asian Policy in Washington

It had seemed to the US that by such measures as the Marshall

Plan, the Western Union, and the North Atlantic Treaty, the West had been able to check the Communist tide in Europe: in brief, the events in Europe seemed very "heartening" to the West.[1] But the Communist victory in China, in territory and population the largest country in Asia, offset much of this satisfaction. Commenting on the successes of the advancing armies of Mao in December 1948, an eastern European Communist, G. M. Dimitrov, wrote that developments in China were "of exceptional importance for the relationship of forces between the two world camps."[2] From the foreign policy announcements of Mao it was apparent at the time that the new regime in China would follow the Soviet line in international affairs. In an article published in November 1948 in the Cominform paper, *For a Lasting Peace, For a People's Democracy*, Mao called for "an anti-imperialist united front headed by the Soviet Union." Condemning the "middle way" or "third way" in foreign affairs as "completely false and bankrupt," Mao said that it was only to deceive the working people that:

...this is so loudly proclaimed by all those who do not like Marxism and who hate the Soviet Union—the Socialist fatherland of the working people of world—by all those who are trying to maintain some kind of intermediate position between the counter-revolutionary front against imperialism and its lackeys in all countries.[3]

Voicing Communist China's unity and solidarity with the Soviets, the article was also broadcast over the Chinese Communist radio.[4] In another article, published in *Pravda*, on 6 July 1949, written on the occasion of the twenty-eighth anniversary of the founding of the Chinese Communist Party, about three months before the proclamation of the Communist regime in Peking, Mao said:

We are told: 'You are leaning to one side.' Exactly. Sun Yat-sen's forty years of experience have firmly convinced us that we must adhere to one side in order to achieve and consolidate victory. The forty years and twenty-eight years of experience show that the Chinese people must, with no exception, take either the side of imperialism or that of socialism. It is impossible to remain in between the two. There is no third way.... It is possible to adhere either to imperialism or to socialism, without exception, not only in China, but throughout the world. Neutrality is a camouflage and a third way a mirage.[5]

With Communist rebellions already going on in many Southeast Asian countries, including India, the Communist success in China could not but be taken as a grave threat to South and Southeast Asian countries. What could Washington do about it? Although there has been talk of a Pacific pact in the past and, as has been seen, the State Department as far back as 1948 was thinking in terms of a military alliance in which not only the European powers but Asian and other countries could also participate, such ideas, as far as Asia was concerned, had remained only at the discussion stage. In fact, the Truman Administration discouraged all such plans. On 18 May 1949, Secretary of State Dean Acheson, although recognizing that "there were serious dangers to world peace existing in the situation in Asia," quoted approvingly Nehru's recent statement that the time for a Pacific defense pact was not yet ripe owing to internal conflicts in Asia. Acheson added that Nehru's view presented "an objective appraisal of the actual practical possibilities at the present time."[6] In July, however, there was a renewed effort in this direction by President Rhee of Korea, President Quirino of the Philippines and Generalissimo Chiang Kai-shek, but there was still no favourable response from the US State Department.[7] On 8 August, President Quirino came to Washington and put before the US Senate his proposal for an Asian defence pact, to be aided by the US, to meet the threat of Communism.[8] But as far as this matter was concerned, the Philippine President failed to convince the Truman Administration.

Thus the idea of forming a US-supported Asian defence pact had not yet taken concrete shape in American thinking. Neither was it given up altogether as a possible means of achieving American objectives in Asia; it was simply considered premature at this time. In fact, the first task was felt to be enlisting the support of non-Communist Asia for America's world policy and objectives. Once this was done, a new policy towards Asia could be given final shape. India, the largest country in Asia after China, with vast potential in manpower and resources, seemed to be the obvious choice to serve as the anchor of any new policy in Asia.

US Relations with India

Engrossed with European problems, the US had not so far paid much attention to India, especially in regard to providing assistance for economic development. An Indian who toured the US soon after the achievement of India's independence found that there was not much concern in the US for India's problems. In a letter to the *Net Work Times* he cited figures to show India's contribution in the Second World War, and then added, "...[today] we are no one's concern. To us it appears that the Japanese, who attacked you, and the Europeans who are far richer than we even today, are worthier objects of your help."[9] An American reader, Arthur Upham Pope, wrote endorsing "every word" of this Indian visitor.[10] But Washington did not take any steps in this direction. The principal reason, no doubt, was that the Communist danger did not yet seem as threatening in Asia as it was in Europe. In a statement on 1 December 1947, Henry F. Grady, the US Ambassador in India, said that it was "tremendously important to keep India on our side in the world struggle."[11] Grady's statement, however, was more a hope than an expression of policy in Washington. Also in other matters which India considered vital, such as the treatment of Indians in South Africa or Kashmir, the US had no policy except to go along with Great Britain, and in regard to both these questions British policy was not sympathetic to India's position. In early 1948, when India tried to buy some medium-range B-25 bombers from the US, Washington first agreed to sell the plane, but then the deal fell through.* Although New Delhi was disappointed at the outcome, Nehru decided to send his top foreign policy official, Girija Shankar Bajpai, on a special mission to Washington to seek both economic (especially for hydro-electric projects) and military assistance, and to make it clear to the US officials that India would not be neutral in any East-West conflict.[12] Bajpai even suggested that India would liked to send a military

---

* Colonel B.M. Kaul, who served as Indian Military Attache in Washington at this time, writes that the US decided not to sell the bombers to India because of British intervention (Kaul, *The Untold Story*, New Delhi, 1967, pp. 97-98). In fact, the US received a request for military equipment for Pakistan at about the same time, and it finally decided that it could not supply any military material to both India and Pakistan as long as the war in Kashmir continued. (Memorandum by the Secretary of State to President Truman, 11 March 1948, *FRUS*, 1948, Washington, DC, 1974, 5: 496-97).

mission to Washington.[13] On the question of military assistance, the US reiterated its position that the ban on exports of any kind of ammunition or military equipment would continue until the cessation of armed conflict in Kashmir.[14] Regarding economic assistance, Loy W. Henderson, Director of the Office of Near Eastern and Economic Affairs, told Bajpai that although Washington sympathized with India's needs:

Unfortunately, at the moment the United States found it necessary to concentrate its efforts and resources on resisting aggression in certain other Parts of the world. We recognized this could only be a short term policy, but we were faced with the problem of meeting an urgent and critical situation. We had every intention of giving proper and essential attention to India just as soon as circumstances permitted.[15]

It thus appears that in these early years India supported the US position on the question of Korea, Indonesia, and the creation of a Little Assembly in the UN, without getting any diplomatic, economic, or military assistance in return.

But the US came to realize India's importance with the advancing tide of Communism in China and the Communist uprisings in many parts of South and Southeast Asia. Although Nehru on several occasions had declared that India would follow an independent policy, India's suppression of Communists at home, her decision to join the Commonwealth, and Nehru's constructive role at the Asian Conference in January 1949, seemed to allay Washington's suspicions about India's policies.[16] Even *Time* magazine, which has rarely been sympathetic to India's nonalignment policy, wrote: "India's decision [to join the Commonwealth] does not balance the loss of China, but it does point the way to a constructive relationship between the Western and Asian democracies."[17] An American magazine, the *New Leader*, wrote, "To people of the Western world, the exciting events that have been going on in India take on even greater significance because of the collapse of China. For India now becomes spokesman for democratic peoples throughout Asia...."[18] Walter Lippman, the well-known American commentator, wrote:

Where, then, shall we look for allies, now that nationalist China, the Netherlands and France are so manifestly unable to play the role in Asia which we had supposed they would play? That, it seems to me, is the fundamental problem which has to be solved in order to form an American policy in Asia.

...Nehru,...is certainly the greatest figure in Asia,.... We would be well advised, I think, to enter into intimate consultations with Nehru about our whole course in China and Indonesia.[19]

Even from Moscow, US Ambassador Alan Kirk recommended that the US should try to mobilize anti-Communist Asia around India.[20]

In March 1949 the Truman Administration invited Nehru to visit the US.[21] The Indian Prime Minister announced his decision to accept the invitation in early May and said that he would visit the US in October.[22] Washington's interest in India was reflected in some of the other steps the Truman Administration took at this time. On 20 January, in his Inaugural Address, President Truman announced what he called "a bold new programme" of technical assistance to the underdeveloped countries.[23] In early 1949 a World Bank mission was sent to India to explore the possibility of a loan to India; the Bank found India a "good risk" and a loan $34 million for railroad rehabilitation was announced in August, which was described as the first World Bank loan to any Asian country.[24] Another loan of $10 million was granted by the Bank in September for agricultural development.[25] These were not direct American loans, but since the United States played a dominant role in the policies of the Bank, one must assume that they were the results of the changed US policy towards India.

Nehru's Visit to the US
American Aims and the Results of the Visit

Even before Nehru began his visit to the US, there were many indications that it might not turn out to be a success. Although Nehru had been invited, as Lippman said for "consultations," US officials continued to view his nonaligned policy inimical to American interests. A State Department memorandum of 6 June—which was only a month after the announcement of Truman's invitation—said that:

One of the most serious obstacles to the achieving of the orientation of the governments and peoples of South Asia towards the United States and the Western democracies is the widespread concept in that area that the United States and the USSR are respectively heads of clearly defined power blocs...and that the role of South Asia should be the creation of a third 'force' to act as a mediator between the two blocs already existing. Most articulate exponent of this concept is Prime Minister Jawaharlal Nehru of India whose great personal prestige in the area provides millions of unquestioning followers.[26]

The US objective, therefore, was not to work out a new policy towards Asia after consultations with Nehru, but to try to persuade the Indian leader to give up his neutralist or nonaligned approach and join the US side in international affairs, especially in Asia, more vocally and, hopefully, on a more concrete basis.

Washington's objectives and expectations were also clearly reflected in many of the American press comments made prior to the Indian Prime Minister's visit. The *New York Times* expressed the American aim in these words: "...the US is seeking a way to reassert Western influence and thus prevent a further spread of Communism in the Far East. To this end Washington is trying to enlist the support of Prime Minister Nehru, the unofficial spokesman for most of South-East Asia."[27] Even a writer in the liberal *Nation* said, "India offers the best hope of holding back the tide of Communism flowing south through Asia. What this country badly wants is a new Asian base and a reliable ally to take the place of the unreliable and incompetent Chinese nationalists."[28] *Time* magazine put it more bluntly. In its issue of 3 October, the magazine reported that a month earlier Acheson, after publicly acknowledging the failure of US policy in China, had asked Philip Jessup, Ambassador-at-Large, to work out a new policy for Asia. Jessup, with two of his associates—Everett Case, President of Colgate University and Raymond Fosdick, ex-President of the Rockefeller Foundation—had worked out a plan by the end of September. *Time* reported that the thinking of this committee was that India should be "the anchor of the new US policy" in Asia. But for this the committee was convinced that "Nehru...must be persuaded to give up his dream of India as a neutral 'third force' between Western democracy and world Communism."[29] In its issue of October 17, the magazine picked India for its cover story (with Nehru's picture on the front cover) with the title, "India: Anchor for Asia."[30] In conclusion, however, it put the US aim and problem very clearly and succinctly:

This week the US seemed inclined to go a long way towards the support of nationalism in Southeast Asia—provided it was not of a Red variety. But the US was dubious of Nehru's Third Force position, his pan-Asiatic leanings, his inclination to see the US and Russia as equally bad imperialist powers. In Washington's view, the problem was to persuade Jawaharlal Nehru that there was only one aggressive power design in the world—the Communist—and everybody was in the same non-Communist boat.[31]

This was obviously not what Nehru intended to do. He had joined the Commonwealth and had gone a long way in supporting Western policies. He had suppressed Communists at home. Shortly before the start of his visit to the US, the Communist Party was outlawed in Madras State. On 29 September 1949, the Indian government published a white paper entitled *Communist Violence in India*, which gave details of Communist terror and violence in India and of the steps taken by the government to meet this threat.[32] The policy of the government was also made quite clear. The White Paper said that the government "cannot and will not permit any group, whatever its political complexion, to preach, incite and organize acts of sabotage and violence."[33] It will, the paper added combat such things "with all the resources at their disposal...."[34] Publication of this document only about a week prior to Nehru's departure for the US seems to have been designed to impress Washington about New Delhi's policy towards Communist subversion in India.

Despite earlier commitments and declarations about nationalization in India, the Indian government also seemed to be moving towards a more flexible policy designed to invite American capital investment in India. In an interview with American correspondents in late August, Nehru said that there was no need to fear for the safety of US investments. He explained the change in the following words:

The original policy laid down when independence was still a dream called for the State to own all defence industries. As regards other industry, private ownership would prevail, subject to certain necessary controls.

Since achieving independence, the policy has been that the defence industries. Since they are the concerns of the State, are completely state-owned. Such utilities as the various river valley projects for irrigation, reclamation and hydroelectricity are paid for by the State and owned by the State.

As to key industries, despite the previous plan for state ownership—for which many Congress (party) leaders still clamour—we've done nothing about them and we are putting off consideration for at least ten years.[35]

Nehru also added that if at any remote period nationalization of certain industries did take place, the investors would be compensated in dollars if that was the currency used in the original investment.[36] This was a significant change in India's policy towards foreign capital considering not only the Congress Party's—especially Nehru's—past declarations but also in view of the suspicion that the common people in India had of capitalism and especially foreign capital.[37] India also began to negotiate for a treaty of friendship, commerce and navigation with the US,[38] despite the protests of many members in the Parliament asking why Nehru's government was not contemplating such a treaty with the Soviet Union.[39]

In spite of these changes, Nehru wanted India to play an independent role in international affairs. In fact, speaking on Independence Day in New Delhi on 15 August, where he spoke of his coming visit to the US and talked of "cooperation [with the US] in the smaller as well as bigger tasks ahead," he also said that India would not align herself with any power bloc in the world.[40] Moreover, if Nehru indicated the importance of India's relations with the US by appointing his sister, Mrs. Pandit, as the new Indian Ambassador to Washington, Dr. S. Radhakrishnan, the eminent Indian philospher, later to become President of the Indian Republic, was appointed New Delhi's new Ambassador in Moscow. Speaking at a reception given to Dr. Radhakrishnan prior to his departure for Moscow, Nehru said that India attached the greatest importance to her mission in the Soviet Union. He added, "We consider our relations with the Soviet Union very important not only because the Soviet Union is a great country in extent, power, prestige, capacity and in so many other ways in playing a very great part in the world today, but also because the Soviet Union is our near neighbour. And neighbours cannot afford to be indifferent to each other."[41] Realizing that his stock in Moscow was not high at the time, Nehru said that the Moscow Embassy was a "difficult" post and that was the reason why

Dr. Radhakrishnan, "who had a capacity to understand and make others understand also," was being appointed.[42]

Towards China also, Nehru could hardly be expected to follow any American policy predicated on a hostile attitude towards the new government in Peking. K.P.S. Menon, who was India's first envoy to China, quotes in his autobiography a note which Nehru sent him in January 1947. This note is worth quoting since it contained the seeds of Nehru's future China policy. Nehru said:

In China the situation is difficult because of the civil war that is going on. I have been on very friendly terms with the Chiang Kai-sheks and we hold each other in esteem. I have been friendly also with some of the prominent Communist leaders of the North-West, though I have not met them. It would appear even from the American reports that neither party in the Chinese dispute is free from blame. If American statesmen say so in spite of their violent dislike to everything Communistic, then it seems clear that the Chinese Communists have no bad case. Our Ambassador in China, while maintaining close and friendly relations with Chiang Kai-shek's government, should not allow himself to become a partisan in the civil conflict. Nor should he say anything disparaging to either side. Some words I have used or written have been exploited by the Chinese Government as against the North-West Communist Government. I have regretted this. If our Ambassador in China has any opportunity, without causing ill-will to the Chinese Government, to visit the North-West areas he should seize it and explain to the leaders there our general policy of friendship and non-interference.[43]

When the Communists did succeed in the Chinese civil war, Nehru's policy was therefore to be one of "friendship and non-interference." As early as April 1949, after the fall of Nanking into Communist hands, India had decided to establish consular relations with the victors. A *Statesmen* dispatch had then said, "Diplomatic relations between India and the Communists, indicating formal recognition of the new 'de facto' regime, are expected to follow in due course."[44]

Nehru's new China policy was not lacking in rationale. While he thought that internally the threat of Communism would be met only by providing what he called "Economic and psychological stability,"[45] he also thought that externally the best policy would be to work for Indian-Chinese friendship so they could work together in Asia by being independent both of Washington and Moscow. To one who believed that Communist rebellions in Asian countries were Moscow-inspired, it must have seemed very urgent, in the interests of peace and security in Asia, that China should be weaned away from Moscow to the greatest possible extent.

China and India could also work together, Nehru believed—China with her contacts in Moscow and India in Washington—for the larger cause of reducing tensions in the world. A British scholar, Peter Calvocoressi, writes, "The Indian Prime Minister, Pandit Nehru, was eager to establish relations with Peking, because he believed that the Chinese Communists could be weaned from Moscow and that India and China could together constitute a third force, which might perhaps build a bridge between Washington and Moscow."[46] Nehru's approach thus excluded joining any anti-Communist bloc. Robert Trumbull reported from New Delhi in August, "The Government [of India], while sternly suppressing Communist violence at home, feels that an out-and-out anti-Communist pact would only strengthen the influence of the Soviet Union with Communist China."[47]

Nehru's foreign policy, as he left New Delhi for his first visit to the US, may be summarized as follows: (1) to work for the friendliest relations possible with the US without entering into a formal alliance with her, hoping also that America would provide support to India's economic development. This approach, he thought, was the best guarantee of averting the Communist threat in India; (2) although he had been attacked by the Soviets for his internal and external policies, he hoped to keep the wires with Moscow open (to use a Bismarckian phrase); and (3) to work for friendship between India and China, thus not only averting the Chinese and Communist threat in Asia but also providing a new channel for communications between Washington and Moscow.

This was quite a formidable strategy and perhaps would have been an ideal approach if India had not had her own problems such as Kashmir. For these, she needed support—both diplomatic and military—from outside sources, which could come only as a part of a close and friendly relationship with one great power or the other. Also, economic aid, including food, could only be an integral part of the diplomacy of those countries which had the capacity to provide them; it was too naive to hope that nations would part with these precious things for humanitarian reasons alone. In any case,

Nehru's approach, as outlined above, was not likely to find favour in Washington, where the US hoped to convert Nehru to its own thinking.

Nehru arrived in Washington on 11 October. The importance attached to the visit by the US was evident from many of the press comments and from the elaborate official arrangements.[48] His major address of the two-week stay was delivered before the US Congress. In this address, Nehru defined his concept of nonalignment in the following words:

We are neither blind to reality nor do we propose to acquiesce in any challenge to man's freedom, from whatever quarter it may come. Where freedom is menaced, or justice threatened, or where aggression takes place, we cannot and shall not be neutral.[49]

But to the US government, hoping for some definite commitment from Nehru, these words, though welcome, were hardly reassuring. Commenting on this speech, Walter Waggoner, a correspondent of the *New York Times*, said:

The disciple of Mohandas K. Gandhi, however, gave no implied promise of forceful intervention, nor did he take sides in the specific struggle between the non-Communist and the Communist worlds.
....
The Prime Minister made no mention of either the Soviet Union in particular or communism in general, and the tone of his speech... itself suggested the role of conciliator for India.[50]

Later, wherever he went in the US, Nehru was invariably asked questions on the possibility of India's joining an anti-Communist Asian alliance. His answer either was that the idea was "premature"[51] on an outright "no."[52]

The US officials, including President Truman, did not put the question so directly, but it became obvious that the two sides differed fundamentally on how to deal with communism.[53] In a wide-ranging discussion with Warren Austin and Philip Jessup of America's delegation at the UN, Nehru did say that "India has lost all faith in Russia and in the dependability of Russia's words," and that "there was very little basis of cooperation [between New Delhi and Moscow] under the present circumstances," but he emphasized a "psychological and indirect" approach in dealing with Communism rather than a direct one, which was what he thought the US was pursuing.[54]

On the question of recognizing Peking, he told President Truman that "India's proximity to China put India in a somewhat different position from that of other countries," thus giving the impression of early recognition by his government.[55] Discussing the question with Warren and Jessup he said "the objective should be to divert the Communists away from Moscow leadership as quickly as possible." Differing with Nehru, Ambassador Austin said pointedly that US policy was to deny recognition because it believed "that no government could live in China without external assistance and support and that whereas this support had formerly meant that one or more of the Western European powers today it is the United Nations as a whole whose recognition and support any Chinese government must have if it is to survive."[56] It was thus obvious that the two sides held completely divergent views on how to deal with Communist China, the emergence of which had, in the first place, occasioned the Truman Administration's new approach to India.

On trade and economic aid, however, Nehru spoke in most favourable terms. He said that India would welcome and encourage American capital, that she would allow profits, and that they could also be taken out of the country.[57] He also praised Truman's Point Four Programme as something that would relieve tensions in the world.[58]

On the question of India's commitment to democatic ideals, Nehru was most emphatic. In Chicago, he even went to the extent of criticizing the Soviet system as "characterized by regimentation."[59]

It was reported that almost ninety per cent of the newspaper and radio stories and the comments released before Nehru's arrival and during his stay had mentioned Nehru's "neutrality" in the Cold War.[60] Therefore, the Indian Prime Minister's statements that India would not give up her independent policy and enter into any formal and firm alliance with the US could hardly be expected to bring about any fundamental change in US-Indian relations. The results of Nehru's US visit have been well summarized in the following words:

The tangible results of Nehru's visit were not striking. Nothing came of his proposal to exchange Indian strategic raw materials for a million tons of American wheat, badly needed to increase the Indian ration and combat inflationary and blackmarket conditions. The unspoken questions concerning India's political orientation, combined with American disapprobation of India's stand in the Kashmir dispute, made for a certain undercurrent of irritability on both sides....India, it was evident, was wholeheartedly in sympathy with those aspects of American policy that were directed towards raising world living standards and eliminating the sources of violence; but its government remained unshakably convinced that its own proper position was above the battle and not in it.[61]*

*Dean Acheson's account of Nehru's visit to Washington provides an interesting insight into the frustration and disappointment this top official of the US State Department felt at the Indian leader's performance in Washington. More in irony than in admiration, Acheson says that "the great man" arrived in Washington "in a prickly mood." Of his private talks with Nehru at his house, which lasted one evening from ten-thirty in the evening to past one o'clock, Acheson says, "I had hoped that uninhibited by a cloud of witnesses, we might establish a personal relationship. But he would not relax. He talked to me, as Queen Victoria said of Mr. Gladstone, as though I were a public meeting." He heard the Indian Prime Minister criticize the Dutch policy in Indonesia and that of the French in Indo-China. On China, Nehru gave the impression of early recognition of the new regime in Peking by New Delhi. Writes Acheson, "The President hoped, as I had, that countries deeply concerned in Asian affairs would consult before recognizing. Although the Prime Minister agreed, I felt that we had our consultation."

As it has so often happened, the US annoyance over Nehru's criticism of Western colonial policies or Washington's stand on some of the Asian problems caused the US to criticize the Indian Prime Minister for his stand on Kashmir. Acheson also says that after hearing from Nehru on the "failings" of the Dutch and French, he "wanted, as innocently as possible, to get him to talk about one of his [Nehru's] own." This was, of course, the problem of Kashmir. But on this, too, "...I got a curious combination of a public speech and flashes of anger and deep dislike of his opponents." Nehru's elaboration of the Indian case on Kashmir made Acheson only "...a bit confused."

Summarizing his long talks with Nehru, Acheson writes, "It made a deep impression on me. I was convinced that Nehru and I were not destined to have a pleasant relationship...he was one of the most difficult men I have ever had to deal." (Dean Acheson, *Present at the Creation: My Years at the State Department*, New York, 1969, pp. 334–36.)

Nehru must have made a "deep impressson" on the Secretary of State, because he continued to speak critically and disparagingly of the Indian leader in later years. See, for example, *The Journals of David E. Lilienthal*, vol. 3, *Venturesome Years, 1950-1955* (New York, 1966), p. 61. Even Truman told Chester Bowles (*Ambassador's Report*, New York, 1954, p. 3) as to how puzzled he was at Nehru's performance. To Lilienthal the US President spoke of Nehru's "unfriendliness." Said Truman, "You know, I think he has a feeling against white pople." (*The Journals of David Lilienthal*, p. 72.)

Unable to convince Nehru or be convinced by him, the US only hoped that India might yet change her policy in the future. The *New York Times* reported: "The feeling in American diplomatic circles is that eventually India will arrive at a point where she cannot stay on the fence in the East-West conflict and that at that point she will choose to stand with the Western democracies."[62] Without waiting for that to happen, the US quickly acted to fashion a new approach towards Asia, in which India was now relegated to a minor role. In a report prepared by the National Security Council on "The Position of the United States with Respect to Asia" (NSC 48/1, 23 December 1949), it was clearly stated that "the current reluctance of the area to align itself overtly with any 'power bloc' leads to the conclusion that it would be unwise for us to regard South Asia, more particularly India, as the sole bulwark against the extension of Communist control in Asia."[63] The report, with some minor changes, was approved (as NSC 48/2) by President Truman on December 30.[64]

Since India continued to "stay on the fence," the US did not take much interest in India's economic problems. By the end of 1950 all India got in economic aid from the US was $4.5 million, while the amount given to Nationalist China (Taiwan) was $35.3 million and to Indo-china $6.2 million.[65] Thus, considering India's size and population, the Indian share was almost insignificant. Nothing came of the proposed treaty of friendship, commerce and navigation for which talks had been going on in New Delhi for such a long time.

The Soviet View of Nehru's US Visit

Throughout the early part of 1949, as we have noted, the Soviets had viewed with concern the increasing activity of Americans in India. Even Truman's Point Four Programme, which had been welcomed in India, was described by a Soviet writer as a "new American colonial 'business'."[66] It was, said another Soviet writer, "an integral part of the programme of the American monopolies to seize world domination," and was designed "to crush the national liberation movement in these countries."[67] In a long dispatch from Delhi, Tass quoted a statement in the pro-Communist Indian weekly, *Blitz*, to the effect that the "terrorist campaign" against the Indian Communist Party had been undertaken by the Government of India " 'to clear the way' for closer economic and political ties with the United States, with which India is now negotiating to conclude a treaty of 'friendship, trade and navigation.' "[68] On the presence of the mission of the International Bank for Reconstruction and Development and its negotiations with the Indian government for a loan, Tass said that "liquidation of the Communist menace" had been stipulated by the Bank as a prerequisite for granting a loan.[69]

We noted in the last chapter that the Indian government refused passports to those Indian Communists or Communist-sympathizers who wanted to attend the World Peace Congress held in Paris in February 1949. In general, the government's policy seemed to be to prevent such elements from either going to the Soviet Union or to other countries to participate in the Communist-sponsored international conferences. In regard to the visit of the Soviet delegations or delegations from Communist-sponsored international organizations, they had been allowed to come to India until early 1948, but then New Delhi found that the visits to India were being used either to incite violence or to discredit the government among certain sections of the Indian population. These visits, therefore, were also discontinued.* In the months prior to Nehru's visit to the US, New Delhi seemed especially determined to implement the above

---

*In Chapter Four we noted that although the Soviets were not directly responsible for Communist violence in India in 1948, the Indian Congress Party leaders, including Nehru, thought that the Indian Communists were indulging in terroristic activities at the dictation of Moscow. Thus while a Soviet youth delegation was permitted to attend the South-East Asian Youth Conference held in Calcutta in February 1948 (I. Schraiber, "Two Weeks in India." *New Times*, no. 17, 21 April 1948, pp. 21–25), no such visits took place later. A delegation on behalf of the International Democratic Women's Federation was allowed to visit India towards the end of 1947 for the express purpose of studying the conditions of Indian women, but when the Indian government found that its real purpose was to establish local branches of the federation and also to call a conference of Asian women in India, New Delhi took action to frustrate its activities. See, for example, T. Morozova's report on the delegation's tour of India in which she accuses the Indian government of arresting representatives of a women's organization of Andhra in order to prevent them from handing over applications for membership to the delegation. (T. Morozova, "India-Burma-Malaya: Tour of a Commission of the International Women's Federation to the Countries of Southeastern Asia," *Soviet Woman*, no. 4, July-August 1948, p. 48.) The Indian government also banned the Asian Women's Conference which had been called by the federation. (Gene D. Overstreet and Marshall Windmiller, *Communism in India*, Berkeley and Los Angeles, 1960, p. 402.)

policy in regard to both the domestic and foreign Communists, including the Soviets.

The Soviets felt irritated at this stance of the Indian government and cited several examples in this connection. *Pravda* reported on 22 April that the Indian government had not allowed the All-India Students' Fedration, a student organization sponsored by the CPI, to send its delegation to the World Congress of Peace Partisans.[70] It also reported that a delegation of prominent Soviet writers, which had been invited by the Association of the Progressive Writers of India, was not given visas by the Indian Embassy in Moscow.[71] Another report said that Mulk Raj Anand, a prominent Indian writer who had been invited by the All-Soviet Committee for the A.S. Pushkin sesquicentennial celebration, was denied a passport to go to Moscow.[72] In July, the Credentials Committee of the Second World Trade Union Congress meeting in Milan, Italy, noted that Indian delegates were not able to come as they had been denied permission by the Nehru government.[73] In September, a Tass report from Delhi cited yet another such act of the Indian government. It said that the All-India Students' Federation had organized a fifteen-member delegation to go to the Soviet Union at the invitation of the Anti-fascist Committee of Soviet Youth, but was not given passports by the Indian government.[74] According to *Pravda*, even Soviet "documentary, scientific, general educational and anti-fascist" films were banned by Bombay and several other state governments. Not that the Nehru government was against the foreign delegations or foreign films. *Pravda* added, "India is flooded with American films and vulgar magazines upon which tens of thousands of dollars, in short supply, are spent."[75] As far as foreign missions were concerned. Tass quoted an Indian "peace partisan": "The Nehru Government very frequently invites and meets missions and delegations from imperialist countries—the US and England."[76]

These reports undoubtedly correctly represented the policy of the Indian government. Nor were the Soviets wrong in noting the increasing importance given to India in American policy. Ye. Zhukov noted in July the America's failure in China "has increased US 'interest' in India...." He added, "As is common knowledge, the Indian reactionary bourgeois leadership is distinguished by particular servility not only toward the British but also toward the American imperialists."[77] The Cominform paper, *For a Lasting Peace, For a People's Democracy*, also devoted considerable space to pointing out the increasing US interest and influence in India. Its political commentator, Jan Marek, wrote that Nehru "has become the hero of his imperialist masters."[78] The paper also expressed concern at the possibility that India might be included in some US-sponsored Asian bloc as a result of Nehru's visit to the US. This danger was pointed out by quoting resolutions of meetings of "peace partisans" held in Calcutta: "The resolutions condemned the Anglo-American warmongers and their Indian allies. Warning of the danger that India may be involved in the Anglo-American imperialistic bloc, the meetings called upon the Indian people to fight this danger and give all-round support to the Soviet Union...."[79]

The Soviet press therefore closely followed Nehru's visit to Washington. Commenting on Nehru's statement, made on the eve of his departure from India, that his visit was a "goodwill mission," *New Times* quoted the United Press as saying that Nehru would be informed by Acheson of the measures the Western powers intended to take to combat Communism in Asia. The article added: "The reference is to the plans for an aggressive Pacific bloc directed against the liberation movement of the peoples of Asia. The British and American imperialists assign a special place in these unscrupulous plans to India and its present reactionary leaders." Since India had become important to the US only after the failure of Chiang Kai-shek, *New Times* concluded, "The vacancy left by Chiang Kai-shek is being offered to Nehru."[80] While in the past the danger of Western bases in Kashmir had been seen by the Soviets through the involvement of the US and British with Pakistan, it was now seen in US-Indian collaboration. A Soviet commentator in *Izvestiia* wrote:

The US is taking an interest in the Kashmir problem not without some purpose. The interference in the mutual relations of India and Pakistan, in spite of the fact that the Kashmir question is being examined in the UN, is evidence of the fact that the United States is trying to possess India not only economically but strategically as well. Kashmir is situated in the north of India and lures the American expansionists solely by its strategical situation.[81]

The Soviets thus feared that if Nehru did enter into some kind of military alliance with the US, it could very well lead to the establishment of American bases in the strategic territory of Kashmir.

However, as we have already noted, during his visit to the US, Nehru, although he spoke in favour of US economic aid and also criticized the Soviet system, on more than one occasion came out against the idea of joining any military bloc in Asia. Soviet commentator did take notice of this. A Soviet writer, Ya. Viktorov, with regard to Nehru's speeches in the US, said that he spoke "lengthily, but vaguely, about the new role which India is called on to play at the present time in the life of the countries of Southeast Asia."[82] On the question of economic relations, however, Viktorov wrote, Nehru was quite explicit. Said Viktorov: "Nehru spoke less vaguely of how he regards the mutual economic relations of India and the USA. He displayad the greatest readiness to make concessions to the American capitalists and to open Indian markets to them both for the sale of goods and for the investment of capital. Nehru stated that India would welcome foreign capital investments ...and would gladly guarantee the investors...."[83] A later commentary by A. D'iakov followed similar lines.[84] Although the Soviet specialist on India noted that after their failure in China, "the US imperialist circles" were paying more and more attention to India and "would like to saddle India with the heavy and disgraceful burden of being the instrument of aggressive plans in Asia,"[85] he did not say that Nehru had agreed to participate in such plans. In fact, when referring to Nehru's declarations during his US visit, D'iakov spoke of his readiness "to grant the most favourable conditions and complete freedom of action to American capitalists...."[86] In regard to India's military involvement with the US, D'iakov only quoted Nehru as saying that India would support the US in any war of "self-defence," probably thinking of Nehru's speech before the Congress which we have quoted above.[87] Although he concluded by saying that "the Nehru government is converting India into an Anglo-American gendarme in the East," D'iakov did not cite any specific agreement between the US and India; the only evidence in this connection he gave was the use of Indian troops in Malaya and New Delhi's agreement with England to extend aid to the Burmese government "in suppressing the people's movement in Burma."[88] But this was nothing new. As we have seen, India's involvement in aiding Burma had been mentioned by the Soviet press in its coverage of the Commonwealth Prime Ministers' Conference of October 1948 and March 1949. We can therefore conclude that the apprehension Moscow had felt at the beginning of Nehru's US visit that he might be selected to head an anti-Communist bloc in Asia had been to a large extent dispelled by the time his visit to Washington came to a close.

THE SEARCH FOR A NEW POLICY IN MOSCOW
OVERTURE TO PAKISTAN

We must return to the Soviet position in May 1949—when Nehru had just announced his acceptance of Truman's invitation to visit the US— in order to understand a very significant diplomatic move of the Kremlin. In Moscow, Nehru's announcement apparently created the fear that the US might be successful in sponsoring an Asian bloc to be headed by India; this, in turn, also raised the danger of American bases in Kashmir—close to the Soviet Union. To counter this American move, the Soviets decided to invite the Pakistani Prime Minister, Liaquat Ali Khan, to pay an official visit to the Soviet Union.[89] It is important to note the promptness of Moscow's new move towards South Asia. The Soviet decision to invite the Pakistani leader was taken almost immediately after the announcement of Nehru's acceptance of the US invitation. It was first conveyed personally to Liaquat Ali Khan in Tehran on May 15 by the Soviet charge d'affaires there. A formal invitation was extended on 2 June.[90]

Even the very idea of Pakistan, as has been noted, had been opposed by the Soviets. When the new state did come into existence in August 1947, Moscow neither sent felicitations nor established diplomatic relations.[91] The two countries exchanged notes agreeing to establish diplomatic relations only in April-May 1948.[92] Furthermore, it does not seem that Moscow at that time was very eager to establish relations with Karachi, since the notes had been exchanged as a result of the initiative taken by Pakistan.[93] The Soviet attitude became apparent when no ambassador was appointed in Karachi following the exchange of notes. But all this did not prevent the Kremlin from taking a step towards more cordial relations with Pakistan when it seemed vital to its interests.

Moscow's overture was most welcome to Pakistan because Washington had not paid much attention to it so far; considering the state of Pakistan-Indian relations, the wooing of Nehru by the US actually created much resentment in the country.[94] The London *Economist* reported that in accepting the invitation from Moscow

Liaquat Ali Khan had done "the most popular thing" since his assumption of power in Pakistan after Jinnah's death.[95] M.A.H. Isphani, Pakistan's Ambassador in the US, called Liaquat's acceptance of the Soviet invitation "a masterpiece in strategy."[96] And a Pakistani wrote at the time:

Pakistan has to find friends—friends not only in name but in actions and relations as well. The forthcoming visit of Mr. Liaquat Ali Khan to Moscow will definitely bring something more realistic and will be more appealing to the Pakistan mind than the mere membership of the Commonwealth.[97]

It was also assumed by many in Pakistan that the Soviet Union might help them against India. Arif Hussain, a Pakistani scholar, writes, "The Kremlin's invitation to Mr. L.A. Khan to visit Moscow was interpreted as an indication that Russia was on the side of Pakistan in her quarrel with India over Kashmir."[98] In accepting the invitation, the Pakistani Prime Minister said that he hoped it would result in good for both the Soviet Union and Pakistan.[99] The importance which Moscow attached to the visit was evident from a PTI (Press Trust of India)-Reuters dispatch from Karachi which said that the Soviet Union would be sending a plane to Karachi to bring the Pakistani Prime Minister and his advisers to the Soviet capital.[100]

It was soon announced that a Soviet economic mission would visit Karachi in July.[101] A 12-member Soviet mission arrived in Pakistan as scheduled and began negotiations with the Pakistani authorities.[102] The delegation included a Muslim,[103] probably to make a favourable impression on the Pakistanis.* The Soviet press gave detailed coverage to its activities in Pakistan. It was reported that on 7 August the Pakistani Minister of Trade and Industry gave

---

*That this was intended to make a favourable impression on the Pakistanis is evident from a special reference made to the Muslim member, Mubarek Hasnulovich Ismaev, in a brief announcement about the visit of the delegation made in the Pakistan Government's publication, *Pakistan Affairs*. It was reported that "Mr. Ismaev is a Muslim and a man of considerable reputation in Russia. He is the President of an important corporation which specializes in commercial problems of the Near and Middle East." ("Russian Trade Delegation Expected in Karachi Shortly," *Pakistan Affairs*, vol. 2, 20 July 1949, p. 2.)

a dinner in its honour, which was attended by Sir Zafrullah Khan, the Foreign Minister of Pakistan.[104] Another reception for the delegation was arranged by the Prime Minister of the province of Sind (Karachi was seat of both the central government as well as the provincial government of Sind), which was attended by many central and provincial ministers.[105] Then, finally, the Foreign Minister held a reception which was attended by the Pakistani Prime Minister himself.[106] The members of the delegation also placed floral wreaths on the grave of Jinnah,[107] the founder of Pakistan and a man whom Moscow had bitterly attacked all his life.

In a country which had been considered completely dependent upon the West for its existence, the Soviet press was now able to discover much anti-Western sentiment. In a dispatch from London, Tass quoted the *Observer's* correspondent in Karachi as saying that anti-English sentiment in Pakistan had increased to the extent that it "will possibly soon declare its intention of becoming a republic, breaking its ties with England..."[108] The Soviet news agency said that the *Observer* report was based on its correspondent's interview with no less an individual than the Pakistani Foreign Minister, Zafrullah Khan.[109] Although all the Muslim League leaders, including Zafrullah, in undivided India and even after the creation of Pakistan had been bitterly criticized by the Soviet press, *New Times* now quoted the Pakistani Foreign minister in order to attack Nehru. The Soviet magazine said that at a press conference in Ottawa, the Pakistani Foreign Minister had expressed the opinion that Communism posed no threat to Pakistan. But, said *New Times,* he soon realized that he had committed a blunder, and therefore added, "From the political standpoint, I should perhaps have said that Communism is threatening Pakistan, because if you say that Communism is not threatening your country, the United States will lose all interest in you."[110] In quoting this statement, *New Times* had nobody else but the Indian Prime Minister in mind, because the magazine hastened to add, "What a simple and convincing explanation Zafrullah Khan gave of the anti-democratic witch-hunt started in India by his neighbour, Prime Minister Nehru, who is at present enjoying the hospitality of Washington!"[111]

Another indication of the Soviet Union's changed relationship with Pakistan was the fact that while a delegation of Soviet writers did go to Pakistan and was welcomed there, the same delegation was not permitted to enter India. An invitation was sent in early

October by the Association of Progressive Writers of Pakistan to the Soviet writers to participate in its conference scheduled to begin in Lahore in mid-November.[112] The Soviets chose a delegation headed by N. Tikhonov, Deputy General Secretary of the Union of Soviet writers.[113] The delegation arrived in Lahore on 13 November.[114] There were receptions in its honour at which hope was expressed by both sides for developing and strengthening cultural relations between the two countries.[115] From Pakistan the delegation wanted to go to India to attend the All-India Conference of Peace Partisans in Calcutta, but Tass reported that the Indian High Commissioner in Pakistan "categorically refused" to give visas to the Soviet writers.[116]

Some definite steps also initiated towards establishing formal diplomatic relations which the two countries had agreed to do, as has been noted earlier, back in April 1948. The Pakistani Prime Minister announced on 14 August that "full diplomatic relations" between Karachi and Moscow would soon be established.[117] It was reported in October that preparations were proceeding towards establishing embassies in each other's capitals.[118] On 30 October, Pakistan announced the appointment of its first ambassador to Moscow.[119] The announcement of the appointment of the Soviet ambassador was also made on 21 November. It was reported that the new Soviet ambassador would soon arrive in the Pakistani capital.[120] Prior to his departure for Moscow, the new Pakistani ambassador to the Kremlin, Shuaib Qureshi, paid warm tribute to the Soviet leaders who, he said, were "striving for international understanding and world peace." He called Stalin and his associates "a band of selfless workers who, working with vision and imagination, have raised their backward country in the short period of 30 years to occupy a prominent place among the leading nations of the world."[121] Qureshi arrived in the Soviet capital towards the end of December[122] and presented his credentials to the Chairman of the Presidium of the USSR, Supreme Soviet, N.M. Shvernik, on 31 December.[123]

However, by this time Moscow's invitation to Liaquat Ali Khan, which had led to all these developments in Soviet-Pakistani relations, seemed to have lost the premise on which it had originally been based. The Soviets had suddenly become interested in Pakistan because there was a definite possibility that during his US visit Nehru might enter into a firm military alliance with the US; this, in trun, had posed the danger of the establishment of US bases near the Soviet borders. But the Nehru visit, which failed to forge any new links between India and the US and proved so disappointing to the Truman Administration, brought tidings of relief, if not of joy, to the Kremlin.

There was another reason why the Soviet move towards Pakistan had now lost the importance it seemed to have only a few months before. As we have noted, Pakistan responded eagerly to Stalin's invitation because of its sense of isolation. In fact, as a former Pakistani diplomat says, Liaquat wanted "to use the Russian gesture to enhance Pakistan's importance."[124] In that it eminently succeeded. As Isphani wrote to his Prime Minister from Washington, DC, on 7 September 1949:

...Until a few months ago, we were unable to obtain anything except a few sweet words from middling State Department officials. We were taken much for granted as good boys: boys who would not play ball with communism or flirt with the left; boys who would starve and die rather than even talk to communists;...we were treated as a country that did not seriously matter. On the other hand, the US Government paid much attention to India. It was out to appease and pamper India...[With the Soviet invitation] overnight Pakistan began to receive the serious notice and considerations of the US Government.[125]

In the US, it was especially reflected in the efforts which were now made by some in the Truman Administration to push Pakistan's case. One of them was Stephen J. Spingarn, Special Assistant to the President. In a memorandum on 23 August 1949, to Clark Clifford, President Truman's Special Counsel, he pointed to Pakistan's strategic location,* said that Liaquat Ali had accepted Stalin's overture only as "an answer" to Truman's invitation to Nehru, and

---

*Pakistan's strategic importance, which would become increasingly significant to US military in later years, was not ignored even as the Truman Administration was trying to evolve a new policy towards India. A memorandum prepared by the Joint Chiefs of Staff on 24 March 1949, on the "Appraisal of United States National Interests in South Asia" stated that "From the military point of view, the countries of South Asia excepting Pakistan have, under present and prospective conditions, little value to the United States." *FRUS*, 1949 (Washington, DC, 1977), 6: 30.

suggested that Washington extend an invitation to Pakistan's Prime Minister "before [he]...goes to Moscow."[126] He followed it up on 25 October with another memorandum to Clifford, enclosing a copy of a dispatch from Karachi by *Washington Evening Star*'s Doris Fleeson with the title, "Pakistan Hurt by US—New State Complains of Our Policies and Greater Friendship with India." As he had done in his memo of August 23, Spingarn again emphasized that the US invitation should be extended before Liaquat's projected visit to Moscow in November.[127] His own "Notes on Pakistan," prepared a day later, reveal that he himself was in touch with some individuals in Pakistan.* He quotes a letter written by "a Pakistani friend," which said that had the US extended an invitation to Liaquat Ali Khan, "he would have been glad to accept, [because] no Muslim likes to fall into the lap of the Bolsheviks unless the UK and USA compel us to do so through indifference."[128]

It is hard to predict whether Spingarn or the British Government would have had any success in frustrating Stalin's move towards Pakistan had the Nehru visit resulted in a closer US-Indian alignment, but the failure of the Indian leader's visit now made the US turn to Pakistan. Nehru had hardly left New York when, on 10 November, President Truman announced that the State Department was considering an official visit to the United States by the Pakistani Prime Minister.[129] At about the same time, it was reported that the Soviet Union had asked Liaquat Ali Khan to postpone his visit which was scheduled for 7 November.[130] If the visit was to begin on this date, this was indeed a last-minute postponement. Later, Pakistan officially denied that the visit had either been cancelled or postponed; she said that no date had ever been finalized and Prime Minister Liaquat Ali Khan might still visit Moscow either towards the end of November or some time in December.[131] In the meantime, a formal invitation came from President Truman, which Prime Minister

---

*G.W. Chaudhury identifies some high officials in Pakistan, including Foreign Minister Zafrullah Khan, who were upset at their Prime Minister's acceptance of Stalin's invitation. They, according to Chaudhury, tried to bring about Western pressure on Liaquat Ali Khan to give up his projected visit to Moscow. He says that this group contacted the British government, which, in turn, brought intense diplomatic pressure on the Pakistani leader. (*India, Pakistan, Bangladesh, and the Major Powers*, New York, 1975, pp. 13–14.) In all probability, the letter cited by Spingarn was written by a member of this group.

Liaquat Ali Khan immediately accepted for a visit to begin in May 1950.[132] This finally ended any remaining possibility of his going to Moscow even at a later date.

Moscow was now in no hurry to send an ambassador to Karachi. The first Soviet Ambassador, A.G. Stetsenko, arrived in Karachi on 18 March,[133] and presented his credentials to the Pakistan Governor-General on 23 March.[134]

The Soviet press, which for a brief moment had spoken well of Pakistan's policies, now returned to its usual attacks on them. On the eve of and during Liaquat Ali Khan's visit to the US, it published several articles attacking Pakistan's policy of seeking aid from the US; the fear that Pakistan might be transformed into an American base was again expressed by several commentators.[135]

During his visit to the US, the Pakistani Prime Minister spoke openly in favour of American policies both at home and abroad. In his speech to the US Senate, Liaquat Ali Khan said that Islam, on which Pakistan was based, "firmly believes in the right of private ownership" to which, among other things, Pakistan was "irrevocably bound."[136] He added: "...no threat or persuasion, no material peril or ideological allurement, can deflect us from the path we have chosen."[137] In general terms, but undoubtedly referring to the Soviet threat, he said, "In our short life as a free nation, we have learned not a little about the world and the times we live in and about ourselves. We have learned that freedom, whether of the individual or of countries, is not everywhere and at all times safe and that the integrity of our own homeland...will demand of us increasing vigilance."[138]

This was the kind of speech which the majority of the US Senators wanted to hear. Vice-President Alben Berkley, who in October 1949 had offered merely a one-sentence formal "thank you" to Nehru after his speech to this very body,[139] was now full of praise for Liaquat Ali Khan. In an obvious reference to Nehru's earlier address, he said: "We have had many distinguished guests who have addressed the Senate of the United States. The Chair would not wish to draw any comparisons, except to say that none has been more inspiring, more appreciated, than this one delivered by the new Prime Minister of a new free country."[140] Commenting on Liaquat Ali Khan's US tour, a Pakistani writer observes, "His speeches in the United States and Canada left no room for doubt that, ideologically, Pakistan was pro-West and put an end to all speculation about the possibility of an alliance with Russia."[141]

THE SOVIET VIEW OF NEHRU'S FOREIGN POLICY IN MID-1950

The changed relationship between the US and Pakistan did not mean that Moscow switched over to the Indian side and accepted Nehru's nonalignment policy as being in its interests. While Liaquat Ali Khan had openly come out in support of the US policies, what Nehru had done was only to refuse to align India with the US on a formal basis: otherwise, his policy orientation continued to have a pro-Western bias. The Indian government still suppressed the Communists at home. And this concern was not confined to India alone. This was evident when in order to combat Communism at home and other countries of Asia, India accepted the Commonwealth mutual aid programme (directed to economic development) at the Commonwealth Foreign Ministers' Conference in January 1950.[142] In order to help the Burmese government to deal with the rebellion of Communists and Karens, India played an important role in providing Commonwealth aid to the Burmese Government and contributed quite a substantial amount herself.[143] Nehru visited several Southeast Asian countries in June 1950, and wherever he went he attacked Communist violence and subversion.[144]

All this, of course, was criticized by the Soviet press. Nehru was accused of helping "anti-popular regimes in Asia, notably the reactionary Thankin Nu government in Burma."[145] His statements against Communists in South and Southeast Asia while he was in Indonesia were called "slanderous outbursts."[146] The Colombo Conference's* objective was viewed as "the organization of an 'anti-Communist' front in Southeast Asia because of the cruel defeat of imperialism in China and the intensification of the national liberation movement in the backward Asiatic countries."[147]

---

*At the invitation of the Ceylonese government, the Commonwealth Foreign Ministers met at Colombo, Ceylon, in January 1950. Nehru attended the conference in his capacity of India's Minister of External Affairs. The most important decision of the conference was its acceptance of a proposal — later known as the Colombo Plan—to provide economic assistance to the South and Southeast Asian countries. This was apparently done to check the spread of Communism in this area. (*Survey of International Affairs*, 1949–1950, p. 531.)

Despite the above criticism of some aspects of Nehru's policies, one finds that by mid-1950 the Soviets do not show much apprehension of India's becoming a part of a Pacific pact sponsored by the US which had seemed such a real possibility a year ago. The second volume of the *Diplomaticheskii Slovar'* published in 1950, in its entry on Nehru, still says that one of the main purposes of the Asian Conference of January 1949 was "the creation of a military-political bloc of Asiatic countries, directed against the democratic and national liberation movement in China and other countries of Southeast Asia and the Far East." But then it adds, "This attempt was unsuccessful."[148] In May 1950, *New Times* published an article[149] to answer questions dealing specifically with India's possible involvement with a Pacific bloc. The questions were put by three Soviet readers who asked the magazine to deal with Nehru's foreign policy, "notably with its attitude to the aggressive plans of the Anglo-American bloc."[150] V. Berezhkov, the author of the article, wrote in reply that India "has...remained dependent on the British imperialists and finds herself increasingly bound to the US imperialists."[151] But when he explained the nature of India's increasing association with the US, the Soviet writer spoke only of economy and trade. Said Berezhkov, "Contrary to India's national interests, her government is impelling the country into ever greater economic bondage to the United States, and is hampering the development of trade relations with the Soviet Union and the People's Democracies."[152] On the specific question of India's joining a Pacific bloc, Berezhkov said that during his trip to the US Nehru did not agree "openly" to be a partner in the "projected aggressive Pacific bloc."[153] Nehru did this for several reasons: first, he "feared complications at home"; second because he and others from the ruling party in India "have learned a lesson from the inglorious fate of the Kuomintang clique."[154] What these "complications at home" would be, was explained in this way: "India's ruling circles are afraid of exposing themselves in the eyes of the masses. They fear their own people, for the movement for national liberation is surging powerfully throughout Asia and the Far East, and in India itself the anti-imperialist movement continues unabated."[155]

In its coverage of the Bagui (Philippines) Conference of 26–30 May 1950,* the Soviet press further noted strong opposition of the non-

*Despite the unenthusiastic response from Washington President Quirino of the Philippines still hoped to organize an anti-Communist alliance of South

aligned countries such as Ceylon, Indonesia, and India to the idea of a Pacific pact. The talk of such a conference had been in the air for quite a long time. In view of his opposition to the idea of a defensive pact of non-Communist nations, Nehru was quite unenthusiastic with regard to the proposal. But finally, when it was made clear that the proposed Bagui Conference was being called "primarily for consultation on common cultural and economic problems," India decided to participate in it.[156] At the conference itself, which was attended by the Philippines, Australia, India, Pakistan, Ceylon, Indonesia, and Thailand, India's delegate, Sir A. Ramaswami Mudaliar, emphasized that "raising the standard of living of the common man" was the key to the future of Asian and Pacific nations.[157] A Soviet commentator on the eve of the conference described the meeting as "a new disguised attempt on the part of the USA to organize a so-called Pacific bloc to complement the Atlantic pact." He said that the declaration that the conference was meeting to discuss "only 'political, economic and cultural'" matters was an attempt "to disguise the true nature of the projected alliance..."[158] *Pravda* put forward the same view in its coverage of the first day's meeting of 26 May.[159] However, when the conference ended it was apparent that no Pacific bloc had come into existence. In a dispatch on 31 May, Tass said, "Upon orders from Washington [Carlos P.] Romulo [delegate of the Philippines] insisted from the very first day of the conference on the formation of a political committee which would draft a plan to establish 'a standing organization for the countries of Southeastern Asia and the Western Pacific', which was the real purpose of convoking the conference." But, said Tass, the conference rejected Romulo's proposal and thus the results of the conference did not "coincide with the initial aims of creating a 'regional anti-Communist bloc.'" Tass also noted that Romulo's suggestion was opposed by a majority of the Asian delegates.[160] In a final commentary on the conference, an article in *Izvestiia* specifically pointed out the role of India, Indonesia and Ceylon:

---

and Southeast Asian countries, including Nationalist China, and was continuing his efforts to call a conference of all these countries. India's policy, as we have noted, was opposed to joining any such alliance. But when on 17 April 1950, President Quirino announced that such a conference—now called to meet at Bagui in May—would neither discuss military matters nor include Nationalist China, India decided to send a delegate. (*Survey of International Affairs*, 1949–1950, p. 35.)

At the Conference itself, the representatives of India, Ceylon and Indonesia came out against the proclamation of any kind of anti-Communist slogan, and they announced that they were not authorized by their government to discuss the question of any permanent union or alliance among the countries of Southeastern Asia.[161]

An article in *New Times* further noted India's emerging attitude of independence vis-a-vis US policies in Asia. The article said that after his recent tour of Asian countries, *New York Times* correspondent C.L. Sulzberger found increasing hostility in Asia towards US policies. In this connection, the article quoted the view of K.M. Panikkar, India's ambassador in Peking, which he had expressed to Sulzberger. Panikkar was quoted as saying that "No country in Asia will accept to be bossed by the United States; any hint of such a desire causes immediate suspicion and hostility."[162]

In terms of specific Soviet gestures to India at this time, one can note the interview granted by Stalin to the new Indian Ambassador to the Kremlin, Dr. S. Radhakrishnan, on 14 January 1950.[163] Although we do not have the account of the half-hour conversation which took place during this first contact between Stalin and a representative of Nehru's government, it was shortly after this meeting that the Indian envoy sent a message to Nehru suggesting a friendship treaty with the Soviet Union.[164] The idea of such a treaty was rejected by Nehru, who thought India could not enter into such a arrangement with Moscow in view of New Delhi's close economic and political ties with London and Washington. As he wrote at the time:

If there is a world war, there is no possibility of India lining up with the Soviet Union whatever else she may do. It is obvious that our relations with the United States as with the United Kingdom in political and economic matters are far closer than with other countries. We have practically no such relations with the Soviet, nor is it likely that they will develop to any great extent for obvious reasons.[165]

In this chapter we have attempted to show the development of the Soviet attitude towards Nehru's foreign policy from the middle of 1949 to the middle of 1950. While in the beginning of this period Moscow feared that India was about to be made the head of a new

US-sponsored bloc in Asia, it was clear by mid-1950 that India had no intention of doing this. To be sure, the explanation offered for this change in Nehru's policy was the growing "anti-imperialist" movement in India and the fear of Nehru and other Indian leaders that they would lose popularity at home. The same interpretation was also given to Nehru's concept of nonalignment or neutralism in foreign affairs. While in the past this policy was seen, as Ye. Zhukov had said in December 1947, as being put forward intentionally by "imperialism and its agents" to "undermine the internal forces of resistance in the colonies and semi-colonies" and "to slander the USSR,"[166] it was now seen as the result of the "anti-imperialist" and "national liberation" movement going on in India or other parts of Asia. On 15 April 1950, *Pravda* published a report by Kiuitsi Tokuda, General Secretary of the Japanese Communist Party, which he had presented at the 18th Augmented Plenary Session of the Japanese Communist Party Central Committee. Referring to Nehru's policy of neutrality, Tokuda said, "The position of India, which is advocating neutrality in the struggle between the revolutionary forces and monopoly capital, is explained by the fact that India cannot ignore the national liberation movement in the countries of Southeast Asia. Therefore the formation of an anti-Communist front by India is impossible."[167] Although this new interpretation of Nehru's foreign policy was quite significant, it did not yet represent Soviet recognition of any positive aspects of India's nonalignment or neutralism. These were, however, to be brought to the attention of Stalin and his associates by the events ushered in by the Korean War which broke out towards the end of June 1950.

NOTES

1. *The United States in World Affairs*, 1949 (New York, 1950), p. 45.
2. Georgi Dimitrov, "Report of Comrade G.M. Dimitrov to the Fifth Congress of the Bulgarian Workers' Party (Communists)," *For a Lasting Peace, For a People's Democracy*, 1 January 1949, p. 3.
3. Mao Tse-tung, "Revolutionary Forces of the World Rally to Combat Imperialist Aggression," *For a Lasting Peace, For a People's Democracy*, 1 November 1948, p. 6.
4. "China's Reds Voice Unity with Russia," *New York Times*, 7 November 1948, p. 30.

5. Mao Tse-tung, "On the Dictatorship of the People's Democracy," *Pravda*, 6 July 1949, p. 3; cited from *CDSP*, 1 (9 August 1949): 5.
6. *Documents on International Affairs*, 1949-1950 (London, 1953), pp. 93-94.
7. *The United States in World Affairs*, 1949, pp. 60-61.
8. US, *Congressional Record*, Senate, 9 August 1949, pp. 11031-32.
9. "An Indian in the United States," Letter to the Editor, *New York Times*, 4 December 1947, p. 30.
10. Arthur Upham Pope, Letter to the Editor, ibid., 15 December 1947, p. 24.
11. Quoted in Lawrence K. Rosinger, *India and the United States* (New York, 1950), p. 51.
12. For Bajpai's discussions in the US see Memorandum of Conversation, by the Assistant Chief of the Division of South Asian Affairs, 2 April 1948, and Memorandum of Conversation, by the Acting Secretary of State, 2 April 1948, in *FRUS*, 1948 (Washington, DC, 1975), 5: 501-508.
13. Memorandum of Conversation, by the Acting Secretary of State, ibid., p. 507.
14. Memorandum of Conversation [between the State Department officials and R.K. Nehru and Brigadier D. Chaudhuri of the Indian Embassy], by Mr. Joseph S. Sparks of the Division of South Asian Affairs, 29 July 1948, ibid., pp. 513-14.
15. Memorandum of Conversation, by the Assistant Chief of the Division of South Asian Affairs, ibid., p. 504.
16. For America's changed view of Nehru's foreign policy, see Vera Micheles Dean, "Should the US Re-examine Its Foreign Policy?", *Foreign Policy Reports* 25 (15 December 1949): 187.
17. "Program for Asia," *Time*, 18 July 1949, p. 22.
18. *The New Leader* 32 (23 April 1949): 15.
19. Walter Lippmann, "America in Asia," *New York Herald Tribune*, 10 January 1949, p. 17.
20. Telegram no. 222, 28 January 1949; cited in the American Ambassador in the Soviet Union to the Secretary of State, 22 July 1949, *FRUS*, 1949 (Washington, DC, 1976), vol. 7, pt. 2, p. 1173.
21. Although we do not have the exact date of Truman's invitation, Nehru said in Bombay on 7 May 1949, that President Truman had extended the invitation "two months ago." (*New York Times*, 8 May 1949, p. 35.) The US officials announced the invitation in Washington on 6 May 1949. (Ibid., 7 May 1949, p. 2.)
22. *New York Times*, 7 May 1948, p. 2 and 8 May 1949, p. 35.
23. *Documents on International Affairs*, 1949-1950, pp. 36-37.
24. "Good Risk," *Time*, 29 August 1949, p. 67; figures also cited in K.C.

Kundra, *Indian Foreign Policy*, 1947-1954 (Groningen, Netherlands, 1950), p. 154.
25. Cited in Kundra, *Indian Foreign Policy*, p. 154.
26. Memorandum by the Directorate of the Office of Near Eastern Affairs to the Acting Secretary of State, 6 June 1949, *FRUS*, 1949 (Washington, DC, 1976), 7: 1146.
27. "Nehru and the US," *New York Times*, 16 October 1949, Section IV, p. 2.
28. Freda Kirchwey, "The Welcome to Nehru," *The Nation* 169 (22 October 1949): 387.
29. "Policies and Principles," *Times*, 3 October 1949, p. 18.
30. "India: Anchor for Asia," ibid., 17 October 1949, pp. 30-34.
31. Ibid., p. 34.
32. *Communist Violence in India* (n.p., Ministry of Home Affairs, Government of India, 1949).
33. Ibid., p. 56.   34. Ibid., p. 57.
35. "Nehru Reassures Investors of US," *New York Times*, 28 August 1949, p. 9.
36. Ibid.
37. For Indian attitudes toward capitalism, see E.P.W. da Costa, *India in Asia, Eastern Economist Pamphlets*, no. 27 (New Delhi, 1954). da Costa speaks of three "hangovers" of Asian peoples: colour, colonialism and capitalism.
38. "Indo-US Treaty of Friendship Being Contemplated," *Statesman Overseas Edition*, 19 February 1949, p. 7; "Discussion on Indo-US Treaty of Friendship," ibid., 13 August 1949, p. 2; "Proposed Indo-US Treaty," ibid., 17 September 1949, p. 8.
39. Ibid., 17 September 1949, p. 5.
40. "Nehru's Address at Red Fort," ibid., 20 August 1949, p. 8.
41. "Delhi Reception to Dr. Radhakrishnan," ibid., 3 September 1949, p. 7.
42. Ibid.
43. K.P.S. Menon, *Many Worlds: An Autobiography* (London, 1965), p. 230.
44. "Indian Relations with Chinese Communists," *Statesman Overseas Edition*, 30 April 1949, p. 8.
45. See Nehru's interview with American correspondents, *New York Times*, 28 August 1949, p. 9.
46. *Survey of International Affairs* 1949-1950, p. 335.
47. Robert Trumbull, "India Opposed to Anti-Red Pact," *New York Times*, 21 August 1949, p. 20.
48. See, for example, James Reston's two dispatches, "Importance of Nehru's Visit Seen in Capital's Attitude; India's Prime Minister Seen

as Key Figure in Asia by US Officials Preparing Reception," and "Nehru Trip Fulfils Vision That Engrossed Roosevelt," *New York Times*, 11 October 1949, p. 26, and 12 October 1949, p. 18.

49. US, *Congressional Record*, vol. 95, pt. 11, 81st Congress, p. 14394.
50. Walter H. Waggoner, "Nehru Bars Neutrality in Injustice; Talk Suggests India as Conciliator," *New York Times*, 14 October 1949, p. 1.
51. See report of Nepru's address at National Press Club in Washington: "Asia Defence Part Put Off by Nehru," *New York Times*, 15 October 1949, p. 7.
52. See Nehru's statement on arrival in New York City: "Nehru City Guest, Says India Will Hold Aloof in 'Cold War,' " ibid., 16 October 1949, p. 1; his answer to a question on this issue at the San Francisco Club: "Nehru Bars Indian Role in Non-Communist Group," ibid., 3 November 1949, p. 6.
53. See Memorandum of Conversation [between Truman and Nehru], by the Secretary of State, 13 October 1949, and Memorandum of Conversation, by Mr. Joseph S. Sparks, Adviser to the United States Delegation at the United Nations, 19 October 1949, in *FRUS*, 1949 (Washington, DC, 1977), 6:1750-1756.
54. Memorandum of Conversation, 19 October 1949, ibid., pp. 1752-53.
55. Memorandum of Conversation, 13 October 1949, ibid., p. 1752.
56. Memorandum of Conversation, 19 October 1949, ibid., pp. 1755-56.
57. *New York Times*, 15 October 1949, p. 7. See also ibid., 20 October 1949, p. 18; ibid., 21 October 1949, p. 9.
58. Ibid., 27 October 1949, p. 6.
59. Quoted in Kundra, *Indian Foreign Policy*, p. 120.
60. J.J. Singh, "Nehru, India aud America," *The New Leader* 32 (17 December 1940), 7.
61. *The United States in World Affairs*, 1949, pp. 440-41.
62. "Nehru's Visit," *New York Times*, 23 October 1949, Section IV p. 2.
63. US Department of Defense, *United States-Vietnam Relations*, book 8, 1945-1967 (Washington, DC, 1971), p. 247. Later, at a conference of the United States Chiefs of Mission in the Far East held in Bangkok on 13-15 February, US ambassador in India, Loy Henderson, said that "lack of constructive leadership makes India irresponsible and not suitable as [a] great power now" (cited in the Ambassador to Thailand to the Secretary of State, 27 February 1950, *FRUS*, 1950, Washington, DC, 1976, vol. 6, p. 27).
64. *FRUS*, 1949 (Washington, DC, 1976), vol. 7, pt. 2, pp. 1215-20.
65. *Survey of International Affairs*, 1949, p. 379.
66. Ye. Zhukov, "New American Colonial 'Business,' " *Pravda*, 21 February 1949, p. 4; cited from *CDSP* 1 (22 March 1949), 39.
67. I. Ivanov, "What is the American Plan for 'Aid' to Backward Coun-

tries?", *Trud*, 6 August 1949; cited from *SPT* 5 (1 February 1950), 76, 78.
68. "The Situation in India," *Pravda*, 27 February 1949, p. 4; cited from *SPT* 4 (15 April 1949). 254–55. See also "Repressii protiv indiiskii kommunistov," *Izvestiia*, 22 February 1949, p. 4.
69. "The Situation in India," p. 255.
70. Trudiashchiesia podderzhivaiut Vsemirnyi kongress storonnikov mira," *Pravda*, 22 April 1949, p. 4.
71. "Indiiskie vlasti prepiatstvuiut deiatel'nosti progressivnykh organizatsii," ibid., 28 May 1949, p. 4.
72. "Vo Vsesoiuznom komiteta po provedeniiu 150-letiia so dnia rozhdeniia A.S. Pushkina," ibid., 8 June 1949, p. 2.
73. Supplement to *New Times*, no. 29 (13 July 1949), p. 34.
74. "Pravitel'stvo Indii otkazalo delegatsii indiiskoi molodezhi v vizakh na vyezd v Sovetskii Soiuz," ibid., 9 September 1949, p. 4.
75. "Zapreshchenie sovetskikh kinofil'mov v Indii," *Pravda*, 26 July 1949, p. 4.
76. "Vseindiiskaia konferentsiia storonnikov mira," *Pravda*, 28 November 1949, p. 3.
77. E(Ye). Zhukov, "Colonial Appetites of the American Monopolies; On the Plan for 'Aid' to Backward Countries," *Pravda*, 9 July 1949, p. 4; cited from *CDSP* 1 (9 August 1949), 44.
78. Jan Marek, "Mr. Nehru Is Congratulated," *For a Lasting Peace, For a People's Democracy*, (16 September 1949), p. 4.
79. "Peace Meetings in India," ibid., 30 September 1949, p. 2.
80. "Chiang Kai-shek's Successor," *New Times*, no. 42 (12 October 1949), pp. 20–21.
81. V.K., "V poiskakh novoi agentury," *Izvestiia*, 23 October 1949, p. 3.
82. Ya. Viktorov, "Nehru's Negotiations in the USA," *Pravda*, 23 October 1949, p. 4; cited from *CDSP* 1 (29 November 1949), 32.
83. Ibid.
84. A. Dyakov (D'iakov), "Anglo-American Plans in India," *Pravda*, 25 November 1949, p. 3; cited from *SPT* 5 (1 February 1950), 80, 82–83.
85. Dyakov, "Anglo-American Plans in India," p. 80.
86. Ibid., p. 82.   87. Ibid.   88. Ibid., p. 83.
89. "Russia Invites Pakistan Head," *New York Times*, 9 June 1949, p. 17.
90. The dates of 15 May and 2 June are mentioned in G.W. Choudhury, *India, Pakistan, Bangladesh, and the Major Powers: Politics of a Divided Subcontinent* (New York, 1975), p. 12. Chaudhuri once held a senior position in the Pakistani foreign office, and his account is based on his study of Pakistani documents, as well as interviews with other Pakistani diplomats.

91. Robert Trumbull, "Pakistanis Desire Support From the US," *New York Times*, (13 October 1947), p. 17.
92. Robert M. Slusser and Jan F. Triska, *A Calendar of Soviet Treaties, 1917-1957* (Stanford, 1959), p. 248.
93. Ibid. See also "Pakistan-USSR: Diplomatic Relations," *Pakistan Affairs*, 1 (14 May 1948), 4.
94. "Pakistan Flirts with Moscow," *The Economist*, 26 November 1949, p. 1172.
95. Ibid.
96. Cited in Chaudhury, *India, Pakistan, Bangladesh*, p. 12.
97. Musheeruddin Ansari, Letter to the Editor, *The Economist*, 13 August 1949, p. 346.
98. Arif Hussain, *Pakistan: Its Ideology and Foreign Policy* (London, 1966), p. 75. See also *The Economist*, 6 August 1949, p. 307.
99. "Mr. Liaquat Ali Khan's Coming Visit to Moscow," *Statesman Overseas Edition*, 18 June 1949, p. 10.
100. "Mr. Liaquat Ali's Visit to Moscow; Russia to Send Plane to Karachi," ibid., 6 August 1949, p. 10. That Russia was making a deliberate and determined effort to show friendship towards Pakistan was reflected in a comment made by Ghazanfar Ali Khan, Pakistan's ambassador in Iran. Enthusiastically reporting to his government Russia's new gestures, Ghazanfar said, "The same Russians who did not attend our Independence Day celebrations last year and did not offer condolence on the death of the Quaid-i-Azam [Pakistan's founder, M.A. Jinnah] are now eating out of our hands" (cited in Chaudhuri, *India, Pakistan, Bangladesh*, p. 14).
101. "Russian Economic Mission to Visit Pakistan" (dateline Karachi, 29 June), Ibid., 9 July 1949, p. 10.
102. "Russo-Pakistan Trade Talks," ibid., 6 August 1949, p. 10; *New Times*, no. 32 (3 August 1949), p. 32.
103. "Russian Trade Delegation Expected in Karachi Shortly," *Pakistan Affairs*, 2 (20 July 1949), 2.
104. "Prebyvanie sovetskoi torgovoi delegatsii v Pakistane," *Pravda* and *Izvestiia*, (9 August 1949), p. 4.
105. "Prebyvanie sovetskoi torgovoi delegatsii v Pakistane," *Pravda*, 11 August 1949, p. 3.
106. "Prebyvanie sovetskoi torgovoi delegatsii v Pakistane," ibid., 14 August 1949, p. 4.
107. "Russian Delegates Visit Mr. Jinnah's Grave," *Statesman Overseas Edition*, 20 August 1949, p. 10.
108. "Anti-English Sentiment in Pakistan," *Pravda*, 16 August 1949, p. 3; cited from *CDSP*, 1 (20 September 1949), 17.
109. Ibid.
110. "A Simple Soul," *New Times*, no. 44 (26 October 1949), p. 18.

111. Ibid.
112. "Predstoiashchaia konferentsiia assotsiatsii progressivnykh pisatelei Pakistana," *Pravda*, 11 October 1949, p. 3.
113. "Ot"ezd delegatsii sovetskikh pisatelei v Pakistane," *Pravda* and *Izvestiia*, 10 November 1949, p. 4.
114. "Delegatsiia sovetskikh pisatelei v Lakhore [Lahore]," *Pravda*, 18 November 1949, p. 3.
115. "Prebyvanie v Pakistane delegatsii sovetskikh pisatelei," *Pravda*, 19 November 1949, p. 4. See also "Delegatsii sovetskikh pisatelei v Pakistane," ibid., 22 November 1949, p. 3.
116. "Prebyvanie v Pakistane delegatsii sovetskikh pisatelei," *Pravda*, 25 November 1949, p. 3; "Russian Delegates Refused Entry into India," *Statesman Overseas Edition*, 26 November 1949, p. 1.
117. "Pakistan and Russia; Full Diplomatic Relations Soon," *Statesman Overseas Edition*, 20 August 1949, p. 10.
118. "Pakistan Embassy in Moscow," ibid., 22 October 1949, p. 11.
119. "Pakistan's First Ambassador to Moscow," ibid., 5 November 1949, p. 10.
120. "Russian Ambassador to Pakistan," ibid., 26 November 1949, p. 10.
121. "Russia 'Striving For World Peace'—Tribute by Pakistani Ambassador-designate," ibid., 19 November 1949, p. 7.
122. "Pribytie v Moskvu Pakistanskogo posla," *Pravda* and *Izvestiia*, 23 December 1949, p. 4.
123. "Vruchenie veritel'nykh gramot Predsedateliu Prezidiuma Verkhovnogo Soveta SSSR N.M. Shverniku pakistanskim Poslom G. Sh. Kureshi," *Pravda* and *Izvestiia*, 1 January 1950, p. 1.
124. Chaudhury, *India, Pakistan, Bangladesh*, pp. 12-13.
125. Cited in ibid., p. 12.
126. Spingarn to Clifford, 23 August 1949, Files of Clark M. Clifford, Harry S. Truman Library, Independence, Missouri.
127. Spingarn to Clifford, 25 October 1949, ibid.
128. Stephen J. Spingarn, "Notes on Pakistan," 26 October 1949, Stephen J. Spingarn Papers, Harry S. Truman Library, Independence, Missouri.
129. "Bid to Pakistani Studied," *New York Times*, 11 November 1949, p. 4.
130. "Premier Puts off Soviet Visit," ibid., 8 November 1949, p. 21.
131. "Liaquat Ali's Visit to Moscow," *Statesman Overseas Edition*, 12 November 1949, p. 10.
132. "US Invitation to Liaquat Ali Welcomed; Karachi Speculation on Russian Visit," ibid., 17 December 1949, p. 8; "Pakistan Prime Minister Accepts US Invitation," *New York Times*, 11 December 1949, p. 51.

133. "Pribytie v Karachi sovetskogo posla v Pakistane tov. Stetsenko," *Pravda*, 19 March 1950, p. 4, and *Izvestiia*, 19 March 1950, p. 3.
134. "Vruchenie veritel'nykh gramot poslom SSSR v Pakistane A.G. Stetsenko," *Pravda* and *Izvestiia*, 24 March 1950, p. 4.
135. "V Uchreditel'nom sobranii Pakistana," *Pravda*, 26 March 1950, p. 3; "Day of Demands," *Pravda*, 18 March 1950, p. 3 (cited from *CDSP*, vol. 2, 13 May 1950, p. 19); "Amerikanskaia ekonomicheskaia ekspansiia v Iugo-Vostochnoi Azii'" *Pravda*, 6 May 1949, p. 3; and "'Aid' to Pakistan," ibid., 22 May 1950, p. 4 (cited from *CDSP*, vol. 2, 8 July 1950, p. 25).
136. US, *Congressional Record*, vol. 96, pt. 5, 81st Congress, 2nd Session, p. 6324.
137. Ibid. 138. Ibid.
139. Ibid., vol. 95, pt. 11, 81st Congress, 1st Session, p. 14394.
140. Ibid., vol. 96, pt. 5, 81st Congress, 2nd Session, p. 6324.
141. K. Sarwar Hasan, *Pakistan and the United Nations* (New York, 1960), p. 55.
142. D.N. Mallik, *The Development of Nonalignment in India's Foreign Policy* (Allahabad, India, 1967), p. 86.
143. Ibid.
144. See his statement in *The Statesman*, 13 June 1950, p. 1; ibid., 18 June 1950, p. 1; ibid., 19 June 1950, p. 1; ibid., 21 June 1950, p. 7; and ibid., 23 June 1950, p. 1. Nehru's anti-Communist statements immensely pleased the US State Department officials. In a memorandum on the "Interpretation of Prime Minister Nehru's Southeast Asian Tour, and Shifts in Indian Foreign Policy," Deputy Assistant Secretary of State Raymond Hare said that Nehru spoke to various gatherings in these countries "as few foreigners would have dared." He also added that "in speaking so frankly Nehru served our interests admirably" (Memorandum by the Deputy Secretary of State for Near Eastern, South Asian, and African Affairs to the Secretary of State, 3 July 1950, *FRUS*, 1950, Washington, DC, 1978, vol. 5, p. 1467).
145. V. Berezhkov, "Foreign Policy Maneuvers of Indian Reaction," *New Times*, no. 22 (31 May 1950), p. 31; see also Arthur Clegg, "Uncle Sam Buys Up Burma," *World News and Views*, 30 (15 April 1950): 178.
146. "Nehru's Smear Campaign," *New Times*, no. 55 (21 June 1950), pp. 21–22.
147. Observer, "Much Advertising and Poor Results," *Izvestiia*, 22 January 1950, p. 4; cited from *CDSP*, 2 (18 March 1950): 19. See also Ya. Viktorov, "The Colombo Conference," *Pravda*, 8 January 1950, p. 4 (cited from *CDSP*, vol. 2, 4 March 1950, pp. 24–25); and Arthur Clegg, "The Colombo Conference and After," *World News and Views*, 30 (23 January 1950): 45.

148. A. Ya. Vyshinsky (chief ed.), *Diplomaticheskii Slovar'* (Moscow, 1950), 2: 239
149. V. Berezhkov, "Foreign Policy Maneuvers," pp. 30–32.
150. Ibid., p. 30.   151. Ibid.   152. Ibid.
153. Ibid., p. 31.   154. Ibid.   155. Ibid.
156. "Indian to Take Part in S.-E. Asia Talks," *Statesman Overseas Edition*, 13 May 1950, p. 1.
157. "Joint Action to Safeguard Common Interests," *The Statesman*, 31 May 1950, p. 1.
158. F. Terentiev, "Plans for a Pacific Bloc," *Pravda*, 17 May 1950, p. 4; cited from *CDSP* 2 (1 July 1950), 17-18.
159. ' SShA skolachivaiut agressivnyi tikhookeanskii blok," *Pravda*, 27 May 1950, p. 3.
160. "Plan to Form Pacific Bloc Is Defeated," *Pravda*, 2 June 1950, p. 4; cited from *SPT* 5 (1 July 1950), 414.
161. An Observer, "The Failure of the Present Attempt to Forge a Pacific Bloc," *Izvestiia*, 6 June 1950, p. 3; cited from *SPT* 5 (15 September 1950), 508.
162. N. Sergeyeva, "Crisis of the 'Cold War' Policy," *New Times*, no. 25 (21 June 1950), p. 6.
163. "Priem I.V. Stalinym posla Indii g-na S. Radhakrishnan," *Pravda* and *Izvestiia*, 15 January 1950, p. 1; Harrison E. Salisbury. "India's Envoy Sees Stalin at Kremlin; Ambassador and Premier in Half-hour Talk on Relations between Two Nations," *New York Times*, 16 January 1950, p. 2.
164. Sarvepalli Gopal, *Jawaharlal Nehru*, vol. 2, 1947-1956 (Cambridge, 1979), p. 64.
165. Cited in ibid.
166. Ye. Zhukov, "Obostrenie kolonial'noi sistemy," *Bol'shevik*, no. 23 (15 December 1947), p. 63.
167. "New Position and Policy of Japanese Communist Party—Report by Kiuitsi Tokuda, General Secretary of the Japanese Communist Party, at 18th Augmented Plenary Session of Japanese Communist Party Central Committee," *Pravda*, 15 April 1950, pp. 3-4; cited from *CDSP* 2 (3 June 1950), 22

VI

From the War in Korea to the Peace Treaty with Japan Moscow Reconsiders India's Nonalignment

The age is dominated by force—by ideas clothed in force: the Red Army of Communism *v.* the gathering might of the imperfectly democratic West. To one or the other of these poles the whole world is compelled. Nehru wants India, and Asia, to be let alone—not to be compelled in either direction. But history is not interested in happy socialist endings, or in wistful fairy tales.—*Time*, 7 May 1951.

...At the same time that our movement in general and our initiative for a five-power peace meeting developed, other movements for peace also developed, movements which may not all have attained the clarity of perspective and almost scientific precision of analysis of causes and consequences that many of us possess, but which nevertheless constitute an important factor in the resistance to war. Such, for instance, is the movement for neutrality, which in India in particular has become an expression of real politics.—Pietro Nenni, Vice-President of the World Peace Council, on 3 November 1951, at the Second Session of the World Peace Council in Vienna (*New Times,* Supplement to no. 47, 21 November 1951, p. 18).

WAR IN KOREA

The full-scale invasion by North Korea across the 38th parallel in the early hours of 25 June 1950,[1] brought the world to a grave crisis.

The response of the United Nations to this offensive was facilitated by the absence of the Soviet representative from the Security Council.* On 25 June the Council adopted a resolution calling for an immediate cessation of hostilities and the withdrawal of all North Korean forces to the 38th parallel.[2] But the invading forces continued to advance and soon the South Korean capital, Seoul, fell into their hands. The Council met again on 27 June and passed a second resolution calling for such assistance by the member states of the United Nations to South Korea "as may be necessary to repel the armed attack and to restore international peace and security in the area."[3]

1. *UN military response to North Korean aggression and the American, Indian and Soviet policies* For the United States, the North Korean act was more than a simple case of aggression: it was "a Russian maneuver, as part of the Kremlin's plan to destroy the unity of the free world."[4] This maneuver, therefore, could not be allowed to succeed. Not only in Korea but in other places of the Far East and Southeast Asia, Communist attempts to extend their control and influence posed a threat to the security of the free world and thus could not be allowed to go unchecked. Even before the Security Council met on 27 June, President Truman set forth the American policy in a major statement.[5] Arguing that the UN in its 25 June resolution had, in fact, called upon the member states "to render every assistance" in the execution of that resolution, he announced several measures on behalf of the United States: (1) The American air and sea forces were to give "cover and support" to the South Korean troops; (2) the Seventh Fleet was "to prevent any attack on Formosa"; and (3) there was to be "acceleration in the furnishing of military assistance to the forces of France and the Associated States in Indo-china and the dispatch of a military mission to provide close working relations with those forces." It was thus not only a measure to repel the aggression of North Korea but a programme to resist Communism in large parts of Asia.

India voted for the Security Council resolution of 25 June,[6] but

---

*The Soviets had withdrawn from the Security Council and other bodies of the UN in January 1950 for the apparent purpose of pressing Communist China's claim to be represented in the UN ("V Sovete bezopasnosti," *Pravda* and *Izvestiia*, 15 January 1950, p. 4).

the Indian delegate abstained from voting on 27 June because he said he lacked instructions from his government.[7] For New Delhi, it was not so easy to come out openly in support of Western military action. It led to intense discussions in the cabinet, during which US Ambassador Loy Henderson met both Nehru and Bajpai to press Washington's viewpoint.[8] In the end, India decided to accept the second resolution as well.[9]

Because of India's position as the largest non-Communist nation in Asia, her decision to accept the 27 June resolution gave great comfort to the United States. Henderson wrote to Acheson that India's action "would help millions of Asian doubters to make up their minds."[10] And the American delegate spoke in the Security Council of the "magnificent response" and "the positive help from a great nation such as India."[11]

The *New York Times* in an editorial observed that India's support

will be received throughout the democratic world with profound satisfaction. One can almost say that it puts the finishing touch to the bulwark that the free world is erecting against the North Korean aggression.[12]

The Reporter described India's support for the UN resolution as "one of the most momentous results" of the North Korean aggression.[13] Even *Time* magazine, which had hitherto found little virtue in India's neutrality or nonalignment, wrote appreciatively that Nehru "amazed his countrymen and the world by lining India up on the side of the UN and the US."[14]

But India was far from wholly lining up with the United States in regard to developments in Asia. She was no doubt aware of the Communist danger and had, as we have seen, devoted much effort and energy to suppressing the Communist revolt in Telengana and Communist activities in other parts of India during the past two years. But her diagnosis of the danger and the efforts she thought were necessary to meet it differed from those of the United States. During his tour of the Southeast Asian countries of Indonesia, Malaya, Singapore and Burma, undertaken just before the outbreak of the Korean War, Nehru repeatedly emphasized the importance of the force of nationalism in Asia. Communism, he said, was failing in India and many other places because "not only...it had parted company with nationalism but also because it had opposed it."[15] Implying that if the West wanted to oppose Communism in Asia it must support the force of nationalism, Nehru said "whatever group or party supported nationalism would go ahead."[16] President Truman's programme to provide military aid to France in Indochina could only be directed to the suppression of nationalist aspirations in the French colonies. The American commitment in Indochina therefore, as Harold R. Isaacs wrote, could only serve as a "source of India's deepest misgivings and suspicions" and was largely responsible for India's delay in accepting the 27 June resolution of the Security Council.[17]

The Indian government expressed these misgivings at the very outset. In a press conference on 7 July Nehru said that while India accepted the two UN resolutions of 25 and 27 June, she did so with reference to North Korean aggression alone;[18] she could not, he said, agree to any enlargement of the resolutions.[19] India also took pains to emphasize that the acceptance of the UN resolutions did not mean any change in her foreign policy—in this case no shift to the West had occurred. A statement of the Indian government of 29 June declared:

This decision [the acceptance of the 27 June resolution] does not, however, involve any modification of their foreign policy. This policy is based on the promotion of world peace and the development of friendly relations with *all* countries, it remains an independent policy which will continue to be determined solely by India's ideals and objectives.[20]

Even Henderson, who had felt elated at India' saction, told Acheson that "we should not assume that Nehru is ready as yet to go along with us all the way."[21]

The underlying motivations and objectives of Indian policy were soon apparent when she took two important decisions relating to the military effort in Korea. First, she abstained[22] on the British-French sponsored resolution in the Security Council creating a unified command in Korea under the UN flag and a commander to be nominated by the US.[23] Second, she decided not to send her forces to fight along with those supplied by other UN members, although she agreed towards the end of July to send ambulance and surgical units of her regular army.[24] The reason, as given by Nehru, for Indian military non-participation was that "the structure and organization of our armed forces is designed strictly to meet requirements of India's own defense"; therefore she could not "spare" any ground forces for Korea.[25] Surely India could have despatched a force; after all she eventually sent troops to Suez and the Congo. And, as a matter of fact, after accepting the 27 June resolution, her participation in the matters of command and ground forces should have followed naturally. However, she did not want to associate herself fully with military action in Korea under the leadership of the United States which might identify her with many aspects of US Far Eastern policy with which she disagreed, and thereby prevent her from playing an independent role in peace efforts undertaken in pursuance of her own policies.[26]

Whether or not the Soviet Union had a hand in the North Korean plan of invasion is a question which cannot be answered with complete certainty.[27] But there was no doubt as to where her sympathies lay once the attack had been launched. The Soviet press immediately accepted the North Korean version[28] of the outbreak of the conflict and reported that "a piratical attack" on the Korean People's Democratic Republic had been launched by "the reactionary Li Seung Man Clique, at the instigation of the American imperialists," and that the North Korean forces were acting only in "counter-offensive."[29]

As regards the action of the Security Council—made possible only by the absence of the Soviet Union—the Soviet press declared that owing to the absence of the "lawful" representatives of China and the Soviet Union, and because a decision by the Security Council required unanimity among the permanent members, the Council could not take any step which would have "the force of law."[30] This view was repeated in the Soviet reply of 29 June[31] to the US *aide-memoire* of 27 June, and in Gromyko's note of 29 June to the UN Secretary General.[32]

At this stage, however, there was no Soviet criticism of India for her support of the 25 and 27 June resolutions. The Soviet press and propaganda media concentrated instead on the themes of American "aggression" and "armed intervention."[33] However, the Soviet Union took notice when on 7 July India abstained on the British-French resolution concerning a United Nations commander in Korea. N.V. Roschin, its ambassador in Peking, told India's ambassador in China, K.M. Panikkar, that "neutral attitude and indifference" of Asian powers like India had "isolated" the United States.[34]

And an editorial in *New Times* noted that the refusal of India and Egypt to support a resolution authorizing, as the magazine put it, the UN flag "to be hoisted over MacArthur's headquarters" and the enormous pressure which the US had to bring to bear on a number of countries to vote for the resolution had, in fact, "thrown a very strong search-light upon the internal antagonisms within the imperialist camp."[35] This comment was quite significant. Moscow recognized that notwithstanding New Delhi's earlier support to the 25 and 27 June resolutions, India's policies differed from those of the US in some respect.

2. *Stalin and Nehru's July proposals* The differences between Indian and US policies were further evident when India made her first move to resolve the Korean problem. On 1 July Panikkar approached Chang Han-fu, the Chinese Deputy Foreign Minister, with the suggestion that the Korean question "could probably be solved by referring it to the Security Council with China taking her legitimate place, and consequently the Soviets giving up their boycott and returning to their vacant seat."[36] On 7 July, at a press conference in New Delhi, Nehru alluded to this Indian attempt to bring about "normality" in the Security Council.[37] On 10 July the Chinese gave an affirmative reply expressing "appreciation" of the Indian approach.[38]

While Panikkar approached the Chinese, S. Radhakrishnan, India's ambassador in Russia, met the Soviet Deputy Foreign Minister V.A. Zorin on 1 July, suggesting that the Soviets return to the Security Council and try to persuade the North Koreans to pull back to the 38th Parallel. Zorin's answer was that Moscow could not return to the Council without Communist China.[39] With these responses from Peking and Moscow, Nehru now decided to make a direct appeal to Stalin and Acheson. In identical letters sent to them, he said,

India's purpose is to localize the conflict and to facilitate an early peaceful settlement by breaking the present deadlock in the Security Council so that representatives of the People's Government of China can take a seat in the Council, the Union of Soviet Socialist Republics can return to it, and, whether within or through informal contacts outside the Council, the United States of America, the Union of Soviet Socialist Republics, and China, with the help and cooperation of other peace-loving nations, can find a basis for terminating the conflict and for a permanent solution of the Korean problem.[40]

On the same day, Indian Ambassador Radhakrishnan was received by Deputy Foreign Minister Andrei Gromyko with whom he had a "cordial" conversation.[41] Stalin sent Nehru a reply welcoming his "peaceable initiatives" and adding that:

I fully share your point of view as regards the expediency of the peaceful settlement of the Korean question through the Security Council with the obligatory participation of the representatives of the five great Powers, including the People's Government of China.[42]

Stalin also asserted that "for a speedy settlement of the Korean question it would be expedient to hear in the Security Council representatives of the Korean people."[43] On 16 July Nehru thanked the Soviet Prime Minister for his "prompt and encouraging" reply and wrote that he hoped to address him again after contacting "other Governments concerned."[44]

The US, however, found Nehru's suggestion unacceptable. In his reply on 18 July, Acheson separated the settlement of the Korean question from the issue of China's admission to the United Nations, which Nehru had tried to link together. On Korea, Acheson said, US policy was "to support by all means at our disposal the determination of the United Nations to repel the armed attack..."[45] On the other hand, the decision "between competing claimant governments" for China's seat should be reached "on its merits"; it could not be "dictated by an unlawful aggression or by any other conduct which would subject the United Nations to coercion and duress."[46]

In a second note to Acheson, Nehru argued that his proposal for Peking's participation in the UN was made "on its merits" and in an effort to break the deadlock in the Security Council.[47] He concluded, "I do not think that the admission of China now would be an encouragement of aggression."[48] Clearly the gulf between the two viewpoints was too wide to be bridged.

The Soviet government did not wait for the outcome of Nehru's approach to the United States before releasing its correspondence with him to the press, which both *Pravda* and *Izvestiia* published on their front pages on 18 July.[49] The Soviets obviously did not expect any positive response from Washington and therefore lost no time in presenting their own people and those of other countries with a "proof" of the peaceful nature of Stalinist foreign policy. The United States alone, they claimed, obstructed the realization of peace in Korea. Stalin's proposal, to quote a Soviet scholar, "became a programme of the fighters of the peace movement, who have come out against the bloody aggression of American imperialism in Korea."[50]

Nehru had, indeed, provided the Soviet government with a unique opportunity and one which it did not fail to exploit.

The correspondence between Nehru and Stalin was simultaneously published and favourably commented upon by the press in virtually all the Communist countries. Both *Pravda* and *Izvestiia* on 20, 21, and 22 July carried reports of press comments from Mainland China, North Korea, Poland, Bulgaria, Rumania, Czechoslovakia, Hungary, the German Democratic Republic, and the Mongolian People's Republic.[51] One typical comment, recorded in Tass dispatch from Ulan-Bator quoting an editorial in Unen, said that:

the whole of progressive mankind and all the Mongolian people have greeted with immense satisfaction Generalissimo Stalin's statement on peaceful settlement of the Korean question. Comrade Stalin's reply, the paper says, again clearly expresses the traditional policy of the great Soviet state, its desire for further strengthening peace throughout the world, its policy of respect for the sovereign rights of large and small peoples and nonintervention in the internal affairs of other countries.[52]

The Soviet press continued to publish favourable commentaries on Stalin's statement originating in Communist countries and in Communist or leftist papers outside them.[53] It also did not fail to take note of any approving comment in the "bourgeois" press. For example, a remark by a British Labour MP, S.O. Davies, that "Stalin's answer to Nehru is like a strong current of fresh air penetrating the stinking fog which hides everything reasonable connected with the Korean tragedy," was quoted in both *Pravda* and *Izvestiia*.[54] Soviet commentators and writers repeatedly made use of Stalin's reply as a manifestation of Moscow's desire for a peaceful settlement in Korea.[55]

In addition to praise for Stalin there were favourable comments on Nehru too. An editorial in the Cominform paper, *For a Lasting Peace, For a People's Democracy,* after praising Stalin's policy, said this of Nehru:

The very fact of the peaceable initiative displayed by Nehru, and also the statements by a number of bourgeois newspapers and politicians who have come out in favour of accepting the proposals of J.V. Stalin, testify to the fact that the most sober minds among the bourgeoisie are beginning to show serious uneasiness with regard to the consequences of the adventurous policy of war provocation being pursued by the US imperialists.[56]

Maurice Thorez, General Secretary of the Communist Party of France (PCF) told a PCF Central Committee plenum on 29 September 1950, that while it was not without significance that the governments of the "colony-owning powers"—Great Britain, France, the Netherlands, Belgium—were the first ones to side with the US, "it was the head of the Indian Government who took the initiative, supported without delay or reserve by Stalin, in suggesting the localization and the rapid and peaceful settlement of the Korean conflict, and the admission of Mao Tse-tung's China to the United Nations."[57]

On the other hand, the negative reply of the US Secretary of State was published in the Soviet press in order to demonstrate that the Western powers did not want peace in Korea. On 21 July *Pravda* and *Izvestiia* carried a Tass dispatch from Washington in which Acheson's letter rejecting Nehru's proposal and also Nehru's second note to Acheson of 19 July were included.[58] Ya. Viktorov wrote in *Pravda* that the rejection of the Indian Prime Minister's "peace initiative" by the US had clearly demonstrated "that American ruling circles intend to continue their aggressive war of aggrandizement against the Korean people."[59] Also, in the Soviet view the "internal antagonisms within the imperialist camp," as had been noted in the *New Times* editorial of 12 July, seemed to be further intensified as differences between India and the US were brought into sharp relief on an important international matter. An editorial in *New Times* observed that "the very fact that Nehru sent his message reflects the virtual isolation in which the United States finds itself after launching the armed intervention in Korea...."[60]

Viktorov, in the article just quoted, took comfort in the US dilemma of having to reject the proposal of a friendly country. He remarked that the Nehru formula for the solution of the Korean question had created "commotion and confusion in US ruling circles" and concluded, "It is no wonder that the American press wrote that Acheson is faced with a 'delicate' problem. The State Department has laboured assiduously over the composition of a reply to Mr. Nehru. As the newspapers reported, this reply has received triple revision."[61]

There is no doubt that Nehru's intervention for peace in Korea had a very adverse impact upon Indo-US relations. "The net effect of the Indian mediation effort," wrote the authors of *The United States in World Affairs, 1950*, "was to confirm the basic divergence between American views and those of a government which, not altogether unwarrantably, claimed to speak for the whole of non-Communist Asia."[62] Given the powerful forces in Congress and the country supporting the Chiang regime, it would indeed have been a bold decision on the part of any American administration to accept Communist China's admission to the United Nations at any time in the past; with the outbreak of the Korean war such a step was simply impossible.[63] The prevailing mood in Washington at the time was that aggression should not be allowed to bear fruit. Interpreted in this mood, Nehru's proposal simply appeared, as the *New York Times* put it, to be "an advance payment...at the point of a gun."[64] William Henry Chamberlin went a step further and described it as a "Munich-Yalta plan."[65] And Alan G. Kirk, US ambassador in Russia, said that "India has given damaging impression of a change in her attitude." He also accused Nehru that by calling Stalin's reply as "encouraging," the Indian leader was actually "play[ing] Stalin's game."[66] Thus although Acheson couched his reply to Nehru in the most diplomatic language, the Indian initiative nevertheless caused "surprised pain"[67] and "annoyance"[68] in Washington.

Even Britain and France, who themselves did not fully agree with the US policy in regard to China, rejected Nehru's proposal outright.[69] *The Economist* sharply criticized Nehru for his suggestion of "a dubious political deal" and for confusing the issue of an "open case of aggression" with the impasse in the Security Council.[70] "The question 'what will you give me if I stop twisting your arm?' has a place in the vocabulary of thugs, but not in the proceedings of the United Nations."[71]

On the Indian side there was unconcealed disappointment at the rigidity of the US position at a time when, in Indian eyes, the world was faced with the threat of a world war.[72] The Indian press was almost unanimous in its criticism of the US rejection of Nehru's proposals. The Madras *Indian Express* wrote, "The extent of [America's] surprise is the measure of the Americans' profound misreading of the Asian mind, which resents any attempt to make this area of the globe a happy hunting ground for power politics."[73] The *Indian News Chronicle,* which heretofore had been friendly to the West, offered even harsher comments: "The American note is sore with a sense of loneliness and breathes a frantic faith in the omnipotence of force—till now associated only with totalitarian regimes...The rebuff administered to Nehru is not a rebuff to an officious peacemonger, but an affront to the spirit of world peace."[74] Clarifying India's position further, and replying to the charge that India sought to appease the aggressor, the Indian President, Rajendra Prasad, said that had Nehru's proposal been accepted, the Indian government would have sought for a solution of the Korean question "on the basis of the two resolutions of the Security Council that it supported."[75] Nehru aired his own views in an emotional speech in the Indian Parliament. He defended his belief in the necessity of bringing Communist China into the United Nations.[76] Then, lamenting that "the future of Asia is still determined by the statesmen of the Western world," he charged:

The policy of the Western Powers is dominated more by European problems than by those of Asia, and they continue to take decisions affecting vast areas of Asia without understanding the effective needs and spirit of these people...We can understand the outlook of the Asiatic countries very much better than the West...I want to emphasize that any attempt to tackle Asian problems without taking Asia into account is bound to prove fruitless.[77]

The *New York Times* retorted in an editorial:"...whether we understand Asians or not, we do by now understand Communism."[78]

3. *The Soviets return to the Security Council: The widening gulf between India and the US* Having perhaps realized that boycotting the Security Council was a mistake, the Soviets now decided to return to it. Nehru's peace initiative, which had "served notice on the

Kremlin of a lively division of opinion in the free world,"[79] also seemed to suggest "a possible policy" to the Kremlin.[80] The question of Communist China's admission to the UN could very well be used to isolate the US from non-Communist Asian opinion.[81] The success of Soviet attempts in this direction was greatly facilitated by two factors: first, the increasing emphasis which countries like India put on Communist China's admission to the UN, and second, the hardening of the United States position against such a course and her increasing commitment to the Chiang government.

The objectives of Soviet policy and their partial attainment became apparent as the Security Council engaged in a procedural debate for three full days, 1–3 August 1950. Even before the debate began, the Soviet representative, Jacob Malik as President of the Council, ruled—clearly against established practice—that the representative of the "Kuomintang group" could not take part in the proceedings.[82] While all the other members except Yugoslavia voted to overrule the President's decison, India voted to uphold it.[83] India, her representative said, attached much more importance to the "grave issue involved" than to "mere points of procedure."[84] The issue, he declared, was the very "disruption" of the UN "as a world organization and, therefore, the Council should have no hesitation in departing from the rules."[85]

With regard to its agenda, the Council was faced with two separate proposals, one from the Soviet Union and the other from the US. The Soviet Union's resolution called for Communist China's recognition and the settlement of the Korean question by peaceful means.[86] The United States, on the other hand, proposed that the Council consider the "Complaint of Aggression upon the Republic of Korea," with which, in fact, it was already engaged.[87]

How much the Nehru peace initiative had played into Soviet hands was again evident when Malik, in a lengthy statement suggested that the Council take the Indian Premier's July correspondence with Stalin and Acheson as "litmus paper, as a reagent to determine who is for peace and the cessation of aggression in Korea and who is for aggression and the continuation of war in Korea."[88] He referred to the "noble initiative" and "endeavours...on behalf of peace" of Nehru and the "prompt and unhesitating response" of the Soviet Union, while the US reply was "the exact opposite."[89]

India supported the adoption of the Soviet agenda.[90] In view of her known stand on the Chinese question, there was hardly any doubt about her approval of the first part of the Russian proposal. But it was her support to the second part that further revealed differences between the American and Indian viewpoints. The US delegate, Warren Austin, expressed opposition to the Soviet proposal because it implied that Russia was "the only nation interested in the peaceful settlement of the Korean question...."[91] However, to India, as her delegate, Sri Benegal Rau, said, a "peaceful and honorable settlement" of the conflict was "the paramount need of the hour."[92] He added, "To exclude any express mention of it from our agenda would create an impression that we regard the matter as being merely of subordinate or incidental importance."[93] As far as India was concerned, therefore, it hardly mattered that the proposal originated with the Soviet Union. But it was more than the mere use of certain words; the disagreement revealed a clear difference of priorities between Indian and US policies which would force them apart in the coming months. India was already putting the emphasis on efforts to achieve peace, while the US was primarily concerned with "the fact of armed aggression"[94] and with efforts to meet it as provided in the US resolution submitted to the Council on 31 July.[95] The divergence became further obvious when India, although she had declared her support for adoption of the agenda proposed by the US,[96] abstained, along with Yugoslavia, when the actual voting on this issue took place; the reason for doing so, Sir Benegal Rau said, was the question of "priority."[97] It was also significant that both India and Egypt, the only two countries which could be said to have represented Asia in the Council (except, of course, Nationalist China), voted to include the Soviet proposal in the agenda; all other members—European as well as Latin American—followed the US lead in voting against it.[98]

India put up the strongest opposition, however, when the Soviet Union insisted that the "representatives of the Korean people," i.e., both North and South Korea, also be invited to the discussions of the Council.[99] Sir Benegal Rau contended that the Council was acting under Article 33 to consider a "breach of peace" and not under Article 32 to deal with a "dispute."[100] He remarked that "when the police were quelling a riot or the fire brigade is putting out a fire, they are not considering a dispute; they are taking action to remove a serious danger."[101] The question of inviting the representative of North Korea, he said, could arise only after the "enforcement action" had been completed.[102] India's opposition to this demand by the Soviets, although noted with "particular satisfaction" by Western countries,[103] angered Malik. He ridiculed Sir Benegal's defence of what the Soviet representative described as "injustice and lawlessness," and termed such an action by a jurist like Sir Benegal "tragic."[104] Despite such harsh words, India went ahead and voted against the Soviet proposal.[105]

On the two Korean resolutions, one submitted by the Soviet Union calling for an end to hostilities and the withdrawal of foreign troops[106] (which in practice would have meant the removal of United Nations forces) and the other put forward by the United States condemning the North Korean authorities for "continued defiance" of the United Nations and asking that all countries refrain from assisting the aggressor in any way,[107] India again voted against the Soviet resolution and in favour of the one sponsored by the United States.[108]

The Soviet Union had also submitted a resolution on 8 August concerning the "inhuman, barbarous bombing of the peaceful population and of peaceful towns and populated areas," which it charged was being carried out by the US Air Force in Korea. The resolution called upon the US to cease all such bombing.[109]

Because General MacArthur's headquarters possessed a "monopoly on destruction from the skies," there were reports even in pro-US countries of heavy bombings by the United Nations forces.[110] In India such reports were carried in many national newspapers, especially those published in the Indian languages.[111] These reports led to a fresh wave of anti-American feeling in India. In a dispatch from New Delhi, the *New York Times* correspondent wrote, "Anti-United States feeling in India never has been so widespread as it is now. With every day of the Korean war bringing more news of bombed cities and flaming villages, the unpopularity of the United States is growing."[112] This dispatch was reprinted by *Pravda* in considerable detail,[113] along with similar reports from India. In a press conference on 24 August Nehru himself referred to these bombings and said that India was opposed to them because they killed innocent people and were likely to create more problems and difficulties. But then, he added, being unaware of the nature of the bombing, "it was difficult for him to judge the issue."[114] Both *Pravda* and *Izvestiia* reported the first part of Nehru's statement, but left out the second part.[115] In fact, as the *New York Times* correspondent reported, the proding of several Indian reporters, mostly from the vernacular press, "failed to draw the Prime Minister into an outright condemnation of the American conduct of aerial warfare in Korea."[116] The Indian government, though concerned with the bombing, did not want to adopt an anti-American position when the issue was such a prominent theme of Soviet propaganda both in India[117] and outside. Nehru was again careful in alluding to this issue when he addressed the annual session of the Congress Party.[118] And when voting finally took place on the Soviet draft resolution, the Indian representative, on the ground that India could not "assume without investigation that all the allegations of bombing are true,"[119] voted against it.[120]

It was, however, the China question which, over-shadowing Indian support for the US in the Security Council during August and early September, again split the US and India apart. The Chinese question thus provided Soviet diplomacy with an ideal opportunity to fish successfully in the troubled waters of American-Indian relations, after Russian anti-American propaganda has failed to win Indian support in the United Nations.

It was India—even before the USSR had the opportunity of doing so—which presented a resolution calling for the admission of Communist China to the United Nations when the General Assembly met for its fifth session.[121] The Indian draft resolution naturally met with the support and approval of the Soviet Union and other Communist countries, but Secretary of State Acheson, confident of the majority the US commanded in the Assembly, opposed it vehemently. He told the delegates that "the orderly and the sensible thing" would be to "vote it down."[122] And so it was.[123]

4. *Crossing the 38th parallel: India opposes the American move*
Although, as Dean Acheson has written, the Far Eastern Division of the US State Department and planners at the Pentagon urged as early as July 1950, that UN forces must eventually cross the 38th parallel,[124] a final decision in this regard was not taken until early September. On 11 September President Truman approved the recommendation of the US National Security Council that General MacArthur "was to extend his operations north of the parallel and to make plans for the occupation of North Korea."[125] Instructions based on this recommendation were sent to MacArthur by the US Joint Chiefs of Staff on 27 September.[126] And although the expressed purpose of these instructions was the "destruction of the North

Korean Armed Forces,"[127] there was little doubt that the real objective of the United States was to free all of Korea from Communist control and influence.[128] In an editorial on 30 September the *New York Times* called the 38th parallel a "purely artificial line" and "a manufactured frontier," and supported the crossing for the establishment of a "free and united democratic state in East Asia."[129]

India's views on this question differed from those held by the United States. She also wanted the establishment of a united and democratic Korea, but she thought that to accomplish this by force could only lead to the enlargement of the war. Also, if the UN tried to achieve reunification by force, she would be adopting the same means which had been employed by North Korea. First, Nehru opposed the crossing of the 38th parallel at a press conference on 30 September, saying that this action should not be taken "until all other means of settlement have been explored."[130] Three days later, at the Pacific Relations Conference which was meeting at Lucknow, he charged that in crossing the 38th parallel General MacArthur would be doing the same thing as had been done by the North Koreans.[131] Agreeing that the North Korean aggression was undoubtedly an "evil," Nehru added, "We have to meet it by armed strength and as we meet it we become infected by that evil. We follow the same way...."[132]

The Chinese, on their part, made it quite clear what they would do if the UN forces crossed the 38th parallel. On 30 September Chou En-lai issued a public warning that China would "not stand aside" if North Korea was invaded.[133] Then, on the morning of 2 October, at 1 a.m., the Indian Ambassador in Peking, K.M. Panikkar, was awakened by the Chinese authorities for a conference with Chou. The Chinese Premier told Panikkar that "no country's need for peace was greater than that of China, but there were occasions when peace could only be defended by determining to resist aggression." Chou then added, "If the Americans crossed the 38th parallel, China would be forced to intervene in Korea. Otherwise he was most anxious for a peaceful settlement, and generally accepted Pandit Nehru's approach to the question."[134] This warning, by the very nature of the odd hour at which it was given, was meant to be conveyed to the American government. India promptly did so.[135]

China's threat, as conveyed through Panikkar, was not the first time when the possibility of Chinese intervention was raised as an issue in Washington. In fact, a Central Intelligence Agency report in mid-August on 'Factors Affecting the Desirability of a UN Military Conquest of all of Korea" had discussed this issue and had come to the conclusion that "grave risks" might be involved in such an undertaking, including "hostilities with the Chinese Communists."[136] Then besides India, the Dutch, who had a mission in Peking, also reported that their charge was "convinced" of a "real danger" of China's entry into the war "if our forces cross 38th and penetrate deeply [into] Korea."[137] Even the State Department specialist on China, O. Edmund Clubb, said that Chou's statement "cannot safely be regarded as mere bluff," because "the political and military stakes are considerable, and Moscow and Peking may be prepared to take considerable risks."[138]

So Truman's contention in his *Memoirs* that Panikker's information could not be taken as "more than a relay of Communist propaganda" because of the Indian envoy's pro-Communist sympathies was not the real reason for not taking China's threat seriously. In fact, it was a question of deciding whether or not to reverse a decision—the decision to liberate North Korea—that had already been made and implemented in the form of military orders sent to MacArthur. As Acheson said on 4 October, "...forces were in motion and plans were being made and that the Unified Command after a period of regrouping would be advancing into North Korea and that it was too late now to stop this process."[139] In addition, there was a sense of confidence and victory in Washington. This, together with a total belief in the justness of its cause, prevented the US from giving the kind of cool-headed and sober considerations that Chou's warning warranted. One official in Washington was quoted as saying, "I don't think that China wants to be chopped up."[140] And on 15 October, MacArthur told Truman that "if the Chinese tried to get down to Pyongyang there would be the greatest slaughter."[141]

In order to get an acceptance of the course of action thus already decided upon by the American government, an eight-power resolution (of which Pakistan was one of the sponsors) was introduced in the Political Committee for the purpose of authorizing UN forces to cross the 38th parallel in order to establish a "unified, independent and democratic Government" in Korea.[142] The USSR, on the other hand, along with the Ukraine, Belorussia, Poland, and Czechoslovakia, proposed that hostilities be stopped immediately, all foreign troops withdrawn, and a "unified Korea" established through elections.[143] India was opposed to crossing of the 38th parallel by the UN troops as implied in the eight-power resolution; however, she also did not agree that all foreign forces, which in practice meant the UN should be withdrawn from Korea at this stage. Nevertheless, she considered that there were certain similar points in both resolutions and that perhaps a common ground between them might be found.[144] Her delegate, therefore, proposed that a subcommittee consisting of six nations, three of which should be Asian, be appointed to consider all draft resolutions and recommend the one "commanding the largest measure of agreement."[145]

Though the US was most eager to secure India's support,[146] she was determined nonetheless to go ahead with her plans concerning Korea and was not prepared to bear the delay which the acceptance of the Indian proposal would have made inevitable. Moreover, in view of the record of Soviet dealings in Eastern Europe, she had no faith in cooperation with the Communists in regard to elections in Korea The *New York Times* frankly stated this when it declared that the forces of the UN and of the US in particular, did not "fight and die in Korea in order to enable the Soviet's to stage Balkan elections in that country as a means of its enslavement."[147] The Soviet Union, on the other hand, chose to support the Indian proposal. Vyshinsky said that "a new situation" had been created by the Indian proposal and the USSR would support it because she wished to bring about conciliation by peaceful means.[148]

One can only speculate whether the Soviets supported the Indian proposal out of a real desire to arrive at a satisfactory compromise. It is clear, however, that Russia was definitely interested in drawing India to her side and thereby weakening the American position in Asia. "Andrei Y. Vyshinsky," wrote an American commentator, "was most eloquent when he conferred in the delegates' lounge with Dr. B. V. Keskar, India's Deputy Minister of External Affairs. His face was bathed in smiles all the while."[149]

The General Assembly approved the eight-power resolution on 7 October.[150] Very soon afterwards American forces crossed the 38th parallel. On 12 October *Pravda* published the full text of a statement by the Chinese Foreign Ministry protesting the 7 October resolution. Analysing the voting in the Assembly in favour of this measure on the basis of population, the statement asserted that in fact it was only the "minority" controlled by the US which voted for it.[151] "On the other hand," the Chinese said, "the chief Asian countries, which are closely connected with the Korean question, China, the Soviet

Union and India, object to or at least do not agree with the resolution."[152] An editorial in *New Times* also analysed the situation on the same basis and, counting India on its side, pointed out that while the eight-power resolution was supported by countries which together counted 660 million people, "the aggression in Korea was disapproved by countries with a total population of 1,196 million inhabitants."[153]

The outcome, from the Soviet viewpoint, was not at all discouraging. In the UN itself, she had the satisfaction of seeing India, the chief Asian power at the UN, split away from the majority commanded by the US. Outside, the approval of the eight-power resolution by the General Assembly served her propaganda purposes well. She could show how the "imperialists" were scheming against the interests of the Asian people while the Soviet Union stood up for them. *New Times,* in the editorial just quoted, took up this theme when it asserted that "the American politicians brought their [voting] machine into action" to bring about the defeat of both the Soviet and Indian proposals and thus to force on the Assembly a resolution which would sanction the "conversion" of Korea "into a base for further imperialist aggression against the people of Asia."[154] It was, perhaps, again with the intention of showing that the Soviets sided with Asian interests that *New Times* added that India, "as one of the biggest of the Asiatic countries," was entitled to a say in the matter.[155]

On the other hand, public opinion in the US was very critical of India's stand. *The Reporter*, which would have liked India to play an important role in the unification of Korea under the new resolution, wrote that "India falls short of the role that could be hers."[156] The *New York Times* spoke some "plain words" to Nehru:

Americans are sorely disappointed with the policies pursued by Prime Minister Nehru...To us it is illogical to condemn the North Korean aggression and then not support the only possible measure to right the wrongs that have been done and to make Korea into a unified, independent state, free of all foreign control.

Pandit Nehru purports to speak for Asia, but it is the voice of abnegation; his criticism now turns out to have been obstructive, his policy is appeasement. Worst of all, one fails to find a valid moral judgment in his attitude. One can feel certain that history will condemn the Nehru policy as well-intentioned but timid, short-sighted and irresponsible...[157]

There was also great resentment and anger in the official circles in Washington at India's refusal to go along with the US move. On 28 September, Acting Secretary of State James E. Webb had written to Henderson that since America considered India's support of "tremendous significance," he should try to persuade New Delhi to support the crossing of the 38th parallel.[158] Having failed in his efforts and now expressing the "views of many American officials," Henderson expressed his criticism of India's stand directly to Bajpai. He told the Indian official that Nehru's position was "frankly unsympathetic with that of rest of free world," and that it was a "great tragedy" that "leaders of Asian free world" had been critical of the UN forces using their victory "in way which would most effectively discourage aggressors and potential aggressors."[159]

Such a strong criticism of Nehru's policies provoked widespread comments in India. M. Chalapathi Rau, editor of the Lucknow *National Herald* and one of India's most prominent journalists, replied to the *New York Times* editorial by reminding the Americans that their main concern seemed to be "to fight communism and, if possible, destroy it." In view of this, he observed, obviously referring to Chiang Kai-shek, "anybody can become a good ally of the United States... if only he fights communism." But India's interests, said Rau, lay in peace and therefore she could not join the US in this crusade. Americans will be "sorely disappointed and constantly shifting their standards," he concluded, "if they expected him [Nehru] to ...become a Chiang Kai-shek."[160] Nehru himself was apparently also stung by the increasing criticism of his policies in the United States. At a press conference on 16 October he concluded a long statement in defense his position with the words:

India has tried to follow in all modesty and humility what she considers the right path and has tried to understand other viewpoints. She does not claim infallibility of judgment nor does she recognize such infallibility of judgment and monopoly of rectitude in any other country...[161]

5. The Pacific Relations Conference, October 1950 Feeling between India and the United States was not improved by the discussions which took place at the Pacific Relations Conference at Lucknow in October 1950. In it the majority of the Indian and many other Asian delegates as well criticized American foreign aid policies.[162] This so outraged the *New York Times* that the paper accused Indian officials of permitting "their intellectuals and journalists to believe that the United States is sending economic aid to Asia simply to enable Wall Street to enslave the Asiatics."[163] Reports of these comments were carried by Indian newspapers on their front pages and in turn "shocked" the Indian public.[164]

These developments could not but be noted with satisfaction by the Soviet press. The USSR had been invited by the Indian organizers to send observers to the Lucknow Conference, but had declined to participate in any capacity in a meeting sponsored by an American organization.[165] The first comments in the Soviet press concerning the gathering were naturally hostile. On 9 October *Pravda* commented that William Holland, the American General Secretary of the Pacific Council, was playing a "leading role" in the meeting and that the discussion were mainly concerned "with the problem of what means and methods would be used to undermine from within the national liberation movement in the countries of the Far East and Southeast Asia."[166] But when news of the criticism of the United States by Indian and other Asian delegates reached the Soviet Union, *Izvestiia* began to see in the conference a "striking evidence of the fact that the Asian peoples place no credence whatever in the utterances of goodwill towards the Asian countries by representatives of American imperialism."[167] The article also quoted the Delhi correspondent of the France Presse agency, who found "deep-seated contradictions existing between the delegates of the eastern and western powers."[168] With apparent satisfaction, *New Times* reported the differences between the US and other Indian and Asian delegates, resulting in what it called the failure of the "American arrangers...to secure endorsement for their expansionist warmongering plans in Asia..."[169]

6. *India and Acheson's 'Uniting for Peace' proposal* The military situation in Korea changed rapidly in September in favour of the UN forces. The landing of the US X Corps at Inchon on 15 September and the offensive which got under way the next day in southeastern Korea altered the course of the war completely. By the end of September the UN troops were heading towards the 38th parallel.

We have already noted the decision of the US government to extend the military operations north of the 38th parallel and not to leave Korea, as Warren Austin, the US Representative in the Security Council, had declared on 19 August, "half slave and half free."[170] The favourable developments on the war front seemed to bring the goal nearer.

On the diplomatic front, however, the return of the Soviet delegate to the Security Council had created some difficulties. Moscow was now in a position to use its veto to block the American moves. This seemed particularly hindering at a time when the US needed the support and approval of the UN for her new move in Korea. It was therefore to avoid the Soviet veto in the implementation for her plans concerning Korea that the US put forward what is known as the Acheson Plan. Frankly spelling out the reasons for the plan, Acheson writes in his memoirs:

When this regime [North Korea] attacked the South and in the process lost most of its military force, the tempting possibility of achieving an independent and united Korea without more military effort or risk beckoned the United Nations. But to make this effort, or even the more modest one of preventing renewal of the attack, required a UN decision that could not be blocked by a Soviet veto in the Security Council. The purpose of my 'Uniting for Peace' speech on September 20 was to make further UN decisions possible by action in the General Assembly.[171]

While presenting the new US plan to the General Assembly on 20 September, Acheson called upon the UN to develop "a more adequate system of collective security," and warned that "it will move back" if it did not do so.[172] A resolution on the lines suggested by Acheson, and passed by the Assembly on 3 November, had four important parts: (1) it provided for the calling of an emergency session of the General Assembly to make "appropriate recommendations to Members for collective measures" if, "because of lack of unanimity of the permanent members," the Security Council failed to take action in case of breach of peace or act of aggression, providing also that such a session could be called if requested by seven members of the Security Council or a majority of the members of the UN; (2) it established a Peace Observation Group to "observe and report on the situation in any area where there exists international tension the continuance of which is likely to endanger the maintenance of international peace and security"; (3) it recommended that each Member maintain within its armed forces UN units which "could promptly be made available...for service as a United Nations unit or units..."; and (4) it established a Collective Measures Committee to report by 1 September 1951, on methods to develop and strengthen collective action, including those provided in (3). [173]

Dominated as the UN was at that time by the US, which could always muster seven votes in the Security Council and a majority in the Assembly, the implications of the Acheson Plan were far-reaching. An Indian scholar, K.P. Karunakaran, goes to the extent of saying that this presented the danger of the UN being transformed into "a global military alliance directed against a group of powers headed by the Soviet Union."[174]

In the UN, India expressed her support to the first two provisions, but bitterly opposed the last two. As her delegate, A.C.N. Nambiar, said in the Political Committee, "...at a time when all the peoples of the world desired peace, that part of the resolution gave the impression that the United Nations was more concerned with perfecting its enforcement machinery than with promoting international cooperation and mutual goodwill."[175] At a press conference in New Delhi Nehru said this of the Acheson Plan:

We did not agree with proposals to create separate armed forces on behalf of the United Nations in each country.... It seemed like converting the United Nations into a larger edition of the Atlantic Pact and made it a war organization more than one devoted to international Peace.[176]

Since the Acheson Plan was aimed at neutralizing the power of Soviet veto, the Soviets—as they had done against all such attempts of the US in the past—criticized Washington's action in very strong language. Addressing the US delegation in the General Assembly, Vyshinsky said:

So there it is, you want to move the centre of gravity in the veto controversy to a point where you are bound by nothing save your majority, which you have under your thumb, and by using the majority to do what you want regardless of anything. Therefore you must at all costs push through the decision which will help you to achieve that end, however illegal it may be.[177]

In the final voting, the Soviet Union and her Communist supporters, as expected, voted against the resolution. India and Argentina were the only two non-Communist countries which abstained; all the other 52 countries, including Pakistan, voted for the Acheson Plan.[178]

7. *The question of Chinese "aggression" in Korea* We have noted above that although the instructions sent to MacArthur on 27 September by the US Joint Chiefs of Staff to extend military operations north of the 38th parallel were conditional, the US seemed determined to abolish the dividing line and unify Korea by force. In fact, only two days later, on 29 September, the US Secretary of Defence, General Marshall, cabled to MacArthur, "We want you to feel unhampered strategically and tactically to proceed north of the 38th parallel."[179] Louis Halle rightly observes that Marshall's cable "virtually authorized him to interpret his instructions so widely as to nullify them."[180]

The parallel was crossed by South Korean troops under MacArthur's command on 1 October 1950. And, after UN approval was obtained for the American plan on 7 October, US troops also crossed the parallel the same day. A week later, on 15 October, MacArthur told President Truman at Wake Island that the victory in Korea had been won, and discounted any possibility of the Chinese entering the conflict.[181] In fact, the Chinese "volunteer" forces had begun their secret movement into Korea only a day earlier.[182]

Still unaware of the movements of the Communist Chinese forces, MacArthur, on 24 October, ordered all his forces to push northward to the very end. This order was, in fact, contrary to his instructions of 27 September which had told him to use only South Korean troops "in the north-east provinces bordering the Soviet Union or in the area along the Manchurian border."[183] Reaching the Yalu two days later, his forces came into direct contact with the Chinese for the first time. By 6 November he was quite alarmed and reported that "Men and material in large force are pouring across all bridges over the Yalu from Manchuria."[184] To prevent this, Truman concurred with his plan to bomb the bridges over the Yalu.[185] But hardly had the new instructions gone out, when, on 7 November, he reported the operations of "hostile planes...from bases west of the Yalu River," and asked for "corrective measures" to deal with the situation,[186] obviously asking permission to bomb these bases across the Yalu. Since any such action posed the danger of a wider conflict, the US government was unwilling to grant him this permission.[187] The Chinese still did not undertake any offensive action against the UN forces. It was MacArthur again who launched a major attack on 24 November. This was what he called a "general offensive...to end the war...," and he told his troops that they would be home by Christmas.[188]

Now it was for the Chinese to strike back which they did two days later in very large numbers. By 28 November, the course of the war seemed to be completely changed as MacArthur's forces were forced to fall back and were found almost fleeing southward. There was much truth in MacArthur's statement that "we face an entirely new war...."[189] He also added that the new situation "poses issues beyond the authority of the United Nations military council—issues which must find their solution within the Councils of the United Nations and chancelleries of the world."[190]

In the UN, India again attempted to cool the situation which, disturbing as it already was, threatened to assume dangerous proportions with the statement by President Truman at a press conference on 30 November that there had been "active consideration" of the use of the atomic bomb in Korea.[191] This time, however, the appeal of India and several other Asian and Arab countries for showing restraint in the war was addressed to Peking. On 5 December, India and ten other states appealed to Communist China "immediately to declare that it is not their intention that any forces under their control should cross to the south of the 38th parallel."[192]

But victory on the battlefield has its own logic. As the US forces in the past had refused to stop at the 38th parallel, so now China failed to respond to the appeal of 5 December.

For the next few weeks, India and the Soviet Union seemed to be working on altogether different planes in the UN. While the Soviet delegate, Vyshinsky, submitted a resolution in the Political Committee calling for immediate withdrawal of all foreign troops from Korea and entrusting the Korean question to the Korean people themselves,[193] India devoted her energies to finding a basis which might be acceptable to both sides. The draft resolution put forward by India on behalf of the thirteen Asian and Arab states requested the President of the General Assembly to form a group of three persons, including himself, "to determine the basis on which a satisfactory cease-fire in Korea can be arranged...."[194] The resolution was approved by the Assembly on 14 December, with the Soviet Union and other countries of the Soviet bloc voting against the resolution.[195] The Soviet view, as expressed in the Political Committee by Jacob Malik, was that this was "...merely a hypocritical and camouflaged attempt to obtain a breathing spell before embarking upon further military action."[196] *New Times*, echoing Malik's words, called it "a disguised attempt to enable the US armed forces in Korea to continue the intervention."[197] Premier Chou En-lai attacked the cease-fire proposal in very strong terms in a broadcast on 22 December.[198]

We must, however, note that the Soviet and Chinese attacks on the cease-fire proposal were not attacks on the sincerity of either India or other sponsors of the proposal. In fact, India's delegate, Sir Benegal Rau, while presenting the Asian-Arab resolution to the Political Committee on 12 December, offered what seemed to be a rationalization of China's intervention in the Korean conflict.[199] Therefore, when Chou attacked the proposal, he did not doubt that the sponsors were motivated by "their desire for peace." But, said Chou, if they really desired "genuine peace," they must "give up the idea of cease-fire first and negotiations afterwards."[200]

In the Soviet statements also, there were nowhere any direct attacks upon the sponsors of the proposal.[201] From the Chinese standpoint—which, as we have seen, the Soviets fully supported—to agree to a cease-fire at a time when she was pushing the UN forces towards the south, would be to miss a unique opportunity. This was the time, if ever, to force the Americans to agree to her admission to the UN and also to withdraw from Formosa. In his broadcast on 22 December, Chou said that "the present issues are definitely not confined to the Korean problem." They must include, he asserted, the withdrawal of "American aggression forces" from Taiwan and the admission of Peking to the UN.[202]

Having rejected the cease-fire proposals, the Communist Chinese felt free to cross the 38th parallel, which they did on 26 December. Their advance, however, continued deep into the territory of South Korea, forcing the UN troops to abandon its capital, Seoul, on 3 January 1951.

The rapid advance of the Chinese forces into South Korea created a grave crisis at the UN. The Group on Cease-fire, which had been created under the resolution of 12 December and which included Sir Benegal Rau of India and Lester Pearson of Canada, in addition to the President of the General Assembly, now framed certain proposals which went a long way towards meeting the Chinese stand. Although these proposals provided for an immediate cease-fire, they sought to satisfy the Chinese in envisaging the eventual gradual withdrawal of all foreign troops and in creating a special body, including the representatives of Peking and Moscow, "...with a view to the achievement of a settlement,...of Far Eastern problems, including...those of Formosa (Taiwan) and of the representation of China in the United Nations."[203] Since the US was hardly prepared to change her stand on the questions of Formosa or China's representation in the UN, she could not have accepted these proposals. But the refusal to do so would have alienated her from her Western allies such as Canada and Great Britain. Explaining Washington's reasons for accepting these proposals, Acheson says:

The choice whether to support or oppose this plan was a murderous one, threatening, on one side, the loss of the Koreans and the fury of Congress and press and, on the other, the loss of our majority and support in the United Nations. We chose, after painful deliberations in the Department—and after I recommended to the President what may well have been, even without hindsight, the wrong alternative—to support the resolution. We did so in the fervent hope and belief that the Chinese would reject it (as they did) and that our allies would then return (as they did) to comparative sanity and follow us in censuring the Chinese as aggressors.[205]

Peking and Moscow therefore gravely miscalculated when they chose to reject[206]* these new proposals after they were adopted by

---

* A Soviet commentator, G. Rassadin, criticized the work of the Group on Cease-Fire in strong terms, calling it "servile" and its recommendation "dictated from Washington and London and...far removed from the aims of a peaceful solution of the Korean problem." But while Rassadin spoke of Nasrollah Entezam of Iran (President of the General Assembly) as one "who is well known for his obsequiousness to the US State Department," and of Lester Pearson of Canada as one "who, during the entire Fifth Session of the General Assembly, made base speeches cribbed from the Americans, on the Korean question rejecting a peaceful solution," no such personal criticism

the Political Committee on 13 January with a huge majority of 50 to 7.²⁰⁷ While doing so, however, Communist China offered her own suggestions regarding the settlement of the war in Korea and other Far Eastern problems. In a telegram to the UN Acting Secretary General, Chou proposed that a conference of the representatives of seven countries—China, Egypt, France, India, the USSR, Great Britain and the US—should be held in China for this purpose.²⁰⁸

To the US, China's rejection of the new cease-fire proposals provided the opportunity to bring up before the UN the question of China's "aggression," about which, writes Acheson, Washington had been trying to rally its friends since the very beginning of Peking's intervention in the war.²⁰⁹ On January 20, Warren Austin, the US delegate, presented a draft resolution which charged that Communist China had "...engaged in aggression in Korea"; it affirmed "the determination of the United Nations continue its action in Korea to meet the aggression"; and it provided for constituting a Collective Measures Committee "...to consider additional measures to be employed to meet this aggression..."²¹⁰ Austin said that while the US believed in a peaceful approach, "...the time to draw the line was now," and he added, "Collective judgment and collective action offered the best hope of opposing aggression."²¹¹

Since India was one of the few countries to warn the US that the crossing of the 38th parallel by its troops would bring in Chinese intervention, New Delhi could not accept the view that Peking had committed "aggression" in Korea.²¹² Rau asserted:

...The Government of India, on the basis of the most authoritative information at its disposal and the deductions it had drawn therefrom was not convinced that the participation of Chinese forces in the fighting in Korea was due to any aggressive intention. It was more probably due to the fears of the Government of the People's Republic of China for China's territorial integrity.²¹³

India, in fact, had considered the Chinese reply of 17 January, 1951, to the latest UN peace proposal as "partly acceptance, partly non-acceptance, partly a request for further elucidation and partly a set of counter-proposals."²¹⁴ In line with this evaluation of the

---

was made against the third member, Sir Benegal Rau of India. G. Rassadin, "Clumsy Maneuvers of the American Aggressors," *Pravda*, 16 January 1951, p. 4; cited from *CDSP* 3 (3 March 1951): 15.

Chinese stand, India therefore joined the other Asian-Arab states in presenting a draft resolution, which called for a conference of the seven powers mentioned in Chou En-lai's reply of 17 January to "meet as soon as possible for the purpose of securing all necessary elucidations and amplifications" of the Chinese proposals.[215] In a revised draft of the resolution, presented to the Political Committee five days later, the Asian-Arab states recommended that the proposed conference should agree, at its first meeting, on a cease-fire in Korea, and once it was put into effect, should proceed to discuss other questions.[216] This, in fact, was what the US had so far insisted on, i.e., a cease-fire first and negotiations afterwards. Next day, on 30 January, Sir Benegal Rau explained the reason for including this provision in the Asian-Arab resolution. He said that China had asked the Indian government to inform the Committee that because of Peking's desire for peace, the Chinese government would agree to a cease-fire at the first meeting of the proposed conference and then would work for the settlement of Far Eastern problems through negotiations.[217]

What seemed to be an apparent change in Peking's attitude was described by Warren Austin as "not much more than a postal card."[218] The Truman Administration seemed determined to go ahead with its own resolution. After what an American writer, Lillie Shultz, described as a "campaign of pressure, the like of which had never been seen before,"[219] the Political Committee rejected the Asian-Arab resolution on 30 January.[220] On the same day, it approved the revised US draft resolution. India and Burma were the only non-Communist countries which voted against the US resolution.[221] The resolution was finally adopted by the General Assembly on 1 February, India voting against it.[222] Sir Benegal Rau, in utter frustration, said that India and the other Asian countries which had sponsored the latest peace proposal, "wished to go on record that when the world had, in their view, been marching towards disaster, most of the Asian Powers had done all they could to halt the march."[223] He later told the General Assembly that had their resolution been adopted, that "would...have produced a cease-fire within perhaps a week..."[224]

In a dispatch from Paris, *The Hindu's* correspondent, K. Balaraman, had described the UN debate over the question of China's "aggression" in Korea as a "tussle between the US and Indian viewpoints."[225] India was therefore much criticized in the US for her stand on this question. Although even at the beginning of Chinese involvement in the Korean War, the *New York Times* had described the Indians as "apologists and supporters" of the Chinese,[226] the US criticism of Indian policy grew more and more bitter as the debate at the UN dragged on,[227] culminating in the US move to brand China an aggressor. Summarizing the US reaction, Balaraman, now reporting from New York, wrote, "American resentment against India has reached a new high and the press, the public, Congressional and official opinion has become highly critical and impatient of the line taken by Mr. Nehru on the Korean problem."[228] In a meeting with Mrs. Pandit, Indian ambassador in the US Acheson told Nehru's sister that the Prime Minister's statement had given "us lots of trouble."[229] But perhaps Washington's anger was best reflected in a comment by Truman when he told a Congressman that "Nehru has sold us down the Hudson. His attitude has been responsible for our losing the war in Korea."[230]

The impact on the Soviet Union of India's vote on this question was just the opposite. Stalin, in reply to a question by a *Pravda* correspondent, described the US resolution as a "shameful" one,[231] and the Soviet press followed this line in criticizing the UN action.[232] But while doing so, the Soviets took special notice of India's vote against the US resolution. An article in the Cominform paper, *For a Lasting Peace, For a People's Democracy*, mentioned the pressure the US had exerted on India in trying to get New Delhi's vote for its resolution.[233] A Tass dispatch from New York pointed out the unfavourable reaction Nehru had caused in the US Congress when... "he condemned the attempts of the US in the United Nations to accuse China as 'an aggressor.' "[234] *Pravda*, in a long commentary on the UN resolution, pointed to the policy of "intimidation" pursued by the US, and specifically mentioned India among the Asian nations which had withstood it and eventually cast her vote against the American resolution. *Pravda* wrote:

The unprecedented and mocking resolution proclaiming the Chinese People's Republic an aggressor was adopted as a result of the threatening and intimidation by the American government of a number of nations which were forced under the pressure of these methods of American diplomacy to vote servilely for the resolution. In this case too the customary 'voting machine' in the General Assembly was set going at full speed. This time, however, the 'voting machine' seriously misfired. Many governments, chiefly those of the Asian nations, saw the prospect of an intensification of the people's anger against the policy of support of and connivance with American aggression. These governments evidently realized the danger to their own interests and their own international positions in supporting the aggressive-adventurous course of American policy directed against the Chinese People's Republic.

...not only the Soviet Union and the people's democracies represented in the UN but also the representatives of a number of countries of Asia and the Near East, including India, opposed the American resolution which was directed towards a further spreading of American aggression in the Far East. This found its expression in the criticism of Rau, the Indian delegate, who declared that this resolution would have no moral force and that it might lead to an extension of the conflict and in the final analysis even to a world war.[235]

In an article in *Sovetskoye gosudarstvo i pravo*, two Soviet writers, V.N. Durdenevsky and A.M. Ladyzhensky, described India and Burma, along with the Soviet Union, as Communist China's "closest neighbours," against whose "will and advice" the UN General Assembly had approved the American resolution.[236]

India, a few days later, voted against the two Soviet resolutions calling on the UN to take action against the US for her "aggression" against Peking in Formosa (blockade of the island by the US Seventh Fleet) and Manchuria (alleged air bombing attacks by the Americans).[237] The reason for India's negative vote, as explained by her delegate, Rajeshwar Dayal, was that "An exchange of charges of aggression is not, in our view, conducive to a peaceful settlement."[238] But India's vote on the US resolution had been considered so crucial that neither the Americans nor the Soviets gave any importance to her vote on the two Soviet resolutions.[239]

India's mediation effort in the Korean War thus came to an end, for the time being at any rate. The two sides still fought on the battle-front, and it would be the realities of that theatre that would lead to negotiations towards the end of 1951. But while India failed in her primary objective of bringing peace in Korea, her role in the whole affair had certainly led to a reappraisal of her foreign policy in both Washington and Moscow.

The War in Korea and India's Own Problems

The Korean War, as we have seen, became an all-important issue in the diplomacy of both Moscow and Washington. We have also noted how India's role in trying to bring about a possible compromise which could be acceptable to both sides led to a reappraisal of her position by the two superpowers. At this time, some of the issues in which New Delhi was itself a party provided important case studies where these changed attitudes of the two Great Powers were not only made more evident but were further sharpened by the results of these issues. Two such problems that confronted India were the Chinese invasion of Tibet and the continuing dispute with Pakistan over Kashmir.

1. *The Chinese invasion of Tibet* The Chinese invasion of Tibet began on 7 October 1950, the day when India abstained on the eight-power resolution in the General Assembly. This resolution, it will be recalled, authorized the UN forces to cross the 38th parallel.

The Soviet Union had fully supported the Chinese contention that Tibet was an integral part of China. A Tass dispatch in January 1950 had stated that what the Tibetan people really wanted was to join "the great democratic family of the Chinese People's Republic."[240] A little later, *New Times* disputed the claim, made in an article published in Great Britain, that Tibet was an independent country.[241]

Moscow therefore concurred in the Chinese act of "liberation." The Soviet press provided wide coverage to the progress of the Chinese forces, although these reports were carried only after the Chinese made the move public on 25 October.[242] *Pravda's* correspondent vividly described how the Tibetan people welcomed the liberating forces at every step.[243]

However, what the Soviet press omitted was the angry exchange of notes between India and China of 26 and 30 October.[244] The Indian government, in its note of 26 October, expressed "deep regret" at the "deplorable" step taken by China to annex Tibet by force and reminded her of the assurances given to India that the problem would be settled by "peaceful means."[245] China, on 30 October, replied by accusing India of "having been affected by foreign influences hostile to China," which could only mean either Great Britain or the United States.

The failure of the Soviet press to publish the Chinese note of 30 October seems to have been deliberate, since the Chinese accusation that India's foreign policy was under foreign influence was not in accordance with Moscow's current evaluation of the role of this policy in Korea; in fact, as we have seen, the Soviet view that Indian policy was becoming independent of American influence had been expressed only five days prior to the above Chinese note.²⁴⁷ That the omission was intentional is further indicated by the fact that the Soviet press carried the 16 November Chinese note to India in full (the reply to the Indian note of 31 October).²⁴⁸ The latest Chinese communication made no mention of India's being under any foreign influence; it merely expressed Peking's "regret" at the Indian attempt to treat "an internal problem of the Chinese government" as an "international conflict" and welcomed "the statement of the Indian government which repeats once more that it does not have any political or territorial claims to Chinese Tibet and does not desire to receive any new privileged positions whatsover there."²⁴⁹

Even when the Soviets pointed to foreign intrigues in Tibet, India was not mentioned; it was the "American-British imperialists" whose aim was to "detach" Tibet and use it "as a springboard for new acts of aggression against the Chinese people."²⁵⁰ And although the Soviet press indicated that in the spring of 1950 American arms were being supplied to Tibet "through" India, the Indian government was not directly accused of involvement in this act.²⁵¹*

The Chinese offensive against Tibet shocked India and shook her faith in the peaceful intentions of the Communist regime in China.²⁵² In the ruling Congress Party the elements which did not

---

*That the Soviet Union avoided implicating India in the alleged American arms shipment to Tibet because of Nehru's policies towards the Korean conflict is evident from a Tass dispatch from Prague of 12 May in which a different view had been taken. Quoting the Telepress Agency that a group of Americans had arrived in Calcutta "to supervise the shipment of American arms and war material to Tibet," the dispatch said, "In accordance with an agreement concluded between Henderson, American Ambassador to India and Nehru, Prime Minister of India, the USA receives the right to transport arms, after they have been unloaded in the port of Calcutta..." ("Deliveries of American Arms to Tibet," *Pravda*, 13 May 1950, p. 4; cited from *CDSP*, vol. 2, 1 July 1950, p. 23.) The accusation of such a deal with the Americans was also made by Moscow Radio. The Soviet statement brought an immediate denial by the Indian Ministry of External Affairs. ("Moscow Radio Report Denied," *The Statesman*, 16 May 1950, p. 3.)

fully endorse Nehru's course in foreign affairs and wanted India to pursue a more pro-Western policy now became more vocal. The Deputy Prime Minister, Sardar Patel, who had been a consistent target of the Soviet press for his anti-Communist views and his measures against the Indian Communists as Home Minister, spoke more critically than Nehru of the Chinese act, saying that it could set off a new world war and urging the Indians to be prepared to meet the danger.[253] This clearly implied a proposal for a stronger action than Nehru was prepared to take. When the Indian Parliament discussed the question on 7 December, there was almost unanimous criticism of the Chinese action and a demand that India change her foreign policy. *The Statesman* reported that "so insistent and outspoken was their [members of Parliament] criticism of the Communist countries that one member remarked: 'The House seems to have turned into an anti-Communist conference.'"[254] But it was Nehru's view that eventually prevailed; he was neither prepared to give up nonalignment nor take any positive steps to prevent the Chinese conquest of Tibet.*

The pro-Western voices raised in India in connection with the Tibetan question brought a severe condemnation from the Soviets. A Tass dispatch on the 7 December debate in the Parliament named two members, Ranga and Kriplani, as "followers of British imperialists" and censured their criticism of Nehru's policy towards China and Tibet.[255] Commenting on Masani's speech, in which he urged the revision of India's foreign policy in favour of accepting "the friendship of the democratic countries," and on the wide publicity reported to be given to it by the American radio, *New Times* noted that "the stocks of the American imperialists have fallen low in India, and this publicity of the Masani** speech on the part of

---

*In a way these policies were related to each other: India could not take any concrete steps—which would have surely involved the use of force—without the active military support of the Western powers, including the United States. This would have meant giving up nonalignment in foreign policy and a major shift to, if not complete alliance with, the United States. How far this policy would have worked for India's national interests and prevented the events of 1962 can only be left to speculation. It can, however, be said that such a step at this stage would have had a very adverse effect on the development of Indo-Soviet relations.

**M.R. Masani, at this time a member of Nehru's Congress Party, later left the Congress to become one of the founders of the Right-wing Swatantra Party. He remained a strong advocate of India's alliance with the United States.

Washington was only an effort to boost them up."²⁵⁶

2. *The continuing dispute over Kashmir* The Kashmir question, which continued to plague Indo-Pakistani relations, was also affected by the crisis in the Far East. Although the American position had never been particularly sympathetic to India's case in the dispute, the US in early 1951 began to plan an assertive role in the matter by forcing resolutions through the Security Council which were widely resented in India. By doing so, the United States contributed to the evolution of the Soviet Union's pro-Indian attitude.

Sir Owen Dixon, the UN Representative for India and Pakistan, was in India at the time of the outbreak of the Korean war. After his stay in the subcontinent, which included an extended visit to Kashmir, he made certain proposals.²⁵⁷ We do not need to go into their details, but suffice it to say that they were unsuccessful in breaking the deadlock between India and Pakistan. One important development may, however, be noted because it had some bearing on the criticism which India and the United States hurled against each other regarding their policies on the question.

On the very first day of the conference between the Indian and Pakistani premiers convened by Sir Owen in New Delhi on 20 July, the UN representative endorsed India's charge that Pakistan had committed aggression in Kashmir. In his own words:

...without going into the causes or reasons why it happened...I was prepared to adopt the view that when the frontier of the State of Jammu and Kashmir was crossed...by hostile elements, it was contrary to international law, and that when, in May, 1948...units of the regular Pakistani forces moved into the territory of the State, that too was inconsistent with international law.²⁵⁸

Pakistan had already admitted to the UN Commission in July 1948 that her forces had gone into action in Kashmir in May 1948, but at that time the Commission chose, as Joseph Korbel* reports, "not to express its opinion openly about this new and most important development in the picture."²⁵⁹ Sir Owen's statement, it should be noted, clearly expressed the same view which Nehru had done as

---

*Professor Korbel represented Czechoslovakia on the Commission at that time.

early as 2 November, 1947. Speaking on the invasion by the armed tribesmen who came "across from Pakistan territory," Nehru had asked, "Is this not a violation of International Law...?"[260]

But to point to Pakistan's action as "inconsistent" with international law was one thing, and to take measures against her was another. As the *New York Times* put it, "It does no good to argue who was at fault two or three years ago."[261] Even Sir Owen's proposals more or less treated India and Pakistan on an equal footing.[262]

Kashmir was again discussed—at Pakistan's insistence—by the Commonwealth Prime Ministers' Conference in Junuary 1951. After the discussions, the Pakistani Premier revealed in a press conference in London that three proposals had been put forward: (1) the stationing of Commonwealth troops in Kashmir; (2) supervision by a joint Indo-Pakistani force during the plebiscite; or (3) authorizing the plebiscite administrator to raise local troops. He also said that he was "willing to accept any one of the proposals, but Mr. Nehru...rejected them all."[263]

This disclosure by Pakistan of what were supposed to be secret discussions had the desired result: India was now considered to be the sole obstacle to the solution of the dispute.[264] In the United States especially, where the irritation over India's policy over Korea was mounting daily, the issue provided an opportunity to attack Nehru.* In view of the importance which both India and Pakistan attached to the disputed territory, the increasing pro-Pakistan emphasis in American policy regarding Kashmir marked the beginning of a fundamental change in the United States' relations with the two Asian countries.

---

*The *New York Times*, in contrast with its earlier comments, now commended Pakistan for "consistently" accepting all proposals and criticized India for rejecting "every suggestion for mediation" and making "impossible terms" for a plebiscite or for any other kind of solution. Apparently annoyed over Nehru's "advice" regarding the settlement of the Korean question, the paper commented, "Evidently he finds it easier to solve the problems of the world than one in his own backyard." ("Kashmir Again," editorial on 17 January 1951, p. 26.) Pakistan felt immensely pleased at the turning of the American position in her favour. Ahmed S. Bokhari, the Permanent Representative of Pakistan at the United Nations, in a letter to the *Times*, said that he felt "encouraged" by "the larger view" taken by the paper. (*New York Times*, 23 January 1951, p. 26.)

The question of stationing foreign troops in Kashmir has been discussed here in some detail because of the possible reaction it might have had in the Soviet Union. Convinced of their unselfish motives and imparital attitude, the Western countries could hardly see any logic in India's opposition to the stationing of Commonwealth or UN troops (unless, of course, they were Soviet or troops from some other Communist country). But, from India's point of view, there were important reasons for not accepting this proposal. First, its acceptance would mean that India must also pull out all its forces and thus be treated like Pakistan, something which far exceeded the original plebiscite resolution of the United Nations. Second, Nehru had personal antipathy to the stationing of foreign troops in any country, which he considered to be a symbol of foreign domination. The third, and perhaps most important, consideration was that in view of certain criticism from the Soviet Union, this would bring the cold war to India's doors. Nehru alluded to this when he said that the presence of foreign troops "might give rise to all kinds of speculation in the prevailing atmosphere of international suspicion."[265]

And, indeed, the Soviets seemed to be increasingly disturbed about the growing Western interest in Kashmir, which, to them at least, could only be military.

In an article written before the Korean War, N. Gladkov, while describing his impressions of Pakistan, also discussed the Kashmir question. Without taking either a pro-Indian or a pro-Pakistani attitude, he merely summarized the argument's of the two countries for their respective positions. And although Gladkov accused Britain of using Kashmir to blackmail the two countries in order to keep "both...under her control," there was no reference to the United States in his article.[266]

But the Korean War changed the picture. India's mediation—despite her initial support to the Western position—was in contrast with Pakistan's open support to the West (though it did not include any military contribution). Soviet criticism was now concentrated on the Pakistani Premier who was accused of showing "servile zeal" and of intending "to take on the job of agent of Anglo-American imperialism in its fight against the national-liberation movement in Asia."[267]

A Tass dispatch from Rome in early August quoted reports in the Italian newspaper *Avanti* and *Paese* regarding American maneuvers "to take advantage of the controversies between India and Pakistan more closely to the chariot wheels of American policy and thus to exert pressure on India."[268] Tass also stated that the American Ambassador in Pakistan had "demanded, in accordance with instructions received from Washington," that Pakistan send a military unit to Korea, in exchange for which Pakistan would get "firm American support" on Kashmir.[269]

As the United Nations forces crossed the 38th parallel and the Korean War began to escalate, the Soviet press reported the increasing interest allegedly shown by the American military in the affairs of the Indian subcontinent. In the middle of October, a Tass dispatch from Peking reported American "espionage and subversive activity" stretching "from South Korea to India with its centre in Tokyo."[270] On 11 October both *Pravda* and *Izvestiia* published a report, quoting the Indian Communist Party paper *Crossroads*, that the American Embassy in Karachi was carrying on talks for leasing "certain military and air bases in strategic areas of Gilgit" (in the part of Kashmir in Pakistan's possession).[271] A month later, a Tass dispatch from Karachi further elaborated the alleged American designs in Kashmir on the basis of reports published in Pakistani Communist and leftist papers. It was reported that the Americans envisaged turning Jammu and Kashmir into an independent territory under the control of the United Nations, which, in effect would mean under the United States. "The object of this plan," Tass quoted the Pakistani paper *Imroz* as stating, "is to secure military bases for America on the territory of this principality, since Kashmir borders upon the Soviet Union."[272] The same accusation was repeated in a Tass dispatch in late December from Kabul.[273]

In the midst of all these accusations it was difficult to judge what the actual position of the Soviets was on the Kashmir question. Moscow had so far avoided taking a well-defined attitude, but the shadow which the Korean War cast over the relations between India and Pakistan with the United States made the Soviets more and more concerned about the possibility that the United States might acquire some military bases in the Gilgit area, which bordered on the Soviet Union.

The US denied that it had any desire to seek military bases in either Pakistan or Kashmir.[274] But there was a new urgency in Washington to force a solution of the Kashmir problem through the United Nations. It could be interpreted only in two ways: either the United States really desired to bring peace to the subcontinent by removing the most important source of the continuing bad relations between India and Pakistan and thus to forestall any possibility of fishing in troubled waters by Moscow; or, in view of the deteriorating international situtation and the United States' decision to erect a new treaty system in the Pacific, Washington was thinking of the possible military advantages of the highly sensitive area of Gilgit. And this, as Nehru's persistent refusal to join any Pacific bloc or to give up nonalignment had shown, could be obtained only if Kashmir were awarded to Pakistan, which, as we have noted earlier, had been increasingly supporting US policies in Asia since Liaquat Ali Khan's visit to Washington in May 1950.

In any event, Washington, along with London, submitted a resolution in the Security Council on 21 February 1951, providing for the conduct of a plebiscite on terms which had already been rejected by India, and which, as should have been clear to any observer of the Indian scene, would not be acceptable to her now.[275] The joint American-British draft resolution solved the main obstacle of demilitarization by providing for the stationing of UN troops in Kashmir during a plebiscite; it enunciated the principle of arbitration in regard to differences likely to arise between India and Pakistan in the interpretation of the terms and conditions of the plebiscite as provided in the plebiscite resolution; and, lastly, it criticized the convening of the Kashmir Constituent Assembly in Srinagar.

The new American-British plan, which was commended by the *New York Times* as "a fair, reasonable, workable solution,"[276] found little favour in India. Although the Indian government's reaction at this stage was mild rejection in diplomatic language,[277] the Indian press bitterly criticized the draft resolution for reviving terms which, it was asserted, Washington and London knew would be rejected by India.[278] As the *New York Times* correspondent reported from India, "the Indian press has seldom, if ever, been so unanimous in its sentiment as it has been in objection to the new Kashmir resolution and it has rarely used such language."[279]

Faced with such strong criticism, the US and Britain submitted a revised draft resolution,[280] which dropped the proposal of patrolling by UN troops, but retained the principle of arbitration.

New Delhi was not more vocal in voicing its criticism, accusing the sponsors of the resolution of taking the side of Pakistan. In a public speech at Agra on 25 March, Nehru said that it would be "dishonorable" to India to accept the new resolution. On the American and British approach he said, "I feel that the British and US representatives either do not understand the Kashmir problem or knowingly misrepresent it."[281] For Nehru, the US and Britain were not only being unfair to India, it was a "deliberate" attempt on their part "to discredit his foreign policy."[282]

Despite clear indication that India would not accept the proposals, the Security Council voted on the revised resolution on 30 March 1951, and adopted it by a vote of 8 to 0, with India, Yugoslavia and the Soviet Union abstaining.[283]

Pakistan was very pleased with the outcome. Apart from the general drift of Washington towards her stand—and the estrangement it was causing between the US and New Delhi—the condemnation of the proposed Constituent Assembly in Kashmir and the acceptance of the principle of arbitration were what she desired. Sir Zafrullah Khan, the Pakistani Foreign Minister, in a triumphant mood after the voting, told the Security Council that Pakistan accepted the resolution "in all its parts and aspects—and particularly paragraph 6 [providing for arbitration]," and pledged his country's "fullest cooperation" to the UN representative to be appointed under the new resolution.[284]

In India's view, the principle of arbitration—besides its dangerous and uncertain implications—now put Pakistan on an equal footing with India and gave her an equal voice in the determination of the process of demilitarization and plebiscite, in which, the Indian delegate had told the Council a day before the voting, Pakistan had "no voice and no right to be consulted at all."[285]

India, therefore, expressed its disapproval in strong terms. On 31 March, Nehru told Parliament that the adoption of the British-American resolution by the Security Council was a "serious matter."[286] He then flew to Kashmir to declare that India rejected the new Kashmir resolution and "would face all the consequences flowing from that stand." He called the arbitration proposal "a challenge to the self-respect of the people of Kashmir, nay, the people of India"; it was a "challenge," he declared, which "we shall meet effectively."[287] At the same meeting Sheikh Abdullah, Premier of the Indian part of Kashmir, echoed the charges already made in the Soviet press when he said that Britain and the United States were supporting Pakistan because "they are sure of war bases in Pakistan in their global strategy."[288] At a press conference in June Nehru himself charged the United States and Britain—without imputing any motivation, however—with supporting and abetting the "completely distorted and false" stand of Pakistan.[289]

India's rejection of the American-sponsored proposal was the final act needed to convince large sections of the press and public in the United States that it was only India which hindered the solution of the Kashmir problem.* But behind their criticism was a tinge of the irritation they felt over India's stand on the question of China's entry into the Korean War. How could India, they wondered, now ask that Pakistan be treated like an aggressor after casting her vote against the UN resolution declaring China an aggressor in Korea? To quote Joseph Korbel:

One would be more readily inclined also to understand the moral motives which underlie the Indian attitude toward the Kashmir conflict if they emanated from principled policy applicable to any international situation. But if India seriously considered Pakistan to be an aggressor in Kashmir, how could she decline to see an act of clear-cut aggression in the participation of Chinese troops in the war against the United Nations in Korea?[290]**

The Soviet delegate, however, continued, as before, to be a silent participant in the UN Kashmir debates, and, in consistency with his past record, again abstained when the voting on the Anglo-American resolution took place on 30 March.[291] Nevertheless *Izvestiia*, in reporting UN debate and voting, quoted in detail the Indian delegate's criticism of the Anglo-American resolution.[292] On

---

*The *New York Times* called India's rejection of the latest Anglo-American rasolution "saddening" and said that every Kashmir plan "has been dashed upon a hard rock of what appears to be more and more an unyielding Indian obduracy." ("The Kashmir Problem," Editorial on 31 March 1951, p. 14.)

**In a dispatch sent just before the latest Kashmir debate at the UN, K Balaraman, *The Hindu's* correspondent at Lake Success, had already warned of the intrusion of Korea into the arguments of this debate: "Echoes of the recent Korean debate are bound to be heard. In private talks, Americans are already asking how India, after refusing to name the aggressor in Korea, can ask the Council to name the aggressor in Kashmir." (*The Hindu*, 11 February 1951, p. 7.)

another occasion, the Soviet press carried reports of a letter of protest which India sent to the Security Council on 29 June regarding her accusation that Pakistan was repeatedly violating the cease-fire agreement.[293] Without signifying any basic change in Moscow's Kashmir policy, it at least suggested the ground of common interests on which India and the Soviet Union would one day meet. At the moment, the more important consideration for the Soviets was to search for the *raison d'etre* of America's increasing interest in Kashmir. *New Times* gave the answer:

Why...do Washington and London now so persistently demand arbitration of the Kashmir dispute? The answer is to be found in the commentaries of the imperialist press, which consistently stress Kashmir's strategic importance, its proximity to the borders of the Soviet Union and its border with the Chinese People's Republic. The imperialists are evidently planning to use this area as a military base and a centre of espionage.[294]

On 12 April *Pravda* quoted the Delhi *Times* as reporting the arrival of an American military mission in Gilgit in the middle of March, and of a "secret agreement" between Karachi and Washington.[295] Three days later *Pravda* (quoting the Indian Communist paper *Swadhinata*) reported on 29 March an American plane, which was said to have taken off from a Pakistani air base, flew over India.[296]

It was this alleged American military activity in northern Kashmir which prompted the hitherto silent Soviet delegate to speak when the name of Dr. Frank Graham, an American, was proposed as the new UN representative to carry out the recently passed Anglo-American resolution. "Why should the candidate nominated for this office," asked the Soviet delegate, Jacob Malik, "...necessarily be a representative of the United States or a representative of any other permanent member of the Security Council?"[297] But when the voting on Dr. Graham's nomination took place, the Soviet Union, as it had done on all the past resolutions on the Kashmir question, merely abstained; Dr. Graham was therefore named to be the UN Representative for India and Pakistan.[298] However, the Soviets continued to attack Dr. Graham's appointment. In fact, a little later, he was directly accused of playing the role of an American rather than a UN representative. *New Times* accused him of fulfiling the aim of American diplomacy which was directed at fanning the conflict by putting pressure on both India and Pakistan.[299] It was alleged that in this way he "hopes...to secure concessions to the American demand for new bases in Kashmir and at the same time to create a pretext for American troops, acting under the flag of the United Nations, to come in and restore 'order'."[300] This accusation was preceded and followed by reports of growing American military activity in the northern part of Kashmir under Pakistan's possession.[301]

Thus Moscow's Kashmir policy remained unchanged. And yet one could read the direction in which her interests would take her. The increasingly pro-Pakistan emphasis in America's Kashmir policy led to the apprehension in Moscow that Washington might acquire some military bases in the strategically located part of northern Kashmir which was under Pakistan's possession. In such an eventuality, an India out of the orbit of American influence could be most valuable. From India's viewpoint, the resolution that was carried through the Security Council on 30 March created a real dilemma: either she must suffer the embarrassment of repudiating a resolution passed by the UN, or modify her basic stand over Kashmir. But since India stuck to her position on Kashmir, she could only be grateful to any permanent member of the Council who would be prepared to rescue her from this dilemma. Neither the change in Soviet policy, however, nor India's appreciative response to Moscow, were clear at this time; the importance of developments regarding Kashmir lay in raising pointers for the future of Soviet-Indian relations.

THE JAPANESE PEACE TREATY

1. *The drafting of the treaty* Although Japan was primarily defeated by American arms in the Second World War, the Soviet Union had also entered the war against Japan during the very last stage (on 8 August 1945) of the military operations. And thus though Moscow came to be a member of both the thirteen-nation Far Eastern Advisory Commission and the four-power Allied Military Council, the real control of occupied Japan was in American hands. The US had insisted that the function of these two bodies should be only advisory and that whatever forces other countries sent should be subordinated to a Supreme Commander to be designated by the

United States. To quote Dean Acheson, the whole arrangement "left the ultimate policy-making power in the United States and the executive power in the Supreme Commander."[302]

A similar role—and with the same determination—was played by the US in preparing a peace treaty with the Japanese to end the military occupation. In fact, Japan occupied an important place in Washington's thinking about the Far East. At a time when even Korea was excluded from the areas which the US said it would defend, Japan and the Ryukyu Island had been considered as "essential parts of the defensive perimeter of the Pacific."[303] The Pentagon had opposed the relinquishing of US defence positions in Japan even before the Korean war,[304] but the outbreak of the war "made it more than ever essential that there be no interruption in the use of the military facilities they provided."[305]

Although President Truman announced on 14 September 1950, that the US would initiate discussions with governments represented on the Far Eastern Commission for a peace treaty with Japan,[306] the Secretary of Defence, Louis Johnson, and the Secretary of State, Dean Acheson, had already signed, on 7 September, a memorandum containing the "governing principles [for a peace treaty], which spelled out the security requirements of the Defense Department..."[307]

John Foster Dulles, who was appointed by Truman on 8 September, as his personal representative to work on the peace treaty, made trips to Japan and such other countries in Asia as the Philippines, Australia and New Zealand, as well as Paris and London. Although the US tried to meet some of the demands of these countries or allay the fears of some who felt apprehensive at the prospects of a remilitarized Japan, the basic principles of the treaty remained the same as they had emerged after deliberations within the US Government. Once the treaty was ready (the draft treaty was made public on 12 July 1951), the US sent it to those fifty states which had been at war with Japan. These states were asked to send their comments on the draft and were invited to attend a conference in San Francisco, to be held on 4 September, to participate in the conclusion of the peace treaty. The US, however, made it clear that no negotiations would take place in San Francisco. The invitation said that the US and Great Britain would "circulate the final text of the Peace Treaty," and that the conference was being convened "for conclusion and signature of a Treaty of Peace with Japan on the terms of that text." Communist China (along with

Nationalist China) was excluded from the invitees because of "special circumstances."[308]

Essentially, the draft peace treaty[309] provided the following: (1) Relations between Japan and the Allied Powers were to be as among "sovereign equals" and Japan was to apply to membership of the UN; (2) Japan renounced all claims to Formosa, the Pescadores, the Kuriles, and "that portion of Sakhalin, and the islands adjacent to it" which Japan had acquired as a result of her victory over Russia in 1905. On the Ryukyus and the Bonins, Japan accepted the right of the US to administer these territories and to concur in any US proposal to place them under UN Trusteeship "with the United States as the sole administering authority"; (3) the treaty recognized "the inherent right of individual or collective self-defence" of Japan under which it "may voluntarily enter into collective security arrangements." Further, although it provided that all occupation forces were to be withdrawn within ninety days after the treaty went into effect, it said that this was not to:

prevent the stationing or retention of foreign armed forces in Japanese territory under or in consequence of any bilateral or multilateral agreements which have been or may be made between one or more of the Allied Powers, on the one hand, and Japan on the other.[310]

This was obviously a reference to the US-Japanese security treaty which was being negotiated. (It was signed on the same day, 8 September, shortly after the signing ceremony of the Peace Treaty.)[311]

2. *The Soviet view of the treaty* The Soviets had, for some time, insisted that the peace treaty with Japan should be prepared by the Council of Foreign Ministers,[312] where they obviously hoped that no settlement without their consent could be worked out. But when on 16 March 1950, Acheson said that there were other nations, besides those represented in the Council of Ministers, who were interested in a peace treaty with Japan, and accused the Soviets of blocking the treaty,[313] Moscow changed its stand. A Soviet commentator, Ya. Viktorov, in an article in *Pravda*, said that "Actually, the Soviet Union insists upon a procedure...which provides for active participation in it of *all* interested countries such as took place in the preparation of the peace treaties with Italy, Bulgaria, Hungary, Rumania, and Finland."[314] This change in the Soviet stand suggested

that the Soviets attached considerable importance to the peace treaty with Japan, so that they were now prepared to work it out in a conference where they would not be able to use their veto.

The US, however, chose the safer course. Aware that the kind of treaty US had in mind—involving, as it did, the continuation of US military presence in Japan and the Ryukyus and the Bonins—would not win the adherence of the Soviets (and most probably of the Indians), Washington thought it better to prepare the draft in bilateral talks with other countries, while "ignor[ing]" the Soviet opposition which was considered "predictable and irreconcilable."[315]

The Soviets, therefore, criticized the treaty vehemently when they were presented with a draft by the American on 29 March 1951. In a note to the US on 7 May, the Soviets voiced these objections: (1) the peace treaty should be the affair of all interested governments and not "of any one Government or of a query conducted by it of the opinion of other Governments..."; (2) Communist China should be included in the preparation of the peace treaty; (3) the proposed treaty is a violation of the Cairo Declaration of 1943, as it makes no provision for returning Formosa and the Pescadores Island to the Chinese; (4) the taking over of the Ryukyus, and Bonins, and other islands by the US had not been done either as a result of an agreement among the powers or a decision of the UN; and (5) the draft "...is directly designed to leave American occupation troops and military bases in Japan even after the conclusion of a peace treaty."[316]

Moscow's greatest concern with regard to the American draft, however, was contained in one of the suggestions it made for a peace treaty with Japan. The Soviet note said that such a treaty should "...provide...that Japan will not enter any coalition directed against any of the States participating with their armed forces in the war against militaristic Japan."[317]

In a subsequent note, on 10 June, the Soviets elaborated further the objections they had raised in the 7 May note, now devoting considerable space to such questions as the "restoration of Japanese militarism" and "the participation by Japan in a coalition against states having an interest in signing a peace treaty with her." Moscow also proposed that a peace conference of all states which had participated in the war against Japan should be called in July or August 1951, "for consideration of the available drafts for a peace treaty with Japan."[318]

The US, however, went ahead with its plans and on 20 July 1951, sent to the Soviets, along with others, an invitation to attend the proposed peace conference in San Francisco.[319] The Americans had hoped that the Soviets would not attend, but Moscow informed Washington that a Soviet delegation led by A. A. Gromyko, Deputy Minister of Foreign Affairs, would go to San Francisco to "present the proposals of the Soviet Government on the question of the peace treaty with Japan."[320] The Soviet decision therefore came as a "big surprise" to the US.[321] Dulles called the Soviets a "wrecking crew,"[322] and the US prepared itself to prevent the Soviets from "wrecking" the conferenee.[323]

In the Soviet press, the US efforts were, of course, criticized. It may, however, be noted that the Soviets concentrated their attacks on two things: (1) the US-Japanese security treaty involving the continuation of the American military presence and the possibility of Japan's remilitarization,[324] and (2) the security treaties which the US was negotiating with the Philippines, Australia, and New Zealand.[325] In the Kremlin's view, these plans, if put together, meant the setting up of an "aggressive Pacific" by Washington.[326] Thus what the US considered a "peace" treaty, was taken by the Soviets as "a treaty for the preparation of war,"[327] a "plot against peace,"[328] and a "new road to Pearl Harbour."[329]

3. *The Indian view of the treaty* India found serious flaws in the treaty as drafted by the US. It applied two criteria to the American draft: (1) "The terms of the Treaty should concede to Japan a position of honour, equality, and contentment among the community of free nations"; and (2) "they should be so framed as to enable all countries, countries especially interested in the maintenance of a stable peace in the Far East, to subscribe to the Treaty sooner or later."[330]

Applying the first criterion, India pointed out that the Ryukyus and the Bonin Islands belonged to Japan because their inhabitants had "a historical affinity" with the Japanese and because Tokyo had not acquired them "by aggression from any other country." And though New Delhi recognized Japan's right to make arrangements for defence, in its view this should be done after Japan became "truly sovereign." The Indian note added, "A provision in the Treaty which suggests that the present occupation force may stay on in Japan as part of such a defensive agreement is bound to give rise to the impression that the agreement does not represent a decision taken by Japan in the full enjoyment of her freedom as a sovereign nation."³³¹

As regards the second criterion, New Delhi said that the treaty did not make any provision for the return of Formosa to China, although the "time and manner" of such return could be negotiated later. The same argument, in India's view, applied to the Kurile Islands and to South Sakhalin.³³² The Indian note thus implied that since the treaty was one which could not receive the adherence of Communist China and the Soviet Union, it would not work for a "stable peace" in the Far East.

Since the American draft fell short of the two criteria set by New Delhi, India said it "cannot be [a] part [y] to the Treaty." The Indian note further added that since the draft treaty would not be open to negotiation at San Francisco, India did not think it necessary to attend the peace conference.³³³*

In a rather lengthy note (almost twice the length of the Indian note of 23 August), and described in an International News Service dispatch published in several American papers as the "hardest slap this country [US] has taken at India since relations between the two nations were strained by the Korean War and India's support for Red China in the United Nations,"³³⁴** Washington replied to India's

---

*President Truman made some marginal comments on the Indian note and then sent to Dean Rusk, US Assistant Secretary of State, as a "souvenir." Two comments are worth quoting, as they reflect very much the prevailing mood in Washington. On India's conclusion that the two criteria set by her in the note were not satisfied by the treaty, Truman wrote, "Evidently the 'Govt' of India has consulted Uncle Joe and Mousie Dung of China!" And on India's assertion that the provision that US troops will stay on in Japan after the treaty might give the impression that the Japanese had not signed the pact voluntarily, the President noted, "Let Stalin come in and decide it—shall we?" (*Frus*, 1951, Washington, DC, 1977, vol. 6, pt. 1, pp. 1289-90.)

**Time* magazine reported that Nehru's refusal to attend the conference and sign the treaty "infuriated" Dulles so much that he got up in the night to draft a reply to the Indian Premier. (*Time*, 17 September 1951, p. 30.) Mrs. Vijaya Lakshmi Pandit, who, as India's ambassador in Washington, had several meetings with Dulles, vividly describes his feeling of frustration and irritation when she conveyed to him India's decision not to sign the peace treaty. She writes, "On the morning when I had to tell him that India refused to sign the treaty as it had been drafted by the United States, tempers were frayed and it was a difficult moment....Mr. Dulles had been hoping against hope for a

objections one by one. While doing so, it charged India with applying "different tests" to the Kuriles and the Ryukyus.[335] Replying not only to India's objection to the US-Japanese security treaty, but also to India's opposition to the military pacts in general, the US note said:

...No less than 32 of the Allied Powers, all members of the United Nations, have freely made or are making collective security arrangements to which the United States is a party. It would, indeed, be surprising if the sentiment which has animated so many free peoples did not manifest itself also in Japan.[336]

Finally, the note said that Washington "regrets" that India was not prepared "to join this united effort for peace."[337]

It was, however, the American press and some members of the Congress who attacked the Indian Prime Minister with unusual vehemence. The *New York Times*, in an editorial, called Nehru "one of the great disappointments of the post-war era." It added, "... with each day we are having to say in despair, as Browning did with his 'Lost Leader': 'One task more declined, one more footpath untrod'."[338] In another editorial, written only a day earlier, the paper had said that "India cannot be allowed to imperil the process of peacemaking by more than forty nations any more than can the Soviet Union."[339]

Other leading American newspapers and journals also joined the *New York Times* in pronouncing judgment on Nehru. The Washington *Evening Star* called Nehru's decision a "gift to the Kremlin" and said that by this "he has demonstrated a surprising degree of muddleheadedness."[340] The *Philadelphia Inquirer* wrote that Nehru's "neutrality" was "one-way neutrality, helpful to the Communists, harmful to those who oppose Communist aggression."[341] The *Evening Sun* of Baltimore said that by his decision Nehru "has

---

change of heart or a miracle that would make India side with America, and he was genuinely staggered by the final response. He was a religious man and believed in the power of the prayer. He walked up and down the room with bent head and his hands behind his back while I waited to leave. Then he swung around and said, 'I cannot accept this. Does your Prime Minister realize that I have prayed at every stage of the treaty?'...I could hardly tell him that my Prime Minister's views disagreed with those of the Almighty." (*The Scope of Happiness: A Personal Memoir*, New York, 1979, p. 255.)

altered the feeling about him throughout the West."³⁴² The *Cleveland Plain Dealer* pointed to Nehru's "strange inconsistency,"and said the Indian Prime Minister "still adheres to the old and blasted theory that...[Russia and Communist China] can be bribed into good behaviour if nothing is done to defend oneself."³⁴³ *The New Leader* termed Nehru's arguments against the treaty "finespun[and]absurdly inconsistent," and using "Nehrutrality" for "neutrality," it commented, "We wonder how many more Koreas and Tibets it will take before India jettisons its unrealistic Nehrutrality and joins the forces fighting to defend freedom in Asia."³⁴⁴ *The Reporter* commented that by announcing that India would not send a representative to San Francisco, Nehru had rather made Acheson's task smoother because the presence of the Indian delegation would only have created "a break in the solid front of non-Communist nations." By doing so, the journal concluded, Nehru had also contributed to "the reduction to the size of the myth of Pandit Nehru."³⁴⁵ A commentator (Polyzoides) in the *Los Angeles Times* went to the extent of calling Nehru a "Soviet stooge":

...it is well from our standpoint the Indian Prime Minister has made his position clear so that when the peace conference opens next Tuesday the United States will know those who are willing to cooperate with us for a free, liberal, cooperative and economically prosperous Asia and those who are adopting the thankless role of Soviet stooges against the best interests of their own countries.³⁴⁶

Among the US Congressmen, Representative John F. Lyle Jr., Democrat of Texas, said that he was getting tired of "these damn fool statements" by Nehru in advising Washington on the Japanese Peace Treaty.³⁴⁷ John Foster Dulles, the architect of the treaty, in a speech in Cleveland, Ohio, charged that by not signing the treaty "India...seemed to align itself with the Chinese Communist line, which is that there cannot be 'Asia for Asiatics' unless all Westerners are rooted out of Asia. That kind of an Asia would, of course, not be 'Asia for Asiatics' but 'Asia for the Russians'..."³⁴⁸

Some US comments referred to the wheat loan granted to India earlier.* While reporting India's answer to the treaty, the *Chicago*

---

*The US had granted a loan of $190 million to India in June 1951 to buy American wheat. Because of the severe food shortage, India had requested a

Tribune lamented that Nehru "backed Russia and Red China against the United States" only three months after getting the wheat loan.³⁴⁹ A commentator, Ivan H. Peterman, called India a "Soviet catspaw throughout the 1950 United Nations General Assembly" and said that in declining to sign the Japanese treaty India has now bowed to "secret threats" delivered by Moscow to New Delhi. It has, added Peterman, showed "...what we may expect from continuing the American policy of Give, against the Kremlin's programme of Grab." Therefore, Peterman said, the US should not give help to "threatened areas" unless "they have guns, guts and courageous leadership." "India," Peterman concluded, "has none of these."³⁵⁰ Representative Wesley A. D'Ewart, Republican from Montana, said that the US should stop all aid to India "while Nehru plays the Kremlin game." Recalling the wheat loan granted to India, he added, "If the government of India choose to follow Stalin, I see no reason why the Government of the United States should continue to bail the Nehru Government out of its domestic crises."³⁵¹

One can only speculate, as Professor Frederick Dunn has suggested in his admirable study of the making of the peace treaty,* whether

---

US loan towards the end of 1950, but during the discussion on the food aid bill in the Congress some members attacked Nehru's policy towards China and Korea and demanded that India must supply strategic raw materials. Eventually the loan was granted, although by that time the issue had poisoned American-Indian relations further. (See J.C. Kundra, *Indian Foreign Policy, 1947-1954; A Study of Relations with the Western Bloc*, Groningen, Netherlands, 1955, pp. 155–57.) Attacks on Nehru's foreign policy made in this connection in the US were widely reported in the Soviet press. See, for example, "Starvation Blackmail," *New Times*, no. 5 (31 January 1951), p. 21; "SShA otkazyvaiut davlenie na Indii," *Izvestiia*, 27 January 1951, p. 4; "Amerikanskaia 'pomoshch,'" *Pravda*, 4 May 1951, p. 4; "Kabal'nye usloviia amerikanskogo zaima Indii," ibid., 19 May 1951, p. 3; "Al Capone Methods," *New Times*, no. 22 (30 May 1951), p. 23; and "V palate predstavitelei SShA," *Pravda*, 24 May 1951, p. 3.

*Discussing the journeys Dulles made to various Asian and West European capitals, but which did not include New Delhi, Dunn writes, "In view of the deep impression he made in Australia and New Zealand, it seems unfortunate that Dulles himself did not find it possible also to pay a visit to India.... The case he [Nehru] made might not at that time have been strong enough to resist the analytical and persuasive powers of Mr. Dulles in person. In any event, he might have gained a better understanding than he seems to have had of the real alternatives that Dulles was facing in negotiating a peace

a greater desire on the part of the US to consult Nehru in the making of the treaty would have produced different results. But in one way, the US decision to ignore Nehru while drawing up the peace treaty represented Washington's view that America had no use for India's "neutral" policy. While erecting a structure of various security treaties, in which the one with Japan was the most important one, the US was, in fact, looking for allies who would accept Washington's leadership in its stand against Communism. The *New York Times* expressed this view clearly when it wrote of Nehru's nonalignment policy:

...Instead of seizing the leadership of Asia for its good, Nehru turned aside from the responsibilities, proclaimed India's disinterestedness, and tried to set up an 'independent,' third-force India, suspended in midair between the two decisive movements of our day—the Communism that Russia leads and the democracy of which the United States is the chief champion.

So he and India went into a limbo. It was an abnegation of greatness—and history is not likely to forgive it.[352]

If India chose to be "suspended in midair," there was another nation in South Asia—Pakistan—which was willing to accept the US leadership. Pakistan not only agreed to sign the treaty but its Foreign Minister, Zafrullah Khan, made one of the most forceful speeches in San Francisco in support of the treaty.[353] James Reston, the *New York Times* columnist, called it a "memorable defence" of the treaty, and said that Zafrullah Khan defended it "not only against the arguments of the Soviet Union but against those of his neighbour, Prime Minister Jawaharlal Nehru of India."[354] Dean Acheson, in his concluding address at the San Francisco Conference, appreciatively referred to Zafrullah Khan's earlier remarks.[355]

4. *Soviet comments on India's stand on the treaty* Even before India's

---

settlement." (Frederick S. Dunn, *Peace-Making and the Settlement with Japan*, Princeton, 1963, pp. 132–33.) Quoting Indian sources, Robert Trumbull reported from New Delhi that Nehru felt "brushed off." (Robert Trumbull, "India Pact Boycott Held Fault of US," *New York Times*, 2 September 1951, p. 3.)

note of 23 August was published, the Soviets seemed to be quite hopeful that India might not sign the treaty. A Soviet writer, O. Prudkov, wrote in an article in *Literaturnaia gazeta* that India's position was "especially provoking anxiety in the US," and added that the Americans had grave doubts whether they would be able to convince India to sign it.[356] When finally India's answer to the US became known, the Soviets approvingly noted many similarities between the Soviet and Indian positions.

In a dispatch from Delhi on 27 August, Tass, while reporting in detail Nehru's statement in the Parliament that India would not sign the treaty, noted India's stand of Formosa. Tass added, "The Indian government recognizes the incontestable right of the Soviet Union on the Kurile Islands and South Sakhalin."[357] Two days later, another Tass report cited several Indian editorials in criticism of the treaty and especially noted India's stand on the Ryukyus and Bonin Islands. It quoted the *Times of India* as saying that US control of these islands was "imperialism in the eyes of the people of the East."[358]

However, it was India's opposition to the treaty, as the largest Asian country after China, that seemed most significant to the Soviets; after all, this enabled Moscow to show that the treaty was being opposed by a majority of the people in Asia. A Soviet commentator, M. Mikhailov, stated in *Izvestiia*:

...This decision by the Indian government makes still more obvious the failure of the American plan to enlist at least a measure of support from the chief Asian countries for the separate peace treaty with Japan.[359]

With India's huge population in mind, I. Romanovsky in *New Times* quoted a Dutch paper, *Algemeen Handelsblad*, as reminding Washington of a "few unpleasant truths":

It must not be forgotten that China, India and Burma represent one-third of the population of the globe and two-thirds of the population of Asia. It is a very dangerous thing that these countries are having no share in the settlement of the Japanese question and do not support the United States proposals for a peace treaty with Japan.[360]

In Soviet comments on the San Francisco Conference, India's absence as a symbol of its position with regard to the treaty was particularly noted. In an editorial, *News* said that the US was not motivated by a desire "to further peace and international cooperation" but by the wish "to build up 'situations of strength," and that was the reason that both India and China refused to accept the treaty.[361] In a statement to the press in San Francisco, A.A. Gromyko referred to India's opposition as that of "the second country in Asia in size and importance."[362] Even the Soviet Foreign Minister, A.Y. Vyshinsky, while commenting on the Japanese Peace Treaty during his speech to the General Assembly, said that it had been opposed by the Soviet Union, the Chinese People's Republic, India, and Burma, "the countries most interested in a peace settlement with Japan,...."[363]

In this chapter we have surveyed the development of Soviet policy towards India from the outbreak of the Korean War in June 1950 to the conclusion of the Japanese Peace Treaty in September 1951. Although India gave its support to the 25 June and 27 June resolutions of the Security Council, it gradually adopted a policy which was deeply resented in the United States. Nehru's proposals to Stalin and Acheson in July 1950 provided perhaps the first strong indication to the Soviets that Nehru's policy did not toe the American line. Whatever doubts they might have had were further reduced by India's opposition to the crossing of the 38th parallel by the UN troops and its strong criticism of Acheson's "Uniting for Peace" proposal. An article published in *Pravda* on 24 October 1950, noted that the:

dictate policy pursued by the ruling circles of the USA meets with a vigorous repulse from the Soviet Union and other peace-loving states. It must be noted that certain countries of Asia and the Near East in no way always follow the Anglo-American bloc obediently. The striving of these countries, although it is still timid and inconsistent, to break away from the influence of aggressive forces and to make their contribution to the cause of international collaboration is reflected...at the present session of the General Assembly.[364]

That the Soviets had primarily India in mind was evident from the instructions sent to the CPI in December 1950 by R. Palme Dutt, a British Communist who had acted on several occasions in the past as a transmitter of Moscow's new line to the CPI.[365] Dutt wrote to the Indian Communists that the "indications of a divergence, even though still hesitant and limited, of Premier Nehru...from the reckless aggressive war policy...are a very important develoment."[366] As to what the CPI was expected to do in these new circumstances, Dutt added, "Supporters of peace in India, while welcoming every step towards disentanglement of India from the Anglo-American war-bloc, will press forward with unspairing vigour for the further steps which are necessary in order that India shall fulfil a firm and consistent peace policy."[367] Later, as we noted in the beginning of this chapter, at the second session of the World Peace Council which met in Vienna in November 1951, Pietro Nenni, its Vice-President, described Nehru's policy of "neutrality" as constituting "an important factor in the resistance to war."[368]

Thus India's position towards several important issues of the Korean War, as well as its stand on the Japanese Peace Treaty as drafted by the US, decisively changed Moscow's view of Nehru's "neutralist" foreign policy; it was now found to be serving the cause of "peace."

It would be a mistake, however, to assume that India's stand on either Korea or Japan represented any leaning towards Moscow. Nehru's basic strategy, as it had evolved in the latter part of 1949, was still to work in concert with the Communist Chinese regarding Asian problems. This was designed, as we have noted earlier, not only to preserve peace in Asia but also to prevent the spread of Communism in other parts of Asia.* In fact, there were some reports at the time that despite its objections to some parts of the treaty, India might yet attend the San Francisco Conference.[369] But as Robert Trumbull reported from New Delhi:

---

*For example, even in his opposition to the Peace Treaty as drawn by the US, Nehru seemed to have been, at least partly, motivated by this consideration. He told Marguerite Higgins in an interview, "India's absence from San Francisco was by no means based on any suspicion of the US motives. We certainly have no fears that America is planning to make a colony out of Japan. What we do fear is that the continued presence of American troops will cause friction that will hurt the cause of freedom. We fear that friction resulting from continued station of American troops in Japan will give excuse for outbursts of nationalist feelings that the Communists will direct against the regime." (*New York Herald Tribune*, 25 September 1951; cited in Kundra, *Indian Foreign Policy*, p. 146.)

India's recommendations for amending the treaty—which have been rejected in the final drafting—happen to fit in with Soviet policy...

India does not wish to further any impression in the United States that she is a consistent follower of the Soviet 'line,' yet that could be one result of speaking her honest opinion at San Francisco.[370]*

There was, therefore, much truth in the comment of an American writer, Blair Bolles, that "...an Indian rebuff to the United States is not automatically an Indian gesture of friendship to Russia."[371]

*This was corroborated in a despatch sent by Loyd V. Steere, US charge in India. Relating to the State Department the account of a meeting of the Foreign Affairs Subcommittee of the Indian cabinet (obtained from a member of Nehru's cabinet through an embassy employee, "whose information in the past generally has proved accurate and authentic") at which the decision was taken not to go to San Francisco, the charge reported:

Nehru explained that at first he was definitely in favour of attending the conference but then changed his mind because of fear that the presence of the Indian delegation might be utilized by the Russian for their own purposes. He asked: "Tell me, what would be the position of the Indian delegation if a Russian arose and said; 'Look here, our stand is correct; even India is not signing. Why? Because it feels the treaty is hopeless!'" Nehru said such embarrassment must be avoided, and since India was not signing, it should not attend the conference.

(The Charge in India to the Department of State, 24 September 1951, *FRUS*, 1951, Washington, DC, 1977, vol. 6, pt. 1, p. 1357.)

NOTES

1. For a report on the invasion by the UN Korean Commisssion, see UN document S/1496, 25 June 1950; text in Security Council, *Official Records*, Fifth Year, S/PV.473, p. 2. India was one of the members of the commission.
2. UN, Security Council, *Official Records*, Fifth Year, S/PV.473, 25 June 1950, pp. 16-18.
3. Text in ibid., p. 445.
4. Harry S Truman, *Memoirs*, vol. 2, *Years of Trial and Hope* (New York,

1956), p. 437. See also Philips Talbot and S.L. Poplai, *India and America* (New York, 1958), p. 117.

5. Text of President Truman's statement in *Documents on American Foreign Relations, January 1-December 31, 1950* (Boston, 1951), pp. 444-45.
6. UN, Security Council, *Official Records*, Fifth Year, S/PV.473, 25 June 1950, pp. 16-18.
7. Ibid., S/PV.474, 27 June 1950, pp. 16-17.
8. See texts of Henderson's telegrams of 27, 28, 29, and 30 June to the Secretary of State in *FRUS*,1950 (Washington, DC, 1976), 7: 204-6, 218-20, 234-37, and 266-67.
9. Text of India's letter of acceptance addressed to the UN Secretary-General, 29 June 1950, in *Documents on International Affairs, 1949-1950* (London, 1953), pp. 635-36.
10. The American Ambassador in India to the Secretary of State, 30 June 1950, *FRUS*, 1950 (Washington, DC, 1976), 7:267.
11. UN, Security Council, *Official Records*, Fifth Year, S/PV.475, 30 June 1950, pp. 9-10.
12. "India's Decision," editorial in the *New York Times*, 30 June 1950, p. 22.
13. "Tribute to India," *The Reporter* 3 (18 July 1950): 1. See also O.F. Mills, "India—Pivot of Asia; It Leads an Orient Just Beginning to Awaken to Communist Imperialism," ibid. 3, (18 July 1950): 6-8.
14. *Time*, 10 July 1950, p. 16.
15. Nehru's statement at a press conference in Singapore on 17 June 1950 in *The Statesman*, 18 June 1950, p. 1. In a speech before the Jogjakarta Parliament in Indonesia on 12 June 1950, Nehru said that the result of the Communist activities in India was "the very negation of the basic principles of revolution." (Ibid., 13 June 1950, p. 1.) In a speech in Singapore on 18 June he condemned Communist terrorism in Malaya, and said "It degraded humanity." (Ibid., 19 June 1950, p. 1.) See also ibid., 21 June 1950, p. 7 and 23 June 1950, p. 1, for his criticism of Communist violence in Malaya and Burma. At a press conference on 7 July—two weeks after the outbreak of the Korean War—Nehru again said that Communism, in going against nationalist movements in Southeast Asia, had performed "a counter-revolutionary act." (*Statesman Overseas Edition*, 15 July 1950, p. 5.)
16. Ibid. See also Robert Trumbull, "Nehru Talks of East and West; He Asks Our Support for Asia's Nationalism but Opposes a 'Crusade' Against Communism," *New York Times Magazine*, 20 August 1950, pp. 9, 27, 29, 31.
17. Harold R. Isaacs, "Korea and the American World Policy," *New Republic* 123 (7 August 1950): 14.
18. In fact, even in taking this position, Nehru was far ahead of Indian public opinion, which tended to look at the conflict as a civil war in which there should be no outside intervention. See Robert Trumbull,

"Bold Act on Korea Ascribed to Nehru," *New York Times*, 7 July 1950, p. 5. For an Indian view that the war in Korea was a civil war see "War in Korea," editorial in *Times of India*, 27 June 1950, p. 6.

19. *The Statesman*, 8 July 1950. See also the discussion, "Views in a Divided World," *University of Chicago Round Table*, no. 641 (9 July 1950), p. 2, in which Mrs. Pandit, India's ambassador in the US, clearly stated that India did not support the second half of President Truman's statement because it was "likely to extend the area of conflict...."
20. *Documents on International Affairs*, 1949–1950, p. 636. Emphasis added.
21. The American Ambassador in India to the Secretary of State, 30 June 1950, *FRUS*, 1950 (Washington, DC, 1976), 7: 267.
22. UN, Security Council, *Official Records*, Fifth Year, S/PV.476, 7 July 1950, p. 8.
23. UN document S/1588, 7 July 1950; text in *Documents on International Affairs*, 1949–1950, p. 657.
24. Even this token support was considered "politically important" by American and other Western delegates at the UN. (A.M. Rosenthal, *New York Times*, 30 July 1950, p. 1.)

    However, when in the later stages of the Korean War, differences between India and the US had considerably increased, there was severe criticism of India, both in official quarters and in the press, for not putting "a man or a gun into the front lines in Korea." (The phrase is from William Henry Chamberlin, *Beyond Containment*, Chicago, 1953, pp. 137, 145.)
25. Jawaharlal Nehru's telegram to the UN Secretary-General document S/1647, 29 July 1950; text in Security Council, *Official Records*, Fifth Year, Supplement for June, July and August 1950, pp. 110–11.
26. "The practical response of the United Nations members to the resolution of 27 June underlined once again the existence of differing attitudes within the free world," according to *The United States in World Affairs 1950*, p. 213. See also *India and the United Nations* (New York, 1957), pp. 147–48.
27. In his memoirs, Nikita Khrushchev says that it was Kim Il-sung who brought the plan of military invasion of South Korea to Stalin for his approval. "Stalin had his doubts," says Khrushchev, but finally he let the North Korean leader proceed with his plan of unifying Korea by force (*Khrushchev Remembers*, trans. by Strobe Talbott, Boston, 1970, p. 368). It should be noted that there is a great deal of controversy about the authenticity of these memoirs.
28. For the North Korean version see "Declaration of Ministry of Internal Affairs of Korean People's Democratic Republic," *Pravda*, 26 June 1950, p. 3, and *Izvestiia*, 27 June 1950, p. 4; cited from *CDSP* 2 (15 July 1950): 12.
29. "The Military Operations in Korea," *New Times*, no. 27 (5 July 1950), pp. 3–4. See also "Concerning President Truman's Statement," *Pravda*, 28 June 1950, p. 1; cited from *CDSP* 2 (22 July 1950): 8.

30. "Meeting of Security Council Members," *Pravda*, 27 June 1950, p. 5, and *Izvestiia*, 27 June 1950, p. 4; cited from *CDSP* 2 (15 July 1950): 13.
31. *Documents on International Affairs*, 1949–1950, p. 635.
32. Ibid., pp. 647–48.
33. See, for example, "How Aggression against Korean People's Democratic Republic Was Prepared," *Pravda*, 29 June 1950, p. 5, and *Izvestiia*, 29 June 1950, p. 3; cited from *CDSP* 2 (22 July 1950): 9.
34. See summary of Panikkar's telegram from Peking in "The Ambassador in India to the Secretary of State," 9 July 1950, *FRUS*, 1950 (Washington, DC, 1976), 6:372.
35. "The American Aggressors and the United Nations," editorial in *New Times*, no. 28 (12 July 1950), pp. 2–3.
36. K.M. Panikkar, *In Two Chinas* (London, 1955), p. 103.
37. *Statesman Overseas Edition*, 15 July 1950, p. 5. The *New York Times* published the report of Nehru's press conference under the title, "Nehru Links Korea to Red China," 8 July 1950, p. 4.
38. Panikkar, *In Two Chinas*, p. 104.
39. The Ambassador in India to the Secretary of State, 3 July 1950, *FRUS*, 1950 (Washington, DC, 1977), 7:248. A brief account of Radhakrishnan's meeting with Zorin was supplied to Henderson by Bajpai.
40. *Documents on International Affairs*, 1949–1950, pp. 705–6.
41. "Talks in Moscow Cordial," *New York Times*, 15 July 1950, p. 3.
42. *Documents on International Affairs*, 1949–1950, p. 707, citing *Soviet News*, 19 July 1950.
43. Ibid.   44. Ibid.
45. Dean Acheson's Reply to Jawaharlal Nehru, 18 July 1950, ibid., p. 706. On Acheson's reaction to Nehru's proposal, see also Dean Acheson, *Present at the Creation: My Years in the State Department* (New York, 1969), pp. 419–20.
46. Ibid., p 707.
47. Jawaharlal Nehru's Second Note to Dean Acheson, 19 July 1950, ibid., p. 708.
48. Ibid.
49. It was also published in *New Times*, Supplement to no. 32 (9 August 1950), p. 1; *World News and Views* 30 (29 July 1950): 349; and *For a Lasting Peace, For a People's Democracy*, 21 July 1950, p. 1.
50. M.N. Pak, *Kak podogotovlialas' amerikanskaia agressiia v Koree* (Moscow, 1951), p. 28.
51. "Foreign Reactions to Comrade J.V. Stalin's Answer to Indian Prime Minister Nehru," *Pravda* and *Izvestiia*, 20 July 1950, p. 3; 21 July 1950, p. 4; and 22 July 1950, p. 4; cited from *CDSP* 2 (2 September 1950): 9–10.
52. "Foreign Reactions to Comrade J.V. Stalin's Answer to Indian Prime

Minister Nehru," *Pravda* and *Izvestiia*, 22 July 1950, p. 4: cited from *CDSP* 2 (2 September 1950): 10.
53. See "Gazeta 'Tribiun' [*Tribune*, Sydney] ob otveta I.V. Stalina na obrashchenie Neru," *Pravda*, 25 July 1950, p. 3, and *Izvestiia*, 25 July 1950, p. 4; "Kitaiskaia gazeta ob otvete I.V. Stalina na obrashchenie Neru," *Pravda*, 27 July 1950, p. 4, and *Izvestiia*, 27 July 1950, p. 3; "Gazeta 'Unen' [published in Mongolia] ob otvete tovarishcha Stalina prem'er-ministru Neru," *Pravda*, 28 July 1950, p. 3; "Initsiativa Neru—priemlemyi put' dlia dostizheniia mira [from the Swedish newspaper *Ny Dag*, reporting the speech of the Chairman of the Swedish Communist Party], *Pravda* and *Investiia*, 30 July 1950, p. 3; and "Gazeta 'Kanadien tribiun' [Ottawa] vystupaet v podderzhku predlozhenii Neru," *Pravda* and *Izvestiia*, 1 August 1950, p. 3.
54. "Reactions of Foreign Bourgeois Press to J.V. Stalin's Reply to Nehru's Appeal—Review of Foreign Dispatches," *Pravda*, 23 July 1950, p. 4, and *Izvestiia*, 25 July 1950, p. 4; cited from *CDSP* 2 (9 September 1950): 6-7.
55. See, for example, Ya. Viktorov, "The Line of Peace and the Line of War," *Pravda*, 24 July 1950, p. 4; cited from *SPT* 5 (1 September 1950); 467-69; V. Korionov, "SSSR otstaivaet delo mira," *Pravda*, 6 August 1950, p. 4; V. Mikheev, "Koreiskii narod v bor'be za edinstvo i nezavisimost'," *Bol'shevik*, no. 15 (August 1950), p. 42; and I. Kravtsov, *Agresiia amerikanskogo imperializma v Koree*, 1945-1951 gg. (Moscow, 1951), pp. 363-65.
56. "Two Worlds—Two Policies," editorial in *For a Lasting Peace, For a People's Democracy*, 28 July 1950, p. 1.
57. "Pour developper et gagner la bataille de la paix; Rapport presente le 29 septembre 1950 devant le Comite Central par Maurice Thorez," *L'Humanite* (Paris), 30 September 1950, p. 3.
58. "Rejection by American Government of Nehru's Proposal for Peaceful Settlement of Korean Question," *Pravda* and *Izvestiia*, 21 July 1950, p. 4, cited from *CDSP* 2 (2 September 1950): 10. Also reported in *New Times*, no. 30 (26 July 1950), p. 32.
59. Ya. Viktorov, "The Line of Peace and the Line of War," *Pravda*, 24 July 1950, p. 4; cited from *SPT* 5 (1 September 1950): 468.
60. "Who Needs Aggression in Korea," editorial in *New Times*, no. 30 (26 July 1950), p. 1.
61. Viktorov, "The Line of Peace and the Line of War," p. 468. See also Obozrevatel', "Isoliatsiia agressorov usilivaitsia," *Izvestiia*, 25 July 1950, p. 3.
62. *The United States in World Affairs*, 1950, p. 228.
63. Writing in the *New York Times*, 16 July 1950 (Section IV, p. 3), James Reston said that the US would not accept Nehru's proposal because it would "alienate powerful forces in Congress and in the country."

64. "Reply to Mr. Nehru," editorial in the *New York Times*, 19 July 1950, p. 30.
65. William Henry Chamberlin, "Korea Must Set the Pattern," *The New Leader* 33 (30 October 1950): 19.
66. The Ambassador in the Soviet Union (Kirk) to the Secretary of State, 19 July 1950, *FRUS*, 1950 (Washington, DC, 1976), 7:426.
67. "Nehru's Peace Mission," editorial in *The New Leader* 33 (29 July 1950): 30.
68. *The United States in World Affairs*, 1950, p. 227.
69. The statements of the British Prime Minister Attlee and French Foreign Minister Schuman to this effect are quoted in the *New York Times*, 20 July 1950, p. 8.
70. "Diplomatic Blackmail," *The Economist*, 22 July 1950, p. 159.
71. Ibid.
72. Cf. Robert Trumbull, "Reply of Acheson Disappoints Nehru," *New York Times*, 20 July 1950, p. 4. Not only in India, there was also, as Trumbull said in another dispatch, "universal disappointment" in Asia at the outright rejection of Nehru's proposal. ("Asia Is Supporting America; But It's Not All the Way," ibid., 23 July 1950, Section IV, p. 4.)
73. Quoted in *The New Leader* 33 (29 July 1950): 30.
74. Quoted in Margaret Parton, "what India is Thinking," *The Reporter* 3 (29 August 1950): 35.
75. *New York Times*, 1 August 1950, p. 5.
76. Pandit Nehru's Speech in the Indian Parliament, 3 August 1950 (Extracts), *Documents on International Affairs*, 1949–1950, p. 709. The *New York Times* published the report of Nehru's speech with the headline, "Nehru Denounces West's Asia Policy," 4 August 1950, pp. 1, 7.
77. Ibid.
78. "India and the West," editorial in the *New York Times*, 5 August 1950, p. 14.
79. "Mr. Malik Comes Back," *The Economist*, 5 August 1950, p. 255.
80. "Mr. Malik's Manoeuvres," ibid., 12 August 1950, p. 297.
81. See Freda Kirchway, "Into a Russian Trap," *The Nation* 171 (12 August 1950): 139–40, and Joseph P. Lash, "What Is Malik Up to?" *New Republic* 123 (4 September 1950): 12–14.
82. UN, Security Council, *Official Records*, Fifth Year, S/PV.480/Rev.1, 1 August 1950, p. 1.
83. Ibid., p. 9.   84. Ibid., p. 5.   85. Ibid.   86. Ibid., p. 1.
87. Ibid., p. 13.   88. Ibid., p. 19.   89. Ibid., pp. 18, 19.
90. Ibid., S/PV. 482, 3 August 1950, p. 22.
91. Warren Austin's speech in the Security Council on 1 August, 1950, in ibid., S/PV.480/Rev.1, 1 August 1950, p. 15.

92. UN, Security Council, *Official Records*, Fifth Year, S/PV.482, 3 August 1950, p. 11.
93. Ibid.   94. Ibid., S/PV.481, 2 August 1950, p. 15.
95. UN document S/1653, 31 July 1950; text in Security Council, *Official Records*, Fifth Session, S/PV.479, pp. 7–8.
96. UN, Security Council, *Official Records*, Fifth Year, S/PV.482, 3 August 1950, p. 11.
97. Ibid., p. 20.   98. Ibid., pp. 22–23.
99. Soviet draft resolution S/1751, 1 September 1940; text in UN, Security Council, *Official Records*, Fifth Year, S/PV.494, p. 10. A proposal on these lines was first included in its draft resolution S/1668, 4 August 1950; text in UN, Security Council, *Official Records*, Fifth Year, S/PV. 483, pp. 1–2.
100. UN, Security Council, *Official Records*, Fifth Year, S/PV.494, 1 September 1950, p. 15.
101. Ibid.   102. Ibid., pp. 15–16.
103. Thomas J. Hamilton, *New York Times*, 2 September 1950, p. 4. See also UN, Security Council, *Official Records*, Fifth Year, S/PV.494, 1 September 1950, pp. 20–21.
104. UN, Security Council, *Official Records*, Fifth Year, S/PV.494, 1 September 1950, pp. 16–17.
105. Ibid., p. 21.
106. UN document S/1668, 4 August 1950: text in Security Council, *Official Records*, Fifth Year, S/PV.483, pp. 1–2.
107. UN document S/1653, 31 July 1950; text in Security Council, *Official Records*, Fifth Year, S/PV. 479, pp. 7–8.
108. UN, Security Council, *Official Records*, Fifth Year, S/PV. 496, 6 September 1950, pp. 18–21.
109. Soviet draft resolution S/1679, 4 August 1950; text in UN, Security Council, *Official Records*, Fifth Year, S/PV.484, p. 20.
110. *The United States in World Affairs*, 1950, p. 232.
111. *New York Times*, 25 August 1950, p. 3.
112. Robert Trumbull, "Anti-US Feeling Is on Rise in India," ibid., 13 August 1950, p. 1.
113. "Rost antiamerikanskikh nastroenii v Indii," *Pravda*, 15 August 1950, p. 3.
114. *Statesman Overseas Edition*, 2 September 1950, p. 5.
115. "Statement by Indian Prime Minister Nehru," *Pravda* and *Izvestiia*, 28 August 1950, p. 4; cited from *CDSP* 2 (14 October 1950): 18.
116. *New York Times*, 25 August 1950, p. 3.
117. Robert Trumbull referred to this Soviet propaganda in India failing on "receptive years" and asked the United States Information Service to

take more effective steps ("Soviet Has India's Ear," *New York Times*, 20 August 1950, Section IV, p. 5).
118. *Statesman Overseas Edition*, 23 September 1950, p. 7.
119. UN, Security Council, *Official Records*, Fifth Year, S/PV. 497, 7 September 1950, p. 15.
120. Ibid., pp. 17–18.
121. UN document A/1365, 19 September 1950; text in General Assembly, *Official Records*, Plenary Meetings, vol. 1, p. 2.
122. UN, General Assembly, *Official Records*, Plenary Meetings, vol. 1, 277th meeting, 19 September 1950, p. 6.
123. Ibid., p. 15. The Indian proposal was voted down by 33 to 16, with 10 abstentions. Its rejection by the "Anglo-American majority" was reported in *New Times*, no. 39 (27 September 1950), p. 32.
124. Acheson, *Present at the Creation*, p. 451.
125. Truman, *Memoirs*, vol. 2, p. 359.   126. Ibid., p. 360.
127. Cited in Acheson, *Present at the Creation*, p. 453.
128. See Acheson's statements in *Military Situation in the Far East*, Hearings Before the Armed Services Committee and Foreign Relations Committee, United States Senate, 82nd Congress, 1st Session (Washington, DC, 1951), p. 2258.
129. "The 38th Parallel," editorial in the *New York Times*, 30 September 1950, p. 16.
130. *The Statesman*, 1 October 1950, p. 9.
131. Ibid., 4 October 1950, p. 5. The *New York Times* reported Nehru's speech with the headline, "Nehru Urges UN Go Slow in Korea," 4 October 1950, p. 8.
132. Ibid.   133. *New York Times*, 2 October 1950, p. 3.
134. Panikkar, *In Two Chinas*, p. 110.
135. Truman, *Memoirs*, vol. 2, pp. 361–62.
136. Memorandum Prepared in the Central Intelligence Agency, 18 August 1950, *FRUS*, 1950 (Washington, DC, 1976), 7:600–1
137. The Ambassador in the Netherlands (Vinton Chapin), to the Secretary of State, 3 October 1950, ibid., p. 858.
138. Memorandum of the Director of the Office of Chinese Affairs (Clubb) to the Deputy Assistant Secretary of Far Eastern Affairs, 4 October 1950, ibid., p. 864.
130. Memorandum of Conversation, by Mr. John M. Allison of the United States Delegation to the United Nations General Assembly, 4 October 1950, p. 868.
140. Cited in "Washington Minimizes Threat," *New York Times*, 2 October 1950, p. 3.
141. Substance of Statements Made at Wake Island Conference on 15 October 1950, *FRUS*, 1950 (Washington, DC, 1976), 7:953.

142. UN, General Assembly, *Official Records*, Fifth Session, Annexes, Agenda Item 24, document A/C.1/558, 30 September 1950, pp. 2–3.
143. Ibid., document A/C.1/567, 2 October 1950, p. 9.
144. See the Indian delegate Sir Benegal Rau's statement in UN, General Assembly, *Official Records*, Fifth Session, First Committee, vol. 1, 350th meeting, 3 October 1950, pp. 33–34.
145. Ibid., A/C.1/571, 7 October 1950, p. 55.
146. A.M. Rosenthal, "India in the US Assembly Courted by All Sides," *New York Times*, 8 October 1950, Section IV, p. 3.
147. "For a Free Korea," editorial in the *New York Times*, 4 October 1950, p. 30.
148. UN, General Assembly, *Official Records*, Fifth Session, First Committee, vol. 1, 353rd meeting, 4 October 1950, pp. 55–56.
149. Rosenthal, "India in the UN Courted by All Sides."
150. UN, General Assembly, *Official Records*, Fifth Session, Supplement no. 20, Resolutions Adopted by the General Assembly During the Period, 19 September to 15 December 1950, no. 376 (V), pp. 9–10.
151. "Zaiavlenie predstavitelia ministerstva inostrannykh del Kitaiskoi Narodnoi Respubliki," *Pravda*, 12 October 1950, p. 3.
152. Ibid.
153. "Move to Undermine United States Exposed," editorial in *New Times*, no. 42 (18 October 1950), p. 3.
154. Ibid., p. 2.   155. Ibid.
156. "Reporter's Notes," *The Reporter* 3 (24 October 1950): 1.
157. "Plain Words to Indians," editorial in the *New York Times*, 12 October 1950, p. 30.
158. The Acting Secretary of State to the Embassy in India, 28 September 1950, *FRUS*, 1950 (Washington, DC, 1976), 7:821.
159. The Ambassador in India to the Secretary of State, 4 October 1950, ibid., p. 872.
160. Letter to the Editor, *New York Times*, 19 October 1950, p. 30.
161. Text of Nehru's statement in the *New York Times*, 17 October 1950, p. 8.
162. The criticisms of the Indian delegates are referred to in Vera Micheles Dean, "Why Asia Doesn't Trust US," *The Nation* 171 (4 November 1950): 406–8. Mrs. Dean attended the conference as an American delegate.
163. "Plain Words to Indians," editorial in the *New York Times*, 12 October 1950, p. 30.
164. Dean, "Why Asia Doesn't Trust US," p. 406.
165. "Russia and China Send No Delegates," *Statesman Overseas Edition*, 7 October 1950, p. 9.

166. "By Order of the USA," *Pravda*, 9 October 1950, p. 4; cited from *CDSP* 2 (25 November 1950): 16.
167. An Observer, "Surprises at the Lucknow Conference," *Izvestiia*, 26 October 1950, p. 4; cited from *SPT* 5 (1 December 1950): 648.
168. Ibid.
169. "The Lucknow Conference," *New Times*, no. 43 (25 October 1950), pp. 14–15.
170. Cited in George F. Kennan, *Memoirs*, 1925–1950 (Boston, 1967), p. 489.
171. Acheson, *Present at the Creation*, p. 450.
172. UN, General Assembly, *Official Records*, Fifth Session, Plenary Meetings, vol. 1, 279th meeting, 20 September 1950, p. 24.
173. UN, General Assembly, *Official Records*, Fifth Session, Supplement no. 20, Resolutions Adopted by the General Assembly During the Period 19 September to 15 December 1950, no. 377 (V), pp. 10–12.
174. K.P. Karunakaran, *India in World Affairs, February 1950–December 1953* (Bombay, 1958), p. 136.
175. UN, General Assembly, *Official Records*, Fifth Session, First Committee, vol. 1, 369th meeting, 19 October 1950, p. 161.
176. Text of Nehru's press conference in the *New York Times*, 17 October 1950, p. 8.
177. UN, General Assembly, *Official Records*, Fifth Session, Plenary Meetings, vol. 1, 301st meeting, 2 November 1950, p. 333. See also George Matthews, "Notes on the 'Veto'," *World News and Views* 30 (21 October 1950): 498–99.
178. UN, General Assembly, *Official Records*, Fifth Session, Plenary Meetings, vol. 1, 302nd meeting, 3 November 1950, p. 347.
179. The Secretary of Defence (Marshall) to the Commander in Chief, Far East (MacArthur), 29 September 1950, *FRUS*, 1950 (Washington, DC, 1976), 7:826.
180. Louis J. Halle, *The Cold War As History* (New York, 1967), p. 222.
181. Truman, *Memoirs*, vol. 2, pp. 365–66.
182. Allen S. Whiting, *China Crosses the Yalu* (New York, 1960), p. 116.
183. See Acheson, *Present at the Creation*, pp. 452–53.
184. MacArthur's message to the US Joint Chiefs of Staff, 6 November 1950; cited in Truman, *Memoirs*, vol. 2, p. 375.
185. Ibid., p. 376.
186. MacArthur's message to the US Joint Chiefs of Staff, 7 November 1950; cited in ibid., p. 377.
187. Ibid., pp. 377–80. 188. Quoted in ibid., p. 381.
189. Special Communique by General MacArthur, Commander-in-Chief, United Nations Command, 28 November 1950; cited from *American Foreign Policy, 1950–1955: Basic Documents* (Washington, DC, 1957), 2: 2585.

190. Ibid. 191. Truman, *Memoirs*, vol. 2, p. 395.
192. The Appeal of Thirteen Asian and Middle East States to Peking and to the North Koreans, 5 December 1950; cited from *Documents on International Affairs* 1949–1950, p. 713.
193. UN document A/C 1/640, 9 December 1950; text in General Assembly, *Official Records*, Fifth Session, First Committee, vol. 1, p. 418.
194. UN document A/C.1/641, 12 December 1950; text in General Assembly, *Official Rscords*, Fifth Session, First Committee, vol. 1, p. 433.
195. UN, General Assembly, *Official Records*, Fifth Session, Plenary Meetings, vol. 1, 324th meeting, 14 December 1950, p. 660.
196. UN, General Assembly, *Official Records*, Fifth Session, First Committee, vol. 1, 416th meeting, 13 December 1950, p. 441.
197. *New Times*, no. 51 (20 December 1950), p. 32.
198. UN, document A/C.1/643, cited from *Documents on International Affairs*, 1949–1950, pp. 716–20.
199. *New York Times*, 13 December 1950, p. 6.
200. *Documents on International Affairs*, 1949–1950, pp. 719–20.
201. See, for example, Malik's statement in the Political Committee on 3 January 1951, in which he gave full support to the stand taken by Chou En-lai in his broadcast of 22 December 1950 (UN, General Assembly, *Official Records*, Fifth Session, First Committee, vol. 2, 419th meeting, 3 January 1951, pp. 459–61).
202. *Documents on International Affairs*, 1949–1950, pp 718-720.
203. UN, General Assembly, *Official Records*, Fifth Session, Annexes, Agenda Item 76, Supplementary Record of the Group on Cease-fire in Korea (A/C.1/645), 11 January 1951, p. 13.
204. Max Beloff, *Soviet Policy in the Far East, 1944–1951* (New York, 1953), p. 199.
205. Acheson, *Present at the Creation*, p. 513.
206. For Moscow's rejection, see Malik's statement in the Political Committee on 11 January 1951 (UN, General Assembly, *Official Records*, Fifth Session, First Committee, 422nd meeting, 11 January 1951, pp. 479–80). For China's rejection, see Chou's telegram of 17 January 1951, in UN, General Assembly, *Official Records*, Fifth Session, Annexes, Agenda Item 76, document A/C.1/653, pp. 14–15).
207. UN, General Assembly, *Official Records*, Fifth Session, First Committee 424th meeting, 13 January 1951, p. 496.
208. UN, General Assembly, *Official Records*, Fifth Session, Annexes, Agenda Item 76, Chou En-lai's Telegram to the Acting Secretary-General of the UN, 17 January 1951 (doc. A/C.1/653), p. 15.
209. Acheson, *Present at the Creation*, p. 512.
210. UN, General Assembly, *Official Records*, Fifth Session, Annexes, Agenda Item 76, doc. A/C. 1/654, 20 January 1951, p. 15.

211. UN, General Assembly, *Official Records*, Fifth Session, First Committee, 428th meeting 20 January 1951, p. 517.
212. For Nehru's criticism of the US proposal, see his interview in Paris with the left-wing French newspaper *Franc-Tireur*, reported in *The Hindu*, 20 January 1951, p. 4, and his statement in Bombay on 21 January, reported in *The Statesman*, 22 January 1951, p. 1.
213. UN, General Assembly, *Official Records*, Fifth Session, First Committee, vol. 2, 435th meeting, 29 January 1951, p. 580.
214. Ibid., 428th meeting, 20 January 1951, p. 523.
215. UN, General Assembly, *Official Records*, Fifth Session, Annexes, Agenda Item 76, doc. A/C.1/642/Rev.1, 24 January 1951, pp. 5–6.
216. Ibid., doc. A/C.1/642/Rev.2, 29 January 1951, p. 6.
217. UN, General Assembly, *Official Records*, Fifth Session, First Committee, vol. 2, 437th meeting, 30 January 1951, p. 590.
218. Quoted in *Time*, 5 February 1951, p. 14.
219. Lillie Shultz, "Peace: Why It Was By-passed," *The Nation* 172 (17 February 1951): 153.
220. UN, General Assembly, *Official Records*, Fifth Session, First Committee, vol. 2, 438th meeting, 30 January 1951, p. 601.
221. Ibid., p. 602.
222. UN, General Assembly, *Official Records*, Fifth Session, Plenary Meetings, vol. 2, 327th meeting, 1 February 1951, p. 696.
223. UN, General Assembly, *Official Records*, Fifth Session, First Committee, 438th meeting, 30 January 1951, pp. 600–1.
224. UN, General Assembly, *Official Records*, Fifth Session, Plenary Meetings, vol. 2, 327th meeting, 1 February 1951, p. 695.
225. *The Hindu*, 20 January 1951, p. 4.
226. "Chinese Troops in Korea," editorial in *New York Times*, 5 November 1950, p. 10.
227. For some of these comments, see *Time*, 18 December 1950, p. 23; ibid., 22 January 1951, p. 23; and "The Aggression of China," editorial in *New York Herald Tribune*, 1 February 1951, p. 20.
228. K. Balaraman, "Indian Request for US Grain—Shelving by Senate Committee; World Diplomats Shocked," *The Hindu*, 28 January 1951, p. 7.
229. The Secretary of State to the Embassy in India, 27 January 1951, *FRUS*, 1951 (Washington, DC, 1983), vol. 7, pt. 1, p. 140.
230. Quoted in Vijaya Lakshmi Pandit to Nehru, 18 December 1950; cited from Sarvepalli Gopal, *Jawaharlal Nehru*, vol. 2, 1947–1956 (Cambridge, 1979), p. 109.
231. *Pravda* and *Izvestiia*, 17 February 1951, p. 1.
232. See G.P. Zadorozhny, "The Shameful Resolution of the UN General Assembly—On the Proclamation of China as an 'Aggressor,'" *Sovetskoye gosudarstvo i pravo*, no. 4, 1951 (cited from *SPT*, vol. 6, 15 July 1951,

pp. 387-95); "A Shameful Decision," *Pravda*, 6 February 1951, p. 1 (cited from *CDSP*, vol. 3, 24 March 1951, pp. 14-15); "Unlawful Decision," *New Times*, no. 6 (7 February 1951), pp. 16-17; and "Shameful Slanderous Decision," *For a Lasting Peace, For a People's Democracy*, 9 February 1951, p. 1.
233. "Shameful Slanderous Decision."
234. "SShA otkazyvaiut davlenie na Indii," *Izvestiia*, 27 January 1951, p. 4.
235. "A Shameful Decision," *Pravda*, 6 February 1951, p. 3; cited from *CDSP* 3 (24 March 1951): 14.
236. V.N. Durdenevsky and A.M. Ladyzhensky, "Aggression and Intervension in the Far East in the Light of International Law," *Sovetskoye gosudarstvo i pravo*, no. 2, 1951 (cited from *SPT*, vol. 6, 15 May 1951, p. 266).
237. For the two Soviet draft resolutions, see UN, documents A/1776, 13 February 1951, and A/1777, 13 February 1951; texts in UN, General Assembly, *Official Records*, Fifth Session, vol. 2, p. 700. For India's negative vote on the two Soviet resolutions, see her delegate's statement in ibid., 328th meeting, 13 February 1951, p. 705.
238. Ibid., 328th meeting, 13 February 1951, pp. 704-5.
239. For a Soviet press report of the voting on the two Soviet resolutions, see *New Times*, no. 8 (21 February 1951), p. 32. In this report, India's vote was not even mentioned.
240. "Against Imperialist Intrigues in Tibet," *Pravda* and *Izvestiia*, 22 January 1950, p. 4; cited from *CDSP* 2 (18 March 1950): 21.
241. "Sir Basil Gould's Latest Researches," *New Times*, no. 5 (1 February 1950), pp. 16-17.
242. "Directive to Chinese People's Liberation Army for the Offensive on Tibet," *Pravda*, 26 October 1950, p. 4, cited from *CDSP* 2 (18 November 1950): 6; "Hsinhua on Progress of People's Liberation Army to Tibet," *Izvestiia*, 3 November 1950, p. 3, and "Sinkiang's Population Warmly Welcomes Chinese People's Liberation Army," *Pravda*, 3 November 1950, p. 4, both cited from *CDSP* 2 (25 November 1950); 9.
243. I. Vysokov, "On the Way to Tibet," *Pravda*, 3 November 1950, p. 4; cited from *CDSP* 2 (25 November 1950): 9.
244. For texts see *Documents on International Affairs*, 1949-1950 pp. 550-54.
245. Ibid , pp. 550-51.   246. Ibid., p. 552.
247. See G. Rassadin and I. Filippov, "Two Paths —On Fifth Anniversary of UN," *Pravda*, 24 October 1950 (cited from *CDSP*, vol. 2, 9 December 1950, p. 18), and "The Lucknow Conference," *New Times*, no. 43 (25 October 1950), pp. 14-15.
248. Statement of Central People's Government of the Chinese People's Republic," *Pravda*, 18 November 1950 p. 4; cited from *CDSP* 2 (16 December 1950): 18-19. See also Ya. Viktorov, "The Chinese People are Struggling to Liberate Tibet," *Pravda*, 20 November 1950, p. 4 (cited from *SPT*, vol. 5, 15 December 1950, pp. 679-80), in which the writer men-

tioned the Chinese statement referring to India's "plan" to prevent the Chinese "from exercising its sovereign rights in Tibet;" he also quoted the Chinese note to India (of 16 November) which stated that Tibet was an inalienable part of China and Peking would not tolerate any external intervention. This was undoubtedly a criticism of India's Tibetan policy, but Viktorov in no way implied that India was involved in the "activity of the Anglo-American imperialists," which he mentioned and criticized separately.

249. Ibid., pp. 18-19.
250. V. Vladimirov, "Tibet—Informational Background," *Trud*, 28 October 1950, p. 4; cited from *CDSP* 2 (9 December 1950): 22-23.
251. Litterateur, "International Reaction: Foiled," *Literaturnaia gazeta*, 2 November 1950, p. 4; cited from *CDSP* 2 (9 December 1950): 33.
252. Cf. "A Blow to Faith," editorial in the *Statesman Overseas Edition*, 4 November 1950, p. 3. Commenting on Nehru's description of India's role between China and the West as "a kind of window," the paper remarked, "This now seems to have been one of those peculiar windows made of what the Americans call 'one-way glass,' with India on the opaque side."
253. *New York Times*, 10 November 1950, p. 1.
254. *Statesman Overseas Edition*, 9 December 1950, p. 1.
255. "Followers of British Imperialists Run Amok," *Pravda* and *Izvestiia*, 9 December 1952, p. 4; cited from *CDSP* 2 (30 December 1950): 12.
256. "Masani to the Rescue," *New Times*, no. 52 (27 December 1950), pp. 22-23.
257. UN document S/1791, 15 September 1950; text in Security Council, *Official Records*, Fifth Year, Supplement for September through December 1950, pp. 24-52.
258. Ibid., p. 29.
259. Joseph Korbel, *Danger in Kashmir* (Princeton, 1954), p. 121.
260. Jawaharlal Nehru, *Independence and After: A Collection of Speeches, 1946-1949* (New York, 1950), p. 59.
261. "Kashmir Deadlock," editorial in the *New York Times*, 25 August 1950, p. 20.
262. See UN document S/1791, 15 September 1950, in Security Council *Official Records*, Fifth Year, Supplement for September through December 1950, pp. 24-47.
263. "Prime Ministers' Comments on Kashmir Dispute—Statements by Mr. Liaquat Ali Khan and Mr. Nehru," *The Times* (London), 17 January 1951, p. 7.
264. Cf. Michael Brecher, *The Struggle for Kashmir* (New York, 1953), p. 115.
265. *The Hindu*, 13 February 1951, p. 4.

266. N. Gladkov, "In Pakistan," *New Times*, no. 21 (24 May 1950), pp. 20-21.
267. "Liaquat Ali Khan Shows Servile Zeal," *New Times*, no. 28 (12 July 1950), pp. 19-20.
268. "The American Are Fomenting Conflict Between India and Pakistan," *Izvestiia*, 9 August 1950, p. 4; cited from *SPT* 5 (15 September 1950), 480.
269. Ibid.
270. "Podryvnaia i shpionskaia deiatel'nost' amerikanskikh imperialistov na Dal'nem Vostoke," *Pravda*, 15 October 1950, p. 4. See also "Amerikanskie proiski v Iugo-Vostochnoi Azii," *Pravda*, 24 December 1950, p. 3.
271. "Increased Interest of American Military in India," *Pravda* and *Izvestiia*, 11 October 1950, p. 3; cited from *CDSP* 2 (25 November 1950): 17.
272. "The Pakistan Newspaper *Zamindar* on American Plans for the Principality of Jammu and Kashmir," *Izvestiia*, 14 November 1950, p. 3; cited from *SPT* 5 (15 December 1950); 695.
273. "SShA khoziainichaiut v Kashmire," *Pravda* and *Izvestiia*, 23 December 1950, p. 3.
274. "Establishment of Bases in S. Asia; US Ambassador Denies Reports," *The Statesman*, 4 October 1950, p. 8.
275. UN document S/2017, 21 February 1951; text in Security Council, *Official Records*, Sixth Year, Supplement for January, February and March 1951, pp. 23-25.
276. "Another Try at Kashmir," editorial in the *New York Times*, 23 February 1951, p. 26.
277. An Indian Foreign Ministry spokesman said on February 23 that India was not "very happy or pleased" with the new US-British plan (*New York Times*, 24 February 1951, p. 3).
278. See, for example, "A Word to the Security Council," editorial in *The Hindu*, 28 March 1951, p. 4.
279. Robert Trumbull, *New York Times*, 25 February 1951, p. 9.
280. UN document S/2017/Rev.1, 21 March 1951; text in Security Council, *Official Records*, Sixth Year, Supplement for January, February and March 1951, pp. 25-27.
281. *The Statesman*, 26 March 1951, p. 1.
282. Nehru to Sir Benegal Rau, 26 February 1951; cited in Gopal, *Jawaharlal Nehru*, vol. 2, p. 114.
283. UN, Security Council, *Official Records*, Sixth Year, S/PV.539, 30 March 1951, p. 15.
284. Ibid., S/PV.540, 2 April 1951, pp. 4-6.
285. Ibid., S/PV.538, 29 March 1951, p. 6.
286. *The Hindu*, 1 April 1951, p. 6.   287. Ibid., 3 April 1951, p. 4.
288. Ibid.

289. *New York Times*, 12 June 1951, p. 8.
290. Korbel, *Danger in Kashmir*, p. 181. 291. Above, note 283.
292. "V Sovete bezopasnosti," *Izvestiia*, 31 March 1951, p. 4.
293. "Obrashchenie Indii v Sovet bezopasnosti," *Izvestiia*, 5 July 1951, p. 4, and *New Times*, no. 28 (11 July 1951), p. 31. For India's letter to the Security Council, see S/2225, 30 June 1951; text in Security Council, *Official Records*, Sixth Year, Supplement for 1 April through 30 June 1951, pp. 185-86.
294. "Kashmir and the Security Council," *New Times*, no. 13 (28 March 1951), p. 23.
295. "Indiiskaia gazeta o proiskikh amerikanskikh imperialistov v Kashmire," *Pravda*, 12 April 1951, p. 4. The allegedly "recently signed" and "secret agreement" between Pakistan and the United States was also reported and discussed by *New Times* in a leading article, "More Base-Grabbing," no. 17 (25 April 1951), p. 21.
296. "Amerikanskii samolet narushil granitsu Indii," *Pravda*, 15 April 1951, p. 4, and *Izvestiia*, 15 April 1951, p. 6.
297. UN, Security Council, *Official Records*, Sixth Year, S/PV.543, 30 April 1951, p. 3. See also the coverage of the meeting of the Security Council in *Pravda* ("V Sovete bezopasnosti"), 3 May 1951, p. 4.
298. UN, Security Council, *Official Records*, Sixth Year, S/PV.543, 30 April 1951, p. 4.
299. "Two Sets of Teeth," *New Times*, no. 35 (29 August 1951), pp. 16-17.
300. Ibid., p. 17.
301. See "Letter from Gilgit," *New Times*, no. 24 (13 June 1951), pp. 31-32; "US Speeds Construction of its Military Bases in Northern Pakistan," *Izvestiia*, 25 August 1951, p. 3 (cited from *CDSP*, vol. 3, 6 October 1951, p. 14); and "Americans' Role in Fanning India-Pakistan Conflict," *Izvestiia*, 14 September 1951, p. 4 (cited from *CDSP*, vol. 3, 27 October 1951, p. 22).
302. Acheson, *Present at the Creation*, p. 428.
303. Remarks by Acheson at the National Press Club, Washington, 12 January 1950; cited from *DSB* 22 (23 January 1950): 115-16.
304. The US Joint Chiefs of Staff in December 1949 said the US must not sign a peace treaty which did not assure the continuation of US bases in Japan. Acheson, *Present at the Creation*, p. 430.
305. *The United States in World Affairs*, 1951 (New York, 1952), p. 189.
306. *DSB*, 25 September, p. 513.
307. Acheson, *Present at the Creation*, p. 434.
308. "US Invites 50 Nations to Sign Peace Treaty with Japan," *DSB* 25 (30 July 1951): 186.
309. Text of Draft Treaty and Declarations in *DSB* 25 (23 July 1951): 132-38.
310. Ibid., pp. 133-34. 311. Acheson, *Present at the Creation*, p. 549.

MOSCOW RECONSIDERS INDIA'S NONALIGNMENT 241

312. See the Reply of the Russian Government (to the United States Proposal of July 11, 1947, Regarding a Peace Treaty with Japan), 22 July 1947 (text in *Documents on International Affairs*, 1947–48, London, 1952, pp. 716–17), and V. Mayevsky, "The USA and the Peace Treaty," *Pravda*, 29 June 1949, p. 3 (cited from *CDSP*, vol. 1, 2 August 1949, p. 18).
313. *New York Times*, 17 March 1950.
314. Ya. Viktorov, "Acheson's 'Total Diplomacy,' in the Service of Policy of Aggression," *Pravda*, 19 March 1950, p. 4; cited from *CDSP* 2 (6 May 1950): 17.
315. Acheson, *Present at the Creation*, p. 428.
316. *Documents on International Affairs*, 1951 (London, 1954), pp. 579–82.
317. Ibid., p. 584.   318. Ibid., pp. 593, 597, and 603.
319. "US Invites 50 Nations to Sign Peace Treaty with Japan," *DSB* 25 (30 July 1951): 186.
320. Russian Note to the US, 12 August 1951, in *Documents on International Affairs*, 1951, p. 605.
321. Acheson, *Present at the Creation*, p. 542.   322. Cited in ibid.
323. For a graphic description of how the US dealt with the Soviets at the San Francisco Conference, see ibid., pp. 542–47.
324. M. Mikhailov, "America's 'New Order' in Japan," *Izvestiia*, 25 March 1951, p. 3 (cited from *CDSP*, vol. 3, 5 May 1951, p. 27); E. Zhukov, "The American Imperialists Are Arming Japan," *Pravda*, 29 March 1951 (cited from *SPT*, vol. 6, 15 April 1951, pp. 203–6); Ya. Viktorov, "Aggressive Pacific Pact," *Pravda*, 29 April 1951, p. 4 (cited from *CDSP*, vol. 3, 9 June 1951, pp. 14–15); "Concerning the Peace Settlement for Japan," editorial in *New Times*, no. 22 (30 May 1951), pp. 1–3; "V narushenie mezhdunarodnykh soglashenii—SShA vosstanovlivaiut voennomorskoi flot Iaponii," *Izvestiia*, 27 June 1951, p. 4; Z. Trigorin, "The US Draft Peace Treaty with Japan," *New Times*, no. 30 (25 July 1951), pp. 4–8; and B. Izakov, "An Instrument of War Instead of a Peace Treaty," *New Times*, no. 32 (8 August 1951), p. 3.
325. Ya. Viktorov, "The Aggressors' Intrigues in Japan," *Pravda*, 20 February 1951, p. 4; cited from *CDSP* 3 (7 April 1951): 19.
326. "US Government Sets Up Aggressive Pacific Bloc," *Pravda* and *Izvestiia*, 25 April 1951, p. 4 (cited from *CDSP*, vol. 3, 26 May 1951, pp. 13, 20); M. Markov, "Imperialist Designs in the Pacific," *New Times*, no. 21 (23 May 1951), pp 3–8.
327. Yu. B. Ulanovsky, "Territorial Issues in the Japanese Peace Settlement," *Sovetskoye gosudarstvo i pravo*, no. 5 (1952); cited from *SPT* 7 (1 September 1952); 332.
328. M. Marinin, "Zagovor protiv mira," *Pravda*, 15 July 1951, p. 4.
329. N. Zhigalov, "Again the Road to Pearl Harbour," review of Herbert Feis' *The Road to Pearl Harbour*, in *News*, no. 6 (30 September 1951), pp. 22–24.

330. Note from the Indian Government to the United States Government, 23 August 1951, in *Documents on International Affairs*, 1951, p. 607.
331. Ibid.   332. Ibid.   333. Ibid., pp. 607-8.
334. See, for example, "India Serves Notice of Japanese Pact Boycott," *Los Angeles Times*, 27 August 1951, p. 1, and "US Raps India's Objections to Japanese Pact as Inconsistent," *The Philadelphia Inquirer*, 27 August 1951, p. 1.
335. *Documents on International Affairs*, 1951, p. 610.
336. Ibid.   337. Ibid., p. 611.
338. "The Lost Leader," editorial in the *New York Times*, 28 August 1951, p. 22.
339. "India and the Treaty," *New York Times*, 27 August 1951, p. 18.
340. "Nehru's Gift to the Kremlin," editorial in the *Evening Star*, 27 August 1951, p. A8.
341. "Nehru Aids Red Drive to Block Peace," editorial in *The Philadelphia Inquirer*, 28 August 1951, p. 18.
342. "Some Second Thoughts on India," editorial in the *Evening Sun* (Baltimore), 28 August 1951, p. 16.
343. "Nehru's inconsistency," editorial in the *Cleveland Plain Dealer*, 27 August 1951, p. 16.
344. "Nehrutrality and Japan," editorial in *The New Leader* 34 (3 September 1951): 10.
345. "Secretary Acheson...and his Helper," *The Reporter* 5 (2 October 1951): 1.
346. Polyzoides, "India Stand on Japanese Treaty No Surprise," *Los Angeles Times*, 27 August 1951, p. 8.
347. *New York Times*, 15 August 1951, p. 5.
348. *Washington Post*, 3 December 1951, p. 2.
349. *Chicago Daily Tribune*, 27 August 1951, p. 1.
350. Ivan H. Peterman, "India, Burma Straddle on Japanese Treaty," *The Philadelphia Inquirer*, 28 August 1951, p. 23.
351. Reported in the *Washington Post*, 30 August 1951, p. 4.
352. "The Lost Leader," editorial in the *New York Times*, 28 August 1951, p. 22.
353. For text of Zafrullah Khan's speech, see the *New York Times*, 7 September 1951, p. 6.
354. James Reston, "Four Asian Nations Support Draft of Japanese Treaty," *New York Times*, 7 September 1951, p. 1.
355. Acheson, *Present at the Creation*, p. 548.
356. O. Prudkov, "Vokrug konferentsii v San-Frantsisko," *Literaturnaia gazeta*, 23 August 1951, p. 4.
357. "Vvstuplenie Neru v indiiskom parlamente," *Pravda*, 28 August 1951, p. 4. *Izvestiia* (28 August 1951, p. 4) published a report of Nehru's state-

ment with the title: "Indiia otkazyvaetsia uchastvovat' v konferentsii v San-Frantsisko." See also *New Times*, no. 36 (5 September 1951), p. 31.

358. "Indiiskaia pechat' ob otkaza Indii ot uchastiia v konferentsii v San-Frantsisko," *Pravda* and *Izvestiia*, 30 August 1951, p. 4.
359. M. Mikhailov, "On India's Refusal to Participate in San Francisco Conference," *Izvestiia*, 1 September 1951, p. 3; cited from *CDSP* 3 (13 October 1951): 20.
360. I. Romonovsky, "The Foreign Press on the San Francisco Conference," *New Times*, no. 36 (5 September 1951), p. 18.
361. "Power Politics Versus the People's Interest," editorial in *News*, no. 6 (30 September 1951), p. 3. For comments on India's absence from San Francisco see also I. Filippov, "Schemes of Enemies of Peace Exposed," *Pravda*, 8 September 1951, p. 3 (cited from *CDSP*, vol. 3, 20 October 1951, p. 13); "For Peace and Security in the Far East," editorial in *For a Lasting Peace, For a People's Democracy*, 7 September 1951, p. 1; and "Not a Peace Treaty, But Treaty for Preparing Another War," editorial in ibid., 14 September 1951, p. 1.
362. Statement to the Press by A.A. Gromyko, 8 September 1951, in *New Times*, Supplement to no. 37 (12 September 1951), p. 17. See also Gromyko's reference to India in his speech at the San Francisco Conference on 5 September 1951, in ibid., p. 12.
363. Quoted in Supplement to *New Times*, no. 46 (14 November 1951), p. 9.
364. G. Rassadin and I. Filippov, "Two Paths—on Fifth Anniversary of UN," *Pravda*, 24 October 1950; cited from *CDSP* 2 (9 December 1950): 18.
365. Gene D. Overstreet and Marshall Windmiller, *Communism in India* (Berkeley and Los Angeles, 1959), pp. 159-194.
366. "Palme Dutt Answers Questions on India," *Crossroads*, 19 January 1951, p. 7; cited from John H. Kautsky, *Moscow and the Communist Party of India* (New York, 1956), p. 130. Dutt's reply was dated December 20, 1950.
367. Ibid.
368. *New Times*, supplement to no. 47 (21 November 1951), p. 18.
369. Robert Trumbull, "India's Acceptance Seen," *New York Times*, 23 August 1951, p. 7.
370. Robert Trumbull, "India Between Two Fires," *New York Times*, 26 August 1951, Section IV, p. 5.
371. Blair Bolles, "Asian Tensions to Tax San Francisco Conference," *Foreign Policy Bulletin* 30 (31 August 1951); 2.

VII

New Directions in Soviet Policy Towards India (1952-53)

> We may differ with the neutralists in our understanding of the common tasks of the struggle for peace, but as soon as the neutralists oppose the aggressive forces, we greet them, support them and go along with them. —Ilya Ehrenburg at the Congress of the Peoples for Peace in Vienna, *Pravda*, 17 December 1952, p. 3; cited from *Current Digest of the Soviet Press* 4 (31 January 1953): 25.

THE EVOLUTION OF SOVIET POLICY TOWARDS INDIA

India's deep difference with the US on several aspects of the Korean War, as well as its refusal to sign the Japanese Peace Treaty as drafted by the US, not only led to a reappraisal in Moscow of India's foreign policy, it also made the Soviet leaders aware of the use they could make of New Delhi's position on these important issues relating to Asia in order to mobilize Asian opinion against American policies in the region. It was evident when, in a major speech delivered at the anniversary of the Bolshevik Revolution in November 1951, L.P. Beria criticized the US for imposing a treaty on Japan that "serves the purposes not of peace but of preparation for war." He then added, "The importance of this treaty is further reduced by the fact that India, the second largest and second most important state in Asia, took no part in it."[1]

That Moscow felt a stake in the continuation of the kind of policies India had pursued recently was evident from a letter which some readers in Paris wrote to the Indian Communist Party paper, *Crossroads*, on 18 January 1951.[2] Signed "A Letter from Readers in Paris," it was written in criticism of an editorial published in *Crossroads* on 29 December 1950, with the title "Commonwealth

Conference for War—Keep India Out of its Tentacles." The editorial, as the title suggested, had bitterly criticized the Commonwealth and advised India to sever all ties with it. But arguing against such a step, the "Paris readers" said that Nehru's "vacillation...in favour of peace" was "a big reality" and "a precious capital in our struggle for peace and independence."[3] Therefore, they added, such slogans as "Down with the British Empire" and "Down with the Commonwealth of War" with which the CPI editorial concluded sounded only like "hollow demagogy." What the CPI should do, the "Paris readers" advised, is to mobilize the people to present a programme for peace which Nehru could carry with him to London. Nehru' absence from the Commonwealth, they argued, could only "annihilate a lot of good peace initiatives in the world today."[4] At the second session of the World Peace Council in Vienna in November 1951, India's "neutrality," as we noted in the last chapter, was openly recognized as "a movement for peace."[5]

Two other Soviet comments in 1952 showed that Moscow continued to have a favourable view of India's foreign policy. In early January a Soviet writer, Y. Nezhdanov, discussed the policy of neutrality. Although asserting that his purpose was not to "define our attitude to the policy of neutrality," Nezhdanov stated:

...What concerns us here is the *reason* for neutrality movements in various countries *today*. This reason has its origin in the present world situation, and the problem of neutrality has now acquired a rather different quality.[6]

Then citing examples of the movements for neutrality in West Germany, Norway and Sweden, Nezhdanov said that in all these countries such movements had become expressions of the people's sentiment against an armament buildup and against participation in the Atlantic Alliance. Therefore, Nezhdanov concluded, such neutrality not only promoted world peace but the interests of the country which followed it.[7] A few months later, in June 1952, a Soviet writer, D.I. Chesnokov, commented on the role of Indian bourgeoisie in these words:

...in the epoch of imperialism the national bourgeoisie, under certain conditions, can play a relatively progressive role insofar as it participates in the national-liberation struggle against foreign oppression, in the struggle against feudal survivals. This applies in our day to the national bourgeoisie of India and of a few other colonial and independent countries which are fighting for their national independence and state autonomy.[8]*

In connection with the Soviet reconsideration of India's nonaligned policy, we may also note two other factors. First, in the Soviet-supported Peace Movement there was more and more emphasis on only one goal—the preservation of international peace; second, the Soviets appeared to completely disregard ideology so as to be able to attract the widest sections of the population in their peace campaign. The first was emphasized by Stalin himself, who in his *Economic Problems of Socialism in the USSR*, published on the eve of the Nineteenth Party Congress in October 1952, said that the aim of "the present-day peace movement" was "not to overthrow capitalism and establish socialism," but that "it confines itself to the democratic aim of preserving peace."[9] Then at the Asia and Pacific Area Peace Conference held in Peking in the same month (attended by a large Indian delegation, including a Member of Parliament belonging to the Congress Party),[10] emphasis was put on cooperation among countries of diverse political systems. A resolution passed by the conference stated, "We reaffirm our firm conviction that countries having diverse social systems and ways of life can coexist in the world and cooperate for the common good."[11] The Soviet delegate even declared, "Each people here represented should have freedom to choose their own way of life, their own political system, and their own ideology."[12] Thus an effort was being made to prepare the ground for more cooperation with countries like India.

---

* This was a revised version of Chesnokov's article, which was first published in 1950. At that time Chesnokov had used exactly the same words in laying down conditions under which the national bourgeoisie could play a "progressive" role. However, the relevant paragraph ended there and no mention was made of India. India's inclusion in the 1952 version was another evidence of how the Soviet view of Nehru's foreign policy had changed in 1950 and 1951. For comments on the role of the national bourgeoisie in the 1950 edition see D.I. Chesnokov, "Marksizm-leninizm ob otechestve i patriotizme," in N.P. Vasil'eva and F.D. Khrustova (eds.), *O sovetskom patriotizme* (Moscow, 1950), pp. 9-10.

New Soviet Moves Towards India

Having thus completed their reappraisal of India's "neutral" policy, the Soviets, in the period after the signing of the Japanese Peace Treaty, seemed to be ready to make some new and bold moves towards India, aimed at reducing American military and economic influence and improving their own relations with New Delhi.

1. *Soviet intervention in the UN Kashmir debate* The most important step taken by the Soviets at this time was their intervention in the UN Kashmir debate after their silence for four long years. Although, as we noted in the last chapter, the Soviets in early 1951 had become increasingly concerned at the interest in Kashmir shown by the US and Great Britain, and had charged Washington with trying to seek military bases in the area, they did not, either in the UN or outside, express any opinion on the merits of the issue. However, when the Security Council met on 17 January 1952, to discuss the Kashmir issue, the Soviet delegate, Jacob Malik, spoke at length on the problem. Referring to various plans put forward by London and Washington, he said that:

the purpose of these plans in connection with Kashmir is to secure the introduction of Anglo-American troops into the territory of Kashmir and convert Kashmir into an Anglo-American colony and a military and strategic base.[13]

These military bases, Malik charged, were to be obtained through Pakistan:

...press reports shed light on the true intentions of the United States and the United Kingdom with regard to Kashmir, and reveal the essence of the Anglo-American plans which are being imposed with such zeal and persistence upon the people of Kashmir. The press in the United States, too, has repeatedly indicated United States efforts to dominate Kashmir and the people of Kashmir and to convert its territory into a United States military base. *The Christian Science Monitor*, for example, reported that in Pakistan and Kashmir the United States hoped to obtain a well-prepared ally of exceptional strategic importance in the event of any future conflict with the Soviet Union.[14]

Although the Soviet delegate did not give any direct support to India, he did refer to the convening of a Constituent Assembly by the National Conference to determine the future of the State and said that both London and Washington "immediately interfered in the matter* so as not to allow the people of Kashmir to decide their own future and determine the affiliations of their country independently."[15] Malik's own proposition was to let such a Constituent Assembly decide the future status of the disputed state:

The USSR Government considers that the Kashmir question can be resolved successfully only by giving the people of Kashmir an opportunity to decide the question of Kashmir's constitutional status by themselves, without outside interference. This can be achieved if that status is determined by a Constituent Assembly democratically elected by the Kashmir people.[16]

Insofar as the proposal to call a Constituent Assembly had the support of India, Malik's statement can be considered a support to India's position on this issue. Quite significant also was his reference to India's opposition to the introduction of UN troops into Kashmir.[17] These forces, in the Soviet view, would have been those of Great Britain and the US "in the guise of 'United Nations armed forces.'"[18]

Some later comments in the Soviet press made it clear that the Soviets now fully supported India on Kashmir. On 9 August *Pravda* published a long Tass dispatch from New Delhi containing a report on the proceedings of the Indian Parliament of 7 August. On that day the lower house of the Parliament had approved the recently reached agreement between Nehru and Sheikh Abdullah on the future of the state. These agreements, Tass reported, were based on the decisions taken earlier by the Kashmir Constituent Assembly. According to the newly reached agreements, the Constitution of India would henceforth apply to Kashmir, with the provision that Kashmir would retain a large amount of autonomy. India also agreed to the "liquidation" of the hereditary monarchy. As regards the criticism of the Constituent Assembly in the UN, Tass quoted Nehru as saying, "I saw no basis whatsoever, and see none now, that any for-

*This was a reference to the Anglo-American resolution submitted in the Security Council on 21 February 1951, in which India was criticized for convening the Kashmir Constituent Assembly.

eign power should have interfered in the mutual relations between Kashmir and India or in the desire of the people of Kashmir to determine their future themselves. If other countries object to the setting up of a Constituent Assembly, then we resolutely object to their objections."[19] If Tass made any criticism of Nehru, it was for his refusal to withdraw the question from the UN, a course which was suggested during the dabate by two CPI members, A. K. Gopalan and Professor H. Mukerjee.[20]

2. *Soviet offer of trade* Another Soviet step was in the area of trade. In October 1951, at the ECAFE (Economic Commission for Asia and the Far East) Trade Promotion Conference in Singapore, the chief Soviet delegate, V. P. Migunov, had said that Moscow was prepared to supply manufactured goods, raw materials and agricultural equipment to the countries in the region in return for materials, such as tin, rubber, jute and spices, etc.[21] This suggested that the Soviets were prepared to sign barter deals with countries in South and Southeast Asia. Since most of these countries, including India, suffered from a shortage of hard currency, such deals should normally have been welcome.

In January 1952, at the International Industries Fair in Bombay in which both Communist China and the Soviet Union participated on a large scale, the Soviet offer was made specifically to India. M.V. Nesterov, President of the USSR Chamber of Commerce, who led the Soviet delegation to the fair, said in Bombay on 10 January 1952, that the Soviets were prepared to supply various machine tools, generators, electric equipment, mining equipment, agricultural machinery and such other things as fertilizers and food grains.[22] Four days later, the Soviet Ambassador to India, M. Novikov, repeated Nesterov's offer and said that the Soviet Union would accept payment in rupees or any other currency. Hinting at a barter deal, Novikov added, "You can buy from us anything you want and we are willing to buy from you what we require."[23] S. Borzenko, *Pravda's* correspondent in India, quoted L.A. Razin, the Director of the Soviet Pavilion, as saying that Soviet participation in the fair would lead to "expansion of trade between these two countries."[24] Tass also quoted some Indian visitors to the Soviet pavilion and a non-Communist paper as culling for increased trade relations between the two countries.[25]

At the International Economic Conference called by the Soviets in Moscow in April 1952, Nesterov spoke of the Soviet desire to expand trade with the underdeveloped countries, making a special reference to India. Nesterov said:

Soviet foreign trade organizations are prepared to establish and develop commercial relations with business interests in India, Indonesia, Pakistan, Ceylon, Burma, Thailand, Malaya and other Southeast Asian countries. The mere mention of such a state as India speaks of the potential broad prospects for expanding trade in this part of Asia.[26]

A significant aspect of the conference was the special effort the Soviets made in emphasizing that the conference was being called solely to promote trade relations. A correspondent of *News* cited clause 10 of the Rule of Procedure which provided that "any discussion of the respective merits of different economic and social systems shall be ruled out of order."[27] In almost all the articles published in the Soviet press on the work of the conference, the writers invariably mentioned that the emphasis was on economic cooperation among countries with diverse political, social and economic systems.[28]

3. *Other Soviet gestures to India* The Soviets also made other gestures to India which, considering the way the Kremlin usually dealt with foreign diplomats, were quite significant. Dr. S. Radhakrishnan, who had come to Moscow in early 1950 as India's Ambassador and had met Stalin then, was again received by Stalin on 5 April on the eve of his departure for India to become India's Vice-President.[29] Not only this, Andrei Vyshinsky, the Soviet Foreign Minister, gave a farewell luncheon in Dr. Radhakrishnan's honour and asked him to work for Indo-Soviet understanding even after leaving the post.[30] Moscow's agreement to the appointment of his successor, K.P.S. Menon, was sent within fifteen days. "This," Menon noted in his diary after presenting his credentials to the Soviet President on 18 October 1952, "reflects the friendlier relations which have grown up between India and the Soviet Union during the last few years."[31] Stalin received Menon on 18 February 1953;[32] in fact, he was the last foreign diplomat to have met the Soviet Premier before his death.[33]

India's Response to Soviet Gestures

While India desired more contact with the Kremlin and welcomed Stalin's gesture in receiving Dr. Radhakrishnan before relinquishing his post in Moscow,[34] it did not respond enthusiastically to Moscow's support on the Kashmir question and the Soviet offer for trade.

Even on a question like Kashmir, on which India had been attacked in the West, New Delhi responded coolly. In the UN, while the Pakistan Foreign Minister, Zafrullah Khan, refuted Malik's charge that Pakistan had agreed to grant military bases to the US,[35] the Indian delegate, M. C. Setalvad, in a long statement did not even refer to Malik's speech.[36] Nehru, who spoke so frequently on the Kashmir dispute, chose to remain silent on Malik's statement. A dispatch in the *New York Times* gave these reasons for New Delhi's attitude:

While Indian officials have resolutely declined comment on the statement by Jacob A. Malik...backing India's claim to Kashmir, there is concern in informed circles here that Moscow should have chosen the Kashmir dispute for having a fling at the Western powers.

The general feeling here is that India wants an early settlement of the long-standing issue before the United Nations and that the manner in which the Soviet delegate delivered his frontal attack against the West has hardly contributed towards that end. It is feared in informed circles that Mr. Malik's speech, although it reflects Indian sentiment, might pose new problems and further complicate the dispute.[37]

The Hindu's Paris correspondent, K. S. Shelvankar, attributed somewhat similar reasons to Nehru's position:

...I understand that this is precisely the sort of development Indian diplomacy had been endeavouring to avoid from the beginning—involvement of the Kashmir dispute in the conflict between the rival Power blocs and the propaganda and passions of the cold war.[38]

India, in fact, took the unusual step in assuring the US that it "was in no way responsible for the Soviet intervention"[39] in the UN debate on Kashmir. Loyd V. Steere, US Charge in New Delhi, reported to Washington:

Bajpai asked me to call today and said GOI [Government of India] was anxious that US Govt and Amb Bowles should know that GOI was as much surprised as they must be at Russian charges Anglo-US interference in Kashmir affairs and their alleged interest in military bases Kashmir. He was at pains to emphasize that GOI had not given Soviet authorities information or lead upon which its charges could be based.[40]

To prove his point, Bajpai even showed to Steere copies of cables that his ministry had sent on 10 January (i.e., a week before the Malik statement) to Indian missions in those countries which were at this time members of the Security Council. As far as Russia was concerned, he told the US embassy official, the same cable had been sent to the Indian mission in Moscow. But even this cable "had not been communicated to Soviet authorities," since the Indian charge in Moscow had been away in Berlin. Explaining the contents of the cable, Bajpai told Steere that it was obvious that it "contained nothing" which could have possibly given any "basis for charges such as USSR had made in Paris."[41]

A prominent Kashmiri leader Gulam Mohammed Sadiq, President of the Constituent Assembly, welcomed the Soviet intervention and asked New Delhi to withdraw the Kashmir issue from the United Nations.[42] When the US brought it to the attention of Bajpai saying that the Sadiq statement was "mischievous" and that New Delhi's official position was not to take any notice of the Russian intervention.[43]

In Pakistan, the Malik statement created surprise because, as a *New York Times* report said, "it was not expected that the Soviet Union would side so strongly with India in this dispute." Some Pakistani officials, however, said that Russia's bold step "probably would result in support for Pakistan from major Western powers."[44]

The Indian government also did not show much enthusiasm about Moscow's offer of more trade. When in November 1952, a CPI member, P. Sundarayya, moved a resolution in the Parliament suggesting the promotion of trade with the Soviet Union through agreements, the Minister of State for Commerce and Industry, D.P. Karamkar, gave the evasive reply that India did not think trade agreements were necessary for the development of commercial relations.[45]

One of the reasons for India's attitude seemed to be her continued suspicion of Moscow's intentions about the CPI. An article in the *Statesman* was not far from the truth when it suggested that the future of Indo-Soviet relations would, to some extent, depend on the activities of the CPI.[46] In fact, in some cases, the Soviets acted in such a way as to add to the suspicions of the Indian government about their involvement with the CPI, For example, many of Radio Moscow's broadcasts on India's first general elections in early 1952 vehemently attacked the elections as unfair and undemocratic, while lauding the victory of the "progressive," i.e., CPI members.[47] As the *Statesman's* columnist "Vedette" reported, although the Indian government did not make much fuss about it, Dr. Radhakrishnan, Indian Ambassador in Moscow, brought up the matter when he met Vyshinsky before his return to India.[48] It was probably against this background that at the luncheon given by Vyshinsky in his honour, the Indian Ambassador made it clear that India was determined to follow her own path. Pointing out that "no country could tear up its own roots," Dr. Radhakrishnan said that India had followed "peaceful methods" in getting rid of the princely rule and intended to follow the same path in ending the evils of landlordism.[49] He then added:

We have faith in the peaceful methods of democracy and will work, aware of the past, alive to the present and unafraid of the future.[50]

A Soviet move in August 1952 to provide food aid did not strengthen its position in New Delhi. On 30 August, *Pravda* published reports of "mass famine" in Southern India and said that in order to provide immediate help to the starving in Andhra, an aid committee "having wide representation" had been formed.[51] Next day, both *Pravda* and *Izvestiia* published the correspondence between the General Secretary of the United Famine Relief Committee of Andhra Region and V. Kuznetsov, Chairman of the Central Council of Trade Unions of USSR, announcing that the Soviets would send 10,000 tons of wheat, 5,000 tons of rice, 500,000 tons of condensed milk and 250,000 rupees [at that time about $50,000] to the committee.[52] However, the Nehru government objected to this method of providing aid. In a statement on 5 September, the Indian government announced that the question of relief "should be kept apart from...political controversies." New Delhi added that if Moscow wanted to help, it could do so through the Indian government or agencies like the Indian Red Cross Society.[53] Moscow had, therefore, no alternative but to agree to New Delhi's suggestion. Solovyov, Secretary of the Central Council of Trade Unions, denied that the Soviets were motivated by "any political consideration." He said they were "actuated by one desire—to aid the starving population..."[54] Apparently to dispel any impression of political considerations, an account of this interview was also published in *Soviet Land*.[55]

However, there was another very important reason for India's coolness to the Soviet gestures on Kashmir and trade. Even before the Soviets made these gestures, Washington had, in October 1951, sent Chester Bowles as its new ambassador to India. Fascinated by India's efforts to bring about economic development by democratic means and determined to persuade the White House and Congress to support this experiment, Bowles declared that his mission in India would be to establish a "living, breathing relationship" between the two countries.[56]

THE BOWLES ERA IN INDO-AMERICAN RELATIONS

During the Cold War years, when many in the US thought in terms of combating Communism by military means, Bowles had come to believe that since it was economic suffering and deprivation that turned people to Communism, it was only by satisfying their economic and political aspirations that one could hope to create real barriers to the expansion of Communist ideology. In his view, the US, with its vast human and material resources, had a historic opportunity to help transform these newly-liberated Asian countries into free and democratic societies. In a speech at Freedom House in New York City in January 1947, he argued that if the American people could invest only two percent of their annual income for twenty years for economic development in these countries, "we may change the tide of history."[57] In another speech at Yale University on 14 May 1951, he did not minimize the importance of military defence, but said that its purpose should only be "to secure the elbow room in which to tackle the broad and fundamental problems with which the great bulk of the peoples of the world are confronted."[58]

As far as India was concerned, he later wrote, "I had come to see India as the political and economic key to a free and stable Asia" and "a testing ground for democratic government in a period of receding colonial dominance."[59] He now had the opportunity to conduct American diplomacy in a major Asian country in accordance with his long-held convictions.

On his arrival in India in October 1951, Bowles found that both Nehru and other Indian officials were receptive to what he had to say. Even before presenting his credentials, he had talks with the officials of Indian Foreign Ministry and reported to the State Department on 24 October 1951, that he was "rather reassured by their viewpoint."[60] Six weeks later, on 6 December, in a detailed memorandum to the Secretary of State, Dean Acheson, he spoke about the feeling of Indians towards Russia and America. About Russia he said, "Every top Indian official with whom I have talked has gone out of his way to condemn the Soviet Union and the Communist approach to economic, social and political problems. Nehru has been most emphatic in his statements to me on two occassions."[61] And about India's view of the US, he told Acheson:

The attitude of the average Indian towards the United States is much friendlier than one might assume from reading Indian or American newspapers. I have talked to scores of peasants and working people, and I have yet to see anyone whose face did not light up when he heard I was from America.[62]

Bowles also came to appreciate the fact that behind the policy of nonalignment was India's determination to remain independent. He told Acheson that since it was unlikely "that India will openly support the free world in a manner that would place her against her great neighbour, China," "any aggressive effort to pressure India with a different position will be ineffective and eventually...alienate a people and a government which are now basically sympathetic to our objectives..." The US, he argued, "will make much faster progress if we let India know that much as we agree with her we respect her desire to remain aloof for the present, and that our only wish is to help her to help herself and to maintain her independence." He felt confident that "such a policy towards India will create far better feeling towards America and it may enable us to draw her to our side."[63] And when New Delhi "moves in our direction," he stated, "it will be in several stages—from her present cool neutralism, to benevolent neutralism, to the kind of association which we deeply desire."[64] He concluded his long memo by telling the Secretary of State that although the views he was expressing were his own, they were "broadly shared by most objective and thoughtful observers here in Delhi—American, European, and Asian."[65]

Since any future economic assistance had to be proposed and approved back in Washington, he devoted a great deal of energy in trying to persuade the members of Congress, officials of the Truman Administration, and prominent newspapermen, to support US economic assistance to India. As one-time owner of an advertising firm which had seen remarkable growth during the Depression years, he knew how to do a public relations job.

As a result of Bowles's efforts, Washington succeeded in establishing a new economic relationship with New Delhi. The first technical cooperation agreement, providing for $50 million for community development projects, was signed by him and Nehru on 5 January 1952.[66] Back in the US, a few days later, Bowles proposed to the Congress a grant of $1 billion over the next four years to help complete India's first Five Year Plan.[67] Although Bowles was not able to get this money from the Congress, whose powerful members like Senator Tom Connally of Texas, Chairman of the Foreign Relations Committee, continued to be critical of Nehru's foreign policy,[68] he was able to make a new beginning in this direction.

India's acceptance of economic assistance also symbolized a friendlier attitude towards US policies than New Delhi had shown for quite some time. As a columnist in the *Statesman* stated that although the US-Indian aid agreements did not imply "acceptance by India of a seat in the Western bloc," it would also be wrong to consider it only "a financial deal, pure and simple..." He added, "There is an unwritten obligation to look upon the USA with greater friendship and deeper appreciation of her viewpoint."[69] In a way, this was expressed in India's acceptance of the provisions of the US Mutual Security Act which provided that the recipient countries will cooperate with the US "in maintaining world peace, and to take such action as may be mutually agreed upon to eliminate the causes of international tension."[70] While Burma had asked for modification in these terms and the Indonesian cabinet had been forced to resign for accepting US assistance under them,[71] Nehru saw no problems in committing India to these conditions. In a statement, the Indian Prime Minister said, "...we have no difficulties with the United States and we are getting on very well indeed."[72] In a rare public gesture, he even praised American assistance to India in glowing terms. At a public meeting in Hyderabad in September 1952, he said:

Some people say no nation such as India...should be dependent upon foreign aid and in general this [is] probably correct. However, aid from America has been given [to] us from [the] very best of motives and without strings of any kind. For this reason we welcome this assistance.[73]

In order to be sure that his remarks about American aid to India would be conveyed to Washington, he, when he met Bowles upon his return from Hyderabad, asked the US ambassador if he had seen the reports of his speech.[74]

It was this favourable turn in New Delhi's relations with Washington, and the expectation that the US would now be coming forward in a significant way to meet India's need for developmental aid, that made India turn a cold shoulder to Soviet offers of trade made at the International Industries Fair in Bombay in January 1952. The fear that Soviet intervention on Kashmir in favour of India might jeopardize its new relationship with Washington was also the real reason for India's efforts to dissociate itself from Malik's statement, although, as an Indian columnist reported, the "private reaction" of Indian officials was *not* of "unreserved disapproval." In fact, he added, "Indians are not entirely unhappy over Russia having even belatedly supported their own contention that Jammu and Kashmir was being turned into a pawn of international power politics."[75]

Limitations of the Bowles Approach to India

Despite the fact that Bowles succeeded remarkably well in improving his country's relations with India and transform the mutual recriminations and distrust that had characterized their relations when he took over charge into a new warmth and trust, he was handicapped by some serious limitations that finally brought about an end to this highly successful diplomatic experiment.

In the first place, Bowles' appointment in India was not part of a new approach in Washington towards Asia in general or India in particular. In fact, it was he who had asked for this assignment. President Truman had offered to send him to some other country, but when Bowles suggested India, the President asked him, "Why in the world would you want to go to India."[76] So in giving a new direction to American policy towards India, he was trying to put in practice his deep-held convictions as to what his country's role towards the newly-liberated countries should be and not implement a new policy decided in Washington's corridors of power.

Although, therefore, the Truman Administration responded favourably to Bowles's personal campaign which he waged indefatigably by letters to a score of Americans in different official and non-official positions, Washington's response was not always to the ambassador's expectations. When he could not get the members of the Department of State and the Mutual Security Agency to recommend adequate resources for India for the next fiscal year, he, in a moment of desperation, wrote to Acheson in October 1952:

...Some members of the Department are still clinging to the mistaken belief that the Indian economic problem can be largely solved by technical assistance. Others, who see the problem more clearly, are reluctant to make recommendations which in their judgment the new Congress might not accept.

Still others insist that the Indian government must produce precise figures on its future economic needs which we would find difficult to provide in our own country. And behind the whole confused situation there seems to be a lack of awareness of the seriousness of the political situation here in India and an unwillingness to face what we believe to be a clear-cut crisis in Asia.

What we need and need urgently is a top level political decision on the following two points:

1. Am I correct in my assumption that a free India is vitally important to world stability and to our future security?

2. Am I correct in my assumption that steady economic progress in the next few years is essential to the survival of a free India?[77]

He then asked Acheson that Washington should either reject or accept his view and then act accordingly:

If the Department feels that I am wrong, I should be told that I am wrong, and my proposals for economic assistance should be modified on the basis of that decision. But if it is agreed that my analysis is reasonably correct we should proceed to build a programme that will fit the requirements of the situation. In other words, I believe that the time has come either to reject my views or to act upon them.[78]

The United States also did not respond as favourably as it might have to India's request for military hardware. To New Delhi's desire to have fifty-four C-119 Fairchild aircraft for its air force, Washington's response was that the number of aircraft supplied to India would depend on "the estimate, by the Department of Defense, of the quantity of aircraft that India's military requirement can utilize effectively."[69] In view of the Truman Administration's reluctance to sell fifty-four, India decided to reduce its request to twenty-six, a figure which now met the US approval.[80] In case of India's request for 200 M4A4 tanks, Washington expressed its willingness to sell them for nineteen million dollars, a price which India found too high. In an effort to persuade Washington to reduce the price, India's Foreign Secretary R.K. Nehru made a special pitch with the US embassy in New Delhi. According to an embassy report, the Indian official:

stated that GOI [Government of India] engaged in great internal economic construction program, in which US assisting, and GOI anxious utilize maximum number dollars that program. However, he continued, India had to look to preservation her security and needed replacement tanks as part that program. He concluded by saying GOI would appreciate receiving tanks at lowest price quoted any other purchaser...[81]

Supporting New Delhi's request for price reduction, Bowles wrote to the Department of State:

...I believe this useful opportunity encourage Ind use US equipment rather than have PriMin Nehru cast about elsewhere incl perhaps Soviet Union for needed mil equipment...I feel a gesture on our part by way of knocked down tank prices wld be gratefully recd, wld probably contribute to improved relations, and wld at some time help strengthen GOI's capacity to fight aggression...[82]

Despite Bowles' urgings, Washington decided that the US could not supply tanks in less than nineteen million dollars as quoted earlier.[83]

Washington's opinion of Prime Minister Nehru, who had been the target of so much criticism in the past, also did not change appreciably despite his warm response to Bowles' overtures. Acheson, who had found the Indian Prime Minister such a difficult person to deal with during his meeting with the Indian leader in Washington, DC in 1949, still thought of him as an "irresponsible person" for bringing up all those Afro-Asian issues to the United Nations.[84] And Admiral Arthur W. Radford, after a visit to India in November 1952, said of his meeting with Nehru that he "was sorry it had taken place," because he found the Indian Prime Minister "an opinionated egotist," a man who had "a basic inferiority complex coupled with incredible ambition." It was this type of personality and egotism, wrote Radford, that "prevented him from being the world figure that he might have been."[85] While Bowles had begun his job in India by trying to understand "this complex, controversial and attractive personality," as he wrote of Nehru,[86] and succeeded in developing "an unusually warm and friendly relationship" with him,[87] the view held by Acheson and Radford, two of the most powerful men in America's foreign policy making apparatus, were indicative of the shaky foundation of Bowles' achievement in India.

This was also evident from the fact that while Bowles' approach to India was based on dealing with the problems of the region primarily by economic means, Washington was already in the process of formulating a different policy aimed at linking the area with American military power. In fact, only a month before Bowles's departure for India in Fall 1951 to take up his assignment, the ambassador-designate had been warned by General Hoyt Vandenberg, then Air Force Chief of Staff, that"...we are going to give you some trouble out there in India because we have our eyes on bases in Pakistan."[88] One individual whose ideas were already pushing the US in the direction of a US-sponsored military alliance in the region was Sir Olaf Caroe, who had served as Foreign Secretary under two British administrations. He had come to believe that because of British withdrawal from the Persian Gulf region, it was necessary to fill the vacuum by a grouping of the countries in the region, and that the pacts bringing about this grouping must be under-written by Western powers. Since India adhered to a policy of nonalignment, Sir Olaf concluded, it is Pakistan that must become a very important part of any such undertaking.[89]

While Bowles was working tirelessly in India to build a new structure of Indian-American relations, Sir Olaf, at the suggestion of British Foreign Office, undertook a tour of the United States in May-June 1952. He held discussions with important officials both in the

Pentagon and the State Department.[90] For those—and their number was significant—who were already thinking along these lines, arguments of this retired British official settled the issue. It now became clear that in order to implement these ideas, the US would have to reconsider her policies towards India and Pakistan. In fact, a high-level interdepartmental estimate in October 1952 specifically spoke of the importance of "a large number of excellent airfields and air base sites" in West Pakistan which were "within medium and heavy bomber range of major industrial and governmental centres in Soviet Central Asia and the interior of Communist China."[91] Also, in a report prepared by the Secretaries of State and Defense and the Director for Mutual Security at the request of National Security Council regarding the threats to America's national security in different regions, Pakistan was mentioned, along with Greece, Turkey, Korea, Japan, and Vietnam, as one of the countries strategically important to the US. The report then pointed out the necesssity of building up Pakistan's military forces "if it can be accomplished without involving unmanageable problems with India..."[92]

At his New Delhi post, Bowles was aware of the discussions taking place in Washington, DC, and of the rumours of a possible US-sponsored military alliance in Asia. In a letter to Charles Murphy, President Truman's General Counsel, he wrote in December 1951 that a military alliance involving American bases in Pakistan would be disastrous for American-Indian relations. He argued, "in fact, nothing could be better calculated to destroy the effort that we are now making to create a more solid basis of understanding and friendship."[93] For the time being, his urgent letters and cables from New Delhi on this question proved quite effective. He was able to convince President Truman that "largescale military assistance to Pakistan would be a serious mistake."[94]

The End of the Bowles Era

But the Truman Presidency soon came to an end. The new administration would be headed by Dwight D. Eisenhower, with John Foster Dulles as his Secretary of State. In fact, Bowles had written several letters to both, apprising them of his work in India in an effort to persuade them to his viewpoint regarding America's policy to India. In a letter to Eisenhower in March 1952, who was then the Commander of NATO forces in Europe, Bowles wrote how American aid was being effectively utilized in India. On Nehru's attitude to the US, he said, "Right now there is no question in our minds that the Indian Government from Nehru on down is emotionally quite close to us, and that this trend in our direction is increasing far more rapidly than we dared hope a few months ago."[95] To Dulles he sent an analysis of Indian economy, arguing for American economic aid of $250 million annually in the next four years, an amount which he characterized as "less than our average economic investment in Greece."[96]

In their replies, while Eisenhower complimented Bowles for the way American assistance was being used and wished him success in his "important mission,"[97] Dulles expressed doubts if in view of "the great complexities of the problems in India" and "the difficulties of religion, language, etc." India could really use any massive assistance from the West in a useful manner. Not only this, he pointed to the serious differences between India and the US on the Chinese issue.[98] His emphasis on the continuing political differences between India and the US were to prove decisive in the future.

Eisenhower's victory in the presidential elections in November and the possibility that it might mean a new policy towards South Asia, one which could perhaps completely undo his work in India, prompted Bowles to make known his desire that he would be willing to stay on as America's envoy even under the new administration. He would do that so he could continue "the most important task I have ever tackled" and to build "on the foundations which have been laid in these first twelve months."[99] But apprehensive that emphasis on military build-up might now be the main goal, he wrote:

All of this is particularly important here in India where the military approach is doomed to failure. I am deeply convinced that if only India and America can work more closely together, we can build a bridge between East and West and we can become less dependent upon some of our tired colonial friends in Europe...[100]

But the Eisenhower Administration decided to replace Bowles. It also soon began to formulate a new American policy towards the region, a policy based on a US-sponsored military alliance which India was bound to reject and Pakistan eager to join. As it worked to forge military ties with Pakistan, which would provide a US base in Peshawar, not far from the Soviet borders, it also decided to withdraw Truman's recommendations in the 1953-54 budget for economic assistance to India to the extent of $200 million a year for the completion of its First Five Year Plan.[101]

There was bafflement and frustration in India, especially on Washington's decision to replace Bowles. How could, the Indians asked, a country recall an ambassador who, for the first time, had transformed the Indian-American relations into a bond of friendship and understanding. In a moving letter to Bowles—a letter which the State Department's South Asian Division head Donald Kennedy said the Ambassador will "treasure" all his life[102]—Prime Minister Nehru paid rich tributes to Bowles. He observed that the Ambassador's stay in India had not only been "full of fresh developments in Indo-American relations," but the Indian people had increasingly begun to look upon him "as a friend of India and as one wishing well for India."[103] Discussing his last meeting with Nehru, Bowles wrote to Kennedy that Nehru was "quite emotional and said over and over again that he had not really believed I would be pulled out." Nehru also said "that this made him doubly certain that drastic changes were in the wind in our foreign policy and that he was fearful of effects."[104]

The end of the Bowles era created a crisis in Indian foreign policy. With decreasing interest and desire in Washington to support its developmental plans, and the increasing support that America gave to Pakistan on the Kashmir question, India had to look for support elsewhere. In a public statement, Nehru reiterated his policy of nonalignment, stating that he would work for a "third area," the members of which would "not wish to align themselves with any bloc."[103] But India had turned to the US for aid in the past and even adopted a Western-oriented foreign policy within the broad framework of nonalignment; she could do the same now by responding to the Soviet overtures more positively than she had done so far. Analysing the reasons for Jacob Malik's intervention in the Kashmir debate at the UN in January 1952, a report prepared by the US embassy in New Delhi had speculated that what Russia was trying to do was to "disrupt improving pol[itical] and econ[omic] relations between India and [the] US."[104] As we have seen, Moscow did not succeed in its efforts but Washington had now brought it about by turning its back on the Bowles' policies and adopting a new posture towards South Asia.

NOTES

1. "134th Anniversary of the Great October Socialist Revolution—Speech by L.P. Beria at Ceremonial Meeting of the Moscow Soviet, 6 November 1951," *Pravda* and *Izvestiia*, 7 November 1951; cited from *CDSP* 3 (December 1951): 6.
2. "A letter from Readers in Paris," 18 January 1951, to the Editor, *Crossroads*; text in Romesh Thapar, et al., *Nehru's Foreign Policy* (Bombay, n.d. [1951?]), pp. 9–15.
3. Ibid., p. 11.   4. Ibid., pp. 13–15.
5. Pietro Nenni, Vice-President of the World Peace Council, on 3 November 1951, at the Second Session of the World Peace Council in Vienna; cited from *New Times*, Supplement to no. 47, 21 November 1951, p. 18.
6. Y. Nezhdanov, "The Atlantic Alliance and the Question of Neutrality," *News*, no. 1 (1 January 1952), p. 7.
7. Ibid., pp. 7–8.
8. D.I. Chesnokov, "Marksizm-leninism ob otchestve i patriotizme," in N.P. Vasil'eva and F.D. Khrustova (eds.), *O sovetskom patriotizme* (2nd ed., Moscow, 1952), p. 10.
9. Joseph Stalin, *Economic Problems of Socialism in the USSR* (New York, 1952), p. 30.
10. On India's participation in the Peking Conference, see Gene D. Overstreet and Marshall Windmiller, *Communism in India* (Berkeley and Los Angeles, 1960), pp. 421–23.
11. "Materialy Kongressa storonnikov mira stran Azii i Tikhogo okeana—obrashchenie k narodam mira," *Pravda*, 16 October 1952, p. 4.
12. Cited in J.M. Mackintosh *Strategy and Tactics of Soviet Foreign Policy* (London, 1962), p. 57.
13. UN, Security Council, *Official Records*, Seventh Year, 570th meeting, 17 January 1952, pp. 13–14.
14. Ibid., p. 17.   15. Ibid., p. 14.   16. Ibid., p. 18.
17. Ibid., p. 15.   18. Ibid., p. 16.
19. "Obsuzhdenie kashmirskogo voprosa v parlamente Indii," *Pravda*, 9 August 1952, p. 8.
20. Ibid.
21. A Press Trust of India-Reuters report, 10 October 1951, in *Indian Press Digests* 1 (May 1942); 125. See also N. Martynov, "The Singapore Economic Conference," *News*, no. 8 (31 October 1951), p. 31.
22. "Russia's Trade Offer to India," *The Sunday Statesman*, 13 January 1952, p. 4.
23. "Soviet Offer of Equipment to India," *The Statesman*, 15 January 1952, p. 10.
24. S. Borzenko, "Industrial Exhibit in India—Interview with L.A. Razin, Director of Soviet Pavilion," *Pravda*, 7 January 1952, p. 3; cited from

CDSP 4 (16 February 1952): 11. Hope for increased trade with India was also expressed in other Soviet press coverage of the fair. See Mikhail Nesterov, "The Bombay International Industries Fair," *News* no. 3 (1 February 1952), pp. 25-26, and "Uspekh sovetskogo pavil'ona na Mezhdunarodnoi promyshlennoi vystavke v Bombee," *Pravda*, 22 January 1952, p. 3.

25. "Indiiskaia obshchestvennost' trebuet ukrepleniia sviazei s SSR," *Izvestiia*, 17 January 1952, p. 4.
26. Speech by M.V. Nesterov, President of the USSR Chamber of Commerce at the International Economic Conference, 5 April 1952, *News*, no. 8 (15 April 1952), p. 15. See also Vasily Nemchinov, "Object and Purpose of the International Economic Conference," *News*, no. 7 (1 April 1952), p. 3. Academician Nemchinov specifically mentioned the necessity of India's trade with the Soviet Union and suggested that it could be a barter trade.
27. V. Matveyev, "Trade Contacts Will Be Broadened," *News*, no. 8 (15 April 1952), p. 7.
28. See, for example, Robert Chambeiron, "Prospects of the International Economic Conference," *New Times*, no. 10 (5 March 1952), p. 7; Vasily Nemchinov, "Object and Purpose of the International Economic Conference," *News*, no. 7 (1 April 1952), p. 5; Vasily Krestyaninov, "International Trade and the Workers," *News*, no. 7 (1 April 1952), p. 9; "On the Eve of the International Economic Conference," editorial in *New Times*, no. 14 (2 April 1952), p. 2; "Communique of the International Economic Conference in Moscow, "*News*, no. 8 (15 April 1952), p. 4; Faddei Mikhalevsky, "International Trade and Finance," *News*, no. 10 (15 May 1952), pp. 15-17; and Stanislav Strumilin, "Summing up the International Economic Conference," *News*, no. 10 (15 May 1952), p. 6.
29. "J.V. Stalin Receives Indian Ambassador S. Radhakrishnan," *Pravda* and *Izvestiia*, 6 April 1952, p. 1; cited from *CDSP* 4 (17 May 1952): 21.
30. "Indo-Soviet Friendship—Tribute to Work of Dr. Radhakrishnan," *The Hindu*, 6 April 1952, p. 7.
31. K.P.S. Menon, *The Flying Troika; The Political Diary of India's Ambassador to Russia*, 1952-61 (London, 1963), p. 2.
32. Ibid., pp. 26-32; "J.V. Stalin Receives Indian Ambassador K.P.S. Menon," *Pravda* and *Izvestiia*, 18 February 1953, p. 1; cited from *CDSP* 5 (28 March 1953): 16; *New Times*, no. 9 (25 February 1953), p. 32.
33. Menon, *The Flying Troika*, p. 32.
34. "Vedette," "Radhakrishnan's Interview with Stalin," *Statesman Overseas Edition*, 26 April 1952, p. 4.
35. UN, Security Council, *Official Records*, Seventh Year, 571st meeting, 30 January 1952, p. 7.
36. Ibid., 572nd meeting, 31 January 1952, pp. 4-7.
37. "Indians Fear Malik Statement on Kashmir May Complicate Settlement of the Dispute," *New York Times*, 21 January 1952, p. 3.

38. *The Hindu*, 19 January 1952, p. 4; cited from *IPD* 1 September 1952): 10.
39. Memorandum by the Acting Secretary of State for Near Eastern, South Asian, and African affairs (Burton Y. Berry) to the Secretary of State, 24 January 1952, *FRUS* (Washington, DC, 1983), vol. 11, pt. 2, p. 1178.
40. The Charge in India (Steere) to the Department of State, 18 January 1952, ibid., p. 1173.
41. Ibid.
42. Cited in the Charge in India (Steere) to the Department of State, 20 January 1952, ibid., p. 1175.
43. The Charge in India (Steere) to the Department of State, 19 January 1952, ibid., p. 1174.
44. "Malik Kashmir View Surprises Pakistan," *New York Times*, 19 January 1952, p. 3.
46. "India and Trade with Russia; Policy Explained," *Statesman Overseas Edition*, 29 November 1952, p. 9.
46. "Indo-USSR Relations—May be Governed to Some Extent by Indian Communists' Role," *Statesman Overseas Edition*, 15 March 1952, p. 16.
47. Several comments broadcast by Radio Moscow in February and March 1952 are quoted in "Vedette," "Moscow Radio Comments on Indian Affairs," *The Statesman*, 22 March 1952, p. 4.
48. "Vedette," "Radhakrishnan's Interview with Stalin," *Statesman Overseas Edition*, 26 April 1952, p. 4.
49. "Indo-Soviet Friendship—Tribute to Work of Dr. Radhakrishnan," *The Hindu*, 6 April 1952, p. 7.
50. Ibid. 51. "Golod na Iuge Indii," *Pravda*, 30 August 1952, p. 4.
52. "Pomoshch' sovetskikh profsoiuzov golodaiushchemu naseleniiu iuzhnykh rainov Indii," *Pravda* and *Izvestiia*, 31 August 1952, p. 3. See also "Aid to the Starving in Andhra Province," *Soviet Land* (publication of the Soviet Embassy in New Delhi) 5 (10 September 1952): 17, and "Soviet Trade Unions Help India," *News*, no. 18 (15 September 1952), p. 2.
53. "Policy of Gifts from Abroad; Russia and China Informed," *Statesman Overseas Edition*, 13 September 1952, p. 9.
54. "On Aid from Soviet Trade Unions to Starving Population of State of Madras (India)," *Pravda* and *Izvestiia*, 13 September 1952, p. 3; cited from *CDSP* 4 (25 October 1952): 8.
55. *Soviet Land* 5 (25 September 1952): 24.
56. Chester Bowles, *Ambassador's Report* (New York, 1954), p. 5.
57. Chester Bowles, *Promises to Keep: My Years in Public Life*, 1941–1969 (New York, 1971), pp. 245–46.
58. Box 61, Folder 876, Chester Bowles Papers, Sterling Memorial Library, Yale University, New Haven, Connecticut (hereafter cited as Bowles Papers).

NEW DIRECTIONS 267

59. Bowles, *Promises to Keep*, p. 247.
60. Bowles to Donald D. Kennedy, 24 October 1951, Bowles Papers, Box 95, Folder 256.
61. "Early Observations on India," Bowles' memorandum to Dean Acheson, 6 December 1951, p. 2, Bowles Papers, Box 94, Folder 233.
62. Ibid.   63. Ibid., p. 9.   64. Ibid., p. 13.   65. Ibid., p. 15.
66. *Statesman Overseas Edition*, 12 January 1952, p. 10.
67. "A Billion for India Sought by Bowles," *New York Times*, 17 January 1952, p. 12.
68. *The Statesman*, 18 January 1952, p. 4.
69. Vedette, "Background of US Aid to India," *Statesman Overseas Edition*, 19 January 1952, p. 8.
70. *United States Statutes at Large*, 82d Congress, 1st Session, 1951 (Washington, DC, 1952), 65: 381.
71. "Nehru Endorses US aid Motives; He Differs with Burma and Indonesia," *New York Times*, 29 February 1952, p. 3.
72. Ibid.
73. Cited in the Ambassador in India (Bowles) to the Department of State, 2 October 1952, *FRUS* 1952–1954 (Washington, DC, 1983), 11, part 2; 1666.
74. Ibid.
75. Vedette, "Unsolved Mystery of 'Devers Plan'—Likely Ammunition for M. Malik," *Statesman Overseas Edition*, 2 February 1952, p. 6.
76. Bowles, *Promises to Keep*, p. 247.
77. The Ambassador in India (Bowles) to the Secretary of State, 28 October 1952, *FRUS* 1952-1954 (Washington, DC, 1983), 11, part 2: 1669.
78. Ibid.
79. Memorandum by the Consultant to the Secretary of State (Myron W. Cowen) to the Director of the Office of Military Assistance in the Department of Defence (Maj. Gen. George Olmstead), 13 May 1952. ibid., p. 1639.
80. Memorandum by the Secretary of State's Special Assistant for Mutual Security Affairs (Edwin M. Martin) to the Director of the Office of Military Assistance in the Department of Defense (Olmstead), 20 October 1952, ibid., p. 1668.
81. The Ambassador in India (Bowles) to the Department of State, 13 August 1952, ibid., pp. 1660-61.
82. Ibid., p. 1661.
83. The Department of State to the US Embassy in India, Telegram 461, 15 August 1952, Department of State file 791.5/8; cited in ibid.
84. Memorandum for the File, by the Ambassador at Large (Philip C. Jessup), 17 September 1952, *FRUS* 1952–1954 (Washington, DC, 1979), 3; 46.

85. Stephen Jurika, Jr. (ed.), *From Pearl Harbor to Vietnam: The Memoirs of Admiral Arthur W. Radford* (Stanford, 1980), pp. 298-99.
86. Bowles, *Ambassador's Report*, p. 99.   87. Ibid., p. 102.
88. Quoted in Selig S. Harrison, *The Widening Gulf: Asian Nationalism and American Policy* (New York, 1978), p. 265.
89. For a critical discussion of Sir Olaf Caroe's views see ibid., pp. 263-64
90. Ibid., p. 264.
91. Special Estimate, 3 October 1952, *FRUS* 1952-1954 (Washington, DC, 1983), vol, 11. pt. 2, p. 1070.
92. Report by the Secretaries of State and Defense and the Director for Mutual Security on Reexamination of United States Programmes for National Security, n. d., *FRUS* 1952-1954 (Washington, DC, 1984), vol. 2, pt. 1, pp. 215 and 217-218. It was submitted to President Truman on 16 January 1953 (Memorandum for the President by the Secretaries of State and Defense and the Director for Mutual Security).
93. Bowles to Murphy, 11 December 1951, Bowles Papers, Box 96, Folder 246.
94. Bowles, *Promises to Keep*, p. 478.
95. Bowles to Eisenhower, 24 March 1952, Bowles Papers, Box 94 Folder 246.
96. Bowles to Dulles, 10 March 1952, Bowles Papers, Box 94, Folder 243.
97. Eisenhower to Bowles, 4 April 1952, Bowles Papers, Box, 94, Folder 246.
98. Dulles to Bowles, 25 March 1952, Bowles Papers, Box 94, Folder 243.
99. Bowles to Ethel B. Gilbert, 26 November 1952, Bowles Papers, Box 95, Folder 254.
100. Ibid.   101. Bowles, *Promises to Keep*, p. 248.
102. Kennedy to Bowles, 18 February 1953, Bowles Papers, Box 95, Folder 268.
103. Nehru's letter to Bowles is cited in Bowles to Kennedy, 9 February 1953, Bowles Papers, Box 95, Folder 268.
104. Bowles to Kennedy, 9 February 1953, Bowles Papers, Box 95, Folder 268. This was his second letter to the State Department on the same day.
105. "Nehru Advocates a Third Area, Discouraging War: A New Alignment in Cause of Peace," *Statesman Overseas Edition*, 21 February 1953, p. 9.

VIII

Conclusions

Whichever country [is] under question—of the countries Near or Far East or the countries of Latin America—everywhere the main enemy of the national liberation movement is American imperialism. This is precisely why it is impossible to regard the national liberation movement in every individual country of the colonial world apart from its connection with the struggle of the two camps, the struggle for the forces of democracy and socialism against the forces of imperialism and reaction.

The progressive character of this or that social movement, the revolutionary or the reactionary nature of this or that party is at the present time determined by its attitude towards the Soviet Union, to the camp of democracy and socialism. Therefore, the controversy as to at what stage the colonial bourgeoisie begins to play a reactionary [or progressive] role, can be solved only under the conditions when an answer is given to this main question.—Ye. Zhukov

Made while summing up the discussions of a three-day joint meeting of the Learned Councils of the Institute of Economics and the Pacific Institute of the USSR Academy of Sciences in June 1949,[1] the above statement came from the foremost Soviet specialist of his time on the problems of the Third World. As the preceding chapters have shown, Moscow's view of India, its leaders, and its foreign policy was determind by the rules formulated by Zhukov. These were the rules of the Cold War, when Moscow and Washington were locked into a rigid confrontation and judged other countries on the basis of their support to one side or the other.

Moscow's policy towards India during the Stalin era was not, as many have asserted, inflexible and doctrinaire, but was shaped by its response to India's changing postures in world affairs. It is important to note that Russia's initial response to India was quite favourable. In fact, when, in 1945, the British proposed the inclusion of India at the forthcoming Paris Peace Conference, Stalin opposed the idea on the grounds that India was still a British colony and Russia did not have any direct diplomatic relations with it. Even while opposing the British proposal, Stalin expressed the hope that his opposition would, in fact, hasten India's freedom.[2] Since Stalin gave up his opposition as a concession to the British, the Russians were not terribly upset when the Indian delegation supported the West on most issues which Moscow considered vital for its national interests. The Soviets nursed the hope that when India became independent, her role in world affairs would be different.

This was borne out by some of Nehru's early actions in foreign affairs—India's opposition to US efforts to limit Moscow's veto right in the Security Council and of the Western colonial policies in general in the fall of 1946, and the establishment of diplomatic relations with Moscow in early 1947—all of which were well received in the Kremlin. The presence of several Soviet delegations at the Asian Relations Conference in New Delhi in April 1947 seemed to give a good start to the relations between the two countries. Although Zhdanov in September 1947 divided the world into two camps—"the imperialist and anti-democratic camp" headed by the US and "the anti-imperialist and democratic" camp headed by the Soviet Union—India was still considered to be sympathetic to the latter. However, shortly afterwards the Soviets watched India taking positions in world affairs which to them appeared to be favouring the interests of their adversaries in the Cold War. On the problems of Korea and Indonesia, on the West's efforts to build up armed forces in Europe, on the US proposal to set up a Little Assembly in the UN in an effort to neutralize the power of the Soviet veto, India supported the West. Nehru, who had so far been considered a "progressive" leader by the Soviets, now became an ally of "imperialism." With India's decision to join the British Commonwealth (known as the "Commonwealth" after India's inclusion), the Soviet suspicions were strengthened that India was about to be made the centre of some Western-sponsored anti-Communist military pact in Asia.

Nehru's visit to the US in October 1949, while turning out to be a great disappointment to the Americans, proved reassuring to the

Soviets insofar as India did not agree to join any military alliance with the US. However, it was the Korean War, and the various developments flowing from it that led to a reappraisal of India's foreign policy in the Kremlin. Although India supported the initial UN decision to resist the North Korean aggression, the deep differences between the US and Indian positions came to the surface when Nehru sent his proposals to solve the Korean problem to Washington and Moscow in July 1950. They were promptly accepted by Stalin and summarily rejected by Acheson. Later, on some of the issues relating to the war—the crossing of the 38th parallel, Acheson's "Uniting for Peace" proposal, China's intervention in the war and the US proposal to brand China an "aggressor"—India opposed the US. The Japanese Peace Treaty, signed in San Francisco in September 1951, provided a climax to the events that had taken place since the North Korean invasion of the South in June 1950. Probably never before had non-Communist leader been criticized and condemned in the American press as Nehru was in August and early September of 1951. The Soviets, on their part lauded the stand taken by India in refusing to sign the treaty.

The Soviets thus came to realize that Nehru's foreign policy was not, as they had believed since December 1947, dictated by London and Washington. In fact, it was now found to be contributing to the Soviet foreign policy objectives. One example of this was the Soviet effort to use India's stand on the Japanese Peace Treaty to mobilize Asian opinion against American policies in Asia.

Having completed appraisal of India's foreign policy and finding a stake in New Delhi's self-proclaimed non-attachment to power blocs, but one which was increasingly at odds with the West, Russia was ready to make some bold gestures towards India. The first was Russia's offer of trade on terms which, it was hoped, India would find attractive. As the Soviet ambassador in India said in Bombay on 14 January 1952, Moscow was ready to supply India "any industrial goods and accept payment in rupees or any other soft currency."[3] More importantly, the Soviets, after a long silence, decided to intervene in the UN debate on Kashmir. Although the Soviet delegate Jacob Malik did not directly side with India, his sharp criticism of England and the United States evoked a positive response from many in India. And his assertion that the Kashmir issue could be decided by an elected constituent assembly was probably as favourable to India as could be possible at this time.

We can only speculate as to the resulting change in Soviet-Indian relations had India given a favourable response to Moscow's overtures. But as the Soviets were preparing for their new moves towards the Nehru government, Chester Bowles arrived in India as America's new ambassador. Unlike the US envoys who had served in India before, his views were close to Nehru's regarding the problems faced by the newly-liberated countries. He, like the Indian leader, believed that the primary issues facing these countries were poverty and inequality, which required social change and economic development. Combating Communism by military means, a view held by many in America, was thus rejected by Bowles. Preparing to embark on its first Five Year Plan, New Delhi responded warmly to Bowles. The measure of his success can be determined by the fact that he was able to persuade Nehru to accept economic assistance under the terms of the US Mutual Security Act of 1951, which required the aid-recipient countries to cooperate with Washington on foreign policy issues. The language of the act on this point, in fact, was stronger than India would agree to in 1971 in the Soviet-Indian Treaty of Friendship and Cooperation.

As it turned out, it was more a Bowles policy than a new approach towards the region adopted by the Truman Administration. Although the ambassador in India put emphasis on economic development and asked for Washington's understanding of India's independent foreign policy, many in the US, especially in the Pentagon, were already devising a military-oriented approach to South and Southeast Asia in order to erect barriers against Communism. Bowles' policy, which was already facing difficulties in the last few months of the Truman Administration, was rejected by the incoming Eisenhower Administration.

The new American policy would be based on a US-sponsored military alliance, with Pakistan as one of its key members. In January 1953, Vice Admiral Jerauled Wright of the US Navy arrived in the country and told a press conference that Pakistan had defiinite strategic importance in a Middle East defence plan. He added, "You only have to look at the map to realize Pakistan's strategic importance."[4] Thomas J. Hamilton wrote in the *New York Times* that the Secretary of State-designate, John Foster Dulles, would shortly visit India and Pakistan. "His principal aim," wrote Hamilton, "is to determine to what extent the Governments are ready to cooperate in the new administration's plans for a coordinated defence against Communist aggression in the Far East."⁵

A corollary of a military-oriented approach to South and Southeast Asia, of which Pakistan was expected to be a member, was also the increasing support that Washington began to give to Pakistan on the Kashmir issue. Although the US position on this issue had never been sympathetic towards India, in the past at least it had concentrated on negotiations between the two sides. But a resolution submitted by London and Washington in the Security Council on 5 November 1952, appeared to favour Pakistan. In their speeches, the British and American delegates treated India and Pakistan at par, ignoring India's original complaint of Pakistan's invasion of the State. A suggestion was also made for the introduction of neutral troops during the plebiscite.⁶ Mrs. Vijaya Lakshmi Pandit, who led India's delegation at this meeting, rejected this approach for the solution of the Kashmir problem. As to the introduction of neutral troops, she said:

...It is surprising that anyone should think of suggesting to us that we should admit or receive back, on our soil, foreign troops whose withdrawal was an essential feature of our independence. It does not matter in what guise they are sought to be introduced or by whom. We shall not permit this to happen.⁷

The Soviet delegate repeated Jacob Malik's January 1952 stand that the Kashmiri people should be allowed to determine their future through an elected assembly.⁸ Moscow also abstained, while the resolution, supported by the remaining members under the guidance of London and Washington, easily passed the Security Council.⁹

This turn of events affected both Moscow and New Delhi. For India, the talk of including Pakistan in a US-sponsored military alliance meant at least two things. First, it indicated that rather than continuing to provide economic assistance for its developmental plans, America would now support the military build up of Pakistan with whom India was still locked up in confrontation on Kashmir. Second, the United States would increasingly be supportive of Pakistan's case on Kashmir in the United Nations. The Indian Prime Minister had once told Chester Bowles that India "would cheerfully accept our moral position in regard to USSR" if, in return, Washington accepted "India's basic case on Kashmir."[10] Although the statement was made only jokingly, it reflected the reality of international life. The United Nations has never been the type of forum where the issues are decided on their merit. As a report prepared for the National Security Council (NSC 135, No. 3) in August 1952 pointed out, India was "still unwilling to become directly involved in the Cold War or openly to take the part of the West."[11] If Pakistan was willing to support the West and become its military ally then it would be Pakistan, not India, that would have Washington's backing on Kashmir.

The Kremlin had already charged in the past that the US was seeking a military alliance with Pakistan in order to obtain military bases in that country; its suspicions were now confirmed. The Soviet press published several Tass dispatches, giving details of the US efforts to bring Pakistan into an "aggressive Middle East bloc."[12] Tass reports from Delhi spoke of the deep anxiety caused in India by the reported move of the US.[13] *Pravda* also published a statement by Nehru in which he expressed his government's uneasiness over this development.[14] The new strategic environment on their Southern flank thus became a matter of great concern for the Soviets. India, now alienated from Washington, would increasingly count in their foreign policy calculations.

What could India gain from a new relationship with Moscow? In addition to trade on barter terms, which the Soviets had already suggested, Russia could also offer aid for India's economic development. It could also offer greater and more open support on Kashmir to save India embarrassment at the UN at seeing those resolutions adopted, as it happened in June 1952, which it was not prepared to accept. The future Russian action, in fact, was forecast by US Secretary of State Acheson when, prior to the June meeting of the Security Council, he expressed his apprehension that the US-British joint resolution might be vetoed by the Soviet Union.[15] A pro-Soviet weekly, *Blitz*, had already suggested it in January 1952 at the time of Moscow's first major intervention in the Kashmir debate.[16]

Most of the students of Soviet foreign policy have discussed the favourable turn in Soviet-Indian relations during 1953–54 in the context of changes in Soviet foreign policy in the post-Stalin period. The changes no doubt became materialized after the death of Stalin, but as we have seen the groundwork for them was well laid during the last two years of the Stalin era. It was during this time when the evolution of Moscow's attitude towards nonaligned movement, especially as practised by India, took place. Although acting more boldly towards Nehru and his foreign policy, Stalin's successors would only carry forward a policy whose main contours had already taken shape in Moscow.

Another mistake generally made is to interpret the turn in Soviet-Indian relations *solely* in terms of what happened in Moscow either under Stalin or his successors. If this study has shown one thing, it is that the relationship between Moscow and New Delhi depended on the needs of both, not moves by only one side. If it was not for a pro-Western shift in Indian policies soon after it achieved independence, Soviet-Indian relations might have developed differently in those early years. Even later, Nehru's suspicions of Russia's objectives, especially his inability to separate its interest in the Indian communist movement from its national interests, prevented him from at least using the Russian overtures as bargaining chips in his dealings with Washington. Diplomacy after all is the game of widening one's optionsa and using them for maximum possible advantage. It is in this respect that nonalignment has been a most useful tool for the developing countries. It, therefore, seems remarkable and, to some extent, evidence of lack of finesse in Indian diplomacy that when the Russians intervened in the Kashmir debate in January 1952, Girija Shankar Bajpai went out of his way to prove to the United States that India had not encouraged Moscow to do so. And to support his point, he even showed copies of the cables his ministry had sent to Indian missions abroad, including the one to Moscow. It was this type of unrealistic reliance on Washington that made Nehru react so emotionally[17] when the US decided to abandon the Bowles approach towards South Asia. Had this approach continued, it is unlikely that India would have responded so warmly to Soviet overtures, now made with greater force by Stalin's successors. But Washington's new approach to the region made it necessary for India to look for other sources for economic and technical assistance and for diplomatic support on the Kashmir question. The Soviet Union was willing to provide both without any conditions and on terms which India could easily accept.

NOTES

1. *Colonial Peoples' Struggle for Liberation* (Bombay, 1950), p. 98.
2. See Memorandum of Conversation, by the First Secretary of [US] Embassy in the Soviet Union (Edward Page), 24 October 1945, *FRUS 1945* (Washington, DC, 1967), 2: 574, and Memorandum of Conversation, by the First Secretary of Embassy in the Soviet Union (Page), 25 October 1945, ibid., p. 576. The two documents give accounts of the talks Stalin had at this time with US Ambassador A.W. Harriman in Moscow.
3. "Soviet Offer to India: Industrial Goods," *Statesman Overseas Edition*, 19 January 1952, p. 6.
4. "Pakistan's Strategic Importance," ibid., 31 January 1953, p. 8.
5. Thomas J. Hamilton, "Dulles Will Visit India and Pakistan for Defense Talks," *New York Times*, 12 January 1953, p. 1.
6. The speeches of the British and American delegates are cited in Sisir Gupta, *Kashmir: A Study in India-Pakistan Relations* (Bombay, 1966), pp. 250–51.
7. Cited in ibid., p. 251.   8. Cited in Ibid., p. 252.   9. Ibid.
10. The Ambassador in India (Bowles) to the Department of State, 10 January 1952, *FRUS 1952–1954* (Washington, DC, 1983). 11, part 2: 1168.
11. Report Prepared by the Office of the Director of Mutual Security (Averell W. Harriman), 18 August 1952, *FRUS 1952–1954* (Washington, DC, 1983), 1, part 1: 552.
12. "Pakistanskaia gazeta razoblachaet agressivnye tseli srednevostochnogo bloka," *Pravda*, 10 January 1953, p. 4. "Amerikanskie proiski v Pakistane—K predyvaniiu v Pakistane amerikanskogo vitseadmirala Raita [Wright]," *Pravda*, 29 January 1953, p. 3, and *Izvestiia*, 29 January 1953, p. 4; "Imperialist Intrigue in Pakistan," *New Times*, no. 6 (4 February (1953), pp. 7–8; "Bear Dancing," ibid., no. 7 (11 February 1953), p. 19.
13. "Reaktsiia v Indii na plany vkliucheniia Pakistana v srednevostochnyi bloc," *Pravda*, 29 January 1953, p. 3; and "Popytki anglo-amerikanskikh imperialistov vkliuchit' Pakistan v agressivnyi srednevostochnyi blok—indiiskaia obshchestvennost' pridaet ser'eznoe znachenie soobshcheniiam ob etikh popytkakh," *Pravda*, 17 January 1953, p. 4.
14. "Zaiavlenie Neru v indiiskom parlamenta," *Pravda*, 15 February 1953, p. 3.
15. The Secretary of State to the Embassy in the United Kingdom, 21 June 1952, *FRUS 1952-1954* (Washington, DC, 1983), vol. 11, pt. 2, p. 1261.
16. *Blitz* (Bombay), 26 January 1952, p. 7; cited from *IPD* 1 (September 1952): 9.
17. See ch. 7, note 104.

Bibliography

1. PRIMARY SOURCES

(a) *Documents*

American Foreign Policy, 1950–1955: *Basic Documents*, 2 vols., Washington, DC: Department of State, 1957.

Asian Relations, Being a Report of the Proceedings and Documentation of First Asian Relations Conference. New Delhi: Asian Relations Organization, 1948.

Foreign Relations of the United States 1945, vol. 2. *General: Political and Economic Matters.* Washington, DC: United States Government Printing Office, 1967.

Foreign Relations of the United States 1946, vol. 1. Washington, DC: United States Government Printing Office, 1972.

Foreign Relations of the United States 1946, vol. 5. Washington, DC: United States Government Printing Office, 1969.

Foreign Relations of the United States 1947, vol. 1. Washington, DC: United States Government Printing Office, 1973.

Foreign Relations of the United States 1948, vol. 5, 2 parts, *The Near East, South Asia, and Africa.* Washington, DC: United States Government Printing Office, 1975.

Foreign Relations of the United States 1949, vol. 6. *The Near East South Asia, and Africa.* Washington, DC: United States Government Printing Office, 1977.

Foreign Relations of the United States 1950, vol. 5. *The Near East. South Asia, and Africa.* Washington, DC: United States Government Printing Office, 1978.

Foreign Relations of the United States 1951, vol. 1. *National Security Affairs: Foreign Economic Policy.* Washington, DC: United States Government Printing Office, 1979.

Foreign Relations of the United States 1952–1954, vol. 1, 2 parts, *General Economic and Political Matters.* Washington, DC: United States Government Printing Office, 1983.

Foreign Relations of the United States 1952–1954, vol. 2, 2 parts, *National*

Security Affairs. Washington, DC: United States Government Printing Office, 1984.

Foreign Relations of the United States 1952–1954, vol. 3. *United Nations Affairs*. Washington, DC: United States Government Printing Office, 1979.

Foreign Relations of the United States 1952–1954, vol. 2, 2 parts, *Africa and South Asia*. Washington, DC: United States Government Printing Office, 1983.

Foreign Relations of the United States 1952–1954, vol. 15, 2 parts, Korea. Washington, DC: United States Government Printing Office, 1984.

Mansergh, Nicholas, ed. *Documents and Speeches on British Commonwealth Affairs*, 1931–1952, 2 vols. London: Oxford University Press, 1953.

Philips, C.H., ed. *The Evolution of India and Pakistan, 1858–1947: Select Documents*. London: Oxford University Press, 1962.

Poplai, S.L., ed. *India, 1947–50*, 2 vols. Bombay: Oxford University Press, 1959.

Royal Institute of International Affairs, *Documents on International Affairs, 1947–1948*. London: Oxford University Press, 1952.

———. *Documents on International Affairs*, 1949–1950. London: Oxford University Press, 1953.

———. *Documents on International Affairs*, 1951. London: Oxford University Press, 1954.

———. *Documents on International Affairs*, 1952. London: Oxford University Press, 1956.

UN, General Assembly, *Official Records*, 1946–1953.

UN, Security Council, *Official Records*, 1946–1953.

US, Congress, Senate, *Congressional Record*, 81st Cong., 1st sess., 1949, 95, pt. 11: 14394.

US, Congress, Senate, *Congressional Record*, 81st Cong., 2nd sess., 1950, 96, pt. 5: 6324.

Zhdanov, A. "The International Situation," *For a Lasting Peace, For a People's Democracy*, 10 November 1947, pp. 2–4.

(b) *Personal Papers*

New Delhi, India. Nehru Memorial Library and Museum. Oral History Project. O.L. Orestov's statement, recorded in Moscow by B.R. Nanda, 2 August 1967.

New Haven, Connecticut. Sterling Memorial Library, Yale University. Chester Bowles Papers.

Independence, Missouri. Harry S. Truman Library. Files of Clark M. Clifford.

Independence, Missouri. Harry S. Truman Library, Henry F. Grady Papers.

Independence, Missouri. Harry S. Truman Library. Stephen J. Spingarn Papers.

Independence, Missouri. Harry S. Truman Library. Harry S. Truman Papers.

(c) *Newspapers and Periodicals*

Aja (a Hindi daily published from Varanasi, India).
Bol'shevik (Moscow).
Current Digest of the Soviet Press.
The Economist (London).
For a Lasting Peace, For a People's Democracy (Organ of the Cominform).
The Hindu (Madras).
Izvestiia (Moscow).
Literaturnaia gazeta (Moscow).
The Modern Review (Calcutta).
New Times (Moscow).
The New York Times.
News (Moscow).
Pakistan Affairs (Washington, DC: Embassy of Pakistan).
Pravda (Moscow).
Soviet Land (New Delhi: Embassy of the Soviet Union).
Soviet Press Translations.
The Statesman (Calcutta).
The Statesman Overseas Edition (Calcutta).
Thought (New Delhi).
The Times (London).
VOKS Bulletin (Moscow).
World News and Views (London).

(d) *Books*

Acheson, Dean, *Present at Creation: My Years in the State Department*. New York: W.W. Norton & Company, 1969.

Akademiia Nauk SSSR, *Uchenye zapiski Tikhookeanskogo Instituta*, vol. 2, *indiiskii sbornik*, Moscow: Indatel'stvo Akademii nauk SSSR, 1949.

Bondarevsky, Grigori and Sofinsky, Vsevolod. *Nonalignment: Its Friends and Adversaries in World Politics*. Moscow: "Social Sciences Today" Editorial Board, USSR Academy of Sciences, 1978.

Bowles, Chester, *Ambassador's Report*. New York: Harper and Brothers, 1954.

———. *A View From Delhi: Selected Speeches and Writings*. New Haven and London: Yale University Press, 1969.

———. *Promises to Keep: My Years in Public Life, 1941–1969*. New York: Harper & Row, 1971.

Chelyshev, Yevgeni and Litman, Alexei. *Traditions of Great Friendship.* Moscow: Raduga Publishers, 1985.

Colonial People's Struggle for Liberation. Bombay: People's Publishing House, 1950.

Communist Violence in India. n.p.: Ministry of Home Affairs, Government of India, 1949.

D'iakov, A.M. *Indiia i Pakistan.* Moscow: "Pravda," 1950.

———. *Indiia vo vremia i posle vtoroi mirovoi voiny, 1939-1949.* Moscow: Izd-vo Akademii nauk SSSR, 1952.

———. ed. *Uchenye zapiski Instituta Vostokovedeniia,* vol. 1. Moscow: Izadatel'stvo Akademii nauk SSSR, 1950.

Djilas, Milovan, *Conversations with Stalin.* New York: Harcourt, Brace and World, 1962.

Dutt, Subimal, *With Nehru in the Foreign Office.* Columbia, Missouri: South Asia Books, 1977.

Dvizhenie neprisoedineniia v dokumentakh i materialakh. Moscow: "Nauka," 1979.

Etinger, Y., and Melikyan, O. *The Policy of Nonalignment.* Moscow: Progress Publishers, n.d.

Gafurov, Bobojan, *Neutralism and the National Liberation Movement.* Moscow: Novosti Press Agency Publishing House, n.d.

Ganiushkin, Boris Vladimirovich. *Neitralitet i neprisoedinenie.* Moscow: Mezhdunarodnye otnosheniia, 1965.

Gopal, Sarvepalli, ed. *Jawaharlal Nehru: An Anthology.* New Delhi: Oxford University Press, 1980.

———. ed. *Selected Works of Jawaharlal Nehru,* Second Series, 3 vols. New Delhi: Jawaharlal Nehru Memorial Fund, 1984-85.

Johnson, U. Alexis, with McAllister Jef Olivarius. *The Right Hand of Power.* Englewood Cliffs, N.J.: Prentice-Hall, Inc., 1984.

Jurika, Stephen, Jr., ed. *From Pearl Harbor to Vietnam: The Memoirs of Admiral Arthur W. Radford.* Stanford: Hoover Institution Press, 1980.

Kaul, B.M. *The Untold Story.* New Delhi: Allied Publishers, 1967.

Kaul, T.N. *Diplomacy in Peace and War: Recollections and Reflections.* New Delhi: Vikas Publishing House Pvt. Ltd., 1979.

Kennan, George F. *Memoirs, 1925-1950.* Boston: Little, Brown and Company, 1967.

Krainov, P. *Amerikanskii imperialism v Isponii.* Moscow: Gospolitizdat, 1951.

Lemin, I. *Britanskaia imperiia.* Moscow: Izdatel'stvo "Pravda," 1947.

———. *Bor'ba dvukh napravlenii v mezhdunarodnykh otnosheniiakh.* Moscow: Izdatel'stvo "Pravda," 1947.

McGhee, George. *Envoy to the Middle World: Adventures in Diplomacy.* New York: Harper and Row, 1983.

Majumdar, A.K., ed., *Advent of Independence*, Bombay: Bharatiya Vidya Bhawan, 1963.
Mende, Tibor. *Nehru: Conversations on India and World Affairs*. New York: George Braziller, Inc., 1956.
Menon, K.P.S. *The Flying Troika*. London: Oxford University Press, 1963.
——. *Many Worlds, An Autobiography*. London: Oxford University Press, 1965.
Moon, Penderal, ed. *Wavell: The Viceroy's Journal*. London: Oxford University Press, 1973.
Nehru, Jawaharlal. *Independence and After: A Collection of Speeches, 1946–1949*. New York: John Day, 1950.
——. *Speeches, 1949–1953*. Delhi: Publications Division, Ministry of Information and Broadcasting, Government of India, 1957.
——. *Soviet Russia: Some Random Sketches and Impressions*. 1929. Reprint. Bombay: Chetana, 1949.
Norman, Dorothy, ed. *Nehru, The First Sixty Years*, 2 vols. New York: The John Day Co., 1965.
Pandit, Vijaya Lakshmi. *Scope of Happiness: A Personal Memoirs*. New York: Crown Publishers, Inc., 1979.
Panikkar, K M. *In Two Chinas, Memoirs of a Diplomat*. London: George Allen and Unwin Ltd., 1955.
Prasad, Bimal, ed. *Indo-Soviet Relations, 1947–1972: A Documentary Study*. New Delhi: Allied Publishers Private Limited, 1973.
Redko, I., and Khazanov, A. *The Non-Alignment Movement: Origin and Development*. Moscow: "Nauka" Publishing House, 1979.
Selezneva, Ekaterina Ivanovna *Politika neprisoedineniia molodykh suverennykh gosudarstv Azii i Afriki*. Moscow: Mezhdunarodnye otnosheniia, 1966.
Slusser, Robert M. and Triska, Jan F. *A Calendar of Soviet Treaties, 1917–1957*. Stanford: Stanford University Press, 1959.
Soviet Views on the Post-War World Economy: An Official Critique of Eugene Varga's 'Changes in the Economy of Capitalism Resulting from the Second World War'. Translated by Leo Cruliow. Washington, DC: Public Affairs Press, 1948.
Stalin, Joseph. *Economic Problems of Socialism in the USSR*. New York: International Publishers, 1952.
Thapar, Romesh, et al. *Nehru's Foreign Policy*. Bombay: Crossroads Publications, n.d. [1951?].
Truman, Harry S. *Memoirs*, vol. 2, *Years of Trial and Hope*. Garden City, New York: Doubleday and Company, Inc., 1956.
Varga, Yevgenii (Eugene). *Izmeneniia v ekonomike kapitalizma v itoge Vtoroi mirovoi voiny*. Moscow: Gospolitizdat, 1946.
Vyshinsky, A. Ya., chief ed. *Diplomaticheskii slovar'*, vol. 2. Moscow: Gosudarastvennoe izdatel'stvo politicheskoi literatury, 1950.

(e) *Articles*

Balabushevich, V. "A New Phase in the National Liberation Struggle of the People of India." *Voprosy ekonomiki*, no. 8 (1949), pp. 30–48. In *Current Digest of the Soviet Press* 1 (3 January 1950): 8–10.

———. "Indiia posle razdela." *Mirovoe khoziaistvo i mirovaia politika*, no. 12 (December 1947), pp. 41–62.

———. "What Is Happening in India." *Trud*, 18 (February 1948). In *Soviet Press Translations* 3 (1 June 1948): 326–29.

Bovin, A.F. "Peaceful Coexistence." In *Great Soviet Encyclopedia*, 16: 625–27. New York: Macmillan, Inc., 1977.

Bushevich, V. "Bor'ba Indii za nezavisimost'." *Mirovoe khoziaistvo i mirovaia politika*, no. 9 (September 1946), pp. 39–52.

D'iakov, A.N. "Krizis angliiskogo gospodstva v Indii i novyi etap osvoboditel'- noi bor'by oe narodov." In Ye. M. Zhukov, ed. *Krizis kolonial'noi sistemy: natsional'no-osvoboditel'naia bor'ba narodov vostochnoi Azii*, pp. 87–123. Moscow: Izdatel'stvo Akademii nauk SSSR, 1949.

Dmitriev, Boris. "What Is Peaceful Coexistence." *Coexistence* 10 (March 1974): 31–33.

"Dvizhenie neprisoedineniia vazhnyi fakto mirovoi politiki." In *Istorii diplomatii*, vol. 5, pt. 2, pp. 662–79. Moscow: Izdatel'stvo politicheskoi literatury, 1979.

Ivanov, I. "What Is the American Plan for 'Aid' to Backward Countries." *Trud*, 6 August 1949. In *Soviet Press Translations* 5 (1 February 1950): 76–78.

Lemin, I. "Sovremennye problemy Britanskoi imperii." *Mirovoe khoziaistvo i mirovaia politika*, no. 6 (June 1947), pp. 3–21.

Petrunicheva, Z. "Natsional'no-osvoboditel'noe dvizhenie v kniazhestve Kashmir." In *Uchenye zapiski Instituta Vostokovedeniia*, edited by A.M. D'iakov, pp. 157–224. Moscow: Izdatel'stvo Akademii nauk SSSR, 1950.

Shabshina, F.I. "Koreia posle vtoroi mirovoi voiny." In *Krizis kolonial'noi sistemy*, edited by Ye. M. Zhukov, pp. 249–89. Moscow: Izdatel'stvo Akademii nauk SSSR, 1949.

Ulyanovsky, Rostislav. "The Legacy of Jawaharlal Nehru." *Social Sciences*, no. 1 (1977), pp. 142–63.

"X" George F. Kennan. "The Sources of Soviet Conduct." *Foreign Affairs* 25 (July 1947): 566–82.

Zhukov, Ye. M. "K polozheniiu v Indii." *Mirovoe khoziaistvo i mirovaia politika*, no. 7 (July 1947), pp. 3–14.

———. "Obostrenie krizisa kolonial'noi sistemy," *Bol'shevik*, no. 23 (15 December 1947), pp. 51–64.

———. "Obostrenie krizisa kolonial'noi sistemy posle Vtoroi mirovoi voiny." In *Krizis kolonial'noi sistemy*, edited by Ye. M. Zhukov, pp. 3–28. Moscow: Izdatel'stvo Akademii nauk SSSR, 1949.

———. "Problems of the National-Colonial Struggle Since the Second World War." *Voprosy ekonomiki*, no. 9 (1949). In *Current Digest of the Soviet Press* 1 (3 January 1950): 3-7.

2. SECONDARY SOURCES

(a) *Books*

Abhayavardhan, Hector. *Russo-American Rivalry in Asia*. Bombay: Vora and Co., 1954.

Appadorai, A. *Domestic Roots of India's Foreign Policy, 1947-1972*. Delhi: Oxford University Press, 1981.

Bandyopadhyaya, J. *Indian Nationalism Versus International Communism: Role of Ideology in International Politics*. Calcutta: Firma K.L. Mukhopadhyay, 1966.

Bernds, William J. *India, Pakistan, and the Great Powers*. New York: Praeger Publishers, 1972.

Bazaz, Prem Nath. *Kashmir in Crucible*. New Delhi: Pamposh Publications, 1967.

Berkes, Ross N. and Bedi, Mohinder S. *The Diplomacy of India: Indian Foreign Policy in the United Nations*. Stanford: Stanford University Press, 1958.

Bhattacharya, Sauripada. *Pursuit of National Interests Through Neutralism: India's Foreign Policy in the Nehru Era*. Calcutta: Firma KLM (Private) Limited, 1978.

Brecher, Michael. *India and World Politics: Krishna Menon's View of the World*. New York: Frederick A. Praeger, 1968.

———. *Nehru: A Political Biography*. London: Oxford University Press, 1959.

———. *The Struggle for Kashmir*. New York: Oxford University Press, 1953.

Budhraj, V.S. *Soviet Russia and the Hindustan Subcontinent*. Bombay: Somaiya Publications Pvt. Ltd., 1973.

Burke, S M. *Mainsprings of Indian and Pakistani Foreign Policies*. Minneapolis: University of Minnesota Press, 1974.

Carr, E.H. *The Bolshevik Revolution, 1917-1923*, vol. 3. New York: The Macmillan Company, 1961.

———. *The Twilight of the Comintern, 1930-1935*. New York: Pantheon Books, 1982.

Chakravarti, P.C. *India's China Policy*. Bloomington: Indiana University Press, 1962.

Chamberlin, William Henry. *Beyond Containment*. Chicago: Henry Regnesy Company, 1953.

Chandrasekhar, S. *American Aid and India's Economic Development*. New York: Frederick A. Praeger, 1965.

Crabb, Ceoil V., Jr. *The Elephants and the Grass: A Study of Nonalignment.* New York: Frederick A. Praeger, 1965.

Dallin, Alexander, ed. *Soviet Conduct in World Affairs.* New York: Columbia University Press, 1960.

Das, M.N. *The Political Philosophy of Jawaharlal Nehru.* New York: The John Day Company, 1961.

Donaldson, Robert H. *Soviet Policy Towards India: Ideology and Strategy.* Cambridge: Harvard University Press, 1974.

Druhe, David N. *Soviet Russia and Indian Communism.* New York: Bookman Associates, 1959.

Dunn, Frederick S. *Peace-Making and the Settlement with Japan.* Princeton: Princeton University Press, 1963.

Edwardes, Michael. *Nehru: A Political Biography.* London: Allen Lane The Penguin Press, 1971.

Fic, Victor M. *Peaceful Transition to Communism in India: Strategy of the Communist Party.* Bombay: Nachiketa Publications, 1969.

Fontnine, Andre. *History of the Cold War: From the October Revolution to the Korean War,* 1917-1950. New York: Pantheon Books, 1968.

George, T.J.S. *Krishna Menon: A Biography.* New York; Taplinger Publishing Company, Inc., 1965.

Gopal, Sarvepalli. *Jawaharlal Nehru: A Biography,* 3 vols. Cambridge: Harvard University Press, 1976-84.

Gupta, Sisir. *Kashmir: A Study in India-Pakistan Relations.* Bombay: Asia Publishing House, 1966.

Halle, Louis J. *The Cold War as History.* New York: Harper and Row, 1967.

Harrison, Selig S. *The Widening Gulf: Asian Nationalism and American Policy.* New York: The Free Press, 1978.

Hasan, K. Sarwar *Pakistan and United Nations,* New York: Manhattan Publishing Company, 1960.

Heimsath, Charles H. and Mansingh, Surjit. *A Diplomatic History of Modern India.* New Delhi: Allied Publishers, 1971.

Higgins, Trumbull. *Korea and the Fall of MacArthur: A Precis in Limited War.* New York: Oxford University Press, 1980.

Hirlekar, K.S. *Soviet Asia: The Power Behind U.S.S.R.* Bombay: Avanti Prakashan, 1945.

Hussain, Arif. *Pakistan: Its Ideology and Foreign Policy.* London: Frank Cass & Co. Ltd., 1966.

India and the United Nations: Report of a Study Group Set Up by the Indian Council of World Affairs. New York; Manhattan Publishing Company, 1957.

Imam, Zafar. *Ideology and Reality in Soviet Policy in Asia: Indo-Soviet Relations,* 1947-60. Delhi: Kalyani Publishers, 1975.

Jansen, G.H. *Nonalignment and the Afro-Asian States.* New York: Frederick A. Praeger, 1966.

Jukes, Geoffrey. *The Soviet Union in Asia.* Berkeley and Los Angeles: University of California Press, 1973.

Karanjia, R.K. *The Philosophy of Mr. Nehru.* London: George Allen and Unwin Ltd., 1966.

Karunakaran, K.P. *India in World Affairs, August 1947–January 1950,* Calcutta: Oxford University Press, 1952.

——. *India in World Affairs, 1950–53.* Calcutta: Oxford University Press, 1958.

Kaushik, R.P. *The Crucial Years of Nonalignment (USA Korean War India).* New Delhi: Kumar Brothers, 1972.

Kautsky, John H. *Moscow and the Communist Party of India.* New York: John Wiley and Sons, Inc., 1956.

Korbel, Joseph. *Danger in Kashmir.* Princeton: Princeton University Press, 1954.

Kulkarni, Maya. *Indo-Soviet Political Relations.* Bombay: Vora and Co., 1968.

Kulski, Wladyslaw W. *Peaceful Coexistence: An Analysis of Soviet Foreign Policy.* Chicago; Henry Regnesy Company, 1959.

Kundra, J.C. *Indian Foreign Policy, 1947-1954* (Bombay: Vora, 1955).

Levi, Werner. *Free India in Asia.* Minneapolis: University of Minnesota Press, 1952.

MacKintosh, J.M. *Strategy and Tactics of Soviet Foreign Policy.* London: Oxford University Press, 1962.

Mallik, D.N. *The Development of Nonalignment in India's Foreign Palicy.* Allahabad: Chaitanya Publishing House, 1967.

Masani, M.R. *The Communist Party of India: A Short History.* London: Derek Verschoyle, 1954.

Melozemoff, Andrew. *Russian Far Eastern Policy,* 1881–1904. Berkeley and Los Angeles: University of California Press, 1958.

Moraes, Frank. *Jawaharlal Nehru: A Biography.* New York: The Macmillan Company, 1956.

——. *Witness to an Era: India 1920 to the Present Day.* New York: Holt, Rinehart and Winston, 1973.

Mosley, Philip E. *The Kremlin and World Politics.* New York: Vintage Press, 1960.

Murty, K. Satchidananda. *Indian Foreign Policy.* Calcutta: Scientific Book Agency, 1964.

Overstreet, Gene D. and Windmiller, Marshall. *Communism in India.* Berkeley and Los Angeles: University of California Press, 1960.

Palmer, Norman D. *South Asia and the United States Policy.* Boston: Houghton Mifflin Company, 1966.

Pandey, B.N. *Nehru.* London: Macmillan London Limited, 1976.

Prasad, Bimla. *The Origins of Indian Foreign Policy.* 2nd ed. Calcutta: Bookland Private Limited, 1962.

Rahman, M.N. *The Politics on Nonalignment*. New Delhi: Associated Publishing House, 1969.

Rana, A.P. *The Imperatives of Nonalignment: A Conceptual Study of India's Foreign Policy Strategy in the Nehru Period*. Delhi: The Macmillan Company of India Limited, 1976.

Ramundo, Lt. Col. Bernard A. *Peaceful Coexistence: International Law in the Building of Communism*. Baltimore, Maryland: The Johns Hopkins Press, 1967.

Ray, Hemen. *Indo-Soviet Relations*. Bombay: Jaico Publishing House, 1973.

Reddy, T. Ramakrishna. *India's Policy in the United Nations*. Rutherford: Fairleigh Dickinson University Press, 1968.

Remnek, Richard B. *Soviet Scholars and Soviet Foreign Policy: A Case Study in Soviet Policy Towards India*. Durham, North Carolina: Carolina Academic Press, 1975.

Rosinger, Lawrence K. *India and the United States: Political and Economic Relations*. New York: The Macmillan Company, 1950.

Rubinstein, Alvin Z. *The Foreign Policy of the Soviet Union*. New York: Random House, 1960.

———. *The Soviets in International Organizations*. Princeton: Princeton University Press, 1964.

Sarbadhikari, P.R. *India and the Great Powers: A Study of the Policy of Nonalignment and of India's Relations with the USA and the USSR, 1947–1961*. The Hague: J.C. Bean, 1962.

Sen, Chanakya. *Against the Cold War*. Bombay: Asia Publishing House, 1962.

Shah, A B. *India's Defence and Foreign Policies*. Bombay: Manaktalas, 1966.

Sheean, Vincent. *Nehru: The Years of Power*. New York: Random House, 1960.

Shulman, Marshall D. *Stalin's Foreign Policy Reappraised*. Cambridge: Harvard University Press, 1963.

Stein, Arthur. *India and the Soviet Union: The Nehru Era*. Chicago: Uinversity of Chicago Press, 1969.

Ulam, Adam B. *Expansion and Coexistence: The History of Soviet Foreign Policy, 1917–67*. New York: Frederick A. Praeger, 1968.

———. *Stalin: The Man and His Era*. New York: Viking Press, 1973.

Uldricks, Teddy J. *Diplomacy and Ideology: The Origins of Soviet Foreign Relations, 1917–1930*. London and Beverly Hills: Sage Publications, 1979.

Venkataramani, M.S. *The American Role in Pakistan, 1947–1958*. New Delhi: Radiant Publishers, 1982.

Ward, Patricia Dawson. *The Threat of Peace: James F. Byrnes and the Council of Foreign Ministers, 1945–1946*. Kent, Ohio: The Kent State University Press, 1979.

Warth, Robert D. *Soviet Russia in World Politics* New York: Twayne Publishers, Inc., 1963.

Whiting, Allen S. *China Crosses the Yalu.* New York: The Macmillan Company, 1960.
Zakaria, Rafiq, ed. *A Study of Nehru.* 2d ed. Bombay: A Times of India Publication, 1960.

(b) *Articles*

Appadorai, A. "Indian Diplomacy." In *Diplomacy in a Changing World*, Edited by Stephen D. Kertesz et al., pp. 266-300. Notre Dame: University of Notre Dame Press, 1959.

Gupta, Karunkar, "A Study of Indo-Soviet Relations, 1946-1955." *Calcutta Review* 139 (April 1956): 37-47.

Gupta, Surendra K. "Indo-Soviet Relations." *Problems of Communism* 22 (May-June 1973): 65-68.

———. "Dilemma of Stalin's Policy Toward the Third World: Moscow and the Indian Food Crises of 1951 and 1952." *International Review of History and Political Science* 19 (August 1981): 12-25.

———. "Indonesian Crisis of 1948-1949: A Study in Great Power Diplomacy and India's Relations with Moscow and Washington." *Asian Profile* 12 (October 1984): 473-83.

Kennan, George F. "Some Thoughts on Stalin's Foreign Policy." *Slavic Review* 36 (December 1977): 590-91.

Kapur, Harish. "The Soviet Union and Indo-Pakistani Relations." *International Studies* 8 (July-October 1966): 150-57.

Karanjia, R.K. "The Foreign Policy of India." *The New Statesman and Nation*, 3 January 1948, p. 6.

Nicolson, Harold. "Peacemaking at Paris: Success, Failure or Farce?" *Foreign Affairs* 25 (January 1947): 190-203.

Tucker, Robert C. "The Emergence of Stalin's Foreign Policy." *Slavic Review* 36 (December 1977): 563-80.

Tidmarsh, Kyril. "The Soviet Re-assessment of Mahatma Gandhi." In *St. Anthony's Papers*, no. 8, South Asian Affairs, pp. 85-115.

Vaidik, Ved Pratap. "Rus ka badalata hua rukh." [The Changing Attitude of the Soviet Union] *Dharmayug* (Bombay) 19 (3 November 1968); 11. 37.

Venkataramani, M.S. and Arya, Harish Chandra. "America's Military Alliance with Pakistan: The Evolution and Course of an Uneasy Partnership." *International Studies* 8 (July-October 1966): 73-125.

290 INDEX

Indian Communism, 11; and India's partition, 53–55
Indian Trade Union Congress, 11
International Democratic Women's Federation, 146
Isphani, M.A.H., 151, 154
Iyengar, H.V.R., 105

Jacobs, Joseph, 90
Jambhekar, R.M., 120–121
Japanese Peace treaty, 247; US and, 213–214, 216; USSR and, 214–217, 244; India and, 216–217, 224–225, 244
Jessup, Philip, 137, 142, 143
Jinnah, Mohammed Ali, 18, 56, 151, 152
Johnson, Louis, 213
Joshi, P.C., 101–102

Karamkar, D.P., 252
Kaul, Lieutenant General B.M., 98–99
Kennan, George F., 60
Kennedy, Donald, 263
Keskar, B.V., 187
Khan, Liaquat Ali, 150–151, 153–155, 157, 208
Khan, Sir Zafrullah, 152, 155–156, 209, 221, 251
Khare, N.B., 22
Khrushchev, Nikita, 12, 64
Kirk, Alan G., 136, 179
Korbel, Joseph, 204
Korotkov, Lieutenant General G.P., 88
Kirplani, J.B., 203
Kuznetsov, V., 253

Lenin, V.I., 4, 5, 7, 9, 76, 104; on peaceful coexistence, 3
Li Seung Man, 174
Lilienthal, David, 144
Litvinov, Maxim, 5
Lovett, Robert A., 73
Lyle, John F., Jr. 219

MacArthur, General Douglas, 91, 175, 183–186, 193–194
Malan, D.F., 109
Malik, Jacob, 92, 181, 183, 195, 211; supports India on Kashmir, 247–248, 263, 271, 273
Manuilsky, D.Z., 70, 77
Mao Tse-tung, 131, 178; on neutrality, 132–133
Marshall, George C., 50, 74, 90, 105, 193
Marshall Plan, 50, 60, 62, 131–132
Marx, Karl, 104
Masani, M.R., 203
Masaryk, Jan, 85
Menon, K.P.S., 28, 35, 88–90, 140; meeting with Stalin, 250
Menon, V.K. Krishna, 16–17, 21, 26
Migunov, V.P., 249
Molotov, V.M., 16–18, 20–21, 23, 35, 99; congratulatory telegram to Jawaharlal Nehru on achievement of independence by India, 59
Mountbatten, Louis, 53, 76, 94, 106
Mountbatten Plan, 54
Mudaliar, Ramaswami, 159
Mukerjee, Hiren, 249
Murphy, Charles, 261
Mutual Security Act, US, 258; India's acceptance of, 256, 272

Nazi-Soviet Non-Aggression Pact (1939), 11
Nehru, Jawaharlal, 9, 17, 18, 31–35, 63, 73–74, 76–78, 87, 94, 99–102, 111, 113, 133–134, 136; and his view of links between Indian Communists and the USSR, 9, 11–32, 103–105, 275; and League Against Imperialism, 10–11; and policy towards the US, 14, 136–145, 224–225, 256–257, 262–263, 270, 273–274; and policy towards the USSR, 14–15, 35–36, 59–60; and the Paris Peace Conference (1946), 18–20; and the

Commonwealth, 106–110, 138; supports the Western Union, 108; and the Indonesian problem, 115–117, 122, 135; and policy towards Communist China, 140–141, 143; on Communist violence in India, 146, 172–173; on Communist violence in Southeast Asia, 157, 172–173; letters to Dean Acheson and Joseph Stalin on ending the Korean War, 175–176; on crossing of the 38th Parallel by UN forces, 185; praises US economic assistance, 263; praises Chester Bowles's work, 263; Soviet comments on, 55–58
Nehru, R.K., 105, 259
Nenni, Pietro, 170, 224
Nesterov, M.V., 249–250
Noon, Firoz Khan, 16–17
North Atlantic Treaty Organization (NATO), 86–87, 112, 132
Novikov, K.V., 104, 249
Nu, Thakin, 157

Pakistan, Soviet view of the creation of, 54–56; on crossing of the 38th Parallel by UN forces, 186; on Dean Acheson's 'Uniting for Peace' proposal, 193; supports Japanese Peace Treaty, 221; and its strategic importance for the US, 154, 260–261
Pandit, Vijayalakshmi, 21, 22, 28–31, 66, 68, 73–74, 77, 99, 104, 139, 199; as Indian ambassador in USSR, 58–59
Panikkar, K.M., 76, 160, 174–175, 185
Patel, Vallabhbhai, 103, 203; Soviet view of, 55, 58
Pearson, Lester, 196
Petrov, A.A., 35
Pijade, M., 76
Pillai, P.P., 90

Prasad, Rajendra, 180

Quirino, Elpidio, 133, 158–159
Qureshi, Shuaib, 153

Radford, Admiral Arthur W., 260
Radhakrishnan, S., 139–140, 175–176, 253; meetings with Joseph Stalin, 160, 250–251
Rajagopalachari, Chakravarti, 110
Ranadive, B.T., 101–102
Ranga, N.G., 203
Razin, L.A., 249
Rau, Sir Benegal, 182–183, 195–198, 200
Rhee, Syngman, 91, 133
Riga, Treaty of, 5
Rio Treaty, 86
Romulo, Carlos P., 159
Roosevelt, Franklin D., 28
Roschin, Nikolai V., 174
Roy, K.S., 103
Roy, M.N., 2
Rusk, Dean, 86, 217

Sadiq, Gulam Mohammed, 252
Sen, B.R., 70
Setalvad, M.C., 251
Shawcross, Sir Hartley, 24
Shvernik, N.M., 59, 153
Singh, Bahadur, 91
Smith, General Walter Bedell, 74
Smuts, Jan Christiaan, 32
Soemitro, D., 116
Sokolovsky, Marshal Vasily, 86
Southeast Asia Youth Conference, 99, 146
Spingarn, Stephen J., 154–155
Stalin, Joseph, 4, 6, 75, 160, 161, 199, 217, 223, 246; on ideology's role in Soviet foreign policy, 1; on peaceful coexistence, 3; message to Nehru, 102; invitation to Liaquat Ali Khan, 154; responds to Jawaharlal Nehru's proposals on the Korean War, 176–177, 271; meets S.

Radhakrishnan, 160, 250–251; meets K.P.S. Menon, 250; on India's participation at the Paris Peace Conference, 270
Steere, Lloyd V., 225, 251–252
Stetsenko, A.G., 156
Sun-Joffe Agreement, 8
Sun Yat-sen, 8
Sundarayya, P., 252
Suslov, Mikhail, 76

Thorez, Maurice, 178
Tikhonov, N., 153
Tokuda, Kiuitsi, 161
Trotsky, Leon, 4
Truman, Harry S., 49–50, 61, 86, 136, 142–143, 145, 150, 154–155, 171–173, 184, 186, 193–194, 199, 213, 217, 257, 261; view of Nehru, 144
Truman Doctrine, 49, 60
Tsiang, T.F., 131

Ukhtomskii, Prince Esper Esperevich, 1
Ukraine, 89, 93; as India's rival for a Security Council seat, 64–68
Union of Soviet Socialist Republics (USSR), 28, 29, 50, 72; view of neutrality or nonalignment, 7, 64, 76–78, 87, 161, 170, 224, 245, 247, 275; and Indian Communism, 11–12, 145, 147; and the Interim Government, 15; and the demand for Pakistan, 18; policy at the Paris Peace Conference, 18–21; and racial discrimination in South Africa, 23–25; and Southwest Africa, 26; and UN Trusteeship Agreements, 26–27; veto right at the UN, 27–28, 75; at the Indian Science Congress (January 1947), 32–35; at the Asian Relations Conference, 33–34; view of the Asian Relations Conference, 34–35, 54–55; on the Mountbatten Plan, 53–58; opposes India's candidacy for a Security Council seat, 66–68; and the Greek question, 69; and the question of Korean unification, 62–71, 75, 88–89, 91–93; and the Kashmir question, 95–99, 206–207, 247–249, 271, 273; on India's membership in the Commonwealth, 99–103, 111–113; and Indonesian question, 117–120; view of Jawaharlal Nehru's visit to the US, 145–146, 148–150, 152, 158; invites Liaquat Ali Khan to Moscow, 150–155; on Jawaharlal Nehru's letters to Joseph Stalin and Dean Acheson to end the Korean War, 176–179; on India's stand on the crossing of the 38th Parallel, 188; on the Pacific Relations Conference (1950), 190; on India's opposition to the US move to declare China an aggressor in Korea, 199–200; and China's invasion of Tibet, 201–204; on India's opposition to the Japanese Peace Treaty, 221–223, 244, 271; and the Communist Party of India, 271; offer of food aid, 253–254; offer of trade, 249–250, 271
United Kingdom, 107–109; on Kashmir, 98, 107, 208–209
United States of America (USA), 58, 61, 85, 86, 113, 119, 143–145; and policy of neutrality or nonalignment, 7, 137, 219, 221, 274; and racial discrimination in South Africa, 23–25; question of Southwest Africa, 25; and UN's Trusteeship Agreements, 27; veto right at the UN, 27–28, 72; on military establishments in foreign territories, 29; on India's candidacy for a Security

Council seat, 65–66; and Greek question, 69; and unification of Korea, 69–70, 87, 90, 92–93; and Kashmir dispute, 107, 205–208, 263, 273; on India's membership in Commonwealth, 110, 113; and Indonesian question, 114–117; policy towards Pakistan, 154–157, 221, 261; on India's stand on crossing of 38th Parallel by UN forces, 188–189; on India's stand on declaring China an aggressor in Korea, 198–199; on India's stand on Japanese Peace Treaty, 217–221; and military sales to India, 259

Vandenberg, General Hoyt, 260
Varga, Eugene, 51–53
Vostochniki, 1

Washington, George, 10
Webb, James E., 189
Western Union, 115, 118, 121, 132
World Peace Council, 170

Vyshinsky, Andrei, 23–24, 28, 59, 66, 68, 187, 192, 194, 223, 250, 253

Wright, Vice Admiral Jerauld, 272

Zhdanov, A.A., 78, 270; and his "two camps" thesis, 62–63
Zorin, V.A., 175